FASCISM

ROGER EATWELL

FASCISM

A History

ALLEN LANE
THE PENGUIN PRESS

ALLEN LANE THE PENGUIN PRESS
Published by the Penguin Group
Penguin Books USA Inc., 375 Hudson Street,
New York, New York 10014, U.S.A.
Penguin Books Ltd, 27 Wrights Lane, London W8 5TZ, England
Penguin Books Australia Ltd, Ringwood, Victoria, Australia
Penguin Books Canada Ltd, 10 Alcorn Avenue,
Toronto, Ontario, Canada M4V 3B2
Penguin Books (N.Z.) Ltd, 182–190 Wairau Road,
Auckland 10, New Zealand

Penguin Books Ltd, Registered Offices:
Harmondsworth, Middlesex, England

First American edition
Published in 1996 by Viking Penguin,
a division of Penguin Books USA Inc.

1   3   5   7   9   10   8   6   4   2

LIBRARY OF CONGRESS CATALOGING IN PUBLICATION DATA
Eatwell, Roger.
Fascism : a history / Roger Eatwell.
p.   cm.
Includes bibliographical references and index.
ISBN 0-713-99147-X
1. Fascism—History.   I. Title.
JC481.E23   1996
320.5'33'09—dc   96-925

This book is printed on acid-free paper.

Printed in the United States of America
Set in Bembo
Designed by Francesca Belanger

For Laura and James

Acknowledgments

Four grants were awarded by the British Academy to support aspects of this work, especially to conduct interviews and to visit specialist libraries. Unfortunately the numbers of people who helped me in this way are too many to list (and some of the activists would not wish to be named). Fellow academics who contributed in various ways include: Luciano Cheles, Nigel Copsey, Chris Husbands, Stein Larsen, Mario Sznajder, Richard Thurlow, Larry Witherell—and especially Michael Pinnock (who read the pre-1945 German chapters) and Roger Griffin (who read the Italian chapters). My father and wife offered various comments on earlier drafts; and my father undertook the laborious task of proofreading. My literary agent, Derek Johns, helped set the book up in the first place. Jonathan Burnham of Chatto and Windus offered advice on style far and above the call of duty. Marion Maneker of Viking Penguin kindly offered me the opportunity to make some additions for the American edition. For all this help, I am most grateful. For any errors of fact or judgment that remain, I alone am responsible—a more than usually necessary caveat, as I am sure that some will disagree with important aspects of what I have written.

Roger Eatwell
University of Bath
January 1996

Contents

PART ONE

IN THE BEGINNING

PART TWO

INTERWAR FASCISM

PART THREE
FASCISM SINCE 1945

Abbreviations

JP *Jeunesses Patriotes* (Young Patriots)
KDF *Kraft durch Freude* (Strength Through Joy)
KPD *Kommunistische Partei Deutschlands* (German Communist Party)
MRP *Mouvement Républicain Populaire* (Popular Republican Movement)
MSI *Movimento Sociale Italiano* (Italian Social Movement)
MVSN *Milizia Voluntaria per la Sicurezza Nazionale* (Voluntary Militia for National Security)
NAR *Nuclei Armati Rivoluzionari* (Armed Revolutionary Nuclei)
ND *Nouvelle Droite* (New Right)
NF National Front
NPD *Nationaldemokratische Partei Deutschlands* (National Democratic Party of Germany)
NSDAP *Nationalsozialistische Deutsche Arbeiterpartei* (National Socialist German Workers' Party)
OAS *Organisation Armée Secrète* (Secret Army Organization)
ODESSA *Organisation der Ehemaligen SS-Angehörigen* (Organization for Former Members of the SS)
ON *Ordre Nouveau* (New Order)
OND *Opera Nazionale Dopolavoro* (National After-Work-Leisure Organization)
OVRA *Organizzazione Vigilanza Repressione Antifascismo* (Organization for Vigilance and Repression of Antifascism)
PCF *Parti Communiste Français* (French Communist Party)
PCI *Partito Comunista Italiana* (Italian Communist Party)
PDS *Partei des Demokratischen Sozialismus* (Party of Democratic Socialism)
PDS *Partito Democratico della Sinistra* (Democratic Party of the Left)
PFN *Parti des Forces Nouvelles* (Party of New Forces)
PFR *Partito Fascista Repubblicano* (Fascist Republican Party)
PNF *Partito Nazionale Fascista* (National Fascist Party)
PPF *Parti Populaire Français* (Popular French Party)
PPI *Partito Popolare Italiano* (Italian Popular Party)
PSI *Partito Socialista Italiano* (Italian Socialist Party)
PSF *Parti Social Français* (French Social Party)
REP *Die Republikaner* (the Republicans)
RNP *Rassemblement National Populaire* (National Popular Rally)
RPF *Rassemblement de Peuple Française* (Rally of the French People)
SA *Sturmabteilung* (Storm Detachment)
SFIO *Section Française de l'Internationale Ouvrière* (French Section of the Workers' International)

SPD *Sozialdemokratische Partei Deutschlands* (German Social Democratic Party)

SRP *Sozialistische Reichspartei* (Socialist Reich Party)

SS *Schutzstaffel* (Elite Guard)

UDCA *Union de Défense des Commerçants et Artisans* (Républicains Union for theDefense of Shopkeepers and Artisans)

UFF *Union et Fraternité Française* (French Union and Fraternity)

UNIR *Union des Nationaux et des Indépendants Républicains* (Union of National and Independent Republicans)

UQ *Uomo Qualunque* (the Common Man)

European Frontiers
1919-1937

Lost by Germany 1919
Saar: League of Nations
control 1919-1935
Demilitarized Rhineland
1919-1939
Austria-Hungary until 1918
Plebiscite Areas
Former Territory of Imperial
Russia

NORWAY

SWEDEN

DENMARK

North Sea

Baltic Sea

FINLAND

●Leningrad

ESTONIA

Riga●
LATVIA

Memel● LITHUANIA

●Minsk

●Vilna

USSR

Danzig●
(Free City) GERMANY

HOLLAND

Berlin ●

●Bonn

GERMANY

Weimar●

Saar

Alsace-Lorraine

Munich●

SWITZERLAND

●Poznan

Breslau●

●Prague

CZECHOSLOVAKIA

Vienna●

AUSTRIA

●Warsaw

POLAND

Cracow●

●Lvov

HUNGARY

ROMANIA

Trieste●

ITALY

Belgrade●

Montenegro●

YUGOSLAVIA

Adriatic Sea

Serbia

BULGARIA

ALBANIA

GREECE

0   300 miles

The German Mastery of Europe
1942

FINLAND

ESTONIA

LATVIA

LITHUANIA

nzig

ERMANY

Leningrad

Moscow

Minsk

R U S S I A

Stalingrad

Warsaw

POLAND   Brest-Litovsk

Lvov

Rostov

SLOVAKIA

HUNGARY

ROMANIA

Belgrade

LAVIA

BULGARIA

Black Sea

ALBANIA

TURKEY

GREECE

Sea

El Alamein

EGYPT

	Axis Powers 1939
	Powers co-operating with Axis
	Territory occupied by Axis
	French-Vichy governed
	Neutrals
	Unconquered

0   300 miles

Europe 1945-1948

Legend:
- 1937 Frontiers
- Allied Control Zones of Germany & Austria
- Cities divided into 4 Occupation Zones
- Annexed by Russia in 1945
- States which became Communist between 1945 and 1948
- Yugoslav gains from Italy 1945
- The 'Iron Curtain' 1948-1989

FINLAND

Leningrad

SWEDEN

ESTONIA

LATVIA

DENMARK

North Sea

Baltic Sea

Memel

LITHUANIA

Königsberg

Vilna

Danzig

GERMANY (annexed by Poland)

Minsk

USSR

HOLLAND

American

British

Berlin

Russian

Poznan

Warsaw

POLAND

GERMANY

Wroclaw (Breslau)

French

American

Prague

Cracow

Lvov

FRANCE

French

CZECHOSLOVAKIA

French

Russian

Vienna

SWITZERLAND

American

AUSTRIA

Budapest

French

British

HUNGARY

ROMANIA

Trieste

Belgrade

ITALY

YUGOSLOVIA

BULGARIA

Adriatic Sea

Rome

0   300 miles

ALBANIA

GREECE

Introduction

i

IMAGES OF FASCISM are part of our culture. For most people, the word *fascism* conjures up visions of nihilistic violence, war, and Götterdämmerung. Fascism has a sexual side too—but it is a world of Germanic uniforms and discipline, of bondage and sadomasochism, rather than love.

These images have a corresponding reality. Fascist movements and regimes were characterized more by what they were against than by what they were for—a Manichaean division of the world into the forces of good and evil. Nazism especially created a Sadean theater of death for those it deemed the enemies of the nation—most notably the racially dangerous Jews. Its political enemies also suffered appallingly. Many of the leaders of the July 1944 bomb plot against Adolf Hitler were dangled by piano wire from meat hooks and slowly garroted. Their excruciating death throes were filmed so that the Führer could later replay the sadistic drama from the comfort of his armchair.

Yet behind this stereotypical fascism, defined essentially by its style and negations, lay a coherent body of thought, whose roots can be traced to seminal intellectual developments made during the late nineteenth and early twentieth centuries. The resulting ideology was elusive because it drew from both the right and left, seeking to create a radical "Third Way" which was neither capitalist nor communist. Its nationalism, which celebrated the strength of the holistic community over the individual, was very different from the liberal nationalism that had been developed by some of the great thinkers of the Enlightenment during the eighteenth century. But fascism's ability to appeal to important intellectuals, such as the philosophers Martin Heidegger and Giovanni Gentile, underlines that it cannot be dismissed as necessarily irrational.

This last point needs to be clear from the outset. To put it another way, the time has come to shed popular stereotypes and to assess fascism as objectively as possible. Fascism has become a latter-day symbol of evil, like the devil in the Middle Ages. Demonizing all aspects of fascism, a founding form of Political Correctness, has its uses. But failure to take fascism seriously as a body of ideas makes it more difficult to understand how fascism could attract a remarkably diverse following in some countries. This book, therefore, begins by stressing the importance of ideas. More specifically, it shows that fascism is not necessarily defined by the record of the two classic fascist regimes—Hitler's Germany and Benito Mussolini's Italy. (General Franco's Spain, often seen as the third major example, was really a form of authoritarian conservatism and lacked true fascism's social radicalism, though it had some of the stylistic trappings that were so central to classic fascism).

The main focus of this work, however, is the world of real politics rather than the history of ideas. One major question raised by this book is, why did fascism become a mass movement in Italy and Germany, and why did it continue to gather support after coming to power? Conversely, why did fascism fail to become a major force elsewhere? Why did France, which had been a crucial seedbed for proto-fascist ideas before 1914, fail to produce a major interwar fascist party—though it produced some of the more sophisticated fascist political thinkers? And why has Britain become the epitome of the European country that remained immune to the fascist temptation—although it produced in Sir Oswald Mosley, a former Conservative and Labor member of Parliament who some mentioned as a likely future prime minister, one of its apparently most charismatic leaders?

The answer to the conundrum of fascism's appeal has most frequently been found in socioeconomic factors—especially the way in which rapid social change produced a "rootless" society, or the way in which economic crises hit particular groups, most notably the "middle class." Both contain important insights and point to the fact that fascism was nothing if not a child of breakdown and fear. They provide a particularly powerful insight when combined, rather than seen—as they normally are—as competing theories. One of the great strengths of fascism was its syncretic ideology's ability to be interpreted differently by various groups: it could appeal both to those who sought some form of collective rebirth and to those whose concerns were essentially individualistic, focusing on personal economic interests. But there was no automatic progression from socioeconomic change, even mass unmployment and despair, to fascism. Several European countries could match Germany's high unemployment rates in the early 1930s without spawning fascist mass movements. Even in Britain there was great misery in many areas during the interwar years, yet Mosley's movement proved incapable of attracting any significant support.

In order to understand more clearly the factors behind the rise of fascism, it is necessary to turn to more political dimensions. One concerns what could be termed political space: was there a place in the party spectrum where fascism could successfully situate itself? Although its ideology drew on both left and right, in most Western European countries fascism was successful where the mainstream right was weak. But space alone was not enough: legitimacy was far more important. Fascism had to be seen as a continuation of important national traditions, as a force capable of achieving goals. This in turn points to two further factors: the impact of national political traditions and the role played by leadership—fascist and nonfascist. Put simply, fascism succeeded where it achieved syncretic legitimation, the ability both to appeal to affective and more individualistic voters, and to convince at least a section of the mainstream elites that it could serve their purpose better than existing parties.

It is not necessary to resort to crude national stereotypes to see that there were aspects of the British and French political traditions that helped to defuse rather than encourage fascism—the British emphasis on constitutionally limited government and on individual rights, for example, or the French Republican belief in "Liberty, Equality, and Fraternity." German nationalism, on the other hand, had a strong Romantic tradition, which underpinned an emotive sense of community and longing for strong leadership. Italian nationalism had a stronger liberal strand, but it also had a strong affinity with another aspect of German nationalism: namely, the attempt to forge a united community by linking nationalism to economic progress. Such features did not lead automatically to fascism, but they were crucial in helping to define what forms of politics were legitimate—and in moderating or intensifying responses to socio-economic crises.

National identity also helps to understand another important question relating to fascism: why did fascism vary significantly from country to country—not simply in terms of success, but also in terms of program and practice? Why, for example, was anti-Semitism ridiculed by Mussolini and most of his leading colleagues before the late 1930s? (Mussolini even had a Jewish mistress for a time, and many Jews were prominent in the Fascist Party until the late 1930s). Why Mussolini's regime was relatively benign compared to Hitler's cannot be answered solely by national identity. The nature of these two regimes raises complex questions about attitudes, knowledge, and the power of social control (and how other peoples would have reacted had they faced the same climate of fear). But when all is said and done, there seems little doubt that national political traditions played their part in molding the fascist regimes. It is especially hard to understand how the Holocaust could have taken place without reference to the strong German tendency to see citizenship in terms of blood, or to important trends within German politics and scientific thought that made racism almost consensual.

The importance of leadership to the question of success and failure can be seen clearly by briefly considering the coming to power of Italian and German fascism. Neither Hitler nor Mussolini especially commanded anything like a majority in parliament. Although they had helped to create major paramilitary and electoral movements, both became heads of government partly because of the decisions taken by a handful of key individuals in the political system. These decisions were influenced by several factors, but crucially by the inability of existing leaders to forge a consensus that could defuse the threat from the radical left and attract sufficient support to secure a governmental majority in parliament—though in some cases this ineptitude would be better described as a lack of desire to maintain the democratic system.

Turning the spotlight from the Establishment to the fascist leadership helps to explain why fascism has frequently been seen as essentially opportunistic, even as lacking a coherent ideology. Before coming to power, both Hitler and Mussolini steered their movements away from their revolutionary origins in an attempt to court both elite and popular support, often tailoring their appeals for particular audiences. After coming to power, pragmatism was a strong element in both regimes, especially during the early days when fascism had to come to terms with powerful forces, notably the Catholic church in Italy and the army and business in Germany. Yet ultimately Hitler and Mussolini were driven by strong ideological motives—a point which can be seen clearly by Hitler's "Final Solution" of the Jewish "problem," or by Mussolini's reversion to a radical form of fascism during the closing days of World War II.

On April 29, 1945, news reached the besieged *Führerbunker* that the Duce had been shot on the previous day by the Resistance. His corpse was taken to Milan, where it was strung up on public display in Piazzale Loreto beside his last mistress, Clara Petacci, who had been executed at the same time. Hitler had no intention of suffering the same fate—or worse—at the hands of the Russians, who were just blocks away from his Berlin Chancery. The attempt to create a new Aryan Europe was over and Hitler finally decided to marry his long-standing mistress, Eva Braun. In a curious reversal of symbolism, the ceremony was an end rather than a beginning—part of the final rites in his religion of death. Having bid farewell to the loyal group who remained with him to the end, Hitler and his devoted bride committed suicide. The final reckoning came just ten days after the Führer's fifty-sixth birthday.

Most historians have held that fascism was essentially a phenomenon of the interwar years, which died as a major force in the ruins of Berlin. In the decades immediately after 1945, pockets of diehards continued to meet, drink, and to fight the occasional election—sometimes with a modicum of success. A smattering of youth provided a few new faces, who were particularly useful when it came to attacking opponents or defending neofascist meetings. Yet all this was insignificant compared to the interwar years, when even in France and Britain fascists could mount major mass rallies. It might be thought, therefore, that the story could safely close with the military defeats of Italy, Germany, and their various satraps (allegedly post–1945 "fascist" regimes in Europe, like the Colonels' Greece, were conservative dictatorships rather than fascist).

But during the 1980s a variety of notable developments began to take place. One concerns the growth of racial violence. Even "tolerant" Britain has not been immune to this virus, though the wave of firebombing and other attacks in Germany has attracted the most worldwide media attention. There has also been a notable growth in fringe political propaganda. This includes a remarkable wave of Holocaust Denial material, which seeks to argue that no Jews were gassed, that the Holocaust is the "Hoax of the Century." This will reach new audiences in the late 1990s by being distributed on the rapidly growing computer Internet. (One of the main North American Holocaust Denial sites already distributes material in German and Spanish as well as English, and has plans to expand into Russia—a country that seems ripe for the revival of anti-Semitism.) Finally, but by no means least, there has been a surprising trend in recent years for neofascist parties to gain in electoral strength. The sudden rise to prominence during the 1990s of the charismatic and shrewd Gianfranco Fini and the Italian Social Movement–National Alliance, which became part of the governing coalition in 1994, serves as a particularly dramatic example of this tendency.

Some of these developments are not necessarily fascist. *Fascism* and *racism* are not synonyms. It is even possible to deny the Holocaust without being a card-carrying Nazi. These points again highlight the importance of defining fascism, for some of the people and groups discussed in the final section of this book are not strictly fascists—though in most cases they have been frequently accused of being fascist. The same point applies to a lesser degree to the pre-1945 sections, but after 1945, *fascism* becomes a particularly problematic term in objective analysis. Since World War II, few people outside an alienated fringe have been willing to term themselves fascist, for obvious reasons: the epithet has become essentially pejorative. Many historians and social scientists have tried to get around this problem by coining new terms, such as "extreme right" or "radical right," which seem to be more neutral, not so burdened by images of the past. But often they are vaguely defined, or raise new problems. The "radical right," for instance, could legitimately include anti–big government populist movements that have little or nothing in common with the fascist tradition. The term "extreme right" fails to pick up the fact that fascism's intellectual pedigree has not been uniquely right-wing.

This book, therefore, uses the term *neofascism* to refer to post-war developments that can be legitimately considered fascist in relation to how the term was defined implicitly at the beginning of this introduction: namely, a serious ideology that emerged at the turn of the twentieth century. As such, describing an individual or group as neofascist is in no way intended to imply that they are necessarily defenders of past dictatorships. (The term *neo-Nazi* is used to highlight those who essentially look back to Hitler's regime for inspiration, the most common form of recidivist neofascism.)

In the 1970s antifascists asked, "Do you have half a mind to be a neo-Nazi? That's all you need." Today the more alienated, violent side of neofascism remains a danger, particularly to ethnic communities. It is also becoming more sophisticated: cyberspace warriors can now find details of how to make bombs and exchange ideas with fellow activists, and potential converts, through the Internet. These include American neofascist and white rights groups, some of whom have clearly been influenced by European fascism. Before the 1995 Oklahoma bombing, most Americans took little interest in such extremism, be it European or native. But the belief that the bombing may have been inspired by *The Turner Diaries,* written by a leading American neofascist, has increased interest in what exactly is happening on the contemporary European neofascist scene. The *Diaries'* call for race war to secure a white homeland also now seems less far-fetched against a background of growing fears for race relations in America, and a white flight to the safety of the suburbs.

Neofascist violence in Europe tends to be aimed at ethnic communities more than the state. In general it lacks any serious strategy, other than perhaps a local version of ethnic cleansing. But there are signs that violence is increasingly inspired by a belief that it will provoke an ethnic backlash, which will polarize politics and push the mass of "complacent" whites into the arms of the extremists. Should this happen, neofascists might gain yet further electoral support. So far, the main breakthroughs in this sphere have been made by groups led by the more sophisticated type of neofascist—people who are often capable of developing a serious level of debate and tactics in order to achieve some legitimacy. For instance, in Italy Fini and the National Alliance have begun to talk of themselves as "postfascists," and at their 1995 Congress specifically rejected totalitarianism and racism—though in other ways they remained more true to core fascist ideology. As the final section of this book reveals, the time has passed when neofascism can be dismissed as style more than content, a living past rather than a political movement with a future. The fascist tradition remains very much alive and kicking—both literally and metaphorically.

In the pages that follow, the story of fascism—from its origins to the present day—is told largely in narrative form. There has for some time been a prejudice against this approach, not least from professional historians: fashion has encouraged the study of neglected groups, a form of history from below, or has stressed the need for close textual study of a relatively limited range of documents (the historians' philosophers' stone). Others, influenced more by psychology or sociology, have focused on fascism as a form of pathology, appealing to those who had been traumatized by war, or who were seeking some form of personal rebirth. This book, aimed essentially at the general reader and student, is based on the assumption that it is necessary to see fascism more a whole. Or perhaps this point should be redefined to say that a concise, but rounded, picture has been presented for four countries—the four that have already been stressed in this introduction as offering vital insights into the nature of fascism: namely, Germany, Italy, France, and Britain. Omitting other forms of fascism, such as the Spanish Falange or its eastern European manifestations, has undoubted disadvantages. But the focused study of four countries should help bring out key linking themes, two in particular. First, for all the national differences, especially as the main parties grew in strength and watered down their radicalism to attract new support, there was a common ideological core based on the attempt to create a *holistic-national radical Third Way*. And secondly, there were common dynamics in the success and failure of fascism. Most notably, it succeeded where it managed to achieve some form of *syncretic legitimation*, in which the insurgent party was able to portray itself as both economically efficacious and a legitimate part of the national tradition, and the Establishment elites were willing to accord to fascism an important element of support.

These last points illustrate that the revival of fascism should not be viewed fatalistically. In a fundamental sense, fascism succeeded for political reasons: hence, this is primarily a political history, which should serve both as a vehicle of instruction and as a warning.

PART ONE

In the Beginning

The Birth
of Fascist Ideology

i

ON OCTOBER 29, 1932, a great exhibition opened in Rome to cele-
brate the tenth anniversary of the first fascist "revolution." At the
heart of the exhibits was Room R, a reconstruction of the newspaper editorial office that had been home to Benito Mussolini during the rise of fascism. Above, in great letters, was the word DUX
("leader") and the dates 1919–1922—a reminder that it had taken
just three years for Mussolini to move from founding a new political movement to the center of power. Flanking these inscriptions
were two slogans: BELIEVE, OBEY, FIGHT and ORDER, AUTHORITY,
JUSTICE—the Holy Trinities of the new order that had replaced the
hated liberal democratic system.

The Italian fascist movement was built on catechisms. Its early
activists often adopted the slogan of the black-shirted wartime shock
troops, "I don't care a damn," which was written in blood on their
bandaged wounds as a badge of pride—a trophy of their many
battles with the hated "Bolshevik" enemy. After the destruction of
the left-wing and other opposition political parties during 1922–5,
Italy was to become a gigantic hoarding site, pasted with slogans
such as: WAR IS TO MAN AS CHILDBIRTH IS TO WOMAN and BETTER
TO LIVE ONE DAY AS A LION THAN A HUNDRED YEARS AS A SHEEP.

It is easy to understand why fascism is widely seen as little more
than a nihilistic, authoritarian, and violent movement that is best
comprehended in terms of psychology rather than rational thought.
It is also easy to see why what is arguably the most influential academic definition of fascism stresses its style (such as its emphasis on
leadership and propaganda) or its negations (like its hostility to
communism), rather than its positive intellectual content.[1] Liberalism, Marxism, socialism, and even conservatism have their great

thinkers and can truly be considered ideologies. Fascism seems devoid of an intellectual pedigree, little more than a ragbag of authoritarian and nationalist slogans.

All too easy, but all too wrong—for in truth fascism was an ideology just like the others.[2] As such, it needs to be identified in terms of a body of ideas—not simply in order to clarify what can truly be termed fascist, but to help understand why fascism could have exerted such a fatal appeal to intellectuals as well as to violent activists, to those who were seeking to become part of a new community as well as to those who were motivated by personal economic concerns. Ideas matter in politics—they inspire and shape action, take on a concrete force.

This does not mean that fascism in practice necessarily mirrored the ideology. There is a sense in which fascist movements and regimes departed significantly from the ideological roots. Although the activist and more emotive side of the fascist style of thought involved clear dangers, it did not necessarily lead to brutal dictatorship and genocidal practice (in the same way that Marxism did not necessarily lead to Joseph Stalin and the Soviet terror, though flaws in Marxist ideology posed similar dangers). Fascism—like all serious ideologies—had a vital core, but in 1919 it was in its infancy rather than fully developed.

ii

IN ORDER TO TRACE the birth of this fascist ideology, it is most fruitful to begin by looking briefly at the Enlightenment—the great intellectual movement that swept over eighteenth century Europe. It ushered in the era of "modernity": the belief that destiny could be shaped, that life was not simply determined by the forces of fate, luck, or God. The Enlightenment celebrated the power of reason and science over the previously dominant monarchical or religious authority. It heralded a new form of democratic politics. After the French Revolution of 1789, "Sovereignty of the People," rather than the "Divine Right of Kings," was the new liturgy. And material progress, rather than spiritual development, became the primary social goal. With this new politics came new forms of political shorthand—with the "left" representing the forces of progress, and the "right" defending the preservation of the past.[3]

Initially, progressive ideas were most clearly encapsulated in liberal ideology, with its emphasis on individualism and the related political doctrine of the limited, constitutional state, and its economic philosophy of laissez-faire. Such views were to become anathema to fascists, who believed that they made the alienating pursuit of money the main focus of life and created a dangerous division between classes and between government and people. By the late nineteenth century, socialism had taken over from liberalism as the main progressive ideological force. There were more points of contact between this ideology and fascism, but most of the central tenets of socialism were similarly rejected by fascists. This was especially true of the more radical forms of socialism, which opposed all private property—or which, like liberalism, proclaimed the existence of a common humanity and sought some form of universal culture.

In this sense, fascism was a negation of the Enlightenment, part of a counterrevolution that rejected the basic assumptions of "modernity."[4] The Enlightenment, however, also gave rise to other radical ideas, especially the belief that violence might be necessary to purge the existing order, and that only a mass-based form of politics could incorporate the will of the people—ideas that fascism was clearly to echo. Paradoxically, in terms of ideas, fascism was both a product of the Enlightenment and a reaction to it. This can be seen by considering some of the men and movements who have been cited as ideological antecedents of fascism by the handful of academics who have accepted that fascist ideology had some form of intellectual core.

The finger has been most often pointed at the eighteenth-century Swiss political philosopher and polymath Jean-Jacques Rousseau.[5] In many ways, Rousseau was a product of the Enlightenment, especially in his belief that it was possible to shape a better world. Yet key aspects of his thought had a more complex paternity. Arguably the most important was his belief that a "general will" could emerge in society—a harmony that would overcome both social divisions and the gulf between citizen and government. Rousseau was particularly interested in the experience of the small city-states of ancient Greece, which he saw as more natural communities than the emerging large states. His emphasis on homogeneity was very different from liberal thought, which tended to stress pluralism and checks and balances. But the most dangerous aspect of Rousseau's thought was the belief that people might not always perceive the true "general will." This meant there might be occasions when they would need to be "forced to be free." In such views, some have seen the seeds of elitist dictatorship (both communist and fascist). Yet it would be misleading to portray Rousseau as the first fascist. His general body of thought was multifaceted, and there were other central elements that were very different from later fascism—most notably his emphasis on universal rules applying to all peoples.

The German philosopher G. W. F. Hegel is also cited as a major intellectual forerunner of fascism, partly because of his interest in the process of history, for fascism was later to stress the validity of historical over rationalistic truth. More often, the similarities of his view of the state with Plato's are emphasized—leading to both being seen as enemies of an "open society" based on diversity and tolerance.[6] In reality, Hegel's view of the state was complex, but his emphasis on the need for a balance of forces in civil society and his fear of the masses are more characteristic of conservative than fascist thought. A more fruitful parallel can be found in Hegel's attack on abstract reason. He saw Enlightenment philosophy, especially liberalism, as severing people from tradition—a trend that was producing alienation rather than liberation. Yet the fact that both left and right variations of Hegelianism emerged during the nineteenth century should serve as a warning to anyone who seeks to trace a simple line of descent from Hegel to fascism.

Turning from individuals to more general intellectual movements, two developments have most frequently been cited as laying the intellectual foundations of fascism: the Romantic movement and the growth of a holistic nationalism, which was related to the rise of new racist political thinking.

The Romantic movement emerged during the eighteenth century, largely as a response to the hyperrationalism of the Enlightenment, and reached its high point in the works of German writers such as Johann von Goethe and Friedrich von Schelling. Among its many aspects was the worship of nature, the glorification of the national and historical against the universal and timeless, and the exaltation of genius over the mediocrity of the masses. This last aspect was sometimes specifically artistic: the tortured, creative soul, unappreciated by bourgeois society. But it could also take on a political form in the quest for the strong leader who could lead a national rebirth. Similarly, diffuse hostility toward material values became increasingly translated during the late nineteenth century into political anti-Semitism. The Jew was pilloried as the epitome of capitalist materialism—a view particularly prevalent in the German *völkisch* movement, which railed against the evils of urban, industrial society.[7]

Völkisch ideas were linked to the spread of a more emotive form of nationalism during the nineteenth century. The first main wave of nationalist ideology during the eighteenth century had largely been associated with liberal democratic ideas relating to the sovereignty of the people, which then raised the question, "Who are the people?" It was a universalistic and humanistic creed, for most Enlightenment philosophers held that all people had a right to rule themselves and that citizenship was open to all. It was also essentially a left-wing creed, for the doctrine of popular sovereignty clearly challenged the dominant ideas of monarchical and religious authority.

During the late nineteenth century, nationalism increasingly took on a more right-wing hue—though the seeds of a reaction to the first wave can be traced back to the eighteenth century. One of the high priests of this new nationalism was the French journalist and writer, Maurice Barrès, who became the prophet of "rootedness" (*enracinement*), involving a mystical social union between the living and dead. Whereas earlier nationalism had been closely associated with modernity, this new form was highly critical of what it saw as the resulting socially divisive and individualistic materialism. Barrès believed that the epitaph of the French had become "Born a man, died a grocer." ("Accountant" would be today's *mot juste*.) Whereas the old nationalism was essentially concerned with legitimating the overthrow of regimes, this form of nationalism was obsessed with the need to secure social unity in order to prevent the collapse of regimes—and to develop the martial values necessary to survive in war. By the 1890s Barrès was talking of "nationalism socialism"—though the term was essentially manipulative, a desire to extend the appeal into the working class, for his social views were conservative more than radical.[8]

This holistic nationalism was highly critical of liberal universalism, a feature that contributed to the rise of a new racism. Hostility to outsiders had existed since primordial times and ancient Greek philosophy had demonized the barbarian "Other." What emerged during the late nineteenth century was a more systematic form of racial thinking. Two names stand out in this development: the French aristocrat Arthur de Gobineau and the Englishman Houston Stewart Chamberlain—who in later life adopted German citizenship and became an admirer of a rising young politician named Adolf Hitler. Gobineau's key work was his *Essay on the Inequality of Human Races*, written in the 1850s but little read until after the 1870s. He saw the world as polarized between white, yellow, and black races (or Caucasian, Mongoloid, Negroid) and argued that the motor of history was the struggle between these races. Chamberlain was deeply influenced by the nationalism of the composer Richard Wagner, who became his father-in-law. His *Foundations of the Nineteenth Century*, published in 1900, was widely read—or more precisely, sold and talked about. Its seminal importance to the emergence of fascism, however, lies in more than simply its influence. It is also related to its style, for Chamberlain's arguments were not just based on Wagnerian historical or mystical notions. He synthesized these ideas with a growing body of scientific and intellectual developments and rejected the pessimism of Gobineau.[9]

Within these developments in Romantic, and especially in nationalist and racist thought, the origins of fascist ideology begin to emerge more clearly. But much of this thinking arose from a mystical hostility to the Enlightenment. Although there was to be an element of this in fascism, it is important to realize that many of its central arguments were based on "reason"—though the conclusions contradicted the Enlightenment's most optimistic and "modern" assumptions. This can be seen clearly by considering two areas of rationalist thought in the late nineteenth and early twentieth centuries: the sciences and the emerging social sciences.[10]

Arguably the most important nineteenth-century scientific development in its impact on political ideology was Darwinism.

Charles Darwin published *The Origins of Species* in 1859. Others quickly realized that some of the key ideas, especially "survival of the fittest" and "natural selection," could be adapted for political ends—though there were disagreements over what the implications were. In one version, Darwinism seemed to point to the need for minimal state intervention in order to allow free competition. In another, Darwinism was taken as highlighting the need for the state to take on the role of selection to ensure survival—especially in the battle with less developed but virile and martial races. The strong appeal of the latter position needs understanding against a more general background of scientific-racial thought. In particular, further impetus toward statist-racism came in the form of eugenics, which was pioneered by leading scientists such as the German Ernst Haeckel. The eugenicists were worried about the way that moral laws prevented the working of natural selection, for example in taboos on euthanasia. A crucial theme of theirs was the need to regenerate national or European racial stock.[11]

The emphasis on leadership found an echo in two key developments in the social sciences. The first was the emergence of elite theory. By 1914 leading sociologists, including the Italian Vilfredo Pareto and the German Robert Michels (who moved to Italy and became a prominent admirer of Benito Mussolini), believed that societies were necessarily ruled by elites.[12] They held that the major difference between forms of government was simply the social composition of elites and the extent to which they were open to talent from rising social groups. The second development came from psychology. The main intellectual figure here was Sigmund Freud, whose work on unconscious drives seemed to undermine much of the Enlightenment's belief in individuals as conscious and rational actors who could shape their own fate. Of even greater immediate political impact was the work of the Frenchman Gustave Le Bon. His most famous work, *The Psychology of Crowds* (1895), depicted the people as an emotive mass, easily swayed by charismatic leaders. This book was to enjoy remarkably wide sales—and both Hitler and Mussolini were aware of its main arguments.

These ideas were reinforced by two philosophers: Friedrich Nietzsche and Georges Sorel. Highlighting the thought of these two major thinkers serves to illustrate the dangers of believing that classic fascist ideology can be placed simply on the left-right spectrum for Nietzsche is commonly seen as one of the most fertile sources of conservative thought, whereas Sorel is seen as having made a crucial contribution to socialism.[13]

There is no doubt that Nietzsche's writings are elusive, often dealing in metaphors like "sickness and health" or in irony rather than clear arguments. They are also written in a radical style, synthesizing literature and philosophy, the abstract and the concrete. Three sets of argument, however, were central to Nietzsche's credo. First, anticipating Freud, was the appreciation of the irrational, unconscious side of human nature. Next, Nietzsche was fearful for the future of the West, which he believed was lapsing into individualistic and material decadence accompanied by irretrievable decline. He related this back to Christianity—which he termed a "slave religion"—and its later secular forms: humanism and socialism. These, he believed, encouraged a false sense of universalism, tending to promote pity for the weak rather than respect for the strong. This led to his final theme, which he set out in works such as *Thus Spake Zarathustra* (1883–5). Here Nietzsche argued that the main lesson of history was that at exceptional times a man of destiny would use his will to rise above the herd of ordinary men. Nietzsche, therefore, eulogized the great leader, the "Superman" who would overcome nihilism and recreate a more spiritual community—the "man" who would turn politics into aesthetics.

Sorel is associated with two key developments that reflect the doubts felt by some socialist theorists at the turn of the twentieth century: together they reflect a less optimistic view of human nature than that held by most socialists, almost a division of society into two types of people—the economic-rational and the emotive-collective. First, influenced by arguments about the survival of the fittest, he held that socialism could be compatible with private property and that socialism needed to be concerned with securing efficient production as well as equitable distribution: equality among paupers could never form the basis of a viable society. Second, influenced especially by Le Bon, Sorel developed the idea that the working class could only be brought to revolutionary consciousness by the use of "myths." He saw these as simple verbal formulae that underpinned social solidarity by crystalizing fundamental beliefs—like "log cabin to White House" as a vivid expression of the dream of social mobility in the Unites States. In *Reflections on Violence* (1907) he sought to popularize the idea of a general strike as the means to bring down the social order. He did not see his task as the setting out of a clear blueprint for such an insurrection. The point was more to offer an inspiring myth, which would raise working-class consciousness and willingness to take action. For Sorelian syndicalists (from the French for trade union, *syndicat*), the word would thus take on a concrete reality. The herd of "human zeros," as one syndicalist described the people, would be aroused from their slumbers.

Hitler was fond of posing for photographs staring at Nietzsche's bust and he frequently visited the Nietzsche museum in Weimar, where the philosopher died in 1900. This probably tells us more about Hitler and especially Nietzsche's sister than about the thinker himself. Elisabeth Nietzsche and her virulently anti-Semitic husband, Bernhard Förster, set up an Aryan paradise in Paraguay during the 1880s. Nueva Germania turned out to be more like hell and Förster poisoned himself at the end of a six-week drinking spree. Back in Germany, Elisabeth increasingly took control of the affairs of her brother, who was lapsing into insanity—probably the result of syphilis. Even before his death, she set about turning him into the great prophet of nationalism and anti-Semitism. This alone would have made him appeal to Hitler, but he had other attractions too, especially his reputation for being a major, albeit difficult thinker. Hitler was not opposed to intellectuals per se; indeed, he saw the advantages of exploiting the authority of people who were perceived as great thinkers. It was more a certain type of intellectual whom he condemned. This was the rationalistic, optimistic believer in the perfectibility of people and human progress—ideas best encapsulated in liberalism and Marxism. Such ideas found in Nietzsche their most fertile critic of the nineteenth century.

In his final major work, *Ecce Homo* (1888), Nietzsche prophesied: "One day there will be associated with my name the recollection of something frightful, or a crisis like no other before on earth . . . I am not a man. I am dynamite." It is all too easy when studying the origins of fascism to accept Nietzsche's implied connection between ideas and events, without realizing that the relationship between thought and practice is elusive. This crucial point is underlined by the fact that it is far from clear that either Nietzsche or Sorel would have supported the fascist movements that emerged after 1919.

In adult life Nietzsche journeyed from ivory tower academic to ailing grand tourist. It is highly doubtful whether he would have felt any affinity with the working-class, unintellectual side of "proletarian" Nazism. Many have stressed that Nietzsche criticized German nationalism and biological theories of race, but this argument needs probing more carefully. Nietzsche's critique of German nationalism was essentially twofold. First, he believed that it was diverting attention from more general European problems, especially the rise of decadence. Second and related to this first point, he saw modern German culture as too materialist, too philistine. But this did not mean that there was nothing about Germany that Nietzsche admired. He had a great respect for Frederick the Great and celebrated a more ancestral, heroic German spirit. Nor was his thinking completely opposed to racism. Central to his beliefs was a desire to save Europe from decadence and from the threat of newer and more virile nations. Ultimately, it is impossible to be sure how Nietzsche would have reacted to the development of the main fascist regimes. On balance, the evidence points to the idea that he would have opposed them—though some who shared many of Nietzsche's views, for instance the major philosopher Martin Heidegger, were to support the Nazis on the grounds that they offered the best vehicle for creating a new world.[14]

The main difference between Nietzsche's philosophy and fascism was not so much nationalism or racism as his pessimistic view of the possibilities of imminent change. In this context, fascist ideology was to owe more to Sorel. His work on myths as a mobilizing force was critical, a point later acknowledged by Mussolini—or rather by Mussolini on those occasions when he sought to stress the intellectual origins of fascism, for in more egocentric moments Mussolini liked to claim that he was the founder of fascism. Vital too was Sorel's movement away from the belief that socialism nec-

essarily involved the end of private ownership, which made possible a synthesis between aspects of left and right. Sorel, like Nietzsche, was not a nationalist in the sense that he believed in the
superiority of his own nation: it was the fate of European civilization that preoccupied him. But by the outbreak of World War I, he
had come to see the usefulness of nationalism as a myth for achieving popular mobilization and the creation of a new society. At first
Sorel showed some sympathy for infant Italian fascism, though he
quickly turned against it as Mussolini watered down fascism's initially radical program in order to attract the backing of the rich and
powerful. He died in 1923 without apparently commenting on
Nazism, but it seems likely that he would have condemned it—
especially as he was opposed to biological racism. Yet it is impossible to be sure. Certainly other radical socialists turned to fascism
when they came to believe that it was the best means of planning
for economic prosperity, welfare, and social unity—for instance the
Frenchman Marcel Déat.[15]

iii

WHAT WAS EMERGING in the period before World War I, especially among groups of younger thinkers and political activists, was
a complex ideological synthesis of old and new, of left and right.
Fascism was embryonic rather than fully formed, and its name was
yet to be coined. The emerging core of fascist ideology was clear,
nevertheless.

There was a growing concern with populist propaganda as the
basis of an appeal to the masses, especially with the use of myths to
encapsulate simple messages. A key metaphor was increasingly "rebirth"—which had the advantage of hiding whether what was
sought was something essentially new or old, and of exploiting a
central theme in Christian culture, thus broadening fascism's appeal.[16] More fundamentally, the key philosophical approach was
synthesis, or more exactly a set of syntheses. Fascist ideology used
primarily rational arguments to hold that people were largely
swayed by irrational motives. It sought to create a new society, but
one in which crucial old values would be retained. The ideological
goal of fascism was the creation of a "new man" (women had little
place in this thinking) based on deep national roots. It sought to

achieve economic development tempered by a sense of national community. People were to be made whole again by bridging the more individualistic and collective aspects of modernity.

Brief definitions of ideologies have inherent flaws, but perhaps the essence of fascist ideology can best be summed up by combining two ideas. The first relates to the basic nature of the community. Fascism was primarily concerned with building, or reviving, the nation (though a few were more concerned with European culture). But there have been nationalists who accept liberal rights, or who welcome diversity. The fascist conception of the nation was more holistic, it sought to overcome divisive differences and to forge a strong sense of shared purpose. The second part relates more to socioeconomic policy. Intellectual fascists were often to term themselves supporters of a "Third Way," neither left nor right, neither capitalist nor communist: they sought to achieve individual prosperity, but linked to communal goals. The term is in some ways misleading, as it could be taken to imply that fascism was a form of centrism, or conservatism. Both would be totally false descriptions for an ideology that sought to launch a social revolution, albeit one that owed more to the right than left. Yet it is a useful shorthand for fascism's syncretic style of thinking.

Fascist ideology is, therefore, a form of thought that preaches the need for social rebirth in order to forge a *holistic-national radical Third Way*—though in practice fascism has tended to stress style, especially activism and the charismatic leader, more than detailed program, and to engage in a Manichaean demonization of its enemies. This is a formulation that clearly excludes many alleged examples of fascism, such as the essentially conservative dictatorship of General Franco in Spain. Yet it is flexible enough to include different varieties of fascism, for instance the biologically based nationalism of the Nazis and the culturally based Italian Fascism.[17] This emphasis on both its more affective-communal and economic-rational sides also opens important perspectives in terms of explaining why fascism could attract so broad a coalition of support in some countries. Underlining the importance of an ideological approach to the definition of fascism has to be intimately related to the question of the appeal of that ideology.

More specifically, there were four main poles to this emerging fascist ideology. First, there was a view of human nature that seemed to synthesize common left- and right-wing positions: people were seen as constrained by nature and talents, but fascism held that they were capable of being remolded in a new, more communal and virile society. Second, there was a view of geopolitics: nation, region, or race were seen as the driving forces of history, a motor that pointed to the need for military preparedness or aggression. Third (and least developed by 1919), there was a view of what political and economic structures were sought. Central to embryonic fascism was a critique of both democracy and capitalism as weak and socially divisive. Finally, there was an emphasis, largely derived from the view of human nature, on the need for propaganda, often related to the celebration of the charismatic leader, to induct people into the new values. (Although fascism at times could appear populist, it was essentially manipulative and often held common people in contempt.)[18]

It is important to underline that tracing the genesis and core of fascist ideology is not the same as identifying all the roots of the first self-styled "fascist" parties and related groups, which were to explode onto the European political scene after World War I. The relationship between the world of ideas and political movements is complex. There is no doubt that ideas—often derived secondhand, rather than from major thinkers—inspired some political activists. But ideas are not completely timeless, nor are they universal. They rise and fall in particular contexts and under the impact of specific events.

Although there is an important sense in which fascism's intellectual roots can be traced back to the period before 1914, there is no doubt that war played a crucial role in the appearance of the first major fascist movements. Even at the level of ideas it had a major effect. For instance, many syndicalists came to believe that nationalism rather than the working class general strike was the crucial mobilizing myth they were seeking. Sometimes this was related to the widespread belief that war had demonstrated the great power of the state to achieve social revolution. Those of more conservative disposition saw it in terms of securing the economic development that could finance the reforms to buy off left-wing revolution (which petrified many on the right after the Bolshevik success in 1917). War unquestionably undermined faith in old elites and in crucial values, such as religion, which had helped underpin the old order. But although it is possible to make generalizations about these trends, their impact varied depending on national traditions and on the way in which war affected different countries. So the hunt for the roots of fascist movements must turn from the abstract history of ideas to the more concrete realm of national histories.

2

The National Roots
of Fascist Movements

i

THE FIRST SELF-STYLED "fascist" movement was founded in Italy in 1919. Within the space of a few years, most European countries witnessed the creation of their own fascist parties—though some, including Hitler's National Socialists, either rarely or never referred to themselves as fascist. To understand why they took different forms, and why some prospered and others failed, it is necessary to begin the story well before World War 1 and to examine specific national traditions.

Stressing the importance of political traditions does not necessarily involve believing that national identity is written on tablets of stone or coded in the genes. Nations are diverse organisms, and capable of evolution. Political systems too are not rigid structures: parties rise and fall, and constitutions change. Even so, some political systems clearly have firmer roots than others, are more capable of sustaining shock or of marginalizing challenges. And the past shapes the present in a variety of ways. It helps to define what is familiar rather than alien, what is legitimate and what is unacceptable—all crucial factors in understanding the actions of both political leaders and the masses.

Recognizing the importance of national traditions points to the importance of studying fascism within different national contexts. Otherwise, it is difficult to distinguish what is accidental, or of minor importance, from crucial explanatory factors. In the pages that follow, four countries will be considered in turn. The reasons for the choice of two seem self-evident. Only Italy and Germany spawned truly mass fascist movements. France too presents a strong case for inclusion, as it was the crucible for key ideas on which fascist ideology was founded. Yet fascism as a movement dismally

17

failed there during the interwar era—though the popularity of the post-1940 authoritarian Vichy regime raises the possibility that a significant potential lurked beneath the surface. The case for including Britain may seem more debatable, but vital lessons can be learned from failure as well as success—and Britain is unquestionably the archetypal European country that has to this day been almost totally immune to fascism (unlike Germany, Italy, and France, which have spawned notable outbursts of post-1945 fascism—further factors for concentrating on these nations).

So how did these four key countries develop in the period before the formation of the first specifically fascist parties? What were the crucial aspects in their political traditions that were to help—or hinder—the emergence and growth of fascism?[1]

ii

MYTHS OF ENGLISH IDENTITY have deep roots—arguably the deepest roots of any country in Europe. Central to English national consciousness has been its association with liberty, which can be traced at least as far back as Anglo-Saxon times. The Magna Carta of 1215 may have been of mainly symbolic value, but it illustrates a continuing quest to secure rights and prevent the abuse of power. The English Revolution in the seventeenth century was a further major step in this process, particularly through the consolidation of parliamentary government. The related rise of Protestantism, with its sense of rights and tolerance, was another crucial foundation stone of national identity.

The refrain of "Rule, Britannia!" that was sung in taverns during the nineteenth century runs "Britons never will be slaves." It is a self-confident phrase that reveals much more than the widespread belief that the British had won first prize in the lottery of life. It illustrates the way in which a British rather than an English identity had become central to political consciousness. This was largely created consciously by elites, who used the religious and military threat from the continent to help forge a new centralized state, which included Welsh and Scots as well as the English.[2] Because Britain was a multinational state, these elites learned not only the power of ethnic identity but the need to use nationalism with care if it was not to be a divisive force. This encouraged a civic rather than a cultural or bio-logical sense of nation, and loyalty to a set of evolved institutions, es-pecially the monarchy and Parliament, rather than to a mystically conceived race. This tendency was reinforced after the French Revo-lution by a preference for pragmatism and decency over foreign "ra-tionalistic" thought and emotive Romanticism.

British democracy was not founded on clearly codified rules; its workings were tacit rather than articulated. It was evolutionary, punctuated by starts and stops—and the occasional step back. A crucial development in the late nineteenth century was the exten-sion of the franchise. There was no grand design behind this, it was more a response to popular pressures, but the extension of the vote to much of the male working class brought in its train the rapid rise of party organization reaching down into the constituencies, where elections were won by a simple majority. The emergence of elected local government after the 1880s also encouraged the development of two mass parties, undermining still further the power of local notables, and helping a new class of political talent to rise. This was especially true in the urban areas, which by 1900 housed the vast majority of the people who lived in the "First Industrial Nation."[3]

It is easy in retrospect to view these developments as inevitable. At the time, many politicians feared the rise of the masses. They realized that the nature of voting was changing, that social class and economic interest was becoming increasingly important. Both Lib-erals and Conservatives, therefore, were tempted to use social im-perialism as a way of rallying new voters, though it was a potentially divisive issue within each party. During the 1860s and 1870s Ben-jamin Disraeli had shrewdly used a mixture of domestic reform and colonial expansion to help found the modern "One Nation" Con-servative Party. But when Joseph Chamberlain sought to introduce a system of tariffs on nonimperial trade, the Conservatives, under the weak leadership of Arthur Balfour, began to split. The Liberals shrewdly responded by using the cry of "free trade" to reunite their party, which had divided badly over the Boer War, thus helping it to a great election victory in 1906.

Although Chamberlain's crusade failed, his ideas influenced a new generation that was coming to prominence. This was a group convinced by elitist and meritocratic ideas—by social Darwinism, eugenics, and the need for "national efficiency." British politics was relatively meritocratic, but there was a feeling that the country was stuck in the nineteenth century and losing out to the growing challenge of Germany on the economic and military front. Chamberlain's failure to carry the cause of tariff reform within the Conservative Party encouraged a further loss of faith in the parliamentary system. This was reinforced by a tendency to see the post-1906 Liberal government as pandering to sectional interests—including a "plunder-bund" of financiers and businessmen, mainly of German-Jewish origin, a sign of a darker side to Britain culture.

This anti-Semitism had several causes, most notably the arrival of new immigrants fleeing Russian pogroms, which meant that the Jewish community increased significantly around the turn of the century. Many settled in the East End of London, a traditional area for new arrivals to Britain. This economically deprived, irreligious area was the hunting ground of Jack the Ripper, sometimes rumored to be Jewish. Predictably, it was to be the home of Britain's first overtly anti-immigrant group. The Brothers' League was founded in 1902 and quickly attracted forty-five thousand members, though it faded as immigration tailed off. Its demise was hastened by the fact that it was shunned by most mainstream politicians. While there was a tendency in British culture to dislike Jews, there was a stronger elite fear of populism's threat to liberal tolerance—and to the established party system.[4]

From 1900 to 1914, radical new forces were emerging in British politics, including the Labor Party and a women's suffrage movement. Political violence was growing in Ireland, which briefly raised the specter of army disloyalty. It is easy to exaggerate the "strange death of liberal England" just before 1914, but this was clearly a time of considerable strain.[5] Although there were strong impediments to the creation of a successful fascist party, the British party system could have fractured in a way that would have opened a clearer space for fascism.[6] Certainly in 1914 it was far from clear that it was the Liberals who would split and wither, rather than the Conservatives—though British deference toward tradition and the Conservatives' nationalism were powerful cards that could help the party survive temporary economic crisis.[7]

World War I helped to consolidate a new party system. It allowed the Conservative Party further to wrap itself in the Union Jack, and underlined its status as the patriotic party. The Liberals, on the other hand, split over support for the war and the subsequent decision to create a coalition government. The schism was carried into the immediate postwar world when the slippery Liberal Prime Minister David Lloyd George fought an election immediately after the war in coalition with the Conservatives. In a triumphant campaign characterized by strong anti-German sentiment, the rump Liberals were badly squeezed between the nationalistic government forces and the rising appeal of Labor. The age of a Conservative-Labor duopoly was about to dawn—though it had to wait until 1922 before the majority of the Conservatives dumped the "Welsh Goat," as Lloyd George had become known to his detractors (a reference to his sexual as well as political cavortings).

World War I also consolidated Germany's replacement of France as Europe's bogeyman, a trend that had begun in the 1890s as Britain faced increasing trade and colonial rivalry from the Germans. During the war, in the most outlandish propaganda the "Beastly Huns" were accused of all forms of horror—including systematically raping nuns and boiling up corpses behind the front lines in order to utilize the fats.[8] The British Tommy, of course, fought honorably to destroy despotism, to make the world safe for democracy, and to create a better tomorrow. This idealistic propaganda helped divert attention both from the horrors of war, made worse by poor leadership at the front, and the less than fully democratic nature of the British political system before the war (though it is important not to ignore antiwar dissent). The upshot after four years of combat was the reinforcement of central planks of national mythology. The British had fought not for selfish gain, but to deter the evil continental aggressor—to make the "world fit for democracy." Victory had proved, once again, that "Britons never will be slaves"—or so it seemed.

iii

FRENCH MYTHS of national identity have similarly deep roots. A sense of cultural unity can be traced back to Frankish times, when Charlemagne fought the Moors. Six centuries later, Joan of Arc rode into history as a powerful symbol of resistance to the foreign invader, this time the English. Shortly afterward, France—like England before it—began to consolidate a relatively centralized state, which ruled over increasingly integrated territories.[9]

Arguably the most fertile source of French national identity is the Enlightenment and the aftermath of the 1789 Revolution. France had overthrown an autocratic Catholic monarchy, and political modernity had triumphed in the shape of a new set of secular ideas. Core themes in the Republican tradition, such as constitutionalism, individual liberty, and universal rights, seem at odds with what were later to emerge as the central tenets in fascist ideology, but there has been more than one strand to the French Republican tradition. The French Revolution, in part inspired by opposition to absolutism, quickly spawned new forms of dictatorship.[10] First came the Jacobins, who legitimized elite-inspired terror in the name of progress. Later, an obscure Corsican outsider, Napoleon Bonaparte, bolstered his plebiscitary-dictatorship with a remarkable display of extravagant ceremony to manipulate the largely illiterate masses: his coronation as emperor in 1804 was more lavish than that of any French king.

Napoleon created his own legend, which would return to bewitch France in times of self-doubt and crisis. In 1848, Bonapartism reemerged when his nephew, Louis Napoleon, won an overwhelming victory in the presidential election that followed the collapse of the restored monarchy. Four years later, he was crowned Emperor Napoleon III. The new imperial regime made great use of symbolism and myth, though "Bonapartism" was more than just style or an attempt to restore national grandeur. It sought to synthesize charismatic leadership with plebiscitary legitimacy. It claimed to be neither left nor right, to be above the parties and social interests that divided the nation. But it is a mistake to see Bonapartism as an early form of fascism.[11] Notable differences include the absence of a serious Bonapartist party and any attempt to mobilize the masses. Most crucially, there was no attempt to forge a new political culture: Bonapartism was populist more than fascist, hostile to mainstream elites, yet curiously defensive of traditional values—especially peasant ones.

France in the 1850s was made up of a small number of urban

oases, surrounded by a rural desert inhabited by savages—this at least is how much of the Parisian elite viewed their country. Some peasants did not even speak French. Much of this was to change during the last fifty years of the century. The growth of education transmitted the values of French history and culture. Civic ceremonies became national rather than local. The Fourteenth of July, commemorating the storming of the Bastille, became a national celebration, not just a chapter in books—though the celebration of an act of rebellion also helped condition a culture of legitimate direct action. Induction into the armed forces was accompanied by a new symbolism too. Traditionally the last days of freedom for the conscripts were celebrated by a group visit to the nearest brothel, led by the village's tricolor. In 1891 at Bray-sur-Seine a group of conscripts was stopped at the brothel door by a constable, who said that the *national* flag could not be dishonored by carrying it into such a place.[12]

A new form of French nationalism was beginning to emerge— the conservative nationalism of Barrès and others, who were concerned with forging social unity and promoting a more martial spirit. A critical event in the emergence of such thought was France's surrender to Prussia in 1870 after the battle of Sedan—a defeat which led to the fall of Napoleon III, the occupation of Paris, and a brief but bloody civil rebellion inspired by left-wing Communards. There was widespread agreement on the need for revenge and the recapture of the two departments which France had been forced to cede to the newly united German state—Alsace and Lorraine. But there were widespread fears too, for the growing economic might of Germany was plain for all to see, while France's population was falling behind that of her martial and virile neighbor.

This desire for revenge explains the sudden popularity of Boulangism in the late 1880s. In January 1886, General Georges Boulanger was made Minister of War, a post he undertook with reforming enthusiasm. When in January 1887 the German chancellor, Otto von Bismarck, named Boulanger as the greatest obstacle to good relations, his elevation as the popular hero "General Revenge" was complete. He lost office later that year when the government fell, but he did not fade from view. France was experiencing one of the periodic scandals and ministerial crises that were to become a feature of the Third Republic after the 1870s. Forces of both left and right began to coalesce around Boulanger. He won multiple election victories, and mobs shouted his name. (Le Bon was influenced by Boulangist hysteria.) Instead of leading the expected coup against the Republic, however, Boulanger chose to flee into exile when the government issued an order for his arrest. Why remains unclear.

Increasingly, the rising tide of "national populism" was to become linked to a new form of anti-Semitism. A key figure in this development was Edouard Drumont, who in 1886 published a book, *France Under the Jews*, which was into its two hundredth edition by 1914. The rise of a more holistic form of nationalism inevitably raised questions about who was *not* part of the community—and the Jew was the traditional outsider within Western culture. The prominence of Jews in finance and parts of industry added fuel to the fire, helping to stereotype them as materialistic and scheming—a characterization made even easier by the fact that several Jews were involved in the financial scandals that afflicted the Third Republic. The popular anger aroused by these *affaires* heightened an awareness that anti-Semitism was a counterweight to the growing force of socialism: the enemy was not so much capitalism as the Jew. (Anti-Semitism had earlier featured in the thought of several notable socialists.)

The strength of anti-Semitism was revealed most dramatically during the 1890s, when a Jewish army officer was wrongly imprisoned for treason.[13] The Dreyfus affair revealed the fault lines of the French party system for years to come. It rallied the forces of the moderate left to the Republic, and a reassertion of a liberal form of nationalism based on universalism and rights. Leading members of the armed forces were also vetted carefully, as many were revealed to have little sympathy for the apparently weak Republic. But the Dreyfus affair also rallied the Republic's old opponents, especially reactionary *haute bourgeois* Catholic opinion, and gave inspiration to the growing forces of radical nationalism and anti-Semitism in their quest to unite the nation and defeat enemies—both internal and external.

The Dreyfus affair helped inspire the creation of a new nationalist group, the Action Française (AF), which was formally founded on June 20, 1899.[14] The man who quickly emerged as its key theorist was Charles Maurras. Maurras came to believe that only a return to a monarchy could unite the nation and provide an impartial rule above sectional divisions, and that a revival of Catholicism was necessary to underpin morality.

Some historians have seen Maurras as an important forerunner of fascism, but while his "integral nationalism" had affinities with fascism, his views in general are better placed within the reactionary right-wing tradition. A clearer premonition of fascism can be found in a series of meetings held after 1910 by some leading members of the AF, notably Georges Valois, with revolutionary syndicalists like Sorel.[15] A case can be constructed that these links made France the seedbed of fascist ideology on the eve of war—which counters the conventional view that fascism came to France as a minor foreign import during the 1920s.[16] However, neither the Action Française nor any of the other anti-Semitic and nationalist leagues that emerged after the Boulanger affair developed a significant electoral or paramilitary base. They were ideological pressure groups rather than mass parties.

Although the Third Republic appeared to be highly unstable, it had notable strengths. The two-ballot election system that it used for most of its existence encouraged alliance formation on the second ballot—which took place if no candidate received fifty percent or more of the votes on the first round. The main beneficiaries of this were the Radicals, whose primarily middle-class leaders cleverly exploited left-wing revolutionary slogans such as "equality" and "freedom," while in reality building strong local clienteles based on a defense of the existing socioeconomic order: it was a powerful mix of self-interest dressed up as principle. The system offered little political space for the radical right to become a successful electoral force, short of alliance with other groups, which was made difficult if not impossible by its challenge to the legitimacy of the basic Republic tradition.

The left also found itself squeezed by the system, though by 1914 support for the Socialist Party (SFIO) was growing. Electoral weakness nurtured the strand in the French socialist movement that had long advocated direct action, and over the summer of 1914 many feared that the left would launch a revolutionary strike in the event of war breaking out. (The leader of the Socialists, Jean Jaurès, was to pay with his life for such fears when he was struck down by an assassin's bullet in July.) But in general French socialism was moderate and weak, in part a reflection of the slow rate of social change in France and the fact that the working class was largely integrated into the national community. There was never a serious chance that most French Socialists would oppose World War I.[17]

The war began with virtually the whole of France resisting the new invasion by the "militaristic" Germans. President Poincaré declared a "sacred union" of French people and deliberately used nationalism to forge social cohesion. Appalling losses of men—proportionately greater than any of the other Western combatants—brought France's army close to mass mutiny in 1917, but a uniting savior was at hand. The appointment as premier of the elderly, but dynamic, Georges Clemenceau helped rally opinion—and brought the military firmly under political control. After the war was over, the wily parliamentarian led a center-right Bloc National to overwhelming electoral victory.

Germany had been forced to accept unconditional surrender in November 1918. The ensuing Treaty of Versailles restored Alsace and Lorraine to France and seemed to weaken Germany for generations to come. France thus emerged from the war terribly scarred by her losses, but essentially contented (though there were signs of troubles to come, especially on the radical left, which had been inspired by the Bolshevik Revolution). Liberty and Fraternity—if not perhaps Equality—seemed to have triumphed.

iv

UNLIKE BRITAIN AND FRANCE, modern Germany was a creation of the nineteenth century. Previously, it had been divided into primarily small states—of which autocratic Prussia was the most important in 1800. But a German identity existed long before the creation of a united German state. It can be found by the sixteenth century, especially in the thought of Martin Luther; it can be seen even more clearly by the eighteenth century in the aspirations of Frederick the Great.[18] In an intellectually more developed form, modern German nationalism can be traced to Johann Gottfried von Herder, an eighteenth century philosopher who challenged the universalist views of the Enlightenment by stressing the uniqueness of different cultures. Napoleon's occupation of the Germanic states after the French Revolution encouraged rejection of liberal-rationalist thought. Romantic sentiment was to be especially strong in Germany. Major elements of this were picked up in the thought of later *völkisch* thinkers, like the academic orientalist Paul de Lagarde and his disciple Julius Langbehn, with their mystical theories of Germanness based on "blood."[19]

The German nationalist tradition was essentially mixed—it cannot be stereotyped simply as aggressive and authoritarian. Herder was antimilitarist and anti-Prussian; he also accepted the national aspirations of other peoples. During the early nineteenth century there was a strong liberal strand in German nationalism, which hoped that unity would be accompanied by the development of parliamentary democracy. The main thrust of German nationalist ideology, nevertheless, was very different from that of Britain and France, and the manner by which Germany was united had a major impact on the development of nationalism. Essentially, Germany was created between 1830 and 1870 by increasing economic integration and Prussian arms (although many "German" people remained outside the Reich in Austria and Eastern Europe).

The key individual in the later stages of this process was Otto von Bismarck. Bismarck became the first chancellor of the Imperial German federation, which was created after the triumph against France in 1870. Predictably, given the authoritarian Prussian tradition, the political system over which he presided was far from democratic even by the standards of the day. The head of state was the kaiser, who together with the court and unelected groups such as the landed gentry (*Junkers*) wielded considerable influence behind the scenes. The rapid rise of German industry, which was soon to eclipse that of Britain, was bringing other new forces into play. By the late 1870s a tacit alliance had emerged between landowners and industrialists to impose protectionism and to force the government to stem the growing tide of socialism.[20]

The rise of socialism after 1870 illustrates that the new Germany was not an autocracy (though the socialists were banned for a time). It had a national parliament, the Reichstag, and there were parliaments in the federal states too. The franchise varied, and was particularly restricted in Prussia, but there was a multiparty system. Although the government was not chosen by Parliament (ministers did not even sit in the Reichstag), it was necessary for budgetary and other purposes that the government had to maintain some form of majority in the Reichstag—at times a delicate task as the Social Democratic Party (SPD) and Catholic Center party were essentially opposition parties, which had their own almost ghettoized social and political organizations outside parliament.

Anti-Semitism was also growing. It was a term that was coined in Germany when a journalist named Wilhelm Marr published *The Victory of the Jew over the German*—a book that went into twelve editions within six years of its publication in 1873. The underlying causes were much the same as in France, though the growing German tendency to define citizenship in terms of blood reinforced the view that the Jews were alien and unassimilable.[21] Anti-Semitism quickly became a potent electoral force, as was clear from the election campaign of the first Independent anti-Semite to be elected to the Reichstag—Otto Böckel. Previously, a small clique had managed elections in a low-key way. For the charismatic Böckel, style was crucial. His rallies in Marburg during 1887 were characterized by marching bands and torchlight processions, accompanied by Lutheran hymns and patriotic songs. It is not surprising that some have seen in Böckel an embryonic form of populist fascism.[22]

The main Conservative Party (DKP) had originally cooperated with the anti-Semites, but by the late 1890s this landowner-dominated party was becoming increasingly wary of the populist side to the movement. Some anti-Semites held highly radical social views, attacking the existing distribution of wealth and income. Many in the DKP's leadership came to fear that the new forces were a threat to the existing social order, rather than a useful prop.[23] Böckel's inability to forge a united and lasting movement further reinforced fears that anti-Semitism could not form the basis of a parliamentary party.

During the early twentieth century, anti-Semitism became a trait of the new leagues that were increasingly becoming a major feature of German politics. Among the most notable were the social imperialist Navy League and the Pan German League, which has been inaccurately described as having a program that was a chilling anticipation of the policies later put into practice by National Socialism. (The main similarity was in foreign policy.)[24] These leagues differed in size and purpose, but their central thrust was a commitment to Germany taking on a world role (*Weltpolitik*), or expanding into Eastern Europe (*Lebensraum*) in order to increase economic prosperity.

Significant tensions developed between the old conservatives and these more strident groups. Their aggressive militarism necessitated rapid industrialization, which threatened agricultural interests and meant the prospect of high taxes to pay for the arms race. Another source of division concerned the nature of the leagues' nationalism, which tended to stress the will of the people—a far cry from the old conservative nationalist idea of the nation as a harmony of interests, or estates.[25] Their emphasis on an emotional pan-Germanism contrasted with the more cautious nationalism of much of the old political elite, which was conscious that Germany was made up of over twenty different states—and that even allegiance to the (Prussian) crown was a potentially divisive issue.

There were, nevertheless, points of contact between the old and new forces of the right in the years immediately before 1914. One critical factor was the result of the 1912 elections, which saw the Socialists emerge for the first time as the largest party. Although the Reichstag did not choose governments, there was a growing feeling that something needed to be done to counter the apparently irresistible rise of the left. In some cases, especially among those who took the SPD's Marxism at face value, this involved an authoritarian response, even the establishment of a dictatorship. More moderate voices on the right could see the need for a new popular party that could create a wider social consensus.[26]

For a time after the outbreak of war these fears diminished, as the call to arms was greeted ecstatically by the vast majority of Germans. Before hostilities began, more radical Socialists had talked of a revolutionary strike against war. But a combination of patriotism and the belief that Russia was an aggressive autocracy led the SPD to vote for war credits. Had the war finished relatively quickly, especially with a German victory, this might have impressed reactionary and conservative elites that socialism was not the enemy within—that, in the words of the kaiser, the Socialists were not "unpatriotic fellows." Certainly it is totally wrong to hold that Germany was necessarily set on a course for dictatorship, ignoring the forces for change even on the right. But as the war dragged on, there were growing signs of left-wing dissent. By 1917 they had led to a serious split within the SPD, and the creation of a breakaway antiwar group which took further inspiration from the success of the Bolshevik Revolution.

The German chancellor, Theobald von Bethmann-Hollweg, had always doubted that outright victory was possible. But the war increased the influence of the self-confident military, which sought to make sweeping territorial gains.[27] Bethmann-Hollweg was duly replaced in 1916 by a more colorless and compliant chancellor. Important sections within both the military and business elites realized that political control required more than just a change of leadership. It was becoming increasingly necessary to counteract growing popular doubts about the war and the revival of working-class militancy. September 1917 witnessed the creation of the German Fatherland Party, which has been described as exhibiting clear proto-fascist features.[28] Its program advocated massive annexations on Germany's eastern frontiers, which it was claimed would lead to significant economic benefits for the working man, and was reinforced by an attempt to divert discontent away from the government and military toward Jewish "profiteers" and "shirkers." By July 1918 the Fatherland Party claimed 1.25 million individual and corporate members. Even allowing for exaggeration, this would make it Germany's first mass right-wing movement—though its lack of social radicalism means that it was not truly fascist.

By October 1918 the dam was near to cracking. The new Bolshevik regime in Russia had sued for peace and conceded vast tracts of land to Germany by the Treaty of Brest-Litovsk. But in the west a major German offensive had failed and the army was in retreat— though it was still fighting on French and Belgian soil. At home the Allied blockade had caused serious shortages of food as well as strategic materials. Much of the military leadership was coming to see the need for an armistice, though men like Field Marshal Ludendorff hoped to evade responsibility for Germany's failure to win in the west. Their hastily devised plan was to pass the reins of government on to a new set of democratic leaders, who could later be blamed for stabbing the army in the back.

On November 9, the moderate leader of the SPD—Friedrich Ebert—took over as chancellor, and Germany was proclaimed a republic. The previous night the kaiser had slipped away to Holland. It had been hoped that a democratic government might secure more favorable terms from the Allies, but in the cold light of the democratic dawn it was found that they still demanded unconditional surrender. The new government was in no position to negotiate, not least as Red Revolution had broken out among a section of the armed forces and in the cities. On November 11, therefore, a formal armistice was signed on behalf of the new government by the Center Party leader, Matthias Erzberger. For many radical nationalists, this was tantamount to issuing his own death warrant.

The Treaty of Versailles, which was pointedly signed in the Hall of Mirrors where Kaiser Wilhelm I had been crowned emperor in 1871, put the seal on Germany's humiliation. Its provisions included the acceptance of responsibility for starting the war; major limitations on German armed forces; the demilitarization of the Rhineland; the restoration of Alsace and Lorraine to France; extensive boundary changes in the East, including the separation of East Prussia from the rest of Germany so that the new Polish state could have a corridor to the sea; the confiscation of Germany's colonies; a commitment to pay "reparations" to compensate the Allies; and a veto on the union of Germany and Austria, which was left as a small rump state.

The new German republic that was established in the town of Weimar (symbolic of German culture rather than militarism and might) could hardly have had a more disastrous start. Far from uniting Germany, war had ended by polarizing society—and leaving important sections of the German Establishment totally alienated from the values of the democratic republic and its "French" values of liberty and equality. Many ordinary German men and women too felt alienated from the new system, or were overwhelmed by the economic, social, and political turmoil that followed the war. They longed for a new German version of fraternity—for the rebirth of a community of blood, which would transcend divisions and—in its more dangerous forms—banish enemies to hell.

v

ON THE SUMMIT of the Capitol in Rome stands a statue: it celebrates Emperor Marcus Aurelius, who died in A.D. 180 at the zenith of the Roman empire. For over a millennium and a half after the fall of Rome, Italy was essentially a geographical expression. The glory that once was Rome flowered again during the Renaissance, but the focus of this rebirth of European culture was a small set of independent city-states. Much of the rest of the peninsula was a backwater, ruled over by autocratic foreign dynasties.

During the early nineteenth century, a movement emerged, known as the Risorgimento, which sought to liberate Italy and turn it into a united and economically developed country. Most of the key figures involved, like Giuseppe Mazzini and Camillo Cavour, were intellectuals or aristocrats: they were liberals more than democrats, and many of them were suspicious of the masses. The doctrine of Italian nationalism was not based on the gospel of a popular rising. And the unification of Italy owed far more to foreign intervention and the actions of a handful of people—most dramatically Giuseppe Garribaldi and his red-shirted thousand volunteers—than to the Italian people in general.

Italy was finally reunited as a state in 1870, but socially the country remained divided. It was really two countries. Although parts of the north were beginning to industrialize and develop new forms of capitalistic agriculture, most of the center and south had hardly changed for centuries. Loyalty was to the family rather than to an extended political community.[29] Nor did language act as social cement, for it differed regionally and there was mass illiteracy, which helps to explain why Italy had a highly restricted franchise. Even those entitled to vote often abstained because unification had involved occupation of the Papal States, which led to a rupture of relations with the Catholic church, and a papal ban on participation in politics.

Politics in Italy during the late nineteenth century was, therefore, essentially a clique-based game, which owed as much to interest as to ideology. Certainly politics was closely connected to economic power, for major agricultural and industrial lobbies emerged which looked to the government to secure their interests. Predictably, most citizens responded by seeing the state as the enemy, occupied by a parasitical and isolated "political class."

Some leading politicians, most notably Giovanni Giolitti, saw the need to defuse these tensions. By the 1890s Giolitti wanted to make concessions to labor and to promote economic growth as a way of providing better wages and helping to fund social welfare. But his name became synonymous with the attempt to build tenuous and corrupt political coalitions, rather than with reform or modernization. His decision to extend the franchise in 1912 to the majority of males was in part based on the belief that it would still be possible to fix the result by a deft combination of promises and bribery.

The Catholic hierarchy was becoming aware of alienation among the poorer classes. In 1891 Pope Leo XIII issued the papal encyclical *Rerum Novarum*, which called on Catholics to adopt a positive attitude toward the problems of work and social welfare. One important development related to this was a growth of what became known somewhat misleadingly as "corporatist" thought, modeled on medieval guilds, in which there had been close relations between master and worker. The goal was to institutionalize social harmony and prevent the intense class antagonism that was clearly developing in Italy—and elsewhere, for social-Catholicism developed across Europe at the turn of the twentieth century.[30]

These reformist developments were prompted in particular by the growth of socialism. The Italian Socialist Party (PSI) brought together highly disparate ideological elements, including anarchists, Marxists, and syndicalists, which meant that the party was prone to schism, as happened during the war to conquer Libya in 1911–12. At the 1912 party congress, the moderates were expelled for supporting the war. Shortly afterward, a new editor was appointed for the Socialists' main theoretical journal, *Avanti!* The rising star who was given this important task was Benito Mussolini—whose radical views at this time included the belief that "the Arab and Turkish proletarians are our brothers" and that "the national flag is a rag to be planted on a dunghill."[31]

The Libyan war was the latest episode in the Italian quest for national glory through territorial expansion. Africa seemed to offer an easier road to victory than recovery of the "unredeemed" Italian soil still controlled by Austro-Hungary. But this first quest for an African empire had resulted in humiliating defeat at Adowa in 1896. Italy's army was emasculated, both metaphorically and literally, at the hands of Ethiopian tribesmen. The military leaders sought to salvage their honor by blaming the politicians for not spending sufficient sums on equipment. Others drew more fundamental conclusions about the relative economic weakness of Italy and the way in which the national flag failed to inspire the devotion of large numbers of Italians.[32]

During the first decade of the twentieth century a new Italian nationalism emerged, especially among intellectuals.[33] The best known figure in this movement was the author Gabriele D'Annunzio—though before 1914 he spent much of his time outside Italy. More important in terms of forging new organizations were Enrico Corradini and Giovanni Papini. Corradini was hostile to parliamentary government, which he saw as weak, divisive, and corrupt. He denounced bourgeois society as unheroic and ultimately doomed to defeat by more disciplined and martial societies. Initially influenced mainly by Germany, after Japan's victory over Russia in 1905 his eyes turned to the new sun that was rising in the east. Corradini sought to found a new Shinto-like secular religion, based around a mythology of "nature and heroes." He believed that Italy, like Japan, was a "proletarian nation," a potentially strong and coming force that would overcome the decadent rival "plutocratic" powers.[34] By 1910 Corradini was speaking of a "national socialism" that could appeal to the working classes by offering new economic opportunities both at home and in colonies.

The desire to integrate the working class into a holistic nation meant that some of the new nationalists took an interest in the socialists' propaganda. Whereas most socialists saw themselves as rationalists, and heirs to the Enlightenment, key nationalist intellectuals drew different conclusions. Papini, who was probably the most widely read Italian writer of his generation, praised the socialists for their energy and programmatic vitality. But he did not believe that their strength was based simply on organization or their appeal to material interests. He believed that they cleverly exploited myths of "international brotherhood" and "equality" to give their movement a moral facade and a sense of being an inevitable part of the movement of history. To him the mythical side of nationalism was critical, and he turned, inevitably, to the glories of ancient Rome as the most fertile source of such myths. Social Darwinism reinforced history: a new "Great War" of imperial expansion was portrayed as vital to national renewal—as the ultimate test of those who were most fit to survive and to prosper.[35]

The emergence of this new nationalism led to the foundation of the Italian Nationalist Association (ANI) in Florence during 1910. Initially a small intellectual coalition, it gained greater coherence after adopting Alfredo Rocco's doctrine of the authoritarian corporate state. Rocco, a professor at the University of Padua, offered a version of corporatism that differed from social Catholicism in two ways. First, it involved a much stronger central state: Rocco wanted to forge an Italian nation, whereas the Catholics were seeking to end class antagonism and maintain religious influence. Second, Rocco focused on the goal of modernism and economic dynamism: he believed that integrating the nation was vital if energies were not to be wasted on divisive and economically damaging class warfare. Predictably, such views appealed to important business interests, as well as to radical nationalist intellectuals.

Remarkably, the new nationalism was beginning to appeal to a section of the left. For some socialists, history had not developed as Marx had predicted. Socialism was growing, but only the most optimistic believed that a mass Italian revolutionary working class was emerging spontaneously. Partly as a result, the revisionist writings of Sorel were gaining a large following in Italy. Initially this strengthened syndicalism and belief in the power of a general strike to overthrow capitalism. But by 1914 there was a dramatic movement toward seeing nationalism as the key myth. Further points of contact between the syndicalists and some of the new nationalists included hostility to bourgeois society and the belief that nationalism could be used to promote rapid economic growth.[36] The desire for Italian greatness was far from exclusively right-wing.

When the war broke out in August 1914, Italy remained neutral. Although formally part of the triple alliance with Germany and Austro-Hungary, at that time Italy was a "great power" only in name.[37] Its armed forces were weak and demoralized. Its economy was relatively small and dependent on key strategic imports. During the summer of 1914 there had been significant social discontent, which raised Establishment fears of social revolution—or a general strike against the outbreak of war. Yet powerful business, military, and political forces were soon pushing the Italian government toward intervention. As war approached, the interventionist camp had been divided over which side to support, but opinion quickly swung in favour of the Entente, which could promise Italy her "unredeemed" lands in the north as well as other prizes. On May 23, 1915, Italy duly informed Austro-Hungary that a state of war would exist between them the next day.

The belief that Italian intervention would ensure a short, glorious campaign soon faded. Stalemate ensued. This bloody standoff was finally broken when during October 1917 the Austrians, with German support, won a great victory at Caporetto. They quickly advanced a hundred miles toward Venice. A wave of nationalism swept over many Italians. It was heightened by a government campaign to make the war popular by promising social reforms after victory—a commitment encouraged by fears about the spread of Bolshevism, which had just toppled the Russian government. Fighting resolve was strengthened and by the time the Central Powers signed the Armistice in November 1918, Italian troops had bravely battled their way back to the old frontier.

Italy had fought and won, but it was a Pyrrhic rather than glorious victory. The "Great War" had not solved but rather increased social divisions. The frequently poor performance of Italian troops—not least the officer class—reinforced the view that Italians needed to be forged into a true nation. Politically, the Risorgimento was completed in 1870. Culturally, much remained to be done: Italy was still a land of museums rather than heroes.

vi

SINCE THE BEGINNING of history Europe has been an ethnic melting pot, with tribal and state boundaries moving to and fro. Within this fluid world, modern national identity, accompanied by a relatively centralized state, began to emerge in Britain and France by the sixteenth and seventeenth centuries. Germany and Italy had to wait until the late nineteenth century before they achieved political unity.

The nature of their nationalist ideologies differed too. The origins of British nationalism lay mainly in a desire to legitimize the existing system, and especially to integrate the non-English nations into the British state. It used the crown and Parliament as symbols of allegiance and stressed the rule of law as part of a demobilizing ethic. Early French national identity was constructed around a defense of the status quo, but with the Enlightenment a nationalist ideology emerged with very different implications. Nationalism became part of the liturgy of "sovereignty of the people," part of a democratic critique of existing monarchical and religious order, but it was double-edged. On the one hand it stressed liberal universal principles and the rule of law; on the other it could legitimate direct, violent action in the cause of "freeing" the nation.

In Germany and Italy, there was no order to defend, as these "nations" were divided into different states with unclear borders. This was especially true of Germany, whose people were spread far eastward. German nationalism differed too because many German intellectuals turned to a very different conception of the nation from the one that developed especially in eighteenth-century France: it was more a cultural affinity, or an emotive bond of blood, linked to the belief that a great leader or the strong state were necessary to forge the nation. In Italy, the liberal strand was stronger, and there was never this emphasis on the community of blood. Yet there was a bond between nineteenth century German and Italian nationalisms. They were both in some ways lacking confidence (though in the German case, this was often married to a paradoxical sense of superiority, particularly among groups such as the military). Both looked to further expansion and economic growth to help resolve internal divisions and problems.

Britain and France had their social and political problems too. Although the modern British party system had clearly emerged by the 1880s, it was under severe strain immediately before World War I. In particular, it was far from clear that it would be the Liberal Party rather than the Conservatives which would crack. In France the party system was far less well established, and on occasion nationalist demagogues like General Boulanger had seriously threatened the existing order. And the Dreyfus Affair underlined a dangerous polarization, though in many ways this was greater among political elites than in the French countryside, especially among the old who were less caught up by the hectic pace of *fin de siècle* intellectual and cultural change.

The fact that Britain and France recovered from these strains was partly a question of luck, but more specifically because of the unifying impact of World War I. Yet there is an important kernel of truth in the generalization that British and French politicians knew how to build consensus, whereas the German and Italian successors to Bismarck and Cavour failed to establish socially broad coalitions. French and British ability to do this lay in their day-to-day parliamentary experience and their greater openness to meritocratic talent. But another important aspect was the nature of the mythology used by elites, especially during World War I. British national identity was reaffirmed by an ability to depict an enemy that was the antithesis of its self-defined national values of freedom and reconciliation. France too depicted the beastly Germans as the opposite of Republican man. Demonizing the "other" proved a far less powerful force in Germany and Italy. Elites in these two countries had always tended to place great emphasis on material factors to legitimize nationalism, thus moving away from the more anti-material values of Romantic and *völkisch* intellectuals.[38] During World War I they could make promises of gains to come, but the future reality was one of economic hardship, especially in Germany after 1928.

Britain and France also fought in order to make a "Land Fit for Heroes," a country that would soon flow with milk and honey. There had always been an element in their nationalism related to economic progress, but the economic side of nationalism was stronger in German and Italian nationalisms. Partly this was because in the nineteenth century these were the more backward countries, with much catching up to do. More importantly, it reflected the belief that prosperity was necessary to integrate the rapidly growing working class during the late nineteenth and early twentieth centuries. Whatever the reason, one thing is sure. Europe was sitting on a time bomb, for these countries were likely to find it difficult to sustain the pressure of an economic recession—especially one that affected large parts of the younger population, which had been particularly influenced by social change and war.

It should be abundantly clear that there is no simple formula that can set out the preconditions that explain the success or failure of fascism. But important insights begin to emerge by noting the concept of "political space." Fascism needed some form of political "space" in which to operate. Its syncretic ideological form meant that it was highly flexible, but in most countries it tended to gather in force where the right was weak. However, space alone was not enough: more importantly, fascism needed a sense of legitimacy, an ability to relate its ideology to what was familiar, respectable: paradoxically, radicalism had to have a familiar face. In particular, it needed to offer the prospect that it could forge some form of national rebirth, which could restore a sense of community and crucial aspects of national identity. In order to do this, shrewd leadership was required by the insurgent forces, particularly by the way in which they managed to combine more affective-traditional and rational-economic appeals and by their ability to hide key aspects of their radicalism. Some form of legitimation by existing mainstream elites, who often sought to turn fascism to their own more conservative purposes, was also important. Yet these decisions too have to be understood within the context of legitimacy and national traditions, for they were taken within a framework of what was considered acceptable, possible—concepts conditioned by history as well as the more immediate force of economic and social circumstance. Put simply, fascism succeeded where it achieved *syncretic legitimation*, the ability both to appeal to affective and more individualistic voters, and to convince at least a section of the mainstream elites that it could serve their purpose better than existing parties.

Socioeconomic crisis after 1919 was a necessary precondition for the emergence of mass fascist movements in the interwar years, for in both Italy and Germany fascism came to power against a background of fear and paralysis. But it is a set of political factors that provides the real key to how potential was turned into reality.[39]

PART TWO

Interwar Fascism

Italy: The Rise
of Fascism

i

THE TERM *fascio* (plural *fasci*) means "bundle" in Italian, though in a political context it is better translated as "union" or "league." The epithet had been used by various groups before 1914, mainly on the left. During late 1914 the term was adopted by a group of revolutionary syndicalists when they set up the *fasci di azione rivoluzionaria,* to rally Italian support for intervention in World War I and press for economic and social change, which they believed would follow the war.

In an attempt to re-create this united front, a young nationalist journalist named Benito Mussolini called a meeting for March 23, 1919. In a hall off Milan's Piazza San Sepolcro just over a hundred people met to found the *fasci di combattimento,* which adopted the ancient Roman *fasces*—an ax bound in rods—as its symbol. They were an ideological ragbag from different parts of the social spectrum, though the main group seems to have come from the professional middle class. Their closest link, as their name implied, was that they had fought in the war—reflecting Mussolini's belief that only a young "trenchocracy" could provide the new elite which he saw as necessary to complete the regeneration of Italy.[1]

Mussolini's presence at this meeting marked a notable political turnaround, for at the beginning of 1914 he had been one of the rising stars of Italian socialism. Debate still rages over whether the path leading to his interventionist fervor is better explained in terms of opportunism or principle.[2] It was a remarkable metamorphosis for a man whose father was a socialist blacksmith and whose first names—Benito Amilcare Andrea—were chosen to commemorate Mexican and Italian revolutionaries. His mother was a poor schoolteacher, who had struggled to provide a good education for her son. As a result Mussolini too qualified as a teacher, though this re-flected his academic rather than his personal attributes, for from childhood the future Duce had shown violent traits. The young Mussolini seems to have felt little vocational calling and after quali-fying he drifted into an itinerant existence in Switzerland, where he came into contact with many socialist émigrés. This experience deepened his awareness of socialist theory, but on returning to Italy he eventually turned to journalism rather than serious political thought. In 1912 he was made editor of the leading socialist journal *Avanti!* At the age of just twenty-nine a bright future seemed to lie ahead for this firebrand socialist.

Yet Mussolini was a most unusual socialist activist. He had never been part of a close-knit community of friends or class that might have ensured his loyalty. This prophet of collectivism was es-sentially a loner, who was later to argue that "the heart should be kept a desert." Nor was his socialism based on the widespread left-wing belief in laws of history that pointed to the inevitable victory of the proletariat. Even before the outbreak of European war, he was influenced by right-wing nationalist-elitist thought. He was also an ardent admirer of Nietzsche (and in 1908 wrote a perceptive article on him for a nonsocialist journal), deriving from him a belief in the importance of discipline and the need for a secular religion to counter anomie.[3] Mussolini was groping toward a synthesis be-tween left and right as a means of uniting society in a way that would enable Italy to emerge as a self-sufficient major power, ca-pable both of self-defense and expansion. He was attracted to the welfare-oriented policies of the left, and the more leader-oriented authoritarian ideas of the right.

Critics have frequently claimed that Mussolini's conversion to the cause of war was a result of opportunism. More specifically, they have pointed to the fact that he took money from business and French interests to set up an interventionist paper, the *Popolo d'Italia.* But this was not the immediate cause of his sacrilege. Rather, the failure of the left to develop as a major popular force in the summer of 1914 seems finally to have convinced Mussolini that working-class revolutionary action was highly unlikely to suc-ceed, especially without the support of the army. Support for the war, therefore, had a dual function. First, it promised to build bridges with the military leadership. And second, Mussolini had come to see war as a chance to transform his country, to capture the minds of the masses and create a more united and dynamic Italy by transcending existing political divisions. Given his political skills, he quickly became one of the key figures in the interventionist agitation.

In due course Mussolini joined the army, serving with enthusiasm but no great distinction, until injured when a shell exploded in a mortar during firing practice. Invalided out, he returned to the editor's desk of *Popolo d'Italia*, where he continued to rail against the parties and government, this time for incompetence and failure to pursue the war energetically enough. His thoughts were turning to dictatorship, for he was coming to see the strong state as a means of uniting the nation and achieving rapid economic development— and thus at last achieving the central goals that had inspired the Risorgimento.

By the end of the war his attempts to synthesize left and right had hardly progressed beyond grafting nationalism and "productivist" economic dynamism onto a shopping list of what he saw as popular radical policies. The first program of the *fasci di combattimento* was something of a ragbag, encompassing among other things the abolition of the monarchy, the confiscation of church property, nationalization of the arms industry, a special tax on war profiteers, an eight-hour working day with a minimum wage, worker participation in industry, the abolition of the nonelected Senate, and votes for women.

ii

In 1919 Mussolini was by no means the best-known radical nationalist. Also present at the Piazza San Sepolcro meeting was Filippo Marinetti.[4] Born into a rich family, Marinetti moved to Florence, which at the turn of the century was the center of Italian intellectual fashion. Here, surrounded by Persian carpets and Oriental hangings, he held extravagant court and planned what was to become known as *The Futurist Manifesto* (1909), which laid the foundations for a cultural movement that glorified "war—the world's only hygiene—militarism, patriotism, the destructive gesture of the anarchists, beautiful ideas worth dying for, and scorn for woman." Marinetti's mentors were international rather than Italian: especially clear is the Nietzschean combination of obsession with contemporary decadence and the will to create something radically new. At the same time, Marinetti's politics were becoming increasingly influenced by the new nationalism, which he saw as the key to energizing Italy. Although he was almost forty, he was an early volunteer to fight in 1915 and was later decorated for bravery.

Marinetti was elected to the central committee of the fascists in 1919, appearing as number two on the list after Mussolini in the national elections. But for all his renown, Marinetti never seriously challenged Mussolini for leadership of radical Italian nationalism. In part this was a question of personality: he was more an obstreperous artistic exhibitionist than a political manipulator. More fundamentally, it was a question of beliefs and morality. Like Mussolini, Marinetti reflected a strange mixture of left and right, but he took his radical-social views seriously. This led to quarrels with Mussolini as fascism became increasingly right wing in an effort to attract broader support (though he later accepted numerous cultural honors from the fascist regime). Mussolini was hungry for power and accepted whatever compromises he believed were necessary to achieve his goal. Marinetti was ultimately an aesthete and intellectual; he did not share Mussolini's understanding of and thrill in the uncultured crowd.

The most illustrious of the Italian nationalists in 1919 was also an aesthete. Gabriele D'Annunzio was born into a comfortably well-off family and quickly developed into a major literary figure.[5] Before World War I, D'Annunzio's life was concerned with art rather than politics, though he did sit briefly in the Chamber of Deputies. In 1897 he was elected as an Independent in Pescara, his mother's birthplace. He had previously described parliamentarians as an elected herd, and had taken little interest in their proceedings. Standing for election was a game, a new experience, which culminated in a dramatic move across the floor from right to left—a symbolic gesture of hostility to the government's suppression of workers rather than a reflection of deep-rooted ideology or opportunistic calculation. In the general election that followed, D'Annunzio stood as a socialist in Florence and was violently attacked both for lack of principle and for his private life. Among the charges labeled against him were adultery, polygamy, incest, sodomy, theft, and even cannibalism. Predictably, he lost.

Like Marinetti, D'Annunzio's intellectual influences were more European than Italian, but he too developed into an ardent nationalist. Although involved in the agitation that took Italy into war over Libya during 1911–1912, it was the outbreak of World War I that launched the career of D'Annunzio the nationalist hero. After a triumphant return from France, with crowds greeting him along the route, he obtained a roving commission in the armed forces. At the age of fifty-two it might be thought that his wartime role would have been largely symbolic: the occasional sniff of cordite before harangues to rally the troops. In fact, he found an intoxication in war that he had never experienced with women—of whom he had had many—or worldly possessions.

Physically he was as unlikely a hero as he was a great lover, being almost a dwarf, a tragic gargoyle. Yet he was the stuff of which heroes are made—the true Nietzschean Superman. He was not only brave, taking part in torpedo-boat raids on the Austrian fleet and flying across the Alps in a fragile single-engine biplane to drop leaflets he had written—feats that brought him a chestful of medals. His persona was made for legend. He climbed into his plane wearing patent-leather boots with high heels. Like a knight going into battle, he was surrounded by pages—handing him gloves, helmet, and fur-lined jacket. Where Mussolini's war service had been mundane, D'Annunzio's was miraculous and exemplary. It was no wonder that by 1919 he was a popular hero among the nationalists.

Though the war left him understandably drained, he was itching for new action. His chance came in September 1919 when, at the head of a small band of nationalist irregulars, he seized Fiume (later Rijeka), a predominantly Italian city on the Dalmatian coast that the other wartime Allies seemed willing to give to Yugoslavia. The Italian government could have suppressed the coup, but many of its members were keen to appease radical nationalists at home. Although the peace conferences had quickly accepted Italy's claims to the Alto Adige and Trentino—which contained many German-speaking Austrians—there was strong opposition to making major territorial concessions along the Dalmatian coast, which with the exception of a few pockets like Fiume was peopled mainly by

Croats and Serbs. Most members of the government accepted that the area was practically indefensible, but the radical nationalists accused them of planning to accept a "mutilated peace."[6]

During the fifteen months in which D'Annunzio held his Adriatic port, he choreographed what were to become many of the characteristic forms of fascism.[7] He dubbed his troops legionaries to recall Roman greatness—he had already invented the Roman salute, straight arm held high, for a 1914 film script. He dressed them in black shirts and daggers, a reminder of the uniform worn by World War I shock troops, the *arditi* ("the daring ones"). He designed elaborate ceremonies, a civil religion with a liturgy of battle cries—again harking back to the war. These sacraments reflected his awareness of the role of symbol and emotion in mass politics, although they also kept his troops from fighting each other or spending too much time plundering inland villages and rustling shepherd boys.

D'Annunzio created in Fiume a model constitution that he hoped could be adopted by both Italy and other countries founding a new social order. The result was the Charter of Carnaro, which was promulgated on September 8, 1920. One critic has described it as reading as if the modernist (and fascist) American poet Ezra Pound had drawn up the Code Napoléon.[8] Yet behind its strange language and allusions lay a serious attempt to institutionalize social unity, while guaranteeing personal freedoms and tolerance, including equality for women. The charter's main author was Alceste De Ambris, a prewar leader of revolutionary syndicalism. His hand can be seen in aspects such as the attempt to bring workers and management together in "corporations," joint decision-making bodies which would provide a new meaning for work and end alienation.[9] De Ambris's presence in Fiume is revealing, for it illustrates D'Annunzio's appeal to the left as well as to more right-wing nationalists. D'Annunzio saw himself as a synthesis not just of left and right, but of poet and man of action, of Dante and Caesar.

Yet in the autumn of 1920 the commandante's remarkable Fiume days were numbered. The best men were leaving. His "Minister of Supply" was finding that raids and piracy did not provide a guaranteed source of public finance. More importantly, the Treaty of Rapallo, signed in November 1920, made Fiume a free city and the Italian government decided that the time had come to end the occupation. After a brief burst of fighting, D'Annunzio accepted that the game was up, making a last dramatic appearance in the city on January 2, 1921, at a funeral for those killed in the clash. From Fiume he returned to Italy, where he retired to a villa on Lake Garda, which he made a shrine to his extravagant taste and wartime exploits.

Was D'Annunzio a fascist? The balance of opinion is that he was not and that he would never have set up a reactionary totalitarian state.[10] There was also a decadence in his life—a residue of the effete sensibility of his early literary phase—that would find no public place in fascism. His legacy to the fascist movement was one of style more than thought: the ceremonies and uniforms, the leader's harangues from the balcony and rhythmic chanting of supporters, the attempt to foster a civil religion. Such a conclusion seems reasonable in light of fascism's practical development, but it is important to remember that fascism can also be viewed as an ideological force. In this sense D'Annunzio can be seen as the first major figure who sought in practice to synthesize Nietzsche and Sorel, to forge a new ideology that would draw from both left and right. His problem was that he did not have the talents to forge a viable political movement to go with it. Even after 1921 he might still have challenged Mussolini for leadership of the nationalists, but tiredness—and perhaps ultimately lack of will—led him to endorse fascism in 1922, thus helping to prepare the way for Mussolini to take the reins of power.

After becoming prime minister in October 1922, Mussolini shrewdly ordered the publication of a complete set of D'Annunzio's works (on which a massive royalty was paid), and he periodically paid homage to the "great writer" and nationalist. Mussolini was nothing if not conscious of the compromises and manipulative skills necessary to achieve power. His attitude to D'Annunzio's invasion of Fiume clearly illustrates this. In *Popolo d'Italia* he had called D'Annunzio "the intrepid one" and solicited funds for the illegal Fiume regime. In reality much of the money went to help the fascists. When D'Annunzio proposed a march on Rome to seize power, Mussolini came up with objections. While there seems little doubt that he was jealous of the great war hero, Mussolini held serious reservations about the commandante's policy. Though some in the armed forces sympathized with the occupation, it brought nationalists and the forces of law and order into conflict. Fiume was also a sideshow, largely irrelevant to creating a major political movement in Italy. By mid-1920 Mussolini believed that fascism needed to make allies on the right and to distance itself from the left if it was to achieve power—and D'Annunzio's Charter of Carnaro was too radical to be a rallying point.

iii

IN THE NOVEMBER 1919 national elections, the fascists had attracted a derisory following. Even in the founding city of Milan they could poll only 5,000 out of 275,000 votes cast. There seemed to be no political space for a movement that combined nationalism with a set of highly radical social and political proposals that frightened off most of the middle and upper classes. Nationalism, on the other hand, had little appeal among the section of the industrial working class that was closely tied to socialist or Catholic organizations that helped provide their sense of community and norms. Lacking an electoral base and with funds drying up, by early 1920 the fascists seemed on the point of collapse. This marked the beginning of an erratic but clear programmatic drift to the right, which helped to stem and then reverse the decline. Amazingly, within three years Mussolini was to become prime minister.

The immediate postwar era was a highly troubled one for Italy. Future difficulties were clear to see even in 1914. One major problem concerned rapid change in some rural areas, a sector of the economy which accounted for fifty percent of the total workforce in 1914. Within a few years at the turn of the century, large parts of the north, such as the Po Valley, had witnessed the emergence of a new capitalist-style agriculture. The onset of capitalism marked a rapid end to the old paternalist labor relations, and the emergence of more conflict-based social relations. The resulting class animosities encouraged a socialism that had a highly radical and violent side to it. Revealingly, in areas where aristocratic paternalism lasted longer, conflict was much lower.[11]

World War I had aggravated social problems: it took people away from their homes and widened their horizons (many had never traveled more than a few miles). In some cases, the move was permanent, as many flocked to work in the munitions industries in the northern cities. In Turin, for instance, the number of industrial workers doubled between 1913 and 1918. At the same time the old communal organizations that had been set up by earlier generations of immigrants—groups which had helped arrange everything from jobs to marriage partners—were breaking down. In some cases, new collective influences emerged in the shape of unions and left-wing parties. But the workers found themselves socially isolated and attracted by a more diffuse nationalist collectivism.[12]

The war heightened regional differences. The south remained virtually untouched in terms of social structure, whereas even in rural areas in the north there was often notable change. Land sales north of Milan were phenomenal, which produced a new group of peasant proprietors who felt neither deference toward the old land-lord nor attraction toward the left, which in general favored com-munal property.[13] War further strengthened regional animosities, as many of those who did the fighting came from the rural areas, espe-cially of the south. The south thus bled, while some in the north prospered.

Inflation quickly eroded these gains, encouraging further wage demands—though the middle class living on savings or fixed in-comes were harder hit. The employers responded by shedding la-bor, a trend reinforced by conversion to peacetime production. By November 1919 unemployment had risen to 2 million, though the real number seeking work was probably much greater; 1919–20 witnessed a wave of strikes during which both workers and peasants occupied factories or plots of land. This was the *biennio rosso* ("the two red years"), when the fear of Bolshevism and revolution stalked the land. Over a million workers withdrew their labor in 1919; the following year the number who downed tools was even higher.

These social troubles contributed to a political crisis. Again there had been difficulties even before 1914, as the old Giolittian system faced new problems posed by an increasing electorate and new ideologies. During the war the system was further tarnished by incompetent management of the fighting and the home front. An image emerged of a government that was losing control of events.

For many on the right, this image was reinforced in the immediate postwar era by the government's response to strikes. During
the summer of 1920, fears of widespread social disorder led the
government to desert its traditional policy of neutrality in conflicts
between employer and worker. It put pressure on employers in
both industry and agriculture to make concessions. Inevitably, this
led to fears that the government was becoming dangerously weak
in the face of left-wing intransigence, especially as some of the
strikes involved sit-in occupations of the factories—which raised
fears that the rapidly growing unions were seeking more than just
improvements in wages or conditions of work.

The government's attempts to raise taxation to finance the public debt, which had grown massively during the war, caused further
alienation.[14] The government even proposed to clamp down on tax
evasion, a time-honored right for wealthier Italians. By late 1920 a
gulf had opened between the political leadership and important sections of the business and landed classes, who, together with a notable section of the middle class, feared a revolution.

An ominous gulf was also opening between the government
and the parliamentary parties. In 1919 a new electoral law had been
introduced, based on universal male suffrage and multimember
proportional representation. This had helped the socialists to win
156 out of 508 seats in the 1919 legislative elections, making them
the largest—albeit highly divided—grouping. The second largest
party, with 100 seats, was the new Italian Popular Party (PPI), a
Catholic organization whose creation reflected the end of the papal
ban on participation in politics.[15] As the socialists and the PPI refused to cooperate with each other or to join with another party to
form a government, there was little room for coalition-making maneuvers among the motley crowd of liberals, conservatives, and
others who made up the rest of the Chamber of Deputies. As a result the first five ministries formed after the war were highly unstable, even when headed by such eminent figures as the economist
Francesco Nitti, or Giolitti.

iv

THE SIXTH MINISTRY was to be headed by Mussolini. Initially the
dramatic growth of fascism during 1920–1 was reflected not so

much in votes as in its paramilitary organization. Even before World War I, Mussolini had held that violence was necessary to obtain political goals, and the *fasci di combattimento* had created squads to attack others and to protect their own meetings and supporters. During 1920–2 the paramilitary side of the movement took on a dynamic of its own, producing personalities and forces which Mussolini struggled to contain. In centers such as Bologna, Cremona, Ferrara, and Florence, local fascist leaders emerged who became known as *ras* (after the Ethiopian word for "chieftain"). Among the most notorious were Italo Balbo in Ferrara, Roberto Farinacci in Cremona, and Dino Grandi in Bologna.[16] They had a variety of backgrounds and views, but were united in their belief that politics now required the violent suppression of opposition.

Fascist squads attacked a wide variety of opponents, though their main targets were the socialists, especially those who by their support of the Bolshevik Revolution were viewed as revealing murderous and treacherous intent. Many historians argue that a revolutionary situation did not exist in Italy during 1919–22 in spite of the various waves of strikes.[17] But at the time there were good reasons to fear the worst. Although fascism had a particular appeal for violent ex-servicemen, the socialists too attracted many former *arditi* and others who were more than willing to use force to achieve their ends. And socialism was not simply an insurgent force. Outside the south, where electoral corruption was still rife, the socialists actually ruled in many localities. In Ferrara, the socialist administration flew the red flag over the municipal buildings, an act that reflected more than just a taste for symbolic politics. The socialists began to use jobs that were once open to competition to reward their own supporters. Money intended for widows and orphans of soldiers was used to finance a Labor Office, on the grounds that this would also benefit the bereaved, though these offices often excluded nonsocialist labor and those who had fought in the war. In 1920 socialist leaders even stated provocatively that while they would not encourage people to sack shops, equally "we shall not move a finger, nor say a word, to prevent the starvers of the people from being strung up from lampposts."[18] Socialist leaders undoubtedly felt that in the past they had been the victims of exploitation and patronage, but the policies they pursued after 1918 were perfectly conceived to frighten as many people as possible.

Fascism became a mass movement in the countryside of central and northern Italy, rather than in the towns and cities where it was difficult to break the hold of the socialists and Catholics over the working class. The socialist and Catholic parties and unions were also well organized in some rural areas, but here the situation was more fluid. Italian agriculture outside the antediluvian south was changing rapidly. Old practices, such as sharecropping, were giving way to more mechanized capitalistic structures. And new ideas were being propagated by the socialists, such as the view that the Russian Revolution was a humble peasant revolution that would transform life. The scene was set for confrontation and initially the advantage seemed to be with the peasants. In July 1920 Tuscan landowners capitulated to the biggest strike in Italian agricultural history. Elsewhere important concessions were wrung from owners by the socialist unions, which used both boycotts and violence to ensure working-class "solidarity" against the "class enemy."

The rise of fascist squads was set against this background. Initially the squads engaged in small-scale violence: a few dozen men would attack opponents—mainly "Bolsheviks." The result was usually a good beating or dosing with castor oil, rather than death. But soon the squads took on a paramilitary role. Combined with neighboring groups, they could rally hundreds—even thousands—for attacks like the raid on the socialist stronghold of Grosseto in Tuscany, which left fifty-five dead and the socialists' headquarters wrecked. At first they were little more than a disheveled rabble, but increasingly the *squadristi* adopted the black-shirted uniform of the wartime *arditi* and D'Annunzio's legions. From the latter they also learned the one-arm salute and a sense of politics as theater. Even funerals for fascists killed in action were turned into symbolic political events, full of quasi-religious ritual stressing sacrifice and rebirth. Their ceremonies were a powerful contrast with the socialists' more rationalist propaganda.

The generals of this emerging disciplined paramilitary force were the *ras,* men whose dynamism and ambitions were matched only by their proclivity for violence. By early 1922, Balbo, Grandi, and Farinacci were effectively full-time party officials, backed by staff and local newspapers. Financial support from agricultural and business interests became vital, as many of the *ras* came from relatively poor backgrounds. In some cases wealthy patrons themselves became active in the *fasci*. In Tuscany *squadristi* leaders included a battery of counts, marquises, and other titled ranks. Among the region's businessmen who were active squad members was Guido Fabricotti, a large marble-industrialist, whose interests were threatened with expropriation by the local administration. He was the commander of a squad of blackshirts led almost entirely by his relatives.

Rank-and-file blackshirts were a more mixed crowd. The *squadristi* were mostly men of action, not thinkers, who knew they were nationalist and antisocialist and that little else mattered. Even this ideological minimum was not always present. Some were clearly attracted to fascism because of the opportunities it offered for violence. A growing number were attracted by its criminal possibilities. This was certainly the case of Gennaro Abbatemaggio, a leader of the Florence *fascio*. Early in life he had joined the Camorra, but when he was arrested he broke its vow of silence. Forced to move north to escape the Neapolitan brotherhood's wrath, he found in the squads' activities ample opportunities for extortion and theft.[19]

It is only too easy to conclude that fascism in practice was nothing more than a tool of reaction, or a vehicle for opportunism and nihilism.[20] There is no doubt that these were part of fascism, but *squadrismo* was a complex and varied phenomenon. Organizationally, the initial impetus for growth sometimes came from merger with other nationalist groups, or from returning D'Annunzian legionaries. In some areas, the fascists may even have been closer to the people than the main parties. The liberal and conservative parties hardly existed as locally organized forces: they were electoral coalitions of notables. The Catholic Popular Party had stronger local roots and in some areas exhibited a radical face, but it too largely reflected the interests of the middle and upper classes. Even the socialists had a tendency to be bureaucratic and to deal in rhetoric that had little meaning outside activist ranks, and they were also willing to use their own form of pressure, even terror, on recalcitrant peasants who would not join their leagues.

The fascists responded by forming their own leagues, which sought to protect the peasants from socialist intimidation. They sometimes managed to obtain favorable wage deals from owners who sought to weaken the left-wing unions or who sympathized with fascism. By early 1921 the fascists had adopted at national level a new agricultural policy that highlighted the left's weak point in the rural areas: the socialization of agriculture. In general the peasants wanted to own their land, rather than to be incorporated into collectives. The fascists promised them land. At a local level, they pressurized landlords to sell or give away plots. They also tried to ensure that landlords paid fair wages to those who remained employees. In Brescia, farmers complained to the prefect that the blackshirts wanted to impose harsher conditions on them than those asked by the socialist and Catholic leagues.[21] The picture, however, varied considerably from area to area, and there were undoubtedly many places where the landlords called the tune.

By the summer of 1921, *squadrismo* was causing increasing concern to Mussolini. Part of the problem was that many *squadristi* were loyal to their local leader rather than to Mussolini, who was not well known in many areas. Mussolini was also worried by the ever-increasing levels of violence. He was not averse to the use of force as a political tactic, but he was worried that some squads were attacking all opponents, including members of the Catholic Popular Party and their agricultural leagues: even priests were not safe. Besides, the violence against the left was beginning to get out of hand, threatening Mussolini's strategy of courting more moderate opinion by portraying fascism as a force of stability.

These anxieties all influenced his decision to sign a pact of pacification with the moderate socialists and the General Confederation of Workers. (The socialists had split earlier in 1921, which had led to the formation of a separate Communist Party [PCI].) It is not clear whether Mussolini wanted to lower the climate of violence, or whether he was seeking an alliance of all Italians outside the Bolshevik camp. The latter was certainly consistent with his basic political strategy. The pact provoked angry opposition from the *ras,* however, who saw it as a threat to their influence and an ominous sign that fascism was becoming "respectable." Mussolini responded by resigning from the central committee of the *fasci,* though he paved the way for his return by calling for the movement's transformation into a formal political party.[22]

When he founded the *fasci di combattimento* in 1919, Mussolini had not termed his group a party because of his disgust with party politics and his search for a new vehicle that would break free from the parliamentary game. He hoped that by making the *fasci* a fluid movement it would be easier to attract members of other parties— a tactic which unquestionably paid dividends. But in the autumn of 1921 Mussolini believed that turning the fascists into a party would both limit the power of the *ras*, and make clear that the fascists were now in a position to grow as a major parliamentary force. Although this posed clear dangers to the *ras*, Mussolini had shrewdly judged that no one *ras* was powerful enough to challenge him as Duce. As a result, at a Fascist Constitutional Congress held in Rome during November a tacit deal seems to have been struck. Mussolini agreed to the recommendation that all *fasci* should set up squads and the pact of pacification was quietly forgotten. In return Mussolini became head of the National Fascist Party (PNF), which gave him a more secure organizational base. The party also provided the opportunity for a new program, which departed further from the left-radicalism of 1919.

It is not clear whether Mussolini saw the creation of a Fascist Party as the signal to run down the squads' activity, or more as a dual strategy in which fighting elections would proceed hand in hand with continuing to fight local enemies. What is clear is that the *ras* had no intention of ending the violence and were now broadening their targets to include the state as well as political opponents. In May, squads invaded Ferrara demanding government-financed public works. Shortly afterward, squad pressure led to the removal of the Prefect in Bologna. In Cremona at the beginning of July, Farinacci proclaimed himself acting mayor. By August, squads had evicted the socialist council from their main Italian stronghold, Milan, following a dismal attempt at a general strike against fascism—which succeeded mainly in raising the fascists' self-confidence and sapping any remaining socialist resolve to resist.

For some time leading members of the government had realized the growing dangers posed by fascist violence. On occasion administrations had tried to clamp down on the squads, but the overall impact was ephemeral and in general fascist violence went unpunished. The problem was partly local. The fascists' squads were usually backed by agricultural and business interests that retained some influence over the civil authorities. Besides, prefects and police forces were only too happy to turn a blind eye to fascist violence, especially when it was aimed at left-wingers who often openly abused them. Even the armed forces helped the fascists at times, for instance by supplying trucks and allowing *fasci* to recruit among soldiers. The main problem in terms of responding to fascist violence, however, has ultimately to be traced back to central government. The prefects in particular were finely tuned to pick up the government's political line, but they found its position was highly ambivalent.

A key development took place early in 1921. Giolitti was prime minister and as usual was looking for ways to broaden the governing coalition. The recent split in the socialists offered hopes that he might tempt the moderates to join him; even some *popolari* too were showing signs of becoming amenable to entering the government. At this point Mussolini hinted that the fascists would be interested in becoming part of Giolitti's electoral coalition. Why Giolitti accepted the offer is unclear. Almost certainly he believed that he could "transform" them, as he had done to so many before. Perhaps significant socialist or Catholic support was not in the cards. Whatever his motives, the fascists won thirty-five seats in the May 1921 elections, giving them a useful propaganda presence in the Chamber of Deputies. Although Mussolini immediately denounced the pact with Giolitto, the alliance had clearly encouraged the impression that the fascists were not beyond the pale. Certainly during the following year fascist support expanded dramatically. At the end of 1920 the PNF claimed that there were 88 *fasci* with a total membership of 20,615. By December 1921 these figures had become 834 and 249,036 respectively.[23]

During the summer of 1922, talk grew of fascist participation in government. A groundswell of influential opinion stated that the fascists could not be kept out of office much longer. This involved contacts between politicians and agrarian and industrial interests which were sympathetic to the fascists, or who at least saw them as useful in the battle against the left.[24] There was speculation in the press about these developments. In general, the fascists' powerful friends advocated their entry into government rather than the creation of a specifically fascist administration, let alone a dictatorship. But the upshot of such maneuvers and speculation was to condition the belief that the fascists would soon be in a position of power.

In September Mussolini prepared the way for his entry into government by announcing that he had been converted to monarchism—though this was combined with a veiled threat. He then encouraged several leading politicians to believe that he wanted them to head a ministry in which he would serve, thus reinforcing the image that fascism was being transformed into a more conventional political force. In fact, by mid-October the blueprints of a more dramatic plan were drawn up. It is not clear whether Mussolini was ever sincere in his offers to serve in a cabinet other than as prime minister, or whether he was trying to sow discord by raising the expectations of several other contenders. What is certain is that many *ras* were opposed to a token fascist participation in parliamentary government. As their leader, Mussolini had to follow them—a decision made easier by the fact that he despised the weakness of parliamentary government. Indeed, he still saw himself as a revolutionary whose task was to transform Italy. Or perhaps it would be more accurate to say that he was a revolutionary who saw the need to proceed at times with caution, for he was convinced that the turmoil that had followed the Bolshevik Revolution revealed the dangers of too rapid change.

At a series of meetings with leading fascists, Mussolini developed a scheme to seize power. Public buildings and key sites in the main cities were to be occupied by the squads, who would be under the control of four "Quadrumvirs." The local risings would be accompanied by a three-pronged March on Rome. During the night of October 27–8 the plan was put into action.

The government lived down to Mussolini's expectations. A witticism of the day held that the prime minister, Luigi Facta, should have been called Verba because he talked rather than acted. Faced with the squads' actions, Facta and his cabinet at last agreed to advise the king to impose martial law. Initially Vittorio

Emanuele agreed, but by the morning of October 28 he had changed his mind. Why remains unclear. He was not an inherently unconstitutional monarch, longing for autocracy. Perhaps he saw that the writing was on the wall for the small band of politicians who had tried to govern Italy since 1918. He certainly despised Giolitti and the others who had opposed the war, and his contempt was reinforced by their postwar failure to provide stable and firm government. Perhaps he feared for his own future. He was undoubtedly aware that his cousin, the Duke d'Aosta, was sympathetic to the fascists and had ambitions for the throne. More likely, he was motivated mainly by fear of splitting the army. While most of the armed forces would have remained loyal, Vittorio Emanuele believed that there were important pockets of support for the fascists in the forces—a belief encouraged by some within the remarkably small band of people he consulted about developments.[25] As result, the army was never called upon to suppress the fascist uprising.

Mussolini had never intended that serious fighting should begin. He had consulted sympathetic military figures and was well aware that the thirty thousand or so *squadristi* who were mobilized during October 27–8 could not defeat the Italian army. But the March on Rome was a *coup de théâtre* during which he could wait in the wings while events unfolded. October 28, 1922, did not dawn with a bemedaled Mussolini traveling at the head of his legions—in the way D'Annunzio had led the attack on Fiume. Mussolini was a showman, but he was also a shrewd politician. He remained in Milan, conveniently near the Swiss border. And luck favored the bold. Mussolini still could have been arrested had the local prefect obeyed his first orders on the night of the twenty-seventh. His plans could also have been seriously disrupted had there been a sustained left-wing show of counter force. But the left by this time was divided and demoralized—and taken by surprise.

Back in Rome, it quickly became clear that Mussolini would accept nothing less than the premiership. The other aspirants realized they had been deceived and retired to plot—so they hoped—against another day. Mussolini traveled overnight to Rome by train, arriving at the royal palace on October 30. He wore a black shirt for his first meeting with the king, returning later to present his list of ministers in the traditional, albeit ill-fitting morning dress of the political class.

The metamorphosis underlines a crucial point about the rise of fascism. It had not succeeded simply because of economic crisis or a threat from the left: if anything, these were receding by October 1922. Success had come more from a form of syncretic legitimation. Mussolini had managed to give his party a dual appeal: one side appealed to specific economic interests, including a section of the peasantry, while a more affective veneer of respectability was achieved by portraying fascism as not so much a radical break with the past as a vital force for the completion of the Risorgimento. The latter aspect encouraged conservative elites, who were worried about the radical Third Way side of fascism, to believe that it could be transformed and help provide a more stable, authoritarian form of government. Marxists tend to portray fascism as a dupe of capital or large agricultural interests. This is untrue, but Mussolini's rise had involved many compromises with the Establishment; and the PNF's rapid growth had sucked in many who did not support fascism's radical ideological core. These constraints rapidly became clear as Mussolini sought to consolidate the fascist "Revolution" after 1922.

Italy: The Development
of the Fascist Regime

MUSSOLINI TERMED his first ministry a "national government," underlining the presence of ten nonfascists among the Cabinet's fourteen members. These included liberals, nationalists, *popolari*, members of the armed forces, and a leading philosopher, Giovanni Gentile. The absence of members of left-wing parties indicates that this was hardly a truly national government, but Mussolini's continued desire to appeal to rank-and-file socialists is demonstrated by his (unfulfilled) wish to include a socialist trade-union leader. His attempt to build bridges with the left may have been why the *ras* were excluded, though the desire to appeal to "respectable" opinion was undoubtedly a more important motive. Mussolini was also eager to focus as much power in his own hands as possible. Setting what was to become a pattern in subsequent fascist administrations, he combined the post of prime minister with other portfolios—in this instance, with the important foreign and interior ministries.[1]

At the first cabinet meeting, Mussolini laid down the general lines of policy for the ministry: a combination of pacification, the creation of national discipline, and the achievement of budget economies.[2] The new ministry easily won a vote of confidence in the Chamber of Deputies, with five liberal ex-premiers voting for it, including Giolitti and Facta. Shortly afterward, the chamber voted the new administration emergency powers to reform the tax system, achieve economies, and to reorganize public services. Since 1918 it had been clear that serious problems existed in the sphere of public finance. Even so, the granting of emergency powers demonstrates that most deputies did not expect Mussolini to launch a social revolution or to pursue radical economic policies. This impression was reinforced in particular by the new finance minister, Alberto De Stefani, who was an economic liberal. He reduced controls on industry, cut taxes, and pursued other free market policies, all of which contributed to a rapid increase in production and decline in unemployment.

The government's economic program—together with foreign policy successes, most notably the annexation of Fiume—bestowed on fascism an air of respectability that belied its *squadristi* local base. Support came not just from the venal political class or antisocialist businessmen and landowners. Further endorsement came from a variety of notable academics. Italy's most famous philosopher, Benedetto Croce, gave his blessing. Although a liberal, he was also a nationalist who believed that a strong state was necessary to provide direction to a country characterized by social divisions and parochialism. Another liberal, Vilpredo Pareto, described fascism as a vigorous new elite which was in the process of replacing an inept one. A similar line was taken by his fellow elite theorist, Robert Michels, who was in the process of making the intellectual journey from being a Sorelian socialist to becoming a leading academic fascist.[3] Unlike Croce and Pareto, Michels was willing to forsake constitutional rule in the pursuit of a dynamic and united society. Gentile also joined the PNF in 1923. He saw fascism as a continuation of a struggle between the two Italies, between idealism and the materialism of the liberals and socialists.[4] Nineteen twenty-three witnessed the merger of the Nationalists and the PNF, which brought into the fascist fold yet more intellectuals, most notably Rocco and Luigi Federzoni.[5]

Growing respectability did not mean that the fascists' parliamentary position was secure. The 1921 elections had only given them 35 seats. Even after amalgamation with the Nationalists, they commanded fewer than 50 seats in a chamber of 535. Support from much of the political class was fickle. Some were seeking to transform fascism into part of the traditional liberal-conservative governing coalition, while others were waiting to return to power themselves at the first sign of fascist failure. Faced with this situation, Mussolini decided to have his under-secretary of state, Giacomo Acerbo, prepare a new electoral law. This proposed that any party or alliance gaining a least twenty-five percent of the vote would receive two-thirds of the seats. A combination of fascist intimidation and perceptions of self-interest on the part of the various center-right parties led to the passing of the bill.

At the beginning of 1924 Mussolini dissolved parliament, and elections under the new system duly followed in April. To consolidate his support, Mussolini decided on an electoral list of government supporters that would include nonfascists. Again, he seems to have been tempted to approach some socialists, but eventually the list was made up mainly of fascists, liberal-conservative notables including two former prime ministers, and the more right-wing members of the PPI.[6]

The campaign was characterized by considerable levels of corruption and intimidation, though this was more a case of degree than a total break with past practice. For example, at Lagostano in the Po Valley there were 747 registered voters, of whom 683 voted—all for the National list. Many opposition candidates were not allowed to speak, and some were threatened with death if they entered their constituencies. This was especially the case in the north, where the left and the PPI still retained important centers of support. Hundreds of rank-and-file supporters were wounded, and one socialist candidate was killed.

The government list did best in the south. Parts of the south had suffered particularly in terms of dead and wounded during the war, but the PNF had hardly any organization in this area before 1923. Clearly there was no automatic progression from the traumas of war to the fascist mass movement. The key to this late upsurge of fascism south of Rome was the influence of opportunistic local notables, although electoral fraud also played its part. One of the government supporters was Francesco Cuccia, the notorious mayor of Pianna dei Greci, and a former protégé of the local socialist deputy. As he was widely suspected of being a *mafioso,* his initial application to join the PNF was rejected by the idealistic small band of fascists who ran the local party. But Cuccia's persistence and the belief of higher fascist authorities that he would be useful had transformed him into a "fascist" by the time of the elections.[7] Perhaps not surprisingly, in southern Italy the government list won 81.5 percent of the vote.

Nationally, the list won sixty-six percent of the vote, giving it 374 seats, including 275 PNF deputies.[8] Although this fascist success owed much to influence, intimidation, and corruption, there was a more positive side to voting for the PNF. The fascist campaign was relatively sophisticated, often tailoring messages for local consumption. Fascism also retained some working-class backing in areas where it had been radical, though more left-inclined fascists were highly critical of government moderation and the presence of the old political class on the 1924 list. In Brescia, for example, some talked of the government's "revisionist stench."[9] Fascism remained strong too among the groups who had helped staff the *squadristi,* though there was a feeling that Mussolini was compromising too much—and sometimes anger that the leaders of the squads had not been rewarded with more government posts. The main growth in support seems to have come from the white-collar middle class, who saw in fascism the main alternative to either the old political class or a renewed threat from the left.[10] In other words, much of the fascist vote was not an endorsement of radicalism or violence: people wanted a change, but fascism had cleverly portrayed itself as an extension of an old Italian tradition rather than a complete break with the past.

The fascists had won a great electoral victory, but opposition was far from dead. The Chamber of Deputies still contained a number of critics, including forty-six socialists, thirty-nine *popolari,* and even nineteen communists. One of the most vociferous members of this group was the leader of the reformist socialists, Giacomo Matteotti. On May 30 he gave a speech in the chamber that bitterly denounced the elections as having been based on fraud and violence. He declared that the fascists did not have the support of the Italian people and tried to have the elections declared invalid. A few days later, while walking along the banks of the Tiber in Rome, he was attacked and forced into a car, which sped off in a northerly direction. His body, with a knife still stuck in the chest, was not found until several weeks later.

The attack had been witnessed and five fascists were eventually arrested. Their ringleader was named Amerigo Dumini, who was well known for violent exploits. At Carrara in 1922 he had slapped a girl who wore a red carnation; when her brother and mother protested, he shot them dead with a revolver. (It says much that he was not even arrested for this crime.)[11] Although Dumini held no position in the government, he maintained an office in Mussolini's press secretary's suite. It was widely believed that from there he organized terror squads. Exactly what led to Matteotti's murder remains a mystery. Possibly it was planned by fascists trying to prevent a rapprochement between Mussolini and moderate socialists. (Matteotti's own position may have been influenced in part by this fear.) A more likely cause was Mussolini's habit of talking about "making life difficult" for various enemies: he may not have given a direct order to kill Matteotti, but he seems to have been morally responsible for incitement.

Shortly after the kidnapping, most of the opposition deputies withdrew from the chamber in protest. They became known as the Aventine Secession (after the followers of Gaius Gracchus, who had taken to the Aventine hills during the ancient Roman republic); they declared themselves to be the true representatives of the people and tried to persuade the king to depose Mussolini. Visitors to Mussolini at this time found him red-eyed and unshaven; he clearly feared his days were numbered. Yet the king declined to act. Although he did not admire politicians, he had quickly come to value Mussolini for his industry, judgment, and quick understanding of problems.[12] He had been unhappy about the new electoral law, but he realized that a viable alternative government would probably have had to include the moderate socialists and others who were highly critical of him for appointing Mussolini in the first place. And the specter of the end of his dynastic line seems to have loomed particularly prominently: in 1914 Europe had forty-two reigning families—by 1924 this figure was sixteen.

Mussolini was under considerable pressure, but he was far from resigning. He countered by making changes in the government to reassure moderates and right-wingers, including moving Federzoni to the Interior Ministry, a post which Mussolini had previously held himself. Damage limitation was helped by the Vatican, which dissociated itself from the members of the PPI who joined the Aventine Secession, and which allowed right-wing Catholics to enter the new ministry. Many leading members of the clergy were grateful to fascism for breaking the left and believed that a formal understanding about church-state relations might be possible with Mussolini. Industrialists too stayed largely faithful, reflecting their basic satisfaction with government policy and to some shrewd patronage by the Duce, such as putting the owner of Fiat, Giovanni Agnelli, in the Senate. Other prominent figures rallied to Mussolini, including Croce. They had varied motives for their support, but many clearly believed that Mussolini deserved a further chance to show that he could provide firm government. Mussolini too played his part, shrewdly exploiting the fear that if he resigned the result would be further political chaos—and a *squadristi* wave of terror.

ii

AFTER HIS APPOINTMENT as prime minister in 1922, Mussolini had allowed the squads gathered around Rome to march through the capital in triumph. Once this brief hour of pseudo-glory was over, they returned to the provinces—to fester. Without the squads' violence Mussolini would probably never have become prime minister. But his response was not one of gratitude. His amoral acceptance of the usefulness of violence in politics was tempered by a realization of the dangers the squads posed. Increasingly he developed a set of bizarre syntheses whose main purpose was to broaden fascist support without losing sight of the demands of the diverse *squadristi*. For instance, he could talk of fascism as being both "law-abiding and law-breaking," "aristocratic and democratic," "conservative and progressive."[13] This helped to keep the unstable coalition together, but it provided little by way of guidance as to where the regime was going.

A small number of fascists sought to give the movement a more substantial set of policies. One important group that emerged during 1922–3 was associated with the ex-anarchist Massimo Rocca. He was interested in the problem of how to marry a largely free market to more collectivist policies that would ensure efficiency and social welfare. To develop these views, he advocated the creation at local and national levels of "technical groups," which would draw experts into the movement. This position seemed to be gathering support during 1923, so the *squadristi* wing voted for his expulsion. Mussolini had this changed to temporary suspension, but Rocca was expelled again in 1924, and by 1926 he was an anti-fascist exile. This episode underlined the power of the violent intransigents and, paradoxically, encouraged many ideologically radical fascists to accept Mussolini's dictatorial leadership: they believed that once he had curbed the power of the *ras* he would return to more serious ideological roots.

Mussolini was certainly eager to bring the *ras* under control. As part of this process, he created in December 1922 a Fascist Grand Council. Supposedly, this was a form of parallel cabinet, which would coordinate the actions of party and government. Mussolini, however, immediately used this forum to endorse the conversion of the blackshirt squads into a state militia (MVSN). Paid for out of public funds, this offered a useful source of patronage. But it did not fully wrest power from the suspicious *ras,* and its formation created tensions with the army, which feared rivalry for funds. Mussolini responded by appointing an army officer to command the militia after Emilio De Bono, one of the Quadrumvirs of the March on Rome, had been forced to resign following allegations that he was implicated in Matteotti's murder. The new commander quickly increased the military presence in the regional commands, causing further resentment among fascist intransigents. This was followed in November by Balbo, another of the Quadrumvirs, being forced out of his position as party head of the militia after he was implicated in the fatal beating of an antifascist priest.

The *ras* were not a unified group and they were on the whole ideologically unsophisticated, but they knew what they did not like: namely, "Bolshevists" and parliamentary democracy. Their idea of a fascist revolution did not include Mussolini tamely reporting to the king on Monday and Thursday mornings, while receiving deportment and protocol lessons in the afternoons. Their idea of a fascist party did not involve it growing fat as its numbers swelled through the influx of latecomers—the PNF grew from 300,000 members in October 1922 to 783,000 by the end of 1923. And the *ras* were certainly hostile to the continued presence of opposition parties, especially left-wing ones, which could criticize fascism.

Growing antagonism set the scene for a confrontation between

Mussolini and the *ras* at the close of 1924. The immediate cause was a report to the king that provided further damning evidence of fascist involvement in torture and murder. A group of leading *ras* visited Mussolini and threatened to depose him unless he prevented the judiciary from investigating the allegations. They made it clear that what they expected was the establishment of a full dictatorship. Behind this visit lay the clear threat that if Mussolini did not comply, he would be replaced as fascist leader.

The man Mussolini probably feared most was Italo Balbo. Born into a schoolteaching family and the holder of a university degree, Balbo was a latecomer to fascism. He joined the Ferrara *fascio* only in early 1921, attracted by the possibilities of rapid success (by 1924 he had married into the minor aristocracy). He was not simply an opportunist, however. In many ways Balbo lived out the fascist ideals of adventure and heroism. It was Balbo who probably more than any other created the organized system of squads, personally taking great risks. But here lay part of the problem for Balbo in terms of achieving national leadership: although blackshirt violence had been crucial to the rise of fascism, he realized that Mussolini's political skills meant that he was able to attract a broad coalition of support. Balbo held some programmatic views: for instance, he supported vaguely corporatist policies and he had a genuine concern for the plight of the poor. He was, nevertheless, ultimately a man of action rather than a manipulator—let alone a thinker or strategist.

Mussolini acted quickly to defuse any challenge from the *ras*. On January 3, 1925, he appeared in the Chamber of Deputies. He claimed that the deeds of Dumini and his friends were too stupid to be blamed on an intelligent person like himself. He asserted that he alone could unite the country and put it to rights, a proclamation which clearly implied the need for dictatorship. Three nonfascist ministers resigned, and some leading liberals including Giolitti sought to move a vote of censure. These actions could have provided the king with a further opportunity to dismiss Mussolini. But he had never believed that Mussolini was personally responsible for Matteotti's murder, and the arguments that had prevented him sacking the Duce in the summer of 1924 seemed just as compelling now. Having played a crucial role in bringing facism to power, the king tamely accepted that Italy was now set on the path to dictatorship.

Reconstruction of the government was followed in February 1925 by a further attempt to please the intransigents: the appointment of Roberto Farinacci as party secretary. Farinacci was working class by birth, socialist by early conviction. Deeply affected by the war and radical nationalist propaganda, he became a *sansepolcrista,* a founding father of the movement. He quickly made Cremona his personal fiefdom, gaining a reputation as one of the most violent of the *ras.*[14] Such was his control over Cremona that during the March of Rome he obtained the surrender of the local army garrison and secured complete control of the city. He was duly appointed to the Grand Council on its formation. But unlike some *ras,* most notably Grandi, Farinacci did not modify his commitment to the need for the immediate creation of a one-party dictatorship. As Mussolini sought to broaden fascism's appeal, such views became dangerous and Farinacci was dropped from the Grand Council in 1923. Lacking a major national role, he began a legal career, having obtained a degree without attending courses and on the basis of a plagiarized dissertation. (He had wished to submit one entitled "Dosing Subversives with Castor Oil on the Part of Fascists Cannot Be Considered an Act of Violence"; a sympathetic professor had suggested that this did not have a sufficiently academic ring.) Farinacci had already developed a relatively affluent lifestyle as a result of support from agricultural and business interests in Cremona. His legal career was to make him even richer, though the prospects of great wealth did not dampen his political intransigence. He set about his task as party secretary with zeal, launching a major purge of the more opportunistic members of the party and sanctioning further violence against enemies.

While Farinacci was beavering feverishly to increase his influence, Mussolini fell ill. For years he had been receiving treatment for venereal disease. A severe gastro-duodenal ulcer was now diagnosed, which was probably the result of stress and overwork. A new diet was prescribed, and the Duce was soon back working long hours, though these seem often to have been filled devouring newspapers rather than attending to the business of state. Mussolini retained a strong professional interest in journalism, and after the introduction of extensive press controls during 1924–6 he was personally keen to ensure conformity. His avid reading reveals another side to his character. Mussolini was a man who had no confidants, apart from his brother Arnaldo, who was to die in 1931. He loathed Rome's social life, often preferring to work on his farm or to seek solace and reassurance in a succession of mistresses. Indeed, he lived frugally, shunning most material goods. (Sometimes he even gave relatively large sums from his journalistic royalties to charity anonymously, rather paradoxical behavior for someone who craved the limelight.) Reading the press, therefore, served as a source of information about the world at large—and the standing of potential rivals.

Farinacci was never really in a position to challenge for the prime ministership—or head of government, as Mussolini came to term it on the grounds that this sounded more Italian. Even many of the other *ras* saw him as too extreme. His tactics reflected his politics: he was the bull at the gate rather than the fox, a man lacking in craft. By early 1926 Mussolini was, nevertheless, becoming increasingly concerned about Farinacci's more extremist statements and especially about his clashes with Luigi Federzoni, who had been appointed interior minister as part of the attempt to cultivate a respectable face. Mussolini's chance came during the trial of Matteotti's murderers, in which Farinacci acted as defense lawyer. His histrionic and demagogic position alienated all but the most violent fascists. Mussolini therefore found it relatively easy to persuade the Grand Council in March 1926 to name Augusto Turati, the *ras* of Brescia, as the new Secretary of the PNF.

A further dimension to the replacement of Farinacci relates to Mussolini's views about the role of party. The PNF had been created partly as a vehicle in his struggle with the local *ras*. Having achieved power, he was now eager to ensure that the PNF did not become a major center of power in its own right. An important further step in this process followed later in 1926 when the Grand Council approved a new party statute. This incorporated the principle of nomination from above for all offices that had previously been elected, a change which helped the rise of local notables and opportunists—often at the expense of the fascist old guard, who were either too violent or who lacked the ability for the more administrative functions the party was now taking on. A further step followed in 1928 when a new statute was adopted for the Grand Council. Drawn up by Alfredo Rocco, who like most former Nationalists was keen to subordinate the party to the state, this accorded the council formal legal status, but in practice it underlined Mussolini's growing control over the party.

Turati remained Secretary of the PNF until 1930. He was in many ways an atypical *ras,* being more concerned with constructive programs than antisocialist violence—programs which were designed to reflect fascism's radical roots. During 1926–30 he advocated in particular the creation of a corporate state that would help shift power toward the workers. He became increasingly concerned by the growing corruption surrounding fascism, which eventually brought him into direct conflict with Mussolini. Although the Duce lived modestly, he could turn a blind eye to those who found power the route to fortune—especially when it involved those close to him, like his brother Arnaldo.

Turati's successor as party secretary was Achille Starace. He was more the Duce's eunuch than potential rival, an accountant by profession who finally emasculated the party as a radical force. Against the wishes of those who sought to keep fascism an elite group, Starace again allowed membership to grow. During 1932–9 it rose from just under a million to 2,633,000, a figure which excludes the many members of youth and women's organizations. The party badge was now a meal ticket rather than a sign of any ideological conviction, especially for those who worked in the public sector, where membership of the party became compulsory.

It was Starace who did much to turn the party into a Ruritanian force, characterized more by uniform and choreography than a clearly stated program. A humorless flatterer, he stood to attention when speaking on the phone to his Duce, and initiated the practice of running to Mussolini's desk at the start of an audience. It was Starace who sought to put Italy into uniform, so that by the mid-1930s a cabinet minister needed at least ten uniforms for different occasions. Yet Starace's efforts in this sphere did little more than amplify the views of his master. From the formation of the first *fasci,* Mussolini's combination of Nietzschean and Sorelian ideas led him to place much greater emphasis on the role of personal leadership and myths than on formally organized political activity.

Although a full propaganda ministry was not to be established until 1935, the Duce had always demonstrated a strong interest in style and manipulation. D'Annunzio's occupation of Fiume served as a major source of inspiration, especially the emphasis on the leader and the theatricality. Mussolini was a brilliant pupil, who became a master of crowd manipulation. His characteristic style involved leaning on a parapet, while swaying to and fro, occasionally throwing his head back or puffing his chest, and finishing with his hands on hips—or holding a hand inside his jacket in a Napoleonic gesture. On some occasions, the image of Mussolini-the-leader changed to man-of-the-people. He was fond of being photographed with peasants, or wearing a bathing costume at the seaside, thus revealing his muscular torso. He also liked being photographed while engaged in various sporting activities: the healthy, relatively young man of action (he was just thirty-nine when he became prime minister). Camera angles were carefully chosen to hide the fact that he was short—an illusion helped when he was photographed with the king by the fact the monarch was even shorter. He also concealed the fact that he wore glasses, and in later years shaved his head to hide a receding hair line.

Yet there was more to fascist propaganda than charismatic populism designed to court mass support—and to fuel Mussolini's massive ego. The relationship between propaganda and a more fundamental ideology can be seen by considering the cult of ancient Rome (*Romanità*) which fascism adopted. From its foundation, fascism had been led by a Duce (from the Latin *dux*), and symbolized by the lictors' ax bound in rods—*fasces*. After 1922 the regime acquired a whole new set of Roman allusions, including a Birth of Rome Day, which replaced Labor Day, and a fascist militia staffed with consuls, centurions, and legionaries. This cult of the *Romanità* served a dual purpose. It undoubtedly had a manipulative side in the sense that it was meant to cut across party lines, helping to attract a variety of supporters. But there was also a more serious set of messages contained within it. In particular, it harked back to days of Italian greatness and helped to justify new dreams of Mediterranean domination.[15] The same mixture of propaganda and ideology can be discerned in the language that emerged to describe the March on Rome. Initially Mussolini was not quite sure how to portray his takeover, and often talked of a restoration or rebirth—clearly with the intention of assuaging moderate opinion. But increasingly the coming to power was referred to as a "revolution," a point reinforced by a change in the calendar so that 1922 became Anno Primo.[16] After 1925, another key word in the fascist vocabulary was *totalitarian,* which further underlined the belief that what was being created was something essentially new.

iii

MUSSOLINI SEEMS to have first used the term *totalitarian* in a speech delivered on January 5, 1925. Initially he appears to have understood the term in relation to the will: a great leader, through the force of his perception and strength of mind, was capable of bringing about total social and political transformation. Gentile, who was to emerge as the most sophisticated philosophical defender of the regime, portrayed "totalitarianism" somewhat differently. For Gentile, one of the crucial faults of liberalism and capitalism was the way in which they divided people socially and created a political "class" that had little contact with the people. Totalitarianism for Gentile, therefore, referred more to a social system that would bring people together and that would break down the gulf between leaders and masses.

In practice, Italian totalitarianism was different again. Although the regime was unquestionably a dictatorship, it differed significantly from academic models of the totalitarian state—with their emphasis on the pervasive role of ideology and highly centralized control.[17] Many developments owed much to chance, or the specific political and economic needs of the moment. And considerable power remained in the hands of the church and business, though neither group ultimately could control the regime.

In his youth Mussolini had written an anticlerical novel, *Claudia Particella, the Cardinal's Mistress.* Early fascism too was marked by strong hostility toward the Catholic church. But the change in the post-1922 calendar so that the modern world no longer began with Jesus Christ did not indicate that Mussolini was set on a course of open conflict with Catholicism. Even after the proclaimed move to dictatorship in 1925, the goal was synthesis rather than repression.[18] Fascism would increasingly take on the role of a secular religion, while the church would become the repository of key fascist ideas.

Mussolini began his rapprochement with the church before coming to power, though the process was in many ways symbiotic. He realized that anticlericalism would lose him more support than it would gain. Many within the church, on the other hand, saw fascism as a crucial vehicle for suppressing the left. The archbishop of Milan even allowed fascist banners to be displayed in the Duomo, an act of great significance because in February 1922 he became Pope Pius XI. During the next three years fascism received useful help from the Vatican. In particular, a group of "clerico-fascists"— a somewhat misleading term, for they were in many ways an extension of the old Catholic right—played a crucial role in the consolidation of Mussolini's power. In its turn, the government adopted policies that pleased the Vatican—especially the rescue of the Catholic Bank of Rome in 1923, various measures relating to abortion and contraception, and a campaign against freemasonry. On a personal level, Mussolini symbolically married Donna Rachele in church in 1925, ten years after their civil marriage.

The growing understanding between the Vatican and fascism reflected a desire to formalize church–state relations, which had lain unresolved since the occupation of Rome during the unification of Italy. The courtship was consummated on February 11, 1929, when Cardinal Gasparri and Mussolini signed the Lateran Pacts, which included three main parts: the recognition of the sovereign independence of the Vatican; the formalization of church–state relations; and financial compensation for losses suffered as a consequence of the unification of Italy.[19] As a result, the church was accorded significant formal powers in civil society. On the other hand, the regime benefited from both the domestic and international prestige of formal recognition. On balance, Mussolini probably gained more in the short run than the church—at least in terms of further support for the regime.

Predictably, the pacts did not fully resolve church–state relations. By the summer of 1931 considerable tension had emerged over the lay organization Catholic Action, which had been founded during the 1860s as the papacy lost its temporal power. The Pope put much faith in this as a means of combating the corruption of the modern world. Most fascists would not have objected—at least in the short run—if Catholic Action's concerns had been purely spiritual. But it had become especially interested in the socialization of youth, which brought it into conflict with fascist youth organizations. Further tension arose after the disbandment of the PPI and suppression of other parties, as Catholic Action served increasingly as a vehicle for antifascist dissent. In September 1931 a compromise was patched up when it was agreed that Catholic Action would pursue only a recreational role and educational activity of a purely religious nature, while former members of the PPI were removed from its leadership. The clash, however, had shown that relations between fascism and Catholicism were mercurial. By 1937–8 new tensions were emerging over Catholic Action and other issues. The Pope was strongly opposed to Mussolini's drift toward the Nazi brand of fascism, which he correctly categorized as pagan and racist. On the other hand, Mussolini's old anti-Christian views were reemerging. He even told the cabinet that Islam was a more effective religion, which was manna to those fascists who had never liked the Lateran Pacts.

Fascist relations with another major source of influence, business, were also changing and complex. Even more than relations with the Catholic church, they help to reveal the divisions within fascism and the ad hoc nature of the fascist state.[20]

During 1919–20 fascists sometimes supported the syndicalist labor organization led by Alceste De Ambris, but he quickly came to reject fascism because of its compromises with landowners and business.[21] Another member of the union, Edmondo Rossoni, broke away, and by January 1922 had emerged as head of the rapidly growing fascist unions—though much of this strength was in rural areas. Rossoni was a radical who wanted to create a corporatist structure that would include both workers and employers, with the intention of ensuring that the capitalist class did most of the cooperating. Like many Italian syndicalists, he sought to create a new society through institutional structures rather than through the manipulative power of myth—a reversal of the Duce's priorities.[22]

This program aroused considerable opposition from business,

which made it clear to Mussolini that its continued support was based on low levels of government interference. As a result, in December 1923 Mussolini called together representatives of the facist unions and industry. The ensuing Palazzo Chigi Pact made no effort to integrate the two sides in corporatist structures. Its main purposes were to simplify industrial relations, by making the fascist unions the sole representatives of labor, and to ensure industrial peace.

The pact encouraged growth in the membership of fascist syndicates, but where necessary, employers continued to negotiate with other unions. Old practices of this type were clearly doomed once Mussolini proclaimed a dictatorship, and during 1925 new pressure was placed on employers both by the government and by a series of fascist-condoned strikes. The result was the Palazzo Vidoni agreement of October 1925. Rossoni's unions were now formally given a monopoly to negotiate contracts, but workers' factory councils were abolished and plans to challenge the authority of management within factories were vetoed. The grateful employer's federation responded with a public statement of adherence to the fascist regime in December.

Not all fascist economic policies met with business approval. Two related issues during 1925–7 clearly illustrate that ideology could play a major part: the Battle for Grain and the debate over the exchange rate. In 1925 Mussolini announced a plan to make Italy self-sufficient in food production as part of the initial moves toward an autarchic war economy. This policy encouraged domestic production, though only at the expense of raising price levels, which fueled wage demands. The following year Mussolini announced that he planned to stabilize the exchange rate. Driven largely by the desire for international prestige, he decided to adopt a rate of 92.46 lire to the pound, far higher than that expected by most business circles. In the short run this policy harmed the Italian economy in general, and small business in particular—though in the longer run some larger companies gained, as the policy encouraged the takeover of small companies in order to make production more efficient.

There was also some business opposition toward the creation from 1926 to 1934 of an authoritarian corporate state. A key figure in this was Rocco, another Hegelian whom some have seen as a more important ideologist of the regime than Gentile.[23] Like most former ANI intellectuals, he had a clearer program than Mussolini. One result of this was his "Law for the Judicial Regulation of Labor Disputes," which allowed only one association of workers for each major sector of production. But, as strikes were abolished, its main effect was to discipline labor and strengthen ("enlarge" might be a more accurate term) the state. Shortly afterward, a Ministry of Corporations was created to organize the syndicates, though this was largely a sham. Indeed, in 1928 Rossoni was fired and the Confederation of Fascist Syndicates was broken up—a decision that both calmed business fears and brought the syndicates more closely under Mussolini's control. The concurrent reform of the Chamber of Deputies was another part of the corporatist illusion. The change involved putting up a slate of candidates, nominated by various social and economic organizations, for endorsement by national referendum. In theory it was meant to underline the importance of functional rather than regional representation. In practice, as the list had to be approved by the Grand Council—which meant Mussolini—the change illustrated the continued destruction of the old liberal state.

Yet corporatism was more than a conservative sham, useful for manipulating the masses or disguising Mussolini's attempts to center all power in his own hands. There was still a radical wing in the fascist party that sought to introduce significant institutional reforms, a group that played an important part in the most serious moves toward the creation of a corporate state—which came during 1930 to 1934. In 1930 a National Council of Corporations was set up, which comprised seven large worker and employer organizations. It had no legislative power, but could issue binding orders in matters covered by contract concerning wages and conditions. By 1934 this had been expanded to include twenty-two sectors of the economy and social life. Fascist propaganda made considerable play of the way that this was supposed to be transforming the nature of industrial relations, and laying the basis for a new political order.

Giuseppe Bottai was the minister of corporations from 1929 to 1932. Bottai was a former futurist and a man with a university degree. He had a taste for ideas, and in 1923 had founded a periodical called *Critica fascista*, which served as a major forum for radical facist debate. During 1923–4 a central concern of the journal had been how to create an elitist combination of liberalism and authoritarianism—Bottai referred to the mass mobilisers in the party as "cattle-raisers."[24] Subsequently it became a notable source of other key intellectual attempts within fascism to synthesize divergent forces, especially between the commitment to nationalism and the belief that fascism was more a defense of European values against the threat from communism, materialism, and other socially corrosive influences.[25] By the early 1930s Bottai saw the corporations as the basis of a "Third Way," a combination of the best aspects of capitalism and socialism. Again, there was an element of mythology in this structure, for the state and business retained considerable power. Even so, the exiled academic critic Gaetano Salvemini could write in 1935 that Italy had become the Mecca of political scientists, economists, and sociologists looking for the basis of a new order in a world trapped between capitalist depression and communist autocracy.[26]

While the edifice of the corporate state was being created, Italy was slipping into recession. The Index of Manufacturing Production, which had stood at 90 in 1929 (the year of the Wall Street crash), fell to 77 by 1931, rising only slightly to 82 in 1933 (1938 = 100). Even before the recession had reached its low point, the government had launched a program of public works, most notably the draining of the Pontine marshes. This was soon broadened to include bailing out failing industries, a policy which had been pursued on occasion by various liberal governments since the end of the nineteenth century. But the creation of the Institute for Industrial Reconstruction (IRI) in 1933 reflected a more radical departure. It purchased from banks the shares they held in business, and used them to exert a major influence in industrial policy and development.[27] The result was that by 1939 the Italian government controlled a greater section of industry than any other government in Europe outside the Soviet Union and Nazi Germany.

There seems little doubt that business in general benefited from these policies. In particular, as the state held mainly the loss-making units, private industry was left free to concentrate on profitable fields and secure a long-term future.[28] Even so, it would be a mistake to think that fascism was merely a tool of the business class. Most industrialists had little time for corporatism unless it was a ve-hicle for controlling the working class. By the late 1930s they also harbored growing suspicions about other aspects of fascist socioeco-nomic programs. Many feared that economic policy was increas-ingly being made with a view to military concerns. Although some sectors stood to gain from a war, most businessmen were in favor of a conciliatory policy after the conquest of Ethiopia in 1936. There were also fears about a revival of social radicalism within fascism as the economy picked up, which opened the prospects of govern-ment-encouraged wage increases in order to court popular opinion.

iv

IF MUSSOLINI'S GOVERNMENT failed to exert total control over the church and business, did it succeed elsewhere? In particular, did it manage to manufacture widespread consent—or was the regime founded more on repression and terror? Unfortunately, no govern-ment department kept reliable and comprehensive records of public opinion, while the media were highly controlled after 1924 and were not allowed to report crime or anything that might detract from the regime's image. But there are good reasons to believe that by the end of the Ethiopian War in 1936 there was a wide level of acceptance of the regime, and admiration for Mussolini especially.[29]

The largest group in society was those who lived on the land, but this was a very differentiated group. There were various forms of ownership and rental, and many near the cities held second jobs outside agriculture. Those living on the land, however, seem to have been among the main losers under fascism in financial terms, and to have been least integrated by nationalist propaganda—a re-sult that might seem strange, as there was an increasing strand in fascism that eulogized peasant life as decent, healthy, and rooted in tradition. But while some fascists genuinely believed in this ruralist (*strapaese*) myth, its main purpose was social control, an attempt to manage a long-term move away from the land. In particular, it was part of a policy designed to keep most peasants from moving to towns, thus reducing unemployment and avoiding further pres-sures on industrial wages. From the point of view of the peasants—

especially in southern Italy—government was a vague concept: the fascists were simply another set of rulers, largely irrelevant to the drudgery of everyday life.

Opinion among industrial workers was mixed. Strong pockets of antifascist sentiment continued to exist, but there were converts too, attracted by some of fascism's policies and successes. The official figure for unemployment in December 1933 was 1.2 million, relatively low by European standards—though fascist official figures must be treated with caution. It would probably have been higher still but for syndical policy. As the unions could not strike, at least legally, it was easier to impose wage cuts, thus helping to keep up the total number of employed. Cutting the working week in some industries also served as a way of sharing jobs. It is difficult to be precise about the impact of fascism on workers' living standards, not least because it is impossible to be sure what would have happened had there not been a fascist government. The balance of evidence seems to be that after falling initially, by the late 1930s real wages had returned to their prefascist levels. But to these wages must be added various fringe benefits, which were a notable feature of social policy during the 1930s. Among the most notable benefits were improvements in sick pay, year-end bonuses, and holidays with pay.

Fascism looked after the leisure interests of workers through the National After-Work Leisure Organization (OND), commonly known as the Dopolavoro.[30] This was formed in 1925 by amalgamating various social organizations that local fascists had created to replace socialist groups broken up by the squads. The organization was mainly commune-based, but occasionally it operated within major factories, especially in the north. In some ways it acted as a further welfare organization, handing out relief to the poor and providing virtually free holidays to some children. Its main activities, however, were leisure-oriented, though there was occasionally an overt political side to them, such as the provision of radios so that propaganda broadcasts could be heard collectively: the number of individually owned sets rose from three hundred thousand in 1932 to one million by 1938.

Perhaps the most popular leisure activities were outings and organized sports. Sport became an increasingly important focus of fascist propaganda. It diverted attention from other matters, especially the lack of opportunity for meaningful political choice. It also could be used to enhance a sense of national pride and belonging. Soccer thus became the second obsession of Italian men after Italy won the 1934 World Cup, which was held in Italy. Cars became the third, as Alfa-Romeo grand-prix cars became frequent occupants of the winner's circle—challenged mainly by the German auto unions and Mercedes. Government sponsorship of sports highlighted values crucial to the "new man" that fascism was trying to create. Sports in the 1930s did not denote vast commercial sponsorship or immense earnings: rather they were the symbol of athleticism and competition—the strongest survived.

The associated iconography was clearly male, underlining the subservient place usually accorded to women in fascist ideology.[31] The 1919 fascist program had promised women the vote and social equality, but the regime quickly went back on these commitments. Indeed, Gentile's educational reform initiated after the March on Rome began the process in terms of policy. Gentile defended the smaller number of opportunities offered for female advancement within education by arguing that one of the problems in society was the influence of women teachers in secondary and university education. In a speech to the Chamber of Deputies on May 15, 1925, Mussolini was to offer a rather different reason for combating the rise of feminism: namely that women were incapable of synthesizing anything, of combining different ideas into a higher form. He proclaimed that their natural role was caring for a new generation of warriors.

After 1925 a variety of policies sought to push women back into the home and to increase the overall population significantly, including further restrictions on contraception. During the 1930s a series of taxes and subsidies encouraged marriage and having children, including taxes on bachelors. In the field of employment, there was discrimination in favor of family men. Continuing male unemployment encouraged the adoption in 1938 of a law that restricted females to ten percent of the workforce, though a 1939 decree defined some exceptions, such as typists, where the percentage could be higher. Women across Europe suffered during the interwar era from the dual pressures of conservative reaction and economic recession, but these policies clearly reflected a fundamental ideological position.

The overall impact of fascism on women was complex, varying across region, class, and age. In many rural areas female labor remained important, and it was also retained by some industrial concerns because it was cheaper. Even the impact on total population, a major concern, is not clear. This rose from 38,450,000 in 1921 to 44,900,000 in 1940, but such growth is explicable by natural trends without invoking the power of fascist propaganda or coercion. Besides, severe penalties did not stop the extensive practice of abortion, which was probably running at about thirty percent of births in 1930. Although support for fascism—and especially Mussolini—seems to have been relatively strong among women, this did not mean that they were willing to bear extra children in order to fight for a greater Italy.

Fascism set up a panoply of organizations to socialize young people.[32] The earliest group, organizing university students, had been formed in 1920, but the main thrust came after the establishment of the dictatorship. The best-known organization was the Ballila, named after an eighteenth century Genoese street boy who had bravely thrown a rock at the city's Austrian occupiers. It catered to boys from the age of eight to fourteen. The equivalent group for girls was the Piccole Italiane. By the 1930s a host of groups dealt with over five million young people from the age of approximately six until well into their twenties. Their functions and impact varied considerably. The groups for the very young tended to be like Wolf Cubs or Scouts in other countries, though there was always a more military side. From a relatively young age activities included drill and carrying toy guns—at least for the boys. (Girls were sometimes allowed bows and arrows.) Boys in all areas were much more likely to join, especially in the south where no respectable young female marched around in uniform. As such, the organization of youth was part of the drive toward conformism and militarism. In the universities, however, fascist organizations sometimes performed a very different role. Among the activities sponsored by these groups were debates, which could be critical because

ideological compliance was enforced much less rigidly on this privileged elite.

After the establishment of a dictatorship, fascist attitudes toward
dissent are difficult to summarize briefly. There was always an element of pluralism within Italian society. The potential for criticism
did not simply stem from the continued independence of the Vatican and its media, which attracted growing audiences during the
1930s. Even after the suppression of political journals, cultural journals continued to carry dissent and advocate a remarkably broad
range of artistic styles. In part this was a reflection of the desire to
court intellectuals, though a more important factor was probably
the realization that a degree of toleration in this sphere strengthened the regime. Croce, for example, turned into a critic of fascism
after the establishment of a dictatorship, using his position within
the Senate—which was directly appointed by the king—to speak
out. But the very fact that he remained in Italy illustrated that some
dissent was possible. Croce was a major international figure, which
gave him special protection. The exhibition held to commemorate
the tenth anniversary of the fascist "revolution," however, underlines the fact that there was no rigidly enforced cultural line. Relatively minor artists from a wide variety of positions were persuaded
to contribute to this celebration of fascism, which attracted remarkably large attendances. The prestigious, government-sponsored *Enciclopedia Italiana*, first published in 1929, contained entries from
numerous nonfascists and even antifascists.

While an element of dissent existed, it is important not to ignore the powerful repressive side of the state.[33] After the fourth assassination attempt on Mussolini within two years, a series of
Exceptional Decrees was passed in November 1926, which banned
all remaining formal opposition and established a Special Tribunal
for the Defense of the State. This was used mainly to try political
cases, though others who came under its jurisdiction included the
Mafia as a major campaign was launched against Mafia influence,
often using brutal methods.[34] Between 1927 and 1939 the tribunal
imposed 3,596 sentences, with the average sentence being approximately 5.25 years. Some of those convicted were guilty of attacks
against individuals and the state—the most notable "terrorist" attack was a bombing of a meeting addressed by the king in Milan

during 1928, in which eighteen were killed and over forty were wounded. But some were imprisoned simply on account of their views: among those in this category was the leading communist Antonio Gramsci, who died of illness while incarcerated.

After 1926 coercion was operated more by the state than the party, and there was no extensive system of terror of the type which characterised the Nazi regime. The chief of police from 1926 to 1940 was Arturo Bocchini, a technocratic career prefect who was opposed to the violence of the *ras* and local fascists. Although Mussolini suddenly announced in 1930 that a secret police called OVRA had been formed, it seems that no new organization specifically dealing with political control had been created: support for fascism at this time was based on acceptance as much as fear. In fact, relatively few people were sentenced to death or even incarceration. Most dissidents who fell foul of the system were sent into internal exile, a punishment which picked up both big and small fry. Among the latter was Pietro Marieta, who was known to the Turin police for expressing socialist ideas and for his love of drink. In June 1937 he was heard by a militia squad leader to exclaim: "What's the Roman Empire?" then to blow on the palm of his hand and announce, "That's all it is—long live justice and liberty."[35] A period of enforced rural retreat ensued.

There were no concentration camps for Jews either.[36] The Jewish community in Italy was small: only forty-seven thousand in 1938. Jews tended to be a socially important group, playing a particularly notable role in banking, commerce, and the professions, but there was little anti-Semitism in Italy. Nor was it a major feature of the early fascist movement. Indeed, Jews played an important part in funding fascism in areas like Ferrara during 1920 to 1922. Subsequently a Jew, Aldo Finzi, held a government post and a seat in the Grand Council, and by the mid-1930s about one in three Jewish adults were members of the PNF—a higher proportion than among the gentile population. Typical of the richer Jews who turned toward fascism was the Ovazza family. At the age of fifty Ernesto signed up with his three sons to fight in World War I, testimony to the strong desire to prove that they were loyal Italians. He saw the defeat at Caporetto as stemming from a lack of discipline and firm leadership. Before his death in 1926 he asked to have three words engraved on his tomb: "Fatherland, Faith and Family." His son Ettore was made in the same mold. He was one of 230 Jews who took part in the March on Rome. Even as the regime began to move toward overt racism in the mid-1930s, Ettore stayed loyal, founding a stridently profascist journal and physically leading an attack on Zionist Jews.

The main cause of the regime's drift toward anti-Semitism was Mussolini. Curiously, he was not a rabid anti-Semite. For a time he even had a Jewish mistress, Margherita Sarfatti, an intelligent and sophisticated woman associated with the Novecento art movement, which tried to synthesize tradition and modernity. But there had always been an element in his thought that saw the struggle between superior and inferior cultures as the motor of history. The acquisition of a new empire in Ethiopia increased this tendency to distinguish between peoples in a hierarchical way. That war also helped to bring home to Mussolini some of the failings within fascism. Although surrounded by sycophants who encouraged delusions, he seems to have realized that it had been accompanied by a high level of incompetence. By the late 1930s Mussolini wanted to launch a second revolution, to give fascism a new lease of life. As he was by this time falling increasingly under Hitler's influence, he almost certainly saw anti-Semitism as a major factor in regenerating fascist radicalism—in separating the men from the time-servers and opportunists who now made up much of the party. This may also have been related to the increasing estrangement from the Catholic church, for anti-Semitism allowed an attack on key elements of Christian doctrine—such as its universalism and humanism—without the dangers that would have been associated with an open attack on the church.

A series of anti-Semitic decrees based on the Nazi model were promulgated in 1938. The new laws involved a variety of restrictions on Jews, including the forbidding of intermarriage and bans from participation in various walks of life. The changes undoubtedly brought hardship to Jews—and even greater torments in view of what was happening across the Alps. Italian anti-Semitism, however, was far less virulent than the Nazi strain. For instance, there was a special category for those who had served in World War I with distinction, or for early fascist members. Jews categorized in this way received more favorable treatment, though usually after considerable bureaucratic troubles. When Ettore Ovazza made a request to be allowed to travel to a well-known resort because he was ill, he was refused—but told that he could go to another town. When he asked permission to continue owning a radio, this was eventually conceded on condition it could only pick up Italian stations.

The impact of the anti-Semitic decrees was mitigated by other factors. The policy met with opposition from the king and armed forces, in which many officers had been Jewish. The Catholic church too tended to provide succor for the Jews—though Pope Pius XII, who was appointed in 1939, has been strongly criticized for his failure to take a stronger public line against anti-Semitism and the Holocaust.[37] While the regime tried to portray anti-Semitism as a continuation of an old church tradition, Catholicism's emphasis on a redemptive power of baptism meant it was difficult to portray a people as irretrievably dangerous or evil. The healthy (in this case) disregard for authority that characterizes Italian political culture further undermined the policy. Even many fascists were opposed to the policy—most notably Italo Balbo, who spoke against it in the Grand Council.

Aiding Jews in Italy cannot be equated entirely with occupied Eastern Europe, where being caught for such "crimes" usually meant death—often for the whole family. Nevertheless, Italians of all walks of life sabotaged attempts by the Germans and anti-Semitic fascists to impose the Final Solution. As a result, a remarkable eighty percent of Italian Jews survived, largely in hiding. A few, including Primo Levi, who was later to write a stunning account of his experiences, even managed to survive the Nazi death camps. Among the 7,682 who perished was Ettore Ovazza, together with his wife and daughter. Having been seized by the SS, they were shot on October 10, 1943, in northern Italy. Their bodies were cut up and burned in a school furnace. It was just days before the twenty-first anniversary of the March on Rome, in which Ettore had participated so proudly.

Mussolini's meteoric rise from obscurity to national leadership meant that he never fully developed a clear vision of the regime he intended to create. His general goal was to conduct a revolution without first destroying the old. Initially, this involved an erratic blend of compromise and radicalism, with the former dominating the synthesis. Later, Mussolini turned more to propaganda in an attempt to make new Italians. In some ways he succeeded. Italians, especially in the center and north, became more "nationalized" and modernized. And there is no doubt that aspects of fascism were popular, especially its social policies and foreign policy up to the conquest of Ethiopia. But at this point a strange combination of delusions of grandeur tinged with a sense of failure pushed Mussolini into the arms of fascism's ideological, but by no means identical, twin: Nazism. It was to prove a fatal alliance—for both the Duce and fascism.

5

Italy: War and Strife

i

IN THE DECADE following the March on Rome, Mussolini was pre-occupied with domestic issues. The need to build a broad basis of consensus for the regime meant that there was relatively little time to devote to the serious study of foreign policy. His portfolio of posts, however, included the Foreign Ministry from 1922 until 1929, and foreign affairs were never far from his thoughts—especially when they promised to bolster domestic popularity.[1]

During August 1923 he provoked an incident with Greece over the island of Corfu. Although international pressure quickly forced Italian troops to withdraw, the episode was a clear warning of his aspirations to dominate the Balkans. Shortly afterward, Italy annexed Fiume, the site of D'Annunzio's short-lived Regency of Carnaro. The removal of this major source of contention might in the longer run have led to improved relations with Yugoslavia. In-stead, Mussolini was more interested in the breakup of the polyglot state. By the early 1930s he had even allowed the Croatian extreme nationalist Ustasha movement to set up a training camp for terror-ists in Italy, from where the leader of the Ustasha, Ante Pavelić, plotted the assassination of King Alexander of Yugoslavia in 1934. (Pavelić was later to become head of the wartime Nazi-puppet Croatian regimen, which launched a barbaric policy of ethnic cleansing against the Serbs, though atrocities were committed on all sides in the Balkans during World War II).

Another traditional focus of Italian aspirations was North Africa.[2] The conquest of Libya during 1911–12 had provided a powerful boost to the new Italian nationalism emerging at this time. Libya was to be Italy's "fourth shore," a promised new home-land for emigrants. The reality was that the country was largely desert—oil had not yet been discovered—and the local population was distinctly unwelcoming. During 1915 to 1918 Italian forces had been pushed back into a handful of coastal enclaves. Following a period of neglect by previous Italian governments, the fascist regime embarked on a policy of ruthless repression. In Cyrenaica this lasted until the early 1930s. A significant minority of the population was killed by Italian troops or starved to death through the slaughter of livestock. By the mid-1930s, the country had been "pacified" and sizable emigration began to take place, encouraged by the dynamic governorship of Italo Balbo, who was "exiled" there in 1934 after a series of international long-distance flying exploits had brought him great popularity—thus encouraging Mussolini to see in him a potential rival. By 1939 more than a hundred thousand Italians lived in Libya, just over a tenth of the country's population. This development was accompanied by a program to make at least the more developed coastal region a fully fledged part of Italy, in the way that Algeria was part of "Metropolitan France."

As part of this plan, Balbo advocated according equal rights to Arabs.[3] There had always been a minority strand in the new Italian nationalism that accepted nationalism in others, or that saw Italy as leading a "civilizing mission" (rather like France's self-proclaimed universalist goal of spreading French values and civilization).[4] For a brief period during the early 1930s Mussolini's monthly magazine, *Gerarchia*, suggested that the age of colonies was over and that white and native peoples should be treated as equals. But the major strand in fascist thought was conquest of a great empire, with little thought for the indigenous people, at least in the short run.

During the late nineteenth century, the "Scramble for Africa" had parceled out most of the dark continent between various European countries, mainly Britain, France, and Germany. Italy's belated quest for a place in the sun had only brought a few scraps of land before it suffered humiliating defeat in 1896 at the hands of the Ethiopians, a trauma which did much to inspire the vision of completing the Risorgimento by truly uniting the Italians and giving them a sense of martial purpose. It was almost inevitable that the fascist regime would seek to avenge the Italian humiliation at Adowa in 1896. Ethiopia lay in the Horn of Africa, between the existing Italian colonies in Eritrea and Somaliland. During the 1920s

Italy had pursued a policy of peaceful economic penetration, but by the early 1930s thoughts were turning more to military intervention. One factor in this change was a desire to divert attention from the mounting economic problems at home. The appointment of Hitler as chancellor of Germany in January 1933 seems, however, to have been the more immediate spur. Mussolini was anxious to complete the conquest before the Nazis became confident enough to pursue union with Austria, a policy he strongly opposed at this time. French and Britain desires to court Italy offered the further prospect of sympathy for Italian aspirations. Indeed, by early 1935 Mussolini believed that both the British and French had effectively given Italy permission to proceed, an important consideration since he was still pursuing the traditional Italian policy of seeking British friendship.

On October 3, 1935, the people of Italy were summoned into the squares and streets by bells and sirens to hear Mussolini proclaim over radio loudspeakers that war against Ethiopia had begun. Mussolini appointed De Bono to head the attack, a man who had done much to convince him that the campaign was militarily feasible. But the aging Quadrumvir quickly proved cautious and indecisive, though initial military problems were not entirely his fault. De Bono was hampered by the fact that much of his "army" came from the fascist militia, which was poorly equipped and trained. Mussolini responded by promoting the career-general Pietro Badoglio to the command and dramatically increasing the levels of military commitment. Against largely ill-armed tribesmen, Badoglio marshaled 254 planes, 30,000 trucks, and 4.2 million artillery rounds—a massive force by the standards of colonial war. Following his tactics during the Libyan war, he fought with the utmost harshness, including the deployment of poison gas. Under such a barrage, the Ethiopians wilted, and in May 1936 Mussolini announced that the new Italy had at last founded its empire. In reality brave resistance continued, which was met by an Italian policy of brutal repression.[5]

There seems little doubt that the victory was greeted with great rejoicing across Italy. This was a marked change from attitudes in 1934, when the prospect of war aroused little enthusiasm. In part, the joy stemmed from relief over the fact that Italian casualties were remarkably light—fewer than three thousand dead. The number of injured was relatively slight too—and included Roberto Farinacci, who managed to blow off a hand while fishing with grenades, an unfortunate fact which was suppressed in order to arrange a hero's homecoming.

Another factor that helped to produce this sea change in public support was the imposition of economic sanctions by the League of Nations. Although this hardly affected the war effort because key countries like the United States and Germany were not members of the league, and oil was excluded, the sanctions seemed hypocritical—especially because they were imposed by countries like Britain and France, which ruled over large colonial empires. International opposition could be construed as a part of a continued tendency to treat Italians as less than equals. The "proletarian nation," therefore, needed to rise up and assert itself. These sentiments were reinforced by the considerable support that existed for the war among the old political class, and even part of the church. The sense of legitimacy was further underpinned by an increasingly shrewd government propaganda campaign, which emphasized the alleged economic advantages of conquest.[6]

In diplomatic terms, the major effect of the war was to push Italy away from France and Britain. This rift was deepened by Italian intervention in the Spanish Civil War, which broke out in July 1936.[7] For some time Mussolini had been dabbling in Spanish politics and had sent financial support to the fascist Falange Party. But a request from rebel right-wing generals to supply military aid was refused initially. Badoglio argued strongly that money was needed to reequip Italy's own armed forces, while opposition also came from Balbo on the grounds that money was required for development in Africa.

It is not clear why Mussolini changed his mind. Possibly General Franco persuaded him that the war would be short and that Italy would be well rewarded with bases in the Balearics, or that a nationalist victory would push the British out of the strategically important Gibraltar. Perhaps Franco implied that he would set up a radical fascist regime—though in reality he was more an authoritarian conservative.[8] Certainly Mussolini was hostile to the Popular Front government elected earlier in 1936, as it was dominated by the left. He seems to have feared that the Popular Front government in Spain would increase the influence of France, which had just elected a Popular Front government too. He may also have been suspicious of Germany's willingness to supply military aid, fearing the expansion of German influence into this area, and into the Mediterranean sphere in general.

Italian intervention started inauspiciously when only nine of the twelve transport planes sent from Sardinia arrived. Bad turned to worse when the Italian expeditionary force suffered a major defeat near Guadalajara in March 1937. Such an outcome might have been predicted: one fascist general described his men as mainly scum who had been drafted from among the unemployed as a form of outdoor relief. But it was not in Mussolini's nature to back down after such a humiliation, and an escalation of Italian support followed. By the time the war ended in March 1939, seventy-two thousand men and five thousand officers had fought in Spain. Possibly as much as a third of Italy's total military material was left behind when the forces returned home. Although most of these arms were obsolete and important lessons had been learned, the cost of the war—especially following so soon after the Ethiopian campaign—made a rapid rearmament policy economically unfeasible.

Even more important was the diplomatic impact of the civil war on Italy. In spite of some tensions at the outset, the war pushed it ever closer to Germany. In its immediate aftermath, shrewd Italian diplomacy might have led to a rapprochement with World War I Western European allies, both of whom were keen to avoid fighting two fascist powers. But in Britain especially, public opinion was turning against concessions to the dictators. And although Mussolini's foreign policy exhibited strong traditional continuities, both his policies and style represented a break with the past. His way of working stressed the personal and sudden impulse over careful planning and subtle diplomacy. Behind such traits was an ideology that led him to an increasing recognition of fascist fraternalism—and a common destiny in war.

ii

DURING THE 1920s, Mussolini had kept in touch with extreme nationalist groups in Germany, including the Nazis, and had occasionally sent them financial support. After the Nazi breakthrough in the 1930 elections, he began to take more interest in events across the Alps. At the same time, Hitler began to solicit advice from the Duce. Within a few hours of being appointed chancellor in January 1933, Hitler sent a personal message to Mussolini, paying homage to his leadership and expressing the hope that there could be close relations between the two countries. Mussolini responded by reciprocating the good wishes. Various pieces of advice followed on how to consolidate power.

Behind these pleasantries lay a complex web of attitudes, especially on the Italian side. In 1933 Mussolini had perceptively concluded, "I should be pleased, I suppose that Hitler has carried out a revolution on our lines. But they are Germans. So they will end by ruining our idea." Many Italian fascists were especially opposed to the biological racism at the heart of Nazism. They feared the impact of a Nazi government on Austrian independence, and on the German-speaking population Italy had acquired after World War I in the Alto Adige and Trentino. Hitler was an Austrian, who was known to support the union (Anschluss) of the two Germanic states. Although he talked in *Mein Kampf* of achieving an alliance with fascist Italy by compensating it elsewhere for accepting the Anschluss, Mussolini was extremely wary of Nazi foreign policy aspirations.

The two dictators met for the first time near Venice in June 1934. Mussolini arrived in his finest uniform, whereas Hitler was rather underdressed in raincoat and suit. Mussolini prided himself on his German, though in truth he was less than fluent, a problem that was compounded by Hitler's Austrian accent and tendency to speak excitedly. Mussolini, therefore, missed much of what was said. Both dictators seem to have been rather unimpressed with each other: Hitler found Italian fascism a comic burlesque and its leader remarkably unassertive. Mussolini, on the other hand, was irritated by Hitler's rambling monologues, seeing himself as clearly more intelligent.

There is no doubt that by 1935 relations between the two countries were strained. On July 25, 1934, Austrian Nazis assassinated Engelbert Dollfuss, the country's right-wing dictator. They occupied government buildings and the radio station, expecting units from Germany to reinforce them. Instead, it was Italian troops who massed on the border. Germany responded by doing nothing and the uprising was suppressed. The failed coup was followed by increased diplomatic activity between Britain, France, and Italy, all of whom sought in differing ways to contain German expansionism. Common concern culminated in the creation of the Stresa Front in April 1935, when the three powers agreed to oppose any unilateral repudiation of treaties that might endanger the peace of Europe.

Italy took this treaty to exclude military action in Africa, for it had already given clear signals of its ambitions in Ethiopia. Franco-British opposition to the subsequent invasion, therefore, marked an important turning point in European diplomacy, which was underlined when Germany reoccupied the Rhineland in 1936, which had been demilitarized by the Versailles Treaty. Mussolini responded by ordering the Italian press to take a more pro-German line. He followed this by advising the Austrian government to negotiate with Germany. This first phase in the growing understanding between Germany and Italy culminated on November 1, 1936, when Mussolini referred for the first time to the existence of a Rome-Berlin "Axis."

The term was symbolic rather than substantive, for no formal political or military alliance had been agreed by the two powers, but they clearly had a growing understanding about spheres of influence. More significantly, there was a mounting affinity between the two dictators; Mussolini especially was falling under the spell of Hitler's charisma and confidence. A crucial event in this process was Mussolini's visit to Germany in September 1937. Hitler pulled out all the stops to create an impression of goodwill—and of German strength. The Duce was duly taken in, though this reveals as much about his powers of self-delusion as about German organization. He even managed to give a speech in German to a vast crowd, which he considered a triumph though his audience appears to have been left confused. Naturally his hosts did not disabuse him of his belief that he was a born linguist.

Two months later Italy adhered to the Anti-Comintern Pact. The agreement had been signed in November 1936 by Germany and Japan, overtly to combat the activities of the Communist International, which sought to promote communism throughout the world. Italy did not adhere initially because of fears that the agreement was part of a drive toward war with Britain and France. Although relations with these two powers had deteriorated in 1935–6, it was far from clear that bridges could not be repaired. Italy's adherence to the pact in late 1937, therefore, was further evidence of the new power bloc that was emerging in Europe. It was also evidence of its ambitions around the Mediterranean periphery, as it was hoped that Japanese pressure would force the British to weaken their military presence in Egypt and the Middle East.

Mussolini's growing commitment to the German camp was further confirmed when in March 1938 Germany took over Austria. Hitler had promised not to act without consulting Italy, but in the event only a few hours' notice was given of the impending Anschluss. Italy did nothing, and Mussolini tried to hide from the Italian people the fact that a remarkable reversal had taken place in foreign policy. Many Italians remained unconvinced, and there was growing criticism of the drift toward Germany. Mussolini, however, had never been a populist in the sense that he responded to opinion or really believed in the wisdom of the masses. He had always sought to shape attitudes, to mold a new Italy, though this did not mean that he was unaware of the need to present developments in a favorable light. Thus the adoption of the goose step by the military was not portrayed as part of growing admiration for Nazism; instead it was accompanied by a campaign to call it the *passo romano,* and eulogies to the goose as the bird that had saved ancient Rome from the Gauls by sounding a warning of impending attack.

Mussolini's presentational skills were revealed to the full during and immediately after the Munich conference, which took place at the end of September 1938. Increasingly during September, war had seemed likely between Germany and Czechoslovakia over German demands for the Sudetenland, which contained many German speakers. The British prime minister, Neville Chamberlain, proposed a conference, using Mussolini as an intermediary. At the ensuing meeting in Munich, Mussolini took center stage, not least because he had a working knowledge of French, German, and English. (He may not have been a brilliant linguist, but he easily outshone most national leaders in this sphere.) Subsequently he was to portray himself as the great mediator, the man who had managed to reconcile apparent opposites. In truth, the final agreement had been largely worked out in advance with the Germans. While Hitler did not get his war, he gained almost all he wanted in the short run peacefully: namely the Sudetenland and the breaching of Czechoslovakia's powerful western defenses as a prelude to driving eastward.

The result of the conference confirmed Mussolini's belief in the decline of the democracies. He saw Britain as a country led by a weak man who was fond of carrying an umbrella, an image which must have fit in with the Duce's stereotypical Englishman—he even believed that the English put on evening dress to take five o'clock tea. He saw French society as divided and undynamic, and its politicians as timid and largely led by the British in the field of foreign affairs. Even his attitude to the United States was beginning to change, though this was not directly related to the Munich conference. While, in the past he had admired America's youth and dynamism, he was now beginning to put more emphasis on its racial mongrelization and excessive materialism. He believed that these traits would weaken its fighting resolve—though on occasion fears of American power were to reemerge in his thinking.[9]

In March 1939 the Germans marched into what remained of the Czech state. The prospect of a major war came a step closer, as the British and French responded by issuing a guarantee to Poland, which was likely to be Hitler's next target. The situation offered Mussolini a chance to build on his image as the great conciliator, and to put out feelers to the British and French. Instead, he ordered the invasion of Albania. The action was a response to growing fears of German ambitions in the Balkans, a region in which Italy had sought hegemony since the late nineteenth century. The invasion of Albania was a warning to Germany rather than a coordinated move. But coming as it did after the occupation of Czechoslovakia, the attack could only serve to confirm British and French fears about the rising tide of fascist expansionism.

In early May 1939 the German foreign minister, Joachim von Ribbentrop, arrived in Milan for further negotiations. Mussolini wanted to avoid any serious military commitment to Germany, but was eager to orchestrate an enthusiastic popular reception for

Ribbentrop to demonstrate that there was strong pro-German feeling in Italy. Unfortunately, the natives proved uncooperative, a discourtesy which received exaggerated treatment in the French press. On the spur of the moment, Mussolini seems to have responded by agreeing to a treaty. Even more remarkably, the Germans were allowed to draft what became known as the Pact of Steel, which in effect committed each party to fight even if the other launched an aggressive war. Mussolini believed that it was understood there could be no question of Italy fighting before 1943. Hitler had very different ideas.[10]

iii

THE PACT OF STEEL was signed for Italy by Galeazzo Ciano, who had been foreign minister since June 1936. He was the son of Costanzo Ciano, a wealthy war hero who became an early fascist and who in 1926 was designated Mussolini's successor as prime minister—although in reality he had little influence within the PNF. This background, combined with his good looks and charm, marked Galeazzo for success from an early age. His prospects took a further turn for the better when he married Mussolini's favorite daughter, Edda, in 1930. By 1933 he was chief of Mussolini's press office and by 1935 minister for press and propaganda. After serving as a bomber pilot in the Ethiopian war, he became head of foreign affairs at the remarkably young age of thirty-three.

Ciano had trained as a diplomat, but his appointment was clearly based on Mussolini's desire to dominate government, rather than on the belief that he was the best man for the job. Indeed, except in terms of social class, he was the very antithesis of the traditional diplomat. Ciano had little time for the routine of diplomacy. He was notoriously indiscreet: one of his girlfriends regularly passed information to the British ambassador. He was also egocentric and traveled with a court of sycophants. Predictably, his expensive tastes led him into the web of corruption that came to characterize many leading figures in the regime. Among his many perks was a luxurious hunting lodge built after the conquest of Albania.

A common joke of the day asked: "Is there anything Ciano can do well?" To which came the answer: "Yes, he is an excellent cuckold—though even here he needs his wife's help." Ciano, however, had his strengths. In particular, whereas the Duce lived a life largely cut off from others, Ciano had some contacts with the real world. Reality may have been a set made up largely of the powerful and wealthy. Even so, Ciano was more in tune than Mussolini with the growing opposition to the drift of Italian foreign policy. By August 1939 he was extremely suspicious of German plans and convinced that Italy should not join in any European conflagrations.[11]

Growing opposition and lack of detailed military preparation meant that the German invasion of Poland on September 1 was not accompanied by an Italian call to arms. Instead, Italy became, in a felicitous term, a "nonbelligerent" in the war between Germany and the Franco-British alliance. (Poland quickly collapsed in the face of the German onslaught.) After a period of embarrassed silence, Mussolini explained to the Führer that Italy was not yet able to enter war because she needed raw materials and other supplies. Germany was therefore presented with a long shopping list. At the same time, Mussolini advocated that Germany should attack the USSR rather than strike against France and Britain, on the grounds that communism was the great enemy. He added that there was the danger of American intervention should Western Europe be threatened.

Hitler was not to be deflected, and on March 10, 1940, Ribbentrop arrived in Rome to inform the Italians that Germany was ready to attack in the west. Eight days later Mussolini met Hitler at the Brenner Pass. Once again the Führer dominated the conversation with a mixture of excessive confidence about the attack to come and expressions of fascist fraternalism. Mussolini responded by agreeing that Italy would enter the war as soon as practicable. In spite of his doubts about war in the west, there was now little question of his remaining aloof. For Mussolini, war was the highest form of activity, the ultimate test of a man's and a nation's strength and will. Not to fight would also mean conceding that Germany was the major fascist power—an impossibility for the Duce, who deluded himself that he was the senior partner in the Axis.[12]

The king was less sure.[13] He still had great faith in Mussolini's ability to steer the right course, but he was suspicious of the Germans. As it became increasingly likely that Mussolini would take

Italy into war on the Nazi side, the king made an effort to have the Fascist Grand Council convened. He was almost certainly aware that leading fascists, including Balbo, Ciano, and Grandi, were either opposed to the war or had strong doubts about it. Although the council could meet only if Mussolini summoned it, the king had a lever he could have used. His approval was necessary for a formal declaration of war, and he could have asked for the advice of the Grand Council as a condition. Whether he would have pursued this course had Germany not won a series of spectacular victories during May-June 1940 will never be known. Probably not, for at this point Mussolini's spell was still unbroken.

Italy declared war on June 10, 1940, just over a week after the British evacuation from Dunkirk and four days before Paris fell. By this time there was a growing chorus of opinion in favor of war. Ciano had been converted to the cause, as had many leading industrialists. Italy, however, received few spoils after the armistice with France, which was signed on June 22. Hitler was anxious to follow a magnanimous policy to minimize the risk of further French resistance—and perhaps to send a signal to the British. Even Mussolini was loath to press Italian demands too strongly, mainly out of embarrassment over Italy's nonexistent part in France's defeat. He was eager to make up for lost time and play his part in the defeat of Britain, which now seemed ripe for the picking. He insisted on sending three hundred planes to Belgium to help in the Battle of Britain. Although accompanied by a battalion of journalists who were supposed to report the pilots' glorious deeds, the force was relegated to the Italians, a view which if anything worsened during the war, though on occasion Italian troops fought with great bravery.

On paper the Italian forces were relatively large. In reality there were not even enough uniforms to go around, let alone modern weaponry. Although some strategists in the early 1930s had begun to develop the idea of a lightning war, there had been little development of tanks and armored vehicles. There had also been no serious attempt to develop aircraft carriers. Part of the problem was lack of money, for military aspirations ran well ahead of national means. But relations between the military and the fascists added to the problems. Although there was some resentment toward fascism within the officer caste, in general it had come to a modus vivendi with the regime. Fascism made no sustained effort to produce a politicized military, though Mussolini consistently interfered to balance groups within the military. In return, there was no serious attempt to confront Mussolini with home truths about equipment and strategy. As a result, Mussolini was more used to toadying than criticism.

Thwarted in playing a major role in the Battle of Britain, and largely unaware of Italian weakness, Mussolini turned to the Balkans. After Italy's invasion of Albania in 1939, he had ordered Badoglio to prepare plans for attacks on both Yugoslavia and Greece. This prompted a riposte from Hitler, who told the Italians that the conquest of Britain was the highest Axis priority. A German move into Romania in October, however, angered Mussolini, who feared that Germany would soon dominate the Balkans.[14] He ordered an attack on Greece, which eventually began on the eighteenth anniversary of the March on Rome. The Italians believed that victory would be easy, partly deluded by a secret service which was more used to spying on dissidents and Mussolini's fascist rivals than to collecting military and diplomatic information. From the outset the Italian attack was plagued by political and military incompetence. It then became literally bogged down after torrential rains. When these stopped, the Greeks began to advance and had soon occupied part of Albania. These events led to the replacement of Badoglio in December, an ironical development, as he had seen the attack as strategically misguided. Eventually the Italians were rescued only by the German invasion of Yugoslavia and Greece in April 1941.

Had the Italians defeated Greece quickly, the war there would probably not have been a strategic disaster. Yet as the fighting progressed it sucked in more and more troops and logistical support. The Germans took it as another sign of Italian military incompetence. It had the additional consequence of encouraging Mussolini to commit Italian troops to the invasion of Russia after Operation Barbarossa commenced in June 1941. He would have been prudent to keep out of this war, but he eventually committed 227,000 high-quality Italian troops to the bitter and bloody Russian campaign.

Italian aspirations in the Balkans were part of traditional foreign policy goals, but the Russian campaign was clearly part of a pan-fascist crusade. Italy would have been better advised, once in the war, to concentrate on another of its traditional foreign policy concerns, namely North Africa. Massing troops there might have closed the Suez Canal, opening vistas of Middle Eastern oil. Instead by the spring of 1941 Italy had been chased across the Libyan desert and out of East Africa. Once again, rescue came from the Germans: on this occasion, in the shape of General Erwin Rommel and his Afrika Korps. For a brief time it even seemed that the Axis would capture Egypt and other parts of Africa. But the battle of El Alamein turned the tide and by May 1943 the Allies had secured the continent.

As the war degenerated into further disasters, public opinion began to turn dramatically against Mussolini. Fascist propaganda in the late 1930s had sought to teach Italians that it was "better to live one day as a lion than a hundred years as a sheep." Lord Perth, the British ambassador in Rome, caught the public mood more shrewdly when he noted that the people were becoming tired of perpetual roaring and would prefer to graze in peace. From the outset there was little enthusiasm for the war. And Germany's crushing victories in 1939–40 raised as many fears as hopes. Defeats disillusioned the troops, many of whom were peasants who had never been fully integrated into a regime that found it difficult to penetrate the archaic ways of the countryside. Appalling incompetence and shortages had their effect. For instance, Davide Lajolo was a sincere fascist, a volunteer for the war in Spain, but he began to question the regime during service in Greece. While his battalion was being massacred, all he saw arrive from Rome were cardboard shoes and boxes of medals.[15]

Such shortages contrasted with what was perceived as the corruption and affluence of leading fascists at home. In the past Mussolini had largely remained immune to such comment—one of the reasons why his personal popularity was considerably greater than that of the party or the regime. By 1941, however, his name was being linked with Clara Petacci, a young mistress with whom he had pursued a relationship since 1932. Many Italians were not particularly puritanical about such matters, but Mussolini had accorded various members of Petacci's family virtual police immunity from prosecution for a variety of unsavory deals and activities. He was becoming personally associated with the general corruption that plagued the fascist system.

After December 1941, further criticism resulted from Mussolini's appointment of Aldo Vidussoni, an inexperienced twenty-seven-year-old who had lost a hand and eye in Spain, as party secretary. Mussolini seems to have decided to rejuvenate the PNF, and found in Vidussoni a suitable ally. The young war veteran shared several views that were reemerging as important themes in the Duce's thought: in particular the effeteness of the bourgeoisie, the deleterious influence of the Catholic church, and the failings of southern Italians. Mussolini seems to have realized belatedly that, for all the talk of having created a totalitarian state, the regime was in many ways a facade and fascist man an illusion.[16] Whether the inexperienced Vidussoni was the best man to launch the new revolution was another matter.

As Mussolini strove to rejuvenate both fascism and the Italian war effort, his health began to fail.[17] During late 1942 he was very ill. By January 1943 he could hardly get out of bed, where he lay under sedation, taking only liquid food. In a despairing move, during the following month he announced sweeping changes among the leading fascists. Ciano, Grandi, and Bottai headed the list of those dropped from the government. Two months later Vidussoni was replaced as party secretary by Carlo Scorza, an old-guard *squadrista,* who as party vice secretary had shown some ability in dealing with the growing number of strikes that were breaking out in northern Italy.[18]

The deteriorating war situation was brought home when during the night of July 9–10, 1943, the Allies invaded Sicily, quickly establishing a bridgehead from which they could invade the rest of Italy. Ten days later the Allies bombed Rome for the first time, an event that aroused public demonstrations of hostility toward the regime. On the same day Mussolini met Hitler. He had promised some leading fascists that he would try to persuade Hitler to allow Italy to withdraw from the war, but his nerve collapsed when he faced the Führer. The issue was not even broached. Back in Italy, Mussolini learned that there were at least two plots to depose him—one organized by fascists, the other by the royal household and the military. Surprisingly, he responded by agreeing to a proposal from Dino Grandi to summon the Fascist Grand Council, which had not met since 1939. (The cabinet had not met since 1937, another revealing insight into the nature of fascist decision making.)

Grandi was the son of a small landowner. He had become active in the early radical nationalist movement and went on to fight with great bravery during World War I. Immediately after the war he returned to his university studies, graduating in law, but by 1921 he had become the *ras* of Bologna. His first clash with the Duce followed later that year over the pact of pacification, when Mussolini had tried to come to an understanding with the moderate socialists. Grandi, however, was not a representative of the most violent, Farinacci-type *squadrista*. Nor was he a tool of reactionary, agrarian money. He was worried that the pact would lead to suppression of the growing fascist union movement, which he believed would be important in the creation of a new "national democracy." There was subsequently some talk of Grandi challenging Mussolini's leadership, but he seems to have accepted that only Mussolini could hold the disparate fascist movement together.

After the March on Rome, during which he was a Quadrumvir, the high point of his ministerial career came between 1929–32, when he was foreign minister. Grandi sought to create a vast African empire, but without involvement in a European war. He believed that this could be done if Italy acted as a balancing force between the European powers, thereby gaining concessions. (This policy seemed to offer notable opportunities, as the French especially were eager to woo Italy.) He even believed that some concessions were possible through the League of Nations. Although Mussolini largely approved of these policies, in 1932 Grandi was moved to Britain as ambassador, part of the regular game of ministerial musical chairs played by Mussolini. (Another reason for the move was opposition from fascists who sought a more radical foreign policy.) In London Grandi moved in high circles and became ever more convinced of the need for conciliation. He played a particularly important part in setting up the Munich conference. Grandi was not opposed to courting Germany if this improved the Italian negotiating position, but he believed that in the event of a European war Italy's place was beside Britain and France. Given the drift of Mussolini's policy, this led to his recall in July 1939, though he continued to try to keep Italy out of the German camp until Germany's sudden victories in the spring of 1940 made an Italian declaration of war inevitable. From July 1939 until February 1943 Grandi was the minister of justice and speaker of the Chamber of *Fasci*—which had replaced the emasculated Chamber of Deputies in 1939. He also fought for a time in Greece, when Mussolini decided that fascist leaders and ministers should experience the taste of battle. (The fact that ministers could be sent to the front says much about both fascist ideology and Mussolini's style of government.) Grandi quickly reverted to an antiwar position, but only with the deteriorating situation in the early summer of 1943 was he in a position to act.

The Grand Council met during the night of July 24–5. In deference to Mussolini, Grandi's attack was oblique. He argued that a serious mistake had been made during Starace's secretaryship of the PNF, when Italy had been turned into a propagandist theater, and that more dissent was necessary to show up faults and to reveal people's true feelings. He moved that some of the powers focused in Mussolini's hands should now be spread more collectively, and that the king should resume effective command of the armed forces and "the supreme initiative in decision-making." Mussolini could have called for a vote of confidence in himself, which he would probably have won, as there were still strong bonds of loyalty to him. Instead, he took a vote on Grandi's motion, which was carried by nineteen votes to seven.

Some critics had come with hand grenades in their pockets, expecting trouble, or at least arrest. They found Mussolini remarkably relaxed. This raises the possibilities that he was looking for a way to break the German alliance with honor, or that he was seeking to create a new and more radical form of fascist regime, in which relatively greater dissent would have been allowed. He certainly told the Japanese ambassador later that day that he wanted to reform the PNF. Or perhaps growing tiredness meant that he was simply looking for someone else to take the decisions.[19]

At this point the king at last found some backbone, realizing that the Duce had become a millstone to the monarchy. His main problem was whom to choose as prime minister. It could not be another fascist. Mussolini had consistently prevented anyone from emerging as a clear successor. Besides, the party was even more disliked than the Duce. The military offered both a symbol of order and the potential to put down fascist opposition, but the king did not like Marshal Caviglia, the most prominent officer who was not compromised by obsequious support for the regime. The main alternative was Badoglio, whom the king did not like either. During July, however, he had come to believe that the appointment of Badoglio as head of government in place of Mussolini would maximize military support for a palace coup.

The Grand Council decision gave him the excuse to act. Later on the day of the fateful vote, he summoned Mussolini, announced that the war was lost and that military morale was collapsing. He informed the dumbfounded Duce that Badoglio was taking over as prime minister immediately. As Mussolini left the palace, he was arrested and taken to a secret hiding place. By the evening, news of his downfall had spread. It must have surprised few apart from fascist hard-liners that this was greeted with widespread demonstrations of approval. More remarkable was the absence of overt opposition from the supposedly vast fascist party. Even his own newspaper quickly replaced the usual picture of the Duce with one of Badoglio.[20]

iv

MUSSOLINI'S DECISION not to oppose the Anschluss had prompted Hitler to promise that he would never forget this act of friendship. In late July 1943 he set in motion a plan that would repay his debt in full—though it would ultimately lead to Mussolini's death. Hitler sent personal orders from his Wolf's Lair headquarters that Otto Skorzeny and an elite SS commando group were to rescue the Duce. Eventually Mussolini was traced to a winter-sports hotel, high in the Abruzzi mountains. Skorzeny and his small band of commandos landed from gliders in a minuscule rock-strewn field next to the hotel. Surprise was total and no shots were exchanged with the garrison guarding Mussolini. (It seems there was some confusion over orders as to whether Mussolini was to be shot in the event of an attack.) Minutes later the Duce, Skorzeny, and an intrepid pilot took off from beside the hotel in a Fieseler-Storch two-man plane. The overloaded frail craft lost a wheel on takeoff before plummeting into the valley, and only pulled out of the dive yards from the ground. It was September 12 and the Duce was free—of his Italian captors, at least.[21]

Mussolini was taken via Rome and Vienna to Germany, where he personally thanked the Führer for his loyalty. Here he met up with other Italian fascist leaders who had refused to recognize Badoglio's regime. It was quickly decided to establish a new fascist regime in northern Italy, though whether Mussolini was the main driving force behind this plan remains unclear. He seems to have perceived that fascism had lost its way and to have sought a new direction even before his fall. And, partly as a result of the attentions of Hitler's own physician, Mussolini's health quickly improved—which led to a return of his old fighting spirit. But he was also being pushed into making a politial comeback, not least by the Germans. The new Italian government had quickly changed sides in the war. The establishment of a new government under Mussolini, therefore, seemed to offer the prospect of rallying Italian support for the German armies in Italy.[22]

The new government became known as the Italian Social Republic, though it is often referred to as the Salò Republic after the town on Lake Garda which was host to one of its ministries—appropriately the propaganda ministry. Its leading members included three people who had been present at the historic Grand Council vote on July 24–5. Of these the most important was Guido Buffarini-Guidi, who became minister of the interior. He had held the position of undersecretary of the interior from 1933 to 1943, a remarkably long tenure. An effective administrator, he had become increasingly critical of growing party bureaucracy. His appointment, therefore, symbolized an attack on the old party, though not its more corrupt practices, for Buffarini-Guidi was another whose finger was in the pie. The most notable Grand Council absentee from among those who had opposed the Grandi motion was Farinacci. Although he had made something of a comeback in the 1930s, Mussolini remained antagonistic toward him—not least because Farinacci was very much a symbol of the early *squadrista* fascism, which had helped carry the fascist movement away from its radical ideological roots.[23]

A few, like the aging Marinetti, counseled dropping the name "fascist." By 1943 it was too associated with negative features, such as repressive violence, corruption, and ultimate failure. Mussolini, however, declined the advice, and Marinetti reluctantly supported the new regime—mainly out of loyalty to the Duce. Mussolini believed that his task was to return to the founding principles of fascism rather than reject its legacy. The new party he duly created, therefore, became known as the Fascist Republican Party (PFR)— its republicanism a clear statement that there was to be no more truck with the monarchy and its conservative cliques. Its leader was Alessandro Pavolini, who had been appointed minister of popular culture in 1939. He should have served as a warning of radicalism to come, for he was a strange mixture of thought and action, an early *squadrista* who went on to gain a university doctorate in law, a cultured yet intemperate man. Farinacci described him in 1943 as a fanatic who knew nothing of politics. While this damning judgment reveals much about Farinacci's bitterness over continued exclusion from office, it was certainly true that Pavolini held violent views and dreamed about utopian social rebirth.

In November the first Congress of the PFR met in Verona, where a series of radical proposals were adopted. These were expanded in the next few months into a sweeping new vision. The Congress recognized that fascism had committed errors. In particular, power had helped to corrupt, as had lack of criticism. New policy proposals, therefore, included a promise to investigate the illicit fortunes that had been made since 1919. Among the political changes mooted were: a more genuinely elective system for choosing parliament; the creation of an independent judiciary; greater freedom for unions; press freedom; and an end to the system that gave preference at work to party members. Most private property was still guaranteed by the regime, though a program of nationalization was promised. Also, uncultivated land or land not used productively was to be divided among laborers or formed into worker-owned cooperatives. Within companies, it was proposed to establish management councils that included workers; in the private sector this would include profit sharing. Overseeing this economic system would be a government that would engage in extensive planning. In terms of foreign policy, the program envisaged the creation of a European Community, which would develop Africa to the benefit of both whites and blacks. The ultimate proclaimed object of the Italian Social Republic was "the synthesis of all the values," a clear return to fascism's syncretic origins.

There seems little doubt that these proposals reflected Mussolini's latest thinking—though he was aided by an old associate, the former communist, Nicola Bombacci, who during the early 1920s had talked of combining the two revolutionary creeds of communism and fascism. (He was subsequently expelled from the PCI.)[24] After moving to Lake Garda, Mussolini seems to have spent more time reading seriously. Gone was the omnivorous devouring of newspapers to check for the right propaganda line— and his own standing. Plato's *Republic*, philosophy, and works in German came to figure more prominently. The fact that he had so much time for thought shows that he had become largely a figurehead, devoid of ultimate responsibility—especially for the conduct of military strategy.

In a different world, at a different time, he might have retired to develop a detailed program or a more refined ideological position. Certainly he showed in a series of interviews with a socialist journalist Carlo Silvestri that he was thinking about many issues. At times he talked as if he were advocating a paternalist social democracy, or Christian democracy without the Catholicism, both views which involved a break with fascism's social and political radicalism. But these musings seem to have been related to daydreams about how to seek allies and revive fascism in the short run. More fundamentally, he was a *sansepolcrista* at heart, a violent radical who believed that fascism had made a mistake in not taking on the power of business.

Most of those who had led the opposition at the July 24–5 Grand Council meeting wisely or fortuitously remained outside the territory controlled by the Salò Republic. But five members of the council found themselves in the wrong place at the wrong time. Those duly imprisoned by the new regime were Ciano, the almost eighty-year-old Quadrumvir De Bono, Giovanni Marinelli, Luciano Gottardi, and Carlo Pareschi. There was strong pressure from the fascist old guard for a show trial. Mussolini concurred, although he was in a weak position to point the finger, for after the Grand

Council vote he had personally written to Badoglio offering "every possible collaboration." After the semblance of a trial, the five were shot on January 11, 1944. Even a dramatic intervention from Mussolini's daughter could not save her husband, who met his death calmly—though the shootings were bungled and took several rounds. The whole episode symbolized the massive difference between Salò's radical promise and its ruthless and chaotic reality.

By this time it was becoming clear that the Salò Republic was a German satellite, ruled over by SS General Karl Wolff and a small clique. Germany had effectively annexed most of northeastern Italy, including all the gains Italy had made at the end of World War I. Within the areas nominally controlled by the new Italian republic, the Germans had no interest in radical social reform. They wanted to maximize production for the war effort, and they used their influence to ensure that factories were run accordingly. For similar reasons, a large number of Italians were used as a labor force in Germany, including soldiers whom the Germans repeatedly refused to return to Italy. The republic was forced into ever more desperate measures to recruit troops. Among the means adopted was making whole families liable for prison and loss of property if their men refused to register for the draft. Such drastic measures rallied some reluctant recruits to the colors, but the belief that Mussolini was an inevitable loser helped send many into the mountains, where they joined the growing numbers of partisans—who by the end of the war constituted a major force fighting the Germans.

The Italian Social Republic was not totally lacking in support. It is true that there were no longer any conservative fellow travelers; industrialists especially were petrified by the socialistic program. And the church at last formally broke with Mussolini. But at the Verona Congress Pavolini reported that 250,000 members had joined the new party. By 1944 the PFR may have had approaching half a million members, who supported it for a variety of reasons. Many joined to safeguard their jobs, especially those in the public sector who had become used to the party card guaranteeing work. Some still believed in the Duce. Yet others sought radical social change, though this was not always in the direction of the Salò Republic's program, for many were attracted to the Nazi brand of fascism, especially its anti-Semitism. Certainly the Salò Republic became a dangerous place for Jews. This aspect seems to have appealed especially to the Italian-resident American poet Ezra Pound, though Pound had always been one of those artists who had found an appealing blend of modernity and tradition in fascism.[25] Last, but by no means least, some joined the new party for the violence—or the possibility of building their own military or financial empires.

The new minister of defense was Marshal Rodolfo Graziani, who turned to the republic largely through jealousy of Badoglio. He wanted to set up an apolitical traditional army, but it quickly proved impossible to raise this type of force in any number. Instead, a series of semi-autonomous military groups emerged over which there was little centralized control. Pavolini set up his own group and operated a policy of fierce retaliation against the partisans, including killing civilians who helped them. Other targets included strike leaders, who were often communist—though the increase in strikes during the closing stages of the war had basic economic as well as political motives. A variety of independent armed groups also emerged. The most important was run by Prince Valerio Borghese, a hero of the naval war against the British, who engaged in brutal campaigns against the Resistance. Others were little more than criminal or sadistic organizations, running their own prisons and torture chambers, and sometimes fighting among themselves.

There was a bestial and violent side to Salò, though this cannot be blamed entirely on the fascists. There is no doubt that the Resistance, which was dominated by the communists, targeted key fascists for assassination. Among those killed was the aging Gentile, who had reluctantly endorsed the republic after a period of growing disillusionment with the pro-German aspects of Mussolini's policies. Some within the Resistance were perfectly willing to court widespread fascist retaliation knowing that this was likely to turn public opinion away from a regime that was clearly losing the war.

As defeat stared him in the face, Mussolini once more became seriously ill. While he had moments of lucidity when he perceived many of fascism's errors, at other times he preferred to blame the Italians for impending defeat. He kept a file on the "immaturity and blameworthiness of the Italian people." He came to believe that too few Italians were descendants of real Romans: there was too much slave blood in the current population. He concluded that if

Michelangelo had been given clay rather than marble to work, he would have been nothing more than a potter. Increasingly weak and fatalistic, he frequently seemed indifferent to the fate of Italians, who died in relatively large numbers in the closing stages of the war fighting each other—and the Germans.

By mid-April 1945 the Allied advance was nearing Bologna. Less than one hundred miles of flat land now separated them from Lake Garda. With the Russians approaching Berlin, and General Wolff negotiating an armistice on the Italian front, the end was clearly near. Mussolini decided to move westward to Milan, the symbolic founding city of fascism. Typically he seems to have had no clear plan in mind. He was probably toying with several alternatives. One possibility was escape over the nearby Swiss border, or perhaps by submarine or plane to Argentina or Spain. But as well as posing practical difficulties, it must have been psychologically difficult for a man whose ideology was deeply imbued with the warrior spirit to cut and run. Perhaps belief in his own powers of persuasion led him to hope that it was possible to make a deal with the important partisan groups based around Milan. Certainly a meeting was arranged on April 25 by the archbishop of Milan. The leaders of the partisans, however, were sworn to execute the Duce summarily if he was caught, and it is impossible to see that there was any basis for an agreement on terms acceptable to Mussolini.

The Duce left Milan for the last time in the early evening of April 25. In 1923 the first European motorway had been built from Milan to Como; it now sped the Duce north. His small party arrived in Como about nine P.M. Mussolini had for some time fantasized about making a last stand in the Valtellina Mountains, which rose steeply to the northeast. Once in Como, it quickly became clear that there were neither the men nor the material for such heroics. He decided instead to join a German unit that was fleeing along the road on the western side of the lake. Again, it is not clear what he planned: Was he now trying to slip into Switzerland? Was he looking for a hiding place before surrendering to the Americans or British? Perhaps he was even trying to flee to Germany, though this seems unlikely, as he became increasingly hostile to his Axis ally during the closing stages of the war.

Nemesis came near the town of Dongo, when a small partisan

group stopped the convoy. They were willing to let it pass north as long as it contained only Germans. In the ensuing search, they found Mussolini and Clara Petacci, huddled inside greatcoats. After a perfunctory trial, the Duce was sentenced to death. A group of communist partisans led by "Colonel Valerio" moved Mussolini and Petacci to the nearby Villa Belmonte in the hamlet of Giulino di Mezzegra, where they were probably shot on the afternoon of April 28. During the early morning of April 29 the corpses of Mussolini, his mistress, and several other fascist leaders who had suffered the same summary fate were strung upside down in Milan's Piazzale Loreto. Crowds quickly gathered to gape and jeer. It was just over twenty-five years after Mussolini had so confidently founded the *fasci di combattimento* only a short distance away, off the Piazza San Sepolcro.

Germany: The Rise
of Nazism

ON MARCH 7, 1918, a locksmith named Anton Drexler set up a discussion group in Munich. Its purpose was to enlighten local workers about Germany's legitimate war aims and to counter socialist peace propaganda, which had grown markedly after the Bolshevik Revolution. The circle made little progress, and in October Drexler joined forces with Karl Harrer, a journalist, to form another group. In the chaotic weeks after German's unconditional surrender in early November, Drexler and Harrer decided that the time had come to form a new political party that could counter the appeal of the left to the masses. The result was the birth on January 5, 1919, of the German Workers' Party, with Harrer as its first chairman.

The infant party would undoubtedly have suffered premature death had it not attracted the attention of the Bavarian military authorities. As part of their campaign to counter left-wing tendencies, they were using reliable members of the forces to check on nationalist groups. One of those involved was a young Austrian corporal. When he first observed a German Workers' Party meeting during September 1919, he was not especially impressed, but he decided to join the new party a few days later. Its youth offered him the possibility of molding its character and destiny—remarkable ambitions for a man of such low rank.

Adolf Hitler's father was an Austrian imperial customs officer. Contrary to the impression that Hitler sometimes gave in later life, the young Adolf led a life of relative ease, adored by his mother, though he lived in fear of his much older father—traits which have led some to seek the key to his later behavior in his early psychological development.[1] Laziness contributed to a weak school record, and while Hitler had some talent for drawing, this was not enough to gain entry into art college. As a result, he drifted into an aimless existence, eking out a lonely living in Vienna by doing odd jobs and selling the occasional drawing.

Hitler began to find his true purpose in the heady days of August 1914 at the outbreak of World War I. The previous year he had moved to Munich, probably to avoid conscription—he saw Austria as a polyglot and weak state. Now, the twenty-five-year-old rushed to enlist in the German armed forces. He served as a regimental runner, a dangerous task which twice led to his decoration with the Iron Cross—though the fact that he ended the war as a corporal rather than a sergeant indicates that he was not viewed by his superiors as leadership material. He was seen as an eccentric loner who did not participate in the great camaraderie that overcame so many others: an object of curiosity rather than respect.

Being so close to the action meant that he was well aware of the horrors of war: as early as 1915 he could write to a Munich friend of "the rivers of blood which here flow day by day." Yet he justified such sacrifices as necessary to defeat Germany's historic external enemies—and to triumph over "inner internationalism."[2] But war did not make Hitler a nationalist; nor did it give him his first revelation of the threat from the left. From a relatively young age, he had believed that he understood the meaning of world history. He even planned to write a monumental history, a book that would develop the ideas of the importance of leadership and racial purity in order to survive. Although it has often been claimed that he read little, he seems to have been influenced before 1914 particularly by Nietzsche and Wagner. He also carried in his wartime backpack some of the works of the nineteenth century philosopher Arthur Schopenhauer, whom he seems to have been able to quote in large chunks.

Hitler had been influenced more directly by Karl Lueger, a brilliant orator who had helped the Christian Social Party to become dominant in Vienna. Among Lueger's themes were nationalism and municipal socialism, while his techniques included a striking turn of phrase (he referred to Budapest as "Judapest"). From Lueger, Hitler learned two main lessons. First, that a well-organized party was necessary to rally support and to provide activists with a sense of belonging. And second, that it was possible to use nationalist and anti-Semitic propaganda to counter the growing appeal of social-ism; though it is not entirely certain whether the highly virulent form of anti-Semitism Hitler exhibited after 1919 had its origins in the prewar era, or whether it emerged from his belief that Jews had led the wave of tumultuous left-wing revolutions that swept over Europe, and Germany, in 1917–19.[3]

From late 1919 Hitler applied these lessons. He became a fre-quent speaker in Munich and quickly mastered the art of holding an audience. He learned to turn his tendency to begin nervously into a form of climactic performance. He adapted his characteristic verbosity into a quasi-religious ceremony, where he seemed pos-sessed by tongues. He could even be funny, having a notable talent for irony and mimicry. He quickly became a consummate actor and began to practice mannerisms in front of a mirror. The meeting hall was his theater, and soon large audiences were flocking to see him preach the gospel of Germany's resurrection.

In April 1920 Hitler gave an early demonstration of his powers of persuasion when he played a leading part in persuading the growing membership of the German Workers' Party to adopt a new name. Henceforth the party would be known formally as the National Socialist German Workers' Party (NSDAP)—though it was to become more commonly known as the Nazi, or Hitler Party. The party was soon to have a new flag too: a swastika (*Hak-enkreuz*) in a white circle surrounded by a red field. The swastika has previously been used by some *völkisch* and occult groups as a symbol of the Aryan race; the new flag cleverly combined this with the old imperial colors and an allusion to the red flag of the left.[4]

A new Twenty-Five Point Program was drawn up by Hitler, Drexler, and an engineer turned anti-Semitic economist named Gottfried Feder, whom Hitler had met in 1919 at an early meeting of the party. It included staple nationalist fare, such as the demand for the abolition of the postwar peace treaties and the creation of a Greater German including all German speakers, in which citizen-ship would be based on blood. The requirement that all large-scale companies be nationalized, or the commitment to abolish unearned income, however, smacked more of the left than the right—of new radicalism rather than the rebirth of old themes.[5] In a speech on October 26, 1920, Hitler sought to explain this synthesis. He argued that the right lacked a social sense, whereas the left failed to see the importance of the national community. Although Hitler's thinking owed far more to the right than Mussolini's, he shared Mussolini's desire for a movement that would appeal across classes and that would break free of the social and regional ghettoization that characterized German parties. He also wanted to set up a movement in which he was totally dominant. This tendency to ride roughshod over colleagues became clear when Harrer was pushed out of the party in 1920. The following year, Drexler and some others sought to curb Hitler's growing influence within the movement, but Drexler was shunted upstairs as honorary president, while Hitler assumed the post of chairman of the NSDAP, with almost unbridled powers.

The young Nazi Party grew from eleven hundred members in June 1920 to fifty-five thousand by the autumn of 1923. Its core was comprised mainly of two groups. First, there was a large group from the *Mittelstand*, people from small business and lower-middle-class occupations. The *Mittelstand* had formed the basis of earlier nineteenth-century *völkisch* groups, often attracted by policies such as the promise to abolish large department stores—a theme picked up in the Nazi Twenty-Five Point Program. The second group was made up of young males who had fought in World War I and who had been deeply affected by the experience. In some cases this encompassed a pathological addiction to violence, but in general their concern was to rebuild the sense of belonging many of them had found in the trenches—to create a community that was not motivated primarily by alienating materialism.

The war did not lead automatically to membership of groups such as the Nazis. The chaotic situation that characterized the birth of the Weimar Republic was also important in this.[6] Germany during 1918 to 1923 was the scene for considerable political violence. Initially, the danger had come mainly from the left. The newly created German Communist Party (KPD) attempted to launch a revolution in Berlin during January 1919, which was brutally suppressed with the aid of the Freikorps—groups made up largely of ex-officers and NCOs which sprang into existence as auxiliary armed forces. Initially these groups had a semi-official existence, as the Social Democrat-led coalition government used them to help patrol the troubled eastern borderlands and to control the radical left. It was a dangerous ploy, as the Freikorps included many who were nihilistically violent, and almost all their members were radical nationalists who were hostile to the new democratic republic and to the left in particular—many made no essential distinction between communists and Social Democrats.[7] In the words of one of their leading members, Ernst von Salomon: "What we wanted we did not know, and what we knew we did not want."

The radical nature of the Freikorps became clear when the government tried to disband them in order to comply with Allied demands to reduce Germany's armed forces in accordance with the Versailles Treaty. In March 1920 the notorious Ehrhardt Brigade responded by marching through Berlin and declaring the government deposed and a new one appointed under the nationalist Dr. Wolfgang Kapp. Although a trade-union general strike and opposition from sections of the Civil Service led to the collapse of the so-called Kapp *putsch,* there were clear signs that important sections of German society were willing to support the violent establishment of an authoritarian nationalist regime. Field Marshal Ludendorff had even greeted the brigade at the Brandenburg Gate, a telling reflection of attitudes toward the new republic among elite sections of the armed forces. Key leaders of the *putsch* received only short prison sentences, while others were protected from arrest. Indeed, it was members of the Ehrhardt group who were later to assassinate Matthias Erzberger, who had signed the Armistice in 1918, and the prominent Jewish businessman and Reich foreign minister Walther Rathenau.

Similar anti-republican sentiments were to help the rise of the Nazis in Munich, where there had been considerable violence during 1918 and 1919. A key figure in this military-political underworld was Captain Ernst Röhm, one of those who had first spotted Hitler's genius for propaganda. Even after Hitler left the army, Röhm continued to take an interest in his career, helping to raise the money during 1920 from military and other sources to buy the first Nazi newspaper, the *Völkischer Beobachter*. During 1921 Röhm's antigovernment activities went even further when he helped to obtain training facilities for the new paramilitary wing of the Nazi Party, the Storm Detachment (SA). In part, Röhm was motivated by essentially military factors. He and his superiors saw paramilitary nationalist groups as a way of building up an embryonic army, thus avoiding the Versailles Treaty's proscription on a large standing army. But Röhm's motives were not purely military. He bore the NSDAP membership card number 623, and he was nothing if not a political and social revolutionary, who saw the overthrow of the Weimar Republic as a necessary prelude to Germany's rebirth.

Most officers at this time did not go as far as Röhm and actually join the Nazi Party, but the passing of time had done little to change the opposition of most of the officer class to the new regime. If anything, by 1923 animosity was growing. On top of the fundamental opposition to democracy, there was a feeling that the republic was deliberately diminishing the memory of those who had fought and died for their country. The failure to build a national monument to the war dead or to issue a commemorative medal aroused particularly strong feelings of resentment.

Growing military antagonism was mirrored by the widespread antipathy of virtually all radical nationalists toward Weimar and its politicians. The immediate cause of antagonism in the autumn of 1923 was the decision by the government to call off passive resistance to French occupation of the Ruhr. The occupation had begun in January as a punishment for German attempts to evade reparations payments to the Allies, which were required under the Versailles Treaty. The German response of passive resistance (backed by financial compensation to companies) was highly costly and had proved a disaster, hastening the onset of hyperinflation. Rising prices had been a problem since the beginning of the war, but now the floodgates burst and the currency lost value at a dizzying rate. Inflation helped to reactivate a radical section of the working class, which suffered considerably as wages lagged behind prices and from the unemployment resulting from general economic dislocation. Middle-class people on fixed incomes, or with cash savings, were hard-hit too—though this was a group which, lacking social organization, was forced to contain its resentment.

By the end of October 1923 Hitler seems to have decided that the time had come to call for a march on Berlin, along the lines of Mussolini's coup the previous year. Although the Nazis were rarely to call themselves fascist, many of their leaders recognized a clear affinity with the Italian fascist movement and looked to Italy for lessons. Hitler, however, realized that the small Nazi Party alone could not accomplish a march on the capital. At this time he seems to have seen himself as the "drummer" for authoritarian nationalism rather than as its great leader. His plan, therefore, was to persuade key right-wing political and military figures in Bavaria to back the uprising. The omens seemed good, for there appeared to be widespread sympathy with the radical nationalists among the forces of law and order. The Munich police chief, when asked whether he was aware of the existence of right-wingers who committed political murders, replied, "Yes, but there are not enough of them."

The night chosen for the beginning of the *putsch* was November 8. A meeting had been arranged at Munich's Bürgerbräukeller, one of the largest beer halls. It was to be addressed by Gustav von Kahr, the Bavarian minister president in 1920–1, who had just returned to office as state commissioner and had sweeping powers. The SA, backed by other nationalist paramilitary groups, duly surrounded the hall. Hitler forced Kahr and representatives of the local military and police into a back room, where he thought he had persuaded them to back a coup against the Berlin government, which would make him interim head of the Reich government, with Ludendorff as commander-in-chief—a move that surprised the politically naive Ludendorff, who had believed that he himself would become dictator.

Hitler, however, departed shortly afterward, and Ludendorff allowed Kahr and other key local notables to leave. Possibly they had a change of heart after leaving the meeting. It is more likely that they never intended to back the coup. Kahr was essentially an authoritarian conservative rather than a budding Nazi, a man who was seeking to exploit tension between the Berlin and Munich administrations in order to restore the Bavarian monarchy. He had sympathized with Hitler when he was the drummer, but now Hitler seemed to have ideas above his station. And while there was some support for the Nazis among junior officers in Bavaria, the head of the Reichswehr, General Hans von Seeckt, sent a telegram from Berlin ordering the military to resist. Seeckt was lukewarm toward the republic (some even viewed him as a potential dictator), but he feared that a Bavarian coup might lead to political problems in other states—from both left and right. He also realized that it would badly divide the armed forces.

As dawn broke on November 9, therefore, military and police units had been deployed who were prepared to fire upon the insurrectionists. Hitler had made no clear plans for this eventuality and was indecisive, until pushed by Ludendorff to march into the center of the city. The aging field marshal cherished the illusion that no troops would fire on units led by him. Hitler, on the other hand, seems to have had little confidence in this act of bravado—though public reaction to the *putsch* indicated that a section of Munich's population could have been rallied with better organization.[8] At the head of the ranked revolutionaries, Hitler and Ludendorff marched into a volley of fire that left sixteen dead—men who were later to be elevated to the highest pantheon in the Nazi mythology of martyrdom. While the brave Ludendorff walked on, Hitler cowered behind one of the fallen, before fleeing with most of the other would-be *putsch*ists.

Shortly afterward Hitler was arrested and put on trial for treason. The proceedings, which lasted from February until April 1924, were front-page national news and offered Hitler the chance to pluck victory from the jaws of defeat. He showed no embarrassment at what some might have considered an ill-judged and badly planned coup, or at his hasty flight. Instead, he turned the tables on the prosecution, putting the republic on trial for its failure to unite the German people. Powerful figures in the judiciary clearly agreed with at least part of this attack. Although convicted of high treason, Hitler was sentenced to only five years in jail. His imprisonment proved to be relatively benign and easy going, for he received a regular flow of visitors, including admirers from Munich's social elite, who brought with them extra comforts like wine. (He still drank a little at this time.) He was, therefore, well stocked for Christmas 1924, which he spent in freedom, having been released after just over seven months in prison.

It was almost certainly during this period that Hitler finally decided that his great role in politics was to be the longed-for leader, or Führer, rather than the drummer. One result of this new conviction was that he started to write down his political thoughts. He was helped by Rudolf Hess, who became effectively his political secretary. Hess was one of the many early Nazis attracted to the party primarily by Hitler's magnetism. He was a useful catch, for he was hardworking and loyal. He also introduced Hitler to geopolitical ideas, as Hess had been to Munich University, where he had been befriended by the noted geopolitical theorist Karl Haushofer, who preached the need for Germany to secure her "natural" frontiers across Central Europe to counter Russian expansion and the power of the Western European colonial nations.

There is little doubt, however, that *Mein Kampf* (*"My Struggle"*), Volume I of which was published in 1925, is essentially Hitler's own work, though it does not accurately reflect all the influences on his thought, especially lessons he seems to have learned from communism (which was both an object of fear and source of inspiration).[9] The book is written in a pretentious and awkward style; its main form of argument is bombastic assertion. But it reveals Hitler's main obsessions, in particular his fear of communism and his belief that the Jews were a separate biological race that was conspiring to destroy healthy Aryan society. In his own words: "Was there any form of filth or profligacy, particularly in cultural life, without at least one Jew involved in it?" *Mein Kampf* provides clear pointers to the development of Hitler's thought at this time. It emphasized the need for a great idea, which Hitler saw as the main motive force of great revolutions; and the importance of propaganda, which now took on a much greater role in Hitler's mind, since he had decided that the Nazis would probably have to come to power by electoral means. Less openly stated in *Mein Kampf* was the belief that electoral politics were clearly going to be expensive; although rank-and-file Nazi members performed remarkable feats in raising money, the party would need major patrons, especially in business. A final conclusion Hitler drew from the Munich *putsch* was that army support could not be taken for granted; more work was required at least to neutralize the army in any future takeover.

ii

HITLER HAD REVEALED remarkable political acumen, but from 1924 to 1929 the change in tactics heralded by *Mein Kampf* produced few tangible results for the Nazis. These years witnessed a period of economic stabilization. Hyperinflation was brought under control by a currency reform introduced in late 1923. Economic confidence was further encouraged during 1924 by the Dawes Plan, which revised reparations payments. This fostered investment in Germany, which stimulated growth, as did the general upturn in other European economies.

Governmental stability, however, improved less markedly. The Weimar Republic's adoption of proportional representation ensured that a large number of parties gained representation in the Reichstag, and militated against interparty coalition building because even the small parties had realistic hopes of gaining some representation. Partly as a result, unstable multiple-party governing coalitions became the norm. Between February 1919 and November 1922, six different cabinets had been formed. After the Grand Coalition of Gustav Stresemann (perhaps the only "strong" figure among the main Weimar politicians), greater continuity in personnel and policies emerged. Even so, there were seven cabinets between August 1923 and 1928, most of which lacked a majority in the Reichstag.

The emergence of minority government stemmed mainly from the decision taken by the SPD, who had formed the core of administrations during the republic's early years, to withdraw from "bourgeois coalitions." SPD influence was further diminished by the retirement in 1925 of President Paul Ebert, one of the founding fathers of the republic. In the ensuing elections, he was replaced by Field Marshal Hindenburg. The new president was a conservative nationalist, who had asked the ex-kaiser for permission to run for office—a reflection of his continued loyalty to the Wilhelmine monarchy.

That Hindenburg stood at all reflected a growing accommodation with the Weimar Republic by at least some of the more ardent nationalists. Nationalist accommodation to the system was also reflected in the declining vote for the more extreme forms of nationalist party. In the May 1924 elections, various radical nationalist groups—including the remnants of the NSDAP—polled nearly two million votes, thus gaining a notable thirty-two seats in the Reichstag. However, they suffered a severe setback when further elections were held in December 1924. Growing electoral marginalization was confirmed by the 1928 elections, when the Nazi Party won just 2.6 percent of the vote and twelve seats. Gloom and despondency ensued in the Nazi camp.

The failure of the Nazis to make further progress during this period was not simply a result of improvements in the general economic and political situation. The party was plagued by a variety of internal problems after its formal refounding during early 1925.[10]

After his release from jail, Hitler found himself banned from speaking in many states throughout most of 1925 and 1926 (and for longer in Prussia, where an SPD–Center Party coalition ruled remarkably successfully throughout the 1920s). He therefore spent much of this period on the Obersalzberg, completing the second volume of *Mein Kampf*. Apart from refounding the party, Hitler did little to resolve a major split that had taken place after the Munich *putsch*. On the one hand, a primarily southern group had emerged, which tended to be slightly older, more concerned with nationalism than social reform, and more obsessed still with fantasies about Jewish conspiracies. A notable example was Julius Streicher, a schoolteacher who founded the rabble-rousing newspaper *Der Stürmer* in 1923. On the other hand, the mainly northern group tended to be more concerned with developing a program—with what it saw as the "socialist" part of National Socialism. The most important member of this group was a thirty-three-year-old named Gregor Strasser. Paradoxically he was a Bavarian and had taken part in the 1923 Munich *putsch*.[11]

The impact of war is often portrayed in terms of brutalization, of a longing for revenge and foreign conquests.[12] Strasser serves as an excellent example of the "front generation," men whose war experience had a very different impact. He had been particularly moved when one of his men had asked the meaning of the word *Fatherland,* as neither he nor his father had owned any property and had often gone jobless and hungry. Such questions led many to take the road to the left, but Strasser believed that left-wing politics were divisive and would fail to provide for either the spiritual or material well-being of the workers. Although he was a pharmacist by profession, Strasser was not a stereotypical member of the *Mittelstand,* concerned with defending the narrow interests of small business. War showed him the importance of duty and social responsibility, and he sought a genuine synthesis of nationalism and socialism as the best way of providing for the needs of the whole people.

These views were shared by a young man with a university doctoral degree, appropriately on the German Romantic movement, named Joseph Goebbels.[13] Goebbels had been rejected for military service because of his club foot, but in spite of this conspicuous deformity he was attracted to the male-activist environment of the Nazi Party, perhaps in psychological compensation. But it seems more likely that this lapsed Catholic had been deeply influenced by Nietzsche and others who preached the need for a new leader, a new faith. Goebbels, like Strasser, was especially interested in the question of how to integrate the working class into the nation, which led him to stress the need for radical economic and social policies to help counter the appeal of the left-wing parties.

Strasser's and Goebbels's "socialism" has often been seen as a myth, a propaganda smokescreen which hides the fact that the misnamed Nazi "left" was anticapitalist and anti-Semitic, rather than socialist in the sense of holding beliefs such as universal human brotherhood.[14] The argument highlights the danger of accepting the word *socialist* at face value, but it is misleading in that the so-called Nazi left contained many who sought a genuine social revolution—which is more than can be said for many twentieth-century "socialists." During late 1925 Strasser and Goebbels supported a communist referendum that would have confiscated the royal family's remaining property in Germany. They also developed a new program for the Nazi Party, which stressed the more left-wing aspects of the 1920 Twenty-Five Point Program, such as nationalization, together with new demands, including the creation of a vaguely defined autarchic and corporatist United States of Europe. Even more remarkably, Strasser and Goebbels showed interest in the self-styled "National-Bolshevist" position, which not only sought domestic links with communists but also a closer understanding with the Soviet Union. This interest was even more pronounced in Gregor's younger brother, Otto, who held a university degree and had a taste for theorizing.[15]

National Bolshevism was a minor and passing phase, but apparently bizarre combinations of political thought were common in Germany after 1918. The growth of Nazism was undoubtedly helped by a climate of relatively similar ideas, especially among a group of "conservative revolutionaries." Oswald Spengler in his best-selling work *The Decline of the West* (1918–22) wrote of the need to reconcile romantic and irrationalist ideas with a commitment to technology. (The original title was to have been *Conservative and Liberal*.) In *Prussian Virtues and Socialism* (1919) he wrote of liberating German socialism from Marx, of understanding that the Prussian sense of service to the state for the common good was a more honorable ideal than Marxist materialism. Similar themes were found in the prolific writings of Ernst Jünger—though initially this much-decorated soldier was associated more with a celebration of the community of the trenches and ideas such as the need for total mobilization, which had connotations similar to the term *totalitarianism* as used by Italian fascists. Arthur Moeller van den Bruck's seminal book *The Third Reich* (1923) was initially and more accurately entitled *The Third Way*: Moeller sought a Nietzschean hero to break free from the conventional forms of political thinking and organization, a synthesis of Western individualism and Eastern collectivism.[16]

Such works, however, were of no great concern to Hitler, especially when they were tainted with a left-wing tinge, which threatened his strategy of courting business and the military (though in 1922 he had shocked a private meeting of notables in Munich when he had proposed a tactical alliance with the extreme left). During 1925 he had watched the rise of Gregor Strasser with increasing concern. Strasser was not a charismatic figure: large and balding, with a thick Bavarian accent, he cut neither a physical nor a verbal dash, but he was a hardworking and capable organizer, who had come to the Nazis via the Freikorps and the SA, rather than as a result of being captivated by Hitler's magnetism. Hitler realized that "Gregor the Great," as he was known to close colleagues, was his most dangerous rival for the leadership.

In early 1926 Hitler decided to strike back by calling a meeting of the party at Bamberg, which was in Streicher's territory and where he could be sure of putting on a show of strength. Hitler arrived in an impressive cavalcade of cars, and during a speech which lasted four and a half hours he argued that the Nazis were not a debating club. The overriding task was to secure power. Hitler had never taken the details of the party's Twenty-Five Point Program very seriously, but he now argued that the document was sacrosanct—a clear challenge to the radicals who sought a new document. In reply, Strasser made a few weak points, but the force of the Führer's confidence and magnetism seems to have overwhelmed him, though it is possible that he was saving his fire for another day. Certainly Goebbels remained unimpressed by Hitler's line, which he commonly referred to as "bourgeois."

Aware that much remained to be done to consolidate his leadership, Hitler followed up the Bamberg meeting with a series of shrewd decisions. He appointed Strasser Reich propaganda leader, and later, chief of party organization. Strasser took to the task with enthusiasm, consolidating existing developments but setting up new structures where required. The period immediately after 1926 witnessed notable developments in both Nazi propaganda techniques and in its organizational structure. It marked the beginning of the major party rallies—men gathered in a sea of brown shirts, immersing themselves in emotional ritual and ceremony. It marked a growing attempt to legitimize policies by presenting them as central to German identity and traditions: anti-Semitism, for instance, was presented in Protestant areas as central to Luther's thought. Less ostentatiously, the party began to set up special organizations for doctors, teachers, lawyers, students, women, and others who found it more comfortable to participate among their peers than among the Nazi rank and file—a tactic copied from the left. Such changes were accompanied by a notable effort to absorb members from the many *völkisch* and extremist groups, who were attracted by the dynamism of the Nazis.[17]

After the Bamberg conference, Hitler also summoned Goebbels to Munich, offering him the position of regional head of the Nazi Party (*Gauleiter*) in Berlin. This was a major challenge, as the party there was ill organized and faced notable opposition from the left. The ambitious twenty-eight-year-old was becoming fascinated by Hitler's mixture of charisma and confidence. "Adolf Hitler, I love you because you are both great and simple," he wrote in his diary. Hitler was not an intellectual and in some ways his views were flexible, but his underlying sense of ideology gave him great certainty. In the future, the sarcastic but sharp intellect of Goebbels would be deployed in the service of the Führer. The key axis of the Nazi left had thus been broken, though on occasion in years to come Goebbels would show that he still hankered after a socially radical line.[18]

Discontent within the more left-wing sections of the party continued to rumble, reaching another peak after 1930. There were particular problems with the SA, which in Berlin had even refused to protect party meetings—though part of the problem was pay. Hitler responded with another shrewd decision. He asked Röhm to return from Bolivia—where he was working as a military instructor—to take up leadership of the SA. This did not end rumblings from some of the SA's old guard against the party's growing acceptance of legality and conservatism, but Röhm's radicalism helped to assuage some malcontents, while his military expertise was put to good service in organizing the rapidly expanding paramilitary force.

Otto Strasser continued to fulminate against Hitler's strategy, especially the way in which Hitler used total acceptance of the leader principle and the Twenty-Five Point Program as means to keep down ideological debate within the party. Hitler finally ordered Strasser's expulsion from the party and Strasser formed his own group, which espoused a form of National Bolshevism—but few followed him. Otto had not been popular in the party; there were even tensions between him and his own brother. More importantly, national elections in September 1930 led to a major Nazi breakthrough, a result which seemed to confirm the potential of

Hitler's strategy. By 1933 Otto had fled into exile, from where he began to write a stream of accounts of revisionist Nazi history.[19]

iii

FEW IN 1928 outside the Nazi hard core could have believed that power was in sight. The prospects for the Weimar Republic had never looked better. This was not simply a case of continued optimism on the economic front, with prices under control and unemployment falling for much of the year. After the 1928 elections the SPD had decided to reenter government. Hermann Müller's cabinet, formed in June 1928, was a grand coalition made up of most of the main parties. As these controlled over sixty percent of the votes in the Reichstag, a period of stable and relatively untroubled government seemed in prospect. Müller's government even repealed the Law for the Protection of the Constitution, which had been introduced in the early 1920s to help stem the flood of vitriolic extremist propaganda. Confidence in the republic's future—and a legalistic belief in free speech—were running strong among mainstream political elites.

Yet after 1928 the republic was struck by a disastrous combination of economic problems. The first signs of crisis came in the agricultural sector. As rural workers and their families made up just over thirty percent of the population, this was an important sector of economy. Agriculture had been in long-term decline, though protection had helped to delay the inevitable for some farmers and World War I had even seen rising prices for their produce. In the late 1920s farmers were hit by a combination of poor harvests, disease, and falling prices. (The farm price index dropped from 138 in 1927 to 83 in 1933.) A wave of bankruptcies and forced repossessions of farms followed; other farmers found themselves saddled with ever-mounting debt. The general mood was one of living in a terminal crisis (*Endsituation*).

Industry too faced increasing problems. The post-1924 boom had never been strong, as it was based largely on foreign investment which was attracted by high interest rates. The Wall Street crash in 1929 meant that many of these loans were recalled. Germany was also highly dependent on exports and was particularly vulnerable to the downturn in world trade. As a result, unemployment began to rocket. (The index of industrial production fell from 100 in 1928 to 58 in 1932.) The official figure for those out of work by November 1930 was 3,252,000 compared to 1,171,000 two years earlier. The true numbers were far higher. At the bottom of the depression in early 1933, six million workers were officially unemployed: in reality, this meant that perhaps forty percent of the workforce was idle, and there was widespread misery and poverty.

Growing economic problems meant increased demands on the state both to solve the basic problems and to alleviate immediate hardship. Such pressures caused further problems. During the late nineteenth century, elites had increasingly encouraged Germans to identify the state with economic prosperity, partly as a way of defusing the rise of the left. This process had been reinforced by the Weimar Republic, whose constitution enshrined numerous economic rights.[20] It had created a variety of proto-corporatist measures, linking workers and employers, and a fairly extensive system of welfare, aimed at tying workers to the system. With tax revenues falling, it became increasingly difficult to meet welfare demands, which in turn encouraged criticism of the state. The basic system also caused friction with employers. Many were hostile to democracy, especially if it meant high taxes, compulsory arbitration in labor disputes, and other policies which they saw as making Germany's position uncompetitive. With the onset of depression, it was inevitable that the parties closest to business would put pressure on the government to cut expenditure and introduce other changes.

Carrying out "economies" proved impossible for the SPD, which for all its basic moderation still had a strong radical wing and indulged in socialist rhetoric. (Why should the workers suffer in a "capitalist crisis"?) The situation culminated in the resignation of Müller's government during March 1930. His successor as chancellor was Heinrich Brüning, the leader of the Center Party. The new ministry's composition was largely the same as Müller's but without the SPD. This was a serious loss, for it meant that the new administration was a minority one. Although previous minority administrations had often cobbled together majorities on crucial votes, this would now be much more difficult because of the economic crisis. Brüning realized that he would need to rely on the powers of presidential decree, which were provided for in the Weimar Constitution. Müller had requested such powers to pass his last budget and had been refused. Brüning, however, believed that the president would be more sympathetic to him, given his admiration for the monarchy and sympathy with the army's aspirations to increase its size.

True to expectations, Hindenburg quickly showed that he was more amenable to Brüning's government. But during the summer of 1930 the chancellor decided to call new elections for September. It seems that Brüning believed the growing economic crisis would strengthen the hand of the moderate parties. He could not have been more wrong. Both the SPD and the Center Party lost ground, while the extremes gained. The communists, who had gradually been gaining support throughout the 1920s, saw their vote increase from 10.6 percent in the 1928 election to 13.1 percent—almost certainly as a result of their appeal to the growing number of unemployed. Even more spectacularly, the Nazis leapt from 2.6 to 18.3 percent.[21]

The Weimar Republic's proportional representation system meant that these votes were immediately translated into seats in the Reichstag. The prospect of achieving stable government receded further from view. The only consolation for Brüning was that he was able to survive in office, as the SPD decided not to bring his ministry down. Its leadership feared that the collapse of the administration would precipitate a political crisis that would bring new elections—and yet further gains from the triumphant Nazis, whose performance had taken them from the electoral fringes to second only to the SPD in support.

iv

THE MAIN LOSERS in the 1930 election in terms of votes were the right-wing conservatives (DNVP), who dropped back from 14.2 percent in 1928 to 7 percent. Not all the lost votes were transferred to the Nazis: some went to the more moderate center-right parties, partly in reaction to the appointment of the former leading member of the extremist Pan-German League and Fatherland Party, Alfred Hugenberg, as DNVP chairman in 1928.[22] But there is little doubt that the Nazis benefited significantly from the DNVP's decline. To some extent this was a reflection of the radicalization of politics in the face of depression. More specifically, it stemmed from increasing public awareness of the Nazi Party and especially of Hitler—a development which owed as much to Hugenberg as to the Nazis' own propaganda efforts.

During 1929 Germany's reparations payments were reduced by the Young Plan. Radical nationalists opposed any payments, and Hugenberg decided to launch a major campaign linking the main opponents of the new plan. He was in a strong position to influence public opinion, for he had used his wealth to purchase a major newspaper network and the main German film production and distribution company. Already film newsreels had begun to give some coverage to the Nazis. The reparations campaign now launched Hitler as a major national figure, bringing him to the attention especially of a "respectable" middle class that earlier Nazi propaganda had found difficult to penetrate—a task made easier by the Nazis' growing tendency to play down the more radical side of their social program.

Media attention was an important factor in the Nazis' appeal to new voters, including the young and those who had not voted before (a group which seems to have been especially alienated from the Weimar Republic, in part a reflection of the recurring economic crises particularly affecting the prospects of the young). The longing for strong leadership was deeply rooted in German culture (it has even been argued that it was a dominant theme in films during the Weimar period).[23] The media focus on Hitler during 1929 and 1930, therefore, encouraged relatively apolitical voters to project their own desires on to the Führer. Sometimes these were simple economic demands, but Hitler was also the object of quasi-religious veneration. Hugo Rönck, a theology student leader of the Göttingen University Nazi group, spoke of Hitler as being like Christ, gathering disciples around him to help his fellow man. Maria von Belli, a woman who had been active in the Nazi Party from before the 1923 *putsch,* saw Hitler as a Messiah figure, a man of destiny sent by God to heal Germany.[24]

The Nazis were also developing an increasingly strong local organizational structure and an ability to tailor their message to specific audiences. Goebbels, for instance, brilliantly choreographed funerals of Nazi activists who had been killed in clashes with the left to appeal both to religious sentiments of sacrifice and martyrdom and to a more pathologically war-oriented sense of brotherhood in death. More specifically, in working-class areas of Berlin, he termed himself—in the argot of criminal gangs—"Number One Bandit." The quest to become a party of all the people did not mean that sectional appeals were ignored, though these appeals were strongly linked to an attempt to portray Nazism as part of the German tradition.

The targeting of voters can be seen even more clearly in the rural areas, which witnessed the Nazis' greatest success in the 1930 elections. Up until 1928 the party had mainly concentrated on urban areas, a reflection both of its origins in major cities like Munich and of its belief that it could appeal to the working class. But growing organizational efforts were put into the rural areas, which even in 1928 had shown notable swings to the Nazis. Although the opening had come from primarily economic reasons, the Nazis exploited the situation well. Whereas the main parties offered little to the average farmer, the Nazis began to promise aid. The "immutable" 1920 Nazi Twenty-Five Point Program had made no mention of protecting the peasantry. Indeed, it included the promise to expropriate land for communal purposes. By 1930 the Nazis had a new agrarian program and a specific organization designed to court the peasants. Headed by Walther Darré, it eulogized the peasants as the guardians of morality and tradition, as islands of decency in a sea of urban corruption that was overwhelming the true Germany.[25] Curiously, like many other Nazi leaders, this high priest of Blood and Soil was born outside the German Reich: perhaps absence made the heart grow fonder.

The importance of Nazi propaganda in attracting support has frequently been played down. Undoubtedly economic crisis was a necessary solvent for the old order, but minimizing the role of propaganda diverts attention from the immense efforts the Nazis put into local politics, not least by infiltrating or seeking to influence local clubs and organizations, and by converting local opinion-makers. For instance, in Schleswig-Holstein—the only region where the Nazis were to gain over fifty percent of the vote in free elections—there was not a strong relationship between the main areas of economic distress and Nazi voting. Instead, the Nazis did well in the more cohesive communities, where their organizational and propaganda efforts had managed to rally key individuals and groups.

The sophistication of much Nazi local campaigning can also be seen in the way in which anti-Semitism was used. Surprisingly, it did not figure prominently in campaigns in many areas.[26] The reason for this was not so much that most Nazis disagreed with Hitler's anti-Semitism—though there were differences within both the leadership and rank and file. Nor was it because anti-Semitism was widely opposed: the remarkable sales of the forged *The Protocols of the Elders of Zion* after 1918 showed there was a notable section of the population with a taste for anti-Semitic conspiracy theory. But in many areas this could be countered by a distaste for anti-Semitism, especially when linked to mass-mobilizing politics. The Nazis, therefore, tended to suppress their anti-Semitic beliefs in areas where they thought it would lose rather than gain votes.

The importance of organization and propaganda can clearly be seen in the 1932 presidential and Reichstag elections.[27] After a characteristic period of dithering, in February 1932 Hitler decided to enter the presidential elections against the eighty-four-year-old Hindenburg, adopting German citizenship in order to do so. Backed by the strong electoral machine created by Gregor Strasser and Goebbels, who took overall charge of propaganda in 1930, Hitler threw himself into the fray with remarkable energy. His campaign involved thirty-four thousand public meetings, attended by large audiences who had usually paid for the privilege. By his pioneering use of aircraft, he personally attended many, usually two or three major rallies a day. In an attempt to maximize Nazi support, Hitler focused on the problem of economic revival rather than pure Nazi ideology. Hitler lost, but the Nazi vote rose to over thirty-six percent on the second ballet.

The extension of Nazi support was confirmed in the July legislative elections, when for the first time they became the largest party, with 37.3 percent of votes cast (the SPD was second with 21.6 percent). The belief has been widespread that the Nazi vote was made up primarily of rural voters, the urban *Mittelstand*, and various other disaffected sections of the middle class, most notably public employees who had been hit by wage cuts and layoffs. In fact, the Nazis made widespread gains across classes, though the main appeal to the working class came outside the large urban centers.[28] Given their highly male-oriented ideology, the Nazis even performed relatively well among women voters, especially younger ones attracted by Hitler's charisma—though the appeal of the Nazi trinity of "children, church, and kitchen" to older women especially should not be underestimated.[29]

Only two main groups remained largely immune to the Nazis' attempt to create a cross-class new people's community (*Volksgemeinschaft*): the practicing Catholics and the active members of the left-wing parties and trade unions, especially those who lived in the larger towns and cities. The main factor linking these groups was not so much economic interest as the fact that they created strong, almost ghettoized, communities that the Nazis could not penetrate at the local level. In the case of Catholics, the barriers often included overt hostility from bishops and priests—whereas the Protestant clergy would sometimes don the brown shirt.

In the case of the left-wing parties, resistance was often physical, for the KPD had its own paramilitary organization complete with iconography and discipline which was very similar to that of the SA. On July 17, 1932, seven thousand members of the SA marched through a working-class quarter of Hamburg and the local communists opened fire. In the ensuing battle seventeen people were killed and sixty-five wounded. In general the Nazis gained the better of these violent exchanges. Such victories were not simply the result of their rapidly growing numbers. The forces of "law and order" also protected the Nazis sometimes. Even when prosecuted, Nazi activists could often receive remarkably lenient treatment from the courts. For instance, Jakob Timplemann seemed pathologically addicted to violence, but when brought before a Thalburg court for assaulting a left-wing opponent he received only a token fine.[30]

A further problem in the left's battle against "fascism" was the attitude of the Moscow-dominated Communist International, which in 1928 had effectively banned cooperation with social democrats.[31] This Marxist analysis held that fascism was the political vehicle of a doomed capitalist class. By continuing to support parliamentary democracy, the social democrats were therefore helping to prop up the collapsing capitalist system. In practice, such communist sectarianism served mainly to weaken the left—and hasten their own brutal demise. It may also have helped to spread more general fears of communism—particularly the fate which would overcome most Germans if domestic communism, or Soviet invasion, should triumph.

Analytically, this Marxist interpretation of fascism has little use, for the links between the Nazis and business were complex.[32] There is no doubt that from an early stage the Nazis had received some support from wealthy patrons. Many were introduced to Hitler by the *völkisch* poet Dietrich Eckart: the title of one of his poems, "Germany Awake," was to become a key Nazi slogan. Eckart helped Hitler to make a socially awkward entry into the salons of some of Munich's rich and famous, where he gathered a small but dedicated following. By the early 1930s Hitler was attracting support from a growing number of industrialists—who were impressed by his attempts to portray himself as a moderate in the party, and by his exploitation of the fear of communist revolution. The most prominent member of this group was the steel magnate Fritz Thyssen—though he was later to break with the Nazis.

Donations were often steered to individuals rather than the party in general—sometimes to the benefit of the recipient as well as the party. One key conduit for such payments by the early 1930s was Hermann Göring.[33] Göring had ended World War I as the much-decorated leader of the famous Richthofen fighter squadron. Unable to adjust to postwar life, he joined the Nazi Party after meeting Hitler in 1922. Badly wounded in the 1923 Munich *putsch,* he became a morphine addict and for a time left Germany, but in 1928 he had been one of the handful of Nazis to be elected to the Reichstag. Coming from a relatively prosperous higher civil servant background, and blissfully married to a Swedish aristocrat, Göring had never been on the left of the NSDAP. He was, therefor, a natural point of social contact between the Nazis and business, as he could easily mix in elevated social circles. But in spite of the efforts of Hitler, Göring, and others to paint a respectable face on the NSDAP, most industrialists viewed the party as too unstable, violent, and radical to be trusted.[34] Even those who made donations normally gave money to other parties as well, most notably the DNVP, which combined fervent nationalism and hostility to the republic with distinctly conservative socioeconomic policies.

Business elites undoubtedly helped to condition the climate of crisis after 1929, but the chancellor bears a more direct responsibility for the downfall of the Weimar Republic. Although Brüning tried hard to combat the rise of the Nazis, his persistent reliance on presidential decree underlined the failure of democracy. His defenders have argued that in policy terms the government lacked room for maneuver because of the nature of the economic crisis. There is no doubt that the situation was very difficult, but a strong case can be made that Brüning made serious mistakes in handling his limited options.[35] Rejecting reflationary policies, his government made a series of expenditure cuts that earned him the name "Chancellor Hunger" from the Nazis. Some of these hit politically sensitive groups, especially disabled war veterans and the survivors of those killed. Predictably, radical nationalists portrayed this as yet another example of the way in which the republic had ignored or trampled over those who had suffered and given so much for their country. Brüning was aware of the political danger from nationalist sentiment, but his main way of countering it was to try to show the former Allies that Germany was in no condition to continue with reparations payments. The problem was that this encouraged the very deflationary policies that helped push Germany yet further into depression.

The continuing economic crisis played its part in the downfall of Brüning's government at the end of May 1932. A more specific factor, however, was the intriguing of the confident and charismatic "Field Gray Eminence," General Kurt von Schleicher, who was a close friend of the president's son and had served in Hindenburg's regiment. Schleicher seems to have been particularly concerned about a decision taken by the government during April to ban the SA. The SA was the cause of considerable violence, but the Nazis had many sympathizers in the armed forces. Banning it therefore raised the specter of how the army would respond if the Nazis decided to launch a *putsch*. Although Hitler had decided to pursue the parliamentary road after 1923, there were many in the Nazi Party who retained a taste for coups—and the ever-growing SA easily outnumbered the armed forces.

Schleicher played an equally important role in persuading Hindenburg to appoint Franz von Papen chancellor, a politically inexperienced and right-wing member of the Center Party, which proceeded to expel him. Schleicher's plan seems to have been to create a ministry that would include the Nazis, thus avoiding the need for rule by presidential decree. He also saw the Nazis as good patriots, and likely to support the army's wish for significant rearmament.[36] In line with this policy of tempting the Nazis, the new government quickly lifted the ban on the SA—a decision the communist leader described as an open invitation to murder. But an increasingly confident Hitler declined to be entrapped, refusing anything less than the chancellorship.

Shortly afterward, Papen's government was defeated in a no-confidence motion and new elections were called for November. These saw the NSDAP vote slip back slightly to 33.1 percent. The Nazis were short of funds after two national and other local elections; this undoubtedly hampered their propaganda efforts. The party may also have been harmed among more right-wing voters by the decision to cooperate with a transport strike in Berlin. In an evaluation of the election, however, Goebbels concluded that the Nazis had already reached their limit as a catch-all party. He argued that only the imminent seizure of power could halt a further decline—a reflection of widespread pessimism within much of the Nazi leadership over the setbacks of late 1932.

The risk of a Nazi coup, therefore, seemed to be reemerging. As in May, Schleicher visited Hindenburg and informed him that the Reichswehr had no confidence in the chancellor. This time, Hindenburg responded by making the general chancellor. Schleicher had still not given up hope of creating a government that could rally Nazi, nationalist, and center support in the Reichstag. But this time he planned—if Hitler was still unwilling to accept the vice chancellorship—to solve the impasse by persuading Gregor Strasser to take the post. Schleicher may well have preferred the support of Strasser and a group of his followers, for his plans included seeking to attract moderate trade-union support around a program of expansion. He must have been aware that Hitler had told Papen earlier in 1932 that he planned to destroy all communist and social democratic organizations, which was hardly compatible with Schleicher's more corporatist views. While Hitler had sought hard since the late 1920s to play down the more radical Nazi economic and social policies, he had made little attempt to hide his contempt for the left and for the Weimar constitution.

Strasser's position had changed noticeably in many ways since the mid-1920s. In 1931–2 he had come to believe that the way forward for the Nazis lay through coalition rather than exclusive power, and a significant group of more moderate Nazis in the Reichstag seem to have shared this perspective. The upshot of Schleicher's maneuver, however, was that Strasser retreated into virtual retirement rather than entering government. Perhaps Strasser thought that a Nazi breakaway would quickly disintegrate without the charismatic force of Hitler to unite it. Perhaps he had never really planned to join Schleicher, and this was his way of showing his belief that the Führer and party were above individuals. The answer will probably never be known.

Having failed to persuade Strasser to enter his cabinet, Schleicher's days were clearly numbered, not least as he had made very powerful enemies. Papen felt bitter about his betrayal, and in early January 1933 met Hitler secretly to discuss a joint ministry. Papen initially thought that Hitler would serve under him, but he quickly realized that the price of Nazi cooperation was the chancellorship. Schleicher had also aroused the fears of powerful agrarian interests, especially in eastern Germany. These already had the ear of the president, who came from this area. The Junkers were a bastion of autocratic, traditional views, but what aroused their fears at the turn of 1933 were Schleicher's plans for land colonization and his threat to publish a report revealing the scandal of extensive "loans" which had been made primarily to large landowners.

Thus, although a serious economic crisis was a precondition to the rise of Nazism, it needed a broader set of factors to lead to power. In particular, it needed an insurgent party whose leadership could shrewdly use propaganda to portray itself as offering both a radical Third Way alternative and as a central part of national traditions: one that could appeal both to those concerned primarily with economics and to those who sought to restore a more affective community. The latter aspect helped encourage nationalistic conservative elites, who were divided and lacking a popular base, to see Nazism as a vehicle that could provide popular legitimation for a more authoritarian regime that could control the rising left.

During 1932 the president had refused to offer the chancellorship to the "Bohemian corporal." Now he came to believe that the impasse could be broken by accepting a ministry in which Hitler would be hemmed in by a majority of non-Nazis. Added to the pressure that came from various groups and individuals, he was impressed by the Nazis' performance in a state election during January, which witnessed their vote rise remarkably—thus appearing to undermine the belief that their star was on the wane. The ever-mounting economic crisis seemed to be giving the Nazis a further constituency, as ever more people turned away from the main-stream parties. After further negotiations, which continued until the last moment, the deed was done. On January 30, 1933, Hitler was duly appointed chancellor.

That evening, he appeared on the balcony of the Reich Chancellery, taking the salute at a giant but disciplined march of Nazi supporters. In some suburbs and towns, other Nazis celebrated the seizure of power in a more violent and ominous way. The "period of struggle" (*Kampfzeit*) was over. The "seizure of power" (*Machtergreifung*) was just beginning.

7

Germany: The Consolidation of the Nazi Dictatorship

i

THE NAZIS termed Hitler's appointment as chancellor the *Machter-greifung*—the seizure of power. At first, this was more a statement of hope than a description of political reality, for the new cabinet appointed on January 30, 1933, included only two Nazis besides Hitler—Göring and Wilhelm Frick—though the posts they held were major ones. Hitler believed that Göring had been important in the maneuvers that led to his accession to the chancellorship, and rewarded him with the posts of minister without portfolio and minister of the interior for Prussia. Frick was a former civil servant and lawyer who, like Göring, could pass muster as a "respectable" Nazi. He became the national minister of the interior, bringing with him valuable experience as a former interior minister in the state of Thuringia, where after 1930 the Nazis had participated in government. Papen was made vice chancellor and various other right-wing figures filled the remaining cabinet positions. Hugenberg took on both the Reich and Prussian ministries of economics and agriculture and four other ministers, including Konstantin von Neurath at Foreign Affairs, kept the portfolios they had held in the previous ministry.

Even with the DNVP votes, the new administration controlled only just over forty percent of the seats in the Reichstag. At the first cabinet meeting, Hitler proposed to break out of this impasse by calling yet more national elections, in the belief that the Nazis could make further gains. Reluctantly, most of the cabinet and Hindenburg agreed, believing that the alternatives—further parliamentary paralysis or military government, which might provoke a left-wing uprising—were even less attractive options. Elections were called for March 5.

Before polling day, large contributions began to pour in to the Nazis from industry, encouraged by hints from Göring that these might well be the last elections for a long time. The influx of cash, and the privileged access to a radio accorded to the government, allowed the Nazis to mount a particularly effective propaganda campaign. On the streets they harried opponents mercilessly: there were sixty-nine political murders during the campaign, including eighteen Nazi dead. Now that the Nazis were in government, there was even less inclination on the part of the forces of "law and order" to control the SA. Believing that total power was at hand, the SA responded by setting up "wild" (namely unofficial) concentration camps. In Berlin's Columbia cinema, in Stettin's Vulkan docks, and in countless other places, enemies were incarcerated and tortured in a microcosm of the hell that was to come.

This violent side of Nazism presented problems in attracting a broad basis of support, but the Nazis countered by strongly stressing the fear of a left-wing uprising, backed up by visions of the bloody terror that had followed the Bolshevik Revolution. They were helped in this task by the dramatic burning down of the Reichstag on February 27—an event that marked a further crucial step in the collapse of civilized government. The Reichstag fire has been seen by many as too much of a godsend not to have been perpetrated by the Nazis: in fact, it seems to have been carried out by a Dutch communist acting alone. While the embers of the parliament building were still smoldering, Hindenburg was persuaded to sign yet another emergency decree, which temporarily removed many basic constitutional rights. Thus was laid one of the legal cornerstones of the Nazi dictatorship, for the order remained in force until the collapse of the regime.

In the ensuing elections, the main losers were the communists, down from 16.9 to 12.2 percent of the vote—though this was a notable achievement in view of the harassment the party had suffered, including a wave of arrests of leaders and activists after the Reichstag fire. The Nazis won 43.9 percent, up just over ten points from the November 1932 figure. As the turnout had risen markedly, it is likely the Nazis mainly gained support from among the more apolitical members of the electorate. While this helps underline the power of Nazi propaganda and Hitler's personal appeal in particular, the result disappointed most Nazis. They had won the support of less than half the German people, though with DNVP support they now had just enough votes to control the Reichstag.

Six days after the elections, Hitler created his first new government department: the Ministry of Public Enlightenment and Propaganda, under the direction of Goebbels. Since 1930 Goebbels had headed a large party propaganda organization based in Munich. Now a department of the state would be responsible for ensuring that Germans were transformed into good Nazis—a task Goebbels, though not all Nazis, saw as vital.[1] Goebbels set to work with characteristic enthusiasm and flair. His first major task was to orchestrate a ceremony that was to be held in the historic Potsdam garrison church to mark the opening of the new parliamentary session. At this emotion-laden gathering, Hitler pledged to Hindenburg and the German people that he would be loyal to the values of the past. He portrayed himself as a reincarnation of German tradition rather than a force for radicalism. Broadcast live on the radio, the ceremony seems to have had a deep impact on many people. It was, of course, entirely an act designed to prepare opinion for the next Nazi coup.

The Weimar constitution provided for the passing of an Enabling Act, which would give decree power directly to the government, if at least two-thirds of the members of the Reichstag supported the measure. This was Hitler's next goal. On March 23 a bill to this effect was put to the Reichstag. In order to ensure a sufficient majority, SA men menacingly surrounded the building, a physical reminder of the dangers of opposition to a regime that had just announced the opening of the first official concentration camp at Dachau, near Munich—a camp which mainly "housed" left-wingers. The only deputies who voted against the Enabling Act came from the SPD, whose leader bravely spoke against Nazi harassment. (The KPD deputies had been effectively banned.) The other opposition deputies had less backbone.

The deputies who had kept silent in the belief that the government would not abuse these powers were quickly proved wrong. The days of political parties and parliamentary trading were numbered at both national and local level. During 1932 the Papen government had, in a move of debatable legality, prorogued the

Prussian parliament, which during the 1920s had been a bastion of SPD–Center Party cooperation. The setting aside of such a major institution helped set a precedent for the Nazi attack on state parliaments in the weeks after the March elections. Often using the pretext that local government was incapable of maintaining order—the main threat to which came from the SA—Reich commissioners were appointed to replace the existing administrations. Although the federal system was not formally ended until January 1934, by the summer of 1933 local democracy was effectively dead.

The demise of party politics followed apace. The SPD leadership, realizing that the Nazis intended to suppress all opposition, moved their headquarters to Prague shortly after the passing of the Enabling Act, providing the pretext for the government to ban the party as hostile to the German state and people. Hugenberg fought a last-ditch battle to preserve the independence of his party, but this only encouraged Nazi attacks on him personally. He resigned from the government in late June after an ineffectual and bad-tempered performance at the World Economic Conference, and the following day his party was dissolved. By the end of July all parties bar the Nazis had been banned, harassed out of existence, or had dissolved themselves.

In the late summer of 1933 the only remaining serious political check on Hitler was the president. Hindenburg was a dying man, but some aspects of Nazism disturbed him enough to prompt intervention. He was unhappy about physical attacks on Jews, and boycotts of their businesses, to the extent that Hitler and the Nazi leadership decided to clamp down on "wild" actions, though there were also fears about international opinion, and a realization that attacking Jewish businesses could harm economic recovery. At the beginning of August 1934 Hindenburg died and Hitler proceeded to abolish the office of president: he claimed that allowing the office to lapse with the revered field marshal was a final mark of honor. The Führer and Reich chancellor, as Hitler now became known, had overcome the last constitutional check.

ii

AFTER 1930 Hitler increasingly sought to portray himself as outside politics, a Christ-like figure sent from above to save the German people. The technique is evident in his first broadcast to the German people as chancellor, made on February 19, 1933. In a speech that began with characteristic nervousness before it built to a crescendo, Hitler depicted the early Nazi Party as a small band of disciples who had gone forth and sowed the seed. He portrayed himself as a modest man willing to sacrifice all for the rebirth of his people.

The imagery can be seen even more explicitly in the opening scenes of Leni Riefenstahl's documentary film of the 1934 Nuremberg Party Rally, *Triumph of the Will*. After the opening credits, dark turns to light and a plane is revealed descending through clouds. Against a background of Wagnerian music, the metaphor at first seems to be pagan-Germanic: the plane as the chariot brings the new Wotan to earth to rekindle his followers with fire. But soon the imagery becomes more Christian. As the plane swoops down over the sleepy medieval city, its shadow forms a cross, "blessing" the disciplined columns of marching men along which it flies. When Hitler descends from the plane's door, backlighting creates a halo effect around his head. As he makes the journey from the airport to his hotel, vast crowds line the streets in order to express their worship for the New Christ who has been sent to save Germany.

Riefenstahl's film is of great interest not only for the way it picks up the dual metaphors that were often central to Nazi propaganda, but also for the way it points to the growing Führer cult. As time progressed, and this worship grew in obsequiousness, the imagery became more complex and even bizarre. Hitler's birthday issue of *Völkischer Beobachter* in 1941 announced: "The Führer is the highest synthesis of his race . . . He embodies the universalism of Goethe, the depth of Kant, the dynamism of Hegel, the patriotism of Fichte, the genius of Frederick II, the realism of Bismarck as well as the tumultuous inspiration of Wagner, the perspicacity of Spengler." Hitler was portrayed as both a priest and a warrior, a man of action and of great thoughts—almost a living god, an ultimate arbiter who could shape fate.

There is a sense in which aspects of the mythical Führer had a corresponding reality. Although Hitler initially paid some attention to the details of politics, increasingly after the death of Hindenburg he left the running of government to others—for instance, in the field of economic policy. He spent long periods of time talking with favored members of his inner court, like Albert Speer, a young architect who was mainly responsible for the design of the remarkable Nuremberg rallies in the 1930s, which themselves were inspired by a mixture of Catholic ceremony and left-wing Expressionist form and lighting.[2] Hitler saw himself as a great artist and architect manqué, and sought in particular to synthesize the classical and Romantic traditions.[3] Together with Speer, who was perhaps the closest thing to a friend that Hitler had, he could idle away many an hour designing great new buildings that would grace the thousand-year Nazi Reich, vast temples in which his people could worship. Hitler also enjoyed passing time in the company of Winifred Wagner, the great composer's English daughter-in-law, and a longtime admirer and confidante of the Führer.

This daydreaming, pseudophilosophical side to Hitler raises an important question. Exactly what role did he play in decision making during the Third Reich? The classic picture has been one of the evil totalitarian leader, personally controlling all major issues of policy. More recently this has been challenged by those who see the Nazi state as akin to a medieval court, with competing barons: a "polyocracy" of rival interests. Some have even portrayed the Führer as a "weak dictator" who took little or no part in crucial policy decisions, not least because he was frequently incapable of making up his mind.[4]

Much of this debate focuses on the relationship between Hitler and the Nazi Party, which by 1939 had grown to five million members. Size in itself did not guarantee influence, as the case of the Italian Fascist Party shows. But there were crucial differences between Italian fascism and Nazism in relation to the party. Italian fascism tended to worship the state, while Nazism often elevated the party above the state. In practice this meant that there were often parallel state and party organizations, which sometimes developed into major empires for those who headed them.[5]

The most feared of these was the party and state police system, which quickly came under the control of Heinrich Himmler. The son of a devout Catholic schoolteacher, Himmler had been attracted to the Nazis in the early 1920s while studying for a diploma in Munich. A timid but ambitious man, Himmler took part in the 1923 *putsch* and subsequently began to rise quickly in the party. A curious mixture of the almost unideological and the fanatical, his views ultimately coalesced around uncritical devotion to Hitler. As a result, by 1929 he had been appointed head of Hitler's small personal bodyguard, the Elite Guard (SS), which by 1933 had grown into an organization of over fifty thousand racially pure, black-shirted men—warriors whom Himmler saw as a future Samurai class. After the *Machtergreifung*, Himmler's empire expanded still further as he acquired new offices, including command of the Prussian police and its political wing, the Gestapo (which had been set up by Göring, partly to spy on rivals).[6]

During 1934 Himmler seized his chance to eliminate a major rival. The SA under Röhm had grown rapidly: from around 100,000 in 1930, to 450,000 members in January 1933, and to 2.5 million by the summer of 1934 (an increase partly caused by the incorporation of formerly non-Nazi militia). Röhm saw this force as the basis for a people's army, which raised strong fears within the Reichswehr and in the Establishment more generally. Their apprehension was further aroused by Röhm's desire for the Nazis to launch a "second revolution," which would bring about sweeping social changes. Röhm's flagrant homosexuality caused further offense. Himmler decided to heighten Hitler's already strong fears by forging evidence that Röhm was plotting a coup. The result was the Night of the Long Knives, which began on June 30, 1934. The main instrument for arresting and executing Röhm, and over a hundred others who had incurred the animosity of Hitler and Himmler, was the SS.

Shortly afterward, Hitler rewarded Himmler by making the SS a separate organization, rather than a branch of the SA, and giving it the task of "safeguarding the . . . embodiment of the National Socialist idea." Himmler used this vague but sweeping injunction to help set up a variety of party institutions, including schools and maternity hospitals where SS children could be given the perfect start to life. (Contrary to popular image, the Lebensborn program was not a giant stud farm for overvirile SS men.) Further powers were accorded to Himmler in 1936, when he became head of the national police, including the Gestapo. This brought him control of the concentration camps, which were often used as sources of forced labor for industrial production, particularly after the outbreak of war. Himmler now headed his own economic empire.

The main rival to Himmler in terms of empire building was Göring. Göring's position immediately after the seizure of power had seemed strong, but the ending of the federal system removed his Prussian base, while Himmler was taking over all aspects of policing. Göring became increasingly marginalized as a result, since he had never held a major party office, nor had he been personally close to Hitler. His chance for renewed aggrandizement came in 1935–6, when the World War I fighter ace became commander-in-chief of the Luftwaffe, then plenipotentiary for the implementation of the Four Year Plan. He used these positions to build up a gigantic industrial enterprise, including the enormous Hermann Göring Works. His empire provided an ever-growing source of funds to fuel his addiction to an ostentatious baronial lifestyle, complete with hunting mansions and orgiastic feasts. Göring's taste for bizarre uniforms and finery became even more outlandish after his appointment as field marshal in 1938—a sop from Hitler, who had declined to appoint him minister of war. On one memorable occasion he turned up to watch the trial of a new weapon wearing bright red Morocco riding boots, a greatcoat of Australian opossum, and sporting a fistful of platinum rings inset with large rubies.

Goebbels too used his empire, built on the state and party propaganda organizations, to secure great wealth. A fawning film industry bought him a fine house near Berlin and copious sweeteners followed from other sectors of the media. In 1938, however, his tendency to avail himself of a certain type of favor came close to producing his downfall. Goebbels was fascinated by female film stars and seduced several, though not Leni Riefenstahl, who was unimpressed when he commenced his wooing by presenting a copy of *Mein Kampf* bound in red leather and a bronze medallion bearing his own head in relief. Goebbels preferred dark-haired Slav women and became particularly infatuated with Lida Baarova, who was just twenty-two years old when she met him. He planned to marry her, but here he made a mistake that Himmler and Göring studiously tried to avoid. Goebbels fell foul of Hitler. The Führer was a great admirer of Goebbels's wife and disapproved of his cavorting: he ordered the propaganda minister to stay with his family.

Goebbels was left desperately seeking a means to impress Hitler with both his efficiency and loyalty. His chance came at the beginning of November 1938. The German Third Secretary at the Paris Embassy was shot and fatally wounded by a Polish Jew. His death on November 9, a holy day in the Nazi calendar because it was the anniversary of the 1923 *putsch,* set in train a pogrom stoked by a wave of propaganda. All over Germany synagogues and Jewish property were attacked on *Kristallnacht* ("crystal night, the night of the broken glass"). Almost a hundred Jews were killed, and twenty-six thousand were taken off to concentration camps. Goebbels, who was one of the most virulent anti-Semites among the Nazi leaders, was back in Hitler's good books.

The Nazi Party quickly developed after 1933 into rival and amorphous fiefdoms. No key decisions were taken in the cabinet, which hardly met after 1934 and never after 1938. Indeed, a notable characteristic of the regime was the way in which many decisions were taken at low levels. The absence of clear bureaucratic structure, however, does not mean that there was a power vacuum. Hitler's authority did not rest ultimately on the rule of law or the rational structures beloved by liberal theorists. Hitler's power was personal, charismatic. He inspired remarkable loyalty—and in general he was loyal to his old comrades in arms. The certainty of his underlying views inspired great confidence (From the early 1920s this confidence had been a crucial factor in dealing with socially "important" nationalist rivals and potential benefactors.) Sometimes he had to divide and rule. On other occasions he had to coerce or threaten. He even seems to have been able to lose his temper on purpose to get his way. But on the whole Hitler's leading colleagues were eager to please, for they realized that no one else could have kept so faction-riddled a party together. Here lies perhaps the key paradox of Hitler's party position: it was precisely because the party was so divided that he had power—and in turn because the party was divided from other key centers of power, such as the army.

iii

THE NATURE OF the Nazi dictatorship cannot be understood simply by considering leaders, the institutions of government, or party structures. It is also necessary to look at their wider relationship to society. Hitler and the Nazis were very conscious that they had come to power with well under fifty percent of the vote in free elections. They also knew that, even after the destruction of other parties, there were many Germans opposed to them or whose loyalty was dubious. Now that the *Machtergreifung* was over, the focus turned to the *Gleichschaltung*: a scientific term used in this context to refer to the way in which social and economic organizations were to be synthesized, "coordinated" with the party and state.

Early major targets were public administration and education. The main immediate task was the purging of enemies, especially left-wingers. Jews were targets too, but they were initially seen as less of a physical and political threat; and as a result of pressure from Hindenburg some Jews, for instance those who had fought in World War I, were initially excluded from the civil service purge. Many public-sector workers responded by joining the Nazi Party in a desperate attempt to keep their jobs. Largely as a result, Nazi Party membership grew from 850,000 in January 1933 to double that figure by May; the party's old guard often disparagingly referred to these converts as "those who had fallen in March."[7]

There were, however, some more genuine converts, especially among those already inclined to authoritarian conservatism or *völkisch* nationalism, views that had long been well represented in the higher civil service and teaching, respectively.[8] One of the most notable converts in this category was Carl Schmitt, a legal and political philosopher who became the "Crown Jurist" of the early regime. He provided a brilliant defense of the strong state as a way of forging a more truly united society, and of the Führer-principle as a vital way of linking the state and the people.[9] Another major convert was Martin Heidegger, one of Germany's most famous philosophers. In his rectorial address to Freiburg University in April 1933, Heidegger defended fascism in sweeping terms, seeing Hitler as Nietzschean Superman and calling for a synthesis between science and the power of the will, between workers and thinkers. His defenders have subsequently argued that he was largely an opportunist, seeking to curry favor. In fact, Heidegger was an active party member who denounced several left-wing and Jewish colleagues during 1933. While he distanced himself from Nazism in the longer run, he was never to make a fundamental ideological break with fascism, which he saw as the basis of a radical Third Way.[10]

Support from heavyweight academics like Heidegger conferred legitimacy on the regime, but Goebbels was well aware that more popular propaganda would be needed to bring all Germans into the *Volksgemeinschaft. Gleichschaltung*, therefore, paid particular attention to the mass media. Although much of the media in 1933 lay in private hands, this did not save it from an extensive purge. Control and intimidation of personnel were reinforced by a variety of other policies, including gradual purchase of sections of the media, a system of censorship, and the provision of subsidies for the production of the right kind of propaganda films. There was also a program to subsidize the price of radio receivers. By 1939 over seventy percent of German homes had radios, the highest percentage in the world.

Gleichschaltung for the churches was to prove a more difficult task. Over ninty percent of Germans claimed to be members of a church, of whom about two-thirds were Protestants and one-third Catholics. Religion was, therefore, potentially a major source of resistance to the creation of a Nazi-imbued *Volksgemeinschaft*.[11] The Evangelical (Lutheran) Church had a long tradition of obedience to political authority and strong historic links with the Prussian state. But the Nazis wanted more than just loyalty. They wanted to coordinate the churches in such a way that Nazism would become part of the basic credo. In order to do this, they sought to create a national organization under a bishop who supported the Nazis. In July 1933 Ludwig Müller, a figure well known for combining Blood and Soil and anti-Semitic views, was appointed Reich bishop.

Müller, however, faced a strong countermovement in the shape of the Confessional church, led by Martin Niemöller. Niemöller was a World War I submarine captain who had been awarded the highest honour for valor, the Pour le Mérite. In 1933 he had initially welcomed the Nazi regime. Like many Germans, he believed there was a vital need to revive the national spirit and he was worried by the advance of communism, but he fundamentally opposed Nazi attempts to control the church and the destruction of the rule of law. By 1937 his critical sermons had led to his imprisonment, though he miraculously managed to survive, spending most of the next eight years in concentration camps. Another leading member of the Confessional church, Dietrich Bonhoeffer, was not so lucky. Arrested in 1943, he was hanged during the closing days of the war.

Before 1933 members of the Catholic clergy had frequently spoken out against the Nazis. Hitler decided, therefore, that the best way forward was to reach an agreement with the Vatican on basic church-state relations. The Pope was suspicious of the Nazis, but this suspicion heightened his belief in the need for a written agreement. The result was the Concordat, signed in July 1933, by which the church was assured of full religious freedom. In return, the Vatican ordered bishops to take an oath of loyalty to the state and agreed to the dismantling of the church's temporal organizations, including the Center Party. The Nazis had gained another important prop for their regime.

Almost immediately, the Nazis began to go back on the agreement, principally by harassing priests who were seen as hostile. The church responded with an overt attack on a central part of Nazi doctrine, focusing on a particular book; *The Myth of the Twentieth Century*, published in 1930 by one of the leading self-styled theorists of the party, Alfred Rosenberg.[12] Cardinal Faulhaber of Munich criticized the book's commitment to "Germanic" racial politics and rejection of Christianity as an alien creed. One result of this was to help sales, and *The Myth of the Twentieth Century* became second only to *Mein Kampf* in the Nazi bestseller list. Paradoxically, Hitler was unimpressed by it, holding that Nazism was a rational creed not a myth, and few leading Nazis seem to have read it: Goebbels even described it as an "ideological belch." The attack on Rosenberg's work, nevertheless, should have made it clear to Catholics that there was a fundamental incompatibility between the doctrine of Christian brotherhood and Nazi racial thought, though some undoubtedly chose not to heed the lesson.

The gulf was underlined by periodic criticism after 1933 of the Law for the Prevention of Hereditary Diseased Offspring, a eugenics-inspired measure that allowed for the forcible sterilization of about four hundred thousand people by 1945. The main victims were women considered capable of transmitting hereditary diseases or to be mentally deficient, a category defined in a remarkably sweeping way. Catholic opposition did not stop this policy, but it was more successful against the euthanasia policy that followed. In 1939 a father petitioned Hitler for permission to have his badly deformed child "put to sleep." Hitler agreed and had his personal doctor carry out the killing. Thus began a program that led to the end of over seventy thousand "worthless lives"—primarily children—before Bishop Galen of Münster, who had failed in private negotiations to persuade the Nazis to stop murdering Catholics, in 1941 bravely denounced the policy as "plain murder." Some Nazi leaders demanded his arrest, but Goebbels warned Hitler of the dangers of antagonizing a large section of German opinion. Hitler heeded the advice and ordered an end to the program for Germans, though in practice it continued, especially for non-Germans.[13].

Together with Catholics, the main group who had proved resistant to the Nazis' appeal during the *Kampfzeit* were union members. From the moment Hitler came to power, most union leaders had recognised the danger of the Nazis suppressing their organizations. The links between the main union federation and the SPD made a particularly obvious target. As a result, in March 1933 its leadership had announced that it was willing to terminate links with the socialists and to cooperate with the new government. Initially, the Nazis' leadership responded cautiously. Goebbels even made May 1 a public holiday, naming it the "Day of National Labor." Celebrations of this newfound recognition were cut short when, on May 2, union premises were occupied and leading officials arrested.

Subsequently all workers were incorporated into a single German Work Front (DAF), which went on to develop into a major social organization—rather like the Italian Dopolavoro. Its leader was the temperance-preaching, hard-drinking Gauleiter of Cologne, Robert Ley. Ley held a university degree, but he was no intellectual. Blunt and violent—he was jailed several times before the *Machtergreifung*—his opinions were characterized by mindless allegiance to Hitler. It was Ley to whom Hitler had turned to run the party organization after the resignation of Gregor Strasser: his brief had been to ensure the total subservience of the party to its leader.[14]

Ley's appointment, therefore, had important implications for the way in which the DAF would develop. The Nazis had never produced clear plans concerning the role of the workers in a Nazi state. Some working-class Nazi activists, especially those who had been attracted by Gregor Strasser's creation of factory cells, believed that unions could remain in existence, albeit with control wrested from the left and placed firmly in Nazi hands. More commonly, vague corporatist ideas could be found throughout the movement, though these had never been developed as clearly as in Italy (where many of the plans came from the Nationalists rather than the fascists). By the summer of 1933 Hitler had decided that it was crucial to subordinate the DAF to the party, and it became a facet of the burgeoning Nazi social machine, lacking significant rights to negotiate wages or conditions.

Gleichschaltung for the employers proved a slower and more confused process. Some have argued that Nazi economic policy was either largely controlled by big business or at least operated in the interests of business.[15] More commonly, it has been claimed that Nazi economic policy was essentially pragmatic, lacking both philosophy and plan—other than a vague commitment to rearmament. Even some of the Nazi government's most noted public works achievements, such as the commencement of a major *autobahn* network, had been planned by earlier administrations.[16] Both interpretations, especially the former, are misleading. The Nazis may not always have had detailed plans, but there was a clear drift to their economic policy and this owed far more to ideology than to business pressures.

In the early days of the regime considerable influence was exerted by Hjalmar Schacht, a banker who had masterminded the stabilization of the currency in 1923. He later participated in negotiations for the Dawes Plan, but in 1930 resigned as president of the Reichsbank in protest against the new reparations scheme. This, with the Nazi breakthrough in the 1930 elections, led him to become a key figure in advising the party on policy and in promoting contacts with the banking and industrial worlds. In March 1933 he returned to the presidency of the Reichsbank, becoming minister of economics in 1934, a post he held until he resigned over personality and policy disputes in 1937.

Schacht was essentially a conservative opportunist, rather than a true Nazi. He was eager to restore Germany to greatness, and realized that this required rearmament. But he believed in the operation of the free market and the restoration of high levels of corporate profitability. He was also pragmatic in dealing with Jewish business.[17] Schacht was conscious both of the harm that could be done to the German economy by the immediate takeover of Jewish business, and of the dangerous impact this might have on foreign opinion. By 1936 he was even advocating slowing down the rearmament program, believing that the economy was showing signs of overheating and was in danger of producing new inflation—a significant fear since the hyperinflation of the 1920s. He argued that Germany could largely restore its former possessions and its economic power through negotiation and trade rather than war.

Predictably, this led to increasing tensions with the Nazi leadership. Hitler especially had never liked the self-confident Schacht, though he respected his technical expertise. Although there was a remarkable diversity of views in the party about economic policy, there was widespread agreement at the top on the need to construct a new system that would stress national goals and long-run stability more than individual profit or short-run gain. In more concrete terms, such views tended to support an autarchic, or largely closed, market—though trade continued to be important and Germany was not closed to foreign goods: for instance, Coca-Cola, had over fifty bottlers in Germany in 1939. Nazi economic philosophy also envisaged a system of direction for industry, though not the total statist planning and ownership that characterized the Soviet economy.[18]

The radical side to Nazi economic policy was often hidden behind support for a cautious, gradualist approach to business elites immediately after 1933. Göring serves as a good example of a leading Nazi who knew little about formal economics, and who on the surface appeared conciliatory toward business. But underneath lurked a radical.[19] By 1937 he had sought to transform relations between the state and the economy through an extensive system of regulatory offices—and where necessary by the state ownership of industry.

Two examples illustrate more clearly how relations with business developed. First, as part of a drive towards autarchy, Göring tried to persuade German mining and smelting interests to develop factories which could use low-grade German ore rather than imported Swedish ore, which used up scarce foreign currency and whose supply was vulnerable in the event of war. When most industrialists proved less than enthusiastic, Göring threatened them with arrest for sabotage. Continued lack of cooperation led to the creation of the Hermann Göring Works to undertake the task. After the incorporation of Austria into Germany and the takeover of Czechoslovakia during 1938–9, this expanded from its Salzgitter base to encompass numerous factories across Central Europe. By the outbreak of war, it had replaced IG Farben as Germany's—and Europe's—largest company.

Relations with IG Farben are also revealing.[20] Before 1933 the company had often been attacked by the Nazis as an example of Jewish capitalism—a charge encouraged by the fact that several Jews sat on the board. Predictably, its directors were hardly pro-Nazi. Nor were they the rapacious working-class bashers of Marxist demonology. Yet the introduction of the first Four Year Plan in 1936 brought them into close cooperation with the party and state, as the Nazis realized they needed the expertise of firms like IG Farben to help produce the maximum degree of self-sufficiency in a series of products and raw materials. By the end of World War II, IG Farben managed a whole series of factories that used slave labor, including part of the Auschwitz concentration camp. A combination of the (usually latent) threat of coercion with an ideological appeal to create a new Germany and corporate self-interest had turned the company into a major prop for the Nazi regime.

This economic system has often been described as disorganized and chaotic. It certainly encouraged bureaucracy and conflicts of priorities, as the failings of the Nazi war economy before 1942 were to reveal. There is also no doubt that the Nazis were lucky in coming to power at the bottom of the depression. Part of their "success" in reviving the economy stemmed from general economic trends. But Nazi policy played a part too. This was not simply a question of the boost given to the economy by rearmament. *Gleich-schaltung* played a part too, especially through policies such as discrimination against foreign companies, the favoring of firms producing new products, the admiration for innovative designers (like Ferdinand Porsche, creator of the Volkswagen), and the general emphasis on good relations between employer and worker. It has even been argued that they helped to lay the basis for West Germany's postwar economic miracle.[21]

Gleichschaltung for the army was initially an even more delicate task than for business. Although formally the servant of the government, the army had a long tradition of being a state within the state.[22] During the closing years of the Weimar Republic, Schleicher had been the *éminence grise* of the military. But he sought to engineer an authoritarian conservative regime rather than a Nazi dictatorship, a rebirth of the Wilhelminian system under which Germany had become a world power. Although there was some sympathy for the Nazis among the officer class, especially in the junior ranks, in general the Nazis were looked down on as social upstarts. More importantly, many in the army viewed the socially radical wing of the party, especially the sizable SA, with suspicion.

Immediately after he became chancellor, Hitler tried to reassure military leaders that the army would remain an important pillar of the state. High priority was given to rearmament and to nationalist foreign policy initiatives, such as withdrawal from the League of Nations. Yet relations with an important section of the military leadership remained strained. During early 1934 these tensions, and Hindenburg's approaching death, encouraged leading conservative critics to believe that the army could be persuaded to depose the Führer. In a speech made by Papen on June 17, 1934, the vice chancellor condemned talk of the need for a second "revolution," and criticized Nazi hostility to the churches and opposing viewpoints. The speech set alarm bells ringing, for it raised the specter of a conservative-Reichswehr plot, possibly linked to a restoration of the monarchy as a means of furthering army support.

Fear of a coup, combined with intrigues by Röhm's many enemies in the Nazi Party, led Hitler in June 1934 to decide to kill two birds with one stone. In the bloody Night of the Long Knives not only radicals and opponents within the Nazi Party were murdered. Many conservatives who had aroused Hitler's fears or wrath were included on the death or imprisonment list. Among the more prominent figures in this category were Schleicher, who was shot in his own home, probably in repayment for his attempt to promote Gregor Strasser. Kahr, who had reneged on his beer hall deal with Hitler at the time of the 1923 Munich *putsch,* was executed. And the former chancellor, Brüning, would have been arrested had he not been out of the country.

Following the purge, relations with the military gradually improved, but the Nazis remained cautious about interfering with the structure and higher ranks of the military. The first major attempt to create a Nazified military did not come until early 1938, and even then developments owed more to chance and internal party scheming than to grand design. On January 12, 1938, the minister of war, Field Marshal von Blomberg, married. His bride quickly turned out to have been a prostitute, which would have been bad enough without the fact that Hitler had been an honored witness at the wedding. (Also present was Göring, who may well have plotted Blomberg's downfall to obtain his office.) Blomberg was duly sent on a lengthy foreign sojourn. Sensing a chance to broaden the attack, Himmler used the Gestapo to concoct evidence which showed that the army's supreme commander, General von Fritsch, was a homosexual. Fritsch was forced to resign in February 1938.

As on many other occasions, Hitler seized on chance and turned it to his advantage. He carried out a major reorganization of the military, abolished Blomberg's office, and took over the position of head of the armed forces himself. A cohort of generals were pensioned off, and the servile General Wilhelm Keitel was appointed chief of staff of the High Command.

The Blomberg affair was a powerful signal that the Nazis had no intention of allowing the military to remain the state within the state. A groundswell of opposition remained, nevertheless, among the officer class, as well as among the ranks, whose numbers were increased by the reintroduction of conscription in 1935. Although the oath of allegiance was an act of great symbolic force for a German officer, some were willing to engage in what amounted to treason. The most notable member of the military opposition was General Beck, an officer of the old school who believed that politics, like war, should be based on moral principles—a concept totally alien to the Nazi leadership. His resignation in August 1938 marked a further important step in the Nazis' control of the military leadership, though he remained active in plots against Hitler. Indeed Beck would probably have become head of state had the July 1944 bomb plot against Hitler succeeded. He was, instead, shot at his own request by a sergeant, having failed to take his own life.[23]

iv

WHAT IF HITLER had been overthrown by a military coup during 1938–9? How would the public have responded? Had the Nazis succeeded in creating a totalitarian consensus of support after 1933? Or was the dictatorship based on fear and more especially coercion? Definitive answers to such questions are impossible. Nevertheless, there is relatively good evidence for the attitudes of key groups during the 1930s.

A plebiscite that took place shortly after Hindenburg's death in 1934 recorded an 84.6 percent vote of approval for the governmental changes that had taken place since Hitler became chancellor. This figure needs to be treated with caution on several counts—including coercion, fear that the vote was not secret, and ballot rigging—but there are good grounds for thinking that Hitler personally enjoyed widespread popularity.[24] Secret reports taken for the SPD organization in exile at the time indicated that there was extensive support for rearmament and a foreign policy that restored national pride. They also indicated that the Führer myth was becoming a truly integrative force, reaching a peak after the fall of France in the summer of 1940. The Nazi Party itself was less popular. Tales quickly spread of Nazis making themselves rich through the spoils of office, while the use of surveillance and terror, or just the petty bureaucracy of having to deal with various party offices, also caused discontent.

The results of a referendum in the Saar region in 1935 also provide interesting evidence about attitudes. The Versailles Treaty had provided that a poll would take place after fifteen years to see if Saarlanders wanted to return to Germany. In free elections 90.9 percent voted to do so. Goebbels had run a shrewd radio propaganda campaign, backed up by whispered propaganda, which claimed that the Nazis would know how people had voted. Even so, it seems clear that most Saarlanders were willing to be part of the "new" Germany. Prior to 1933, the Saar had exhibited relatively weak Nazi support. In part this was a result of limited Nazi organizational and propaganda activity, but it also reflected the fact that the area had strong concentrations of Catholics and industrial workers. The 1935 referendum vote, therefore, underlines an important dimension in analyzing popular attitudes: support for Hitler and the Nazi Party came in different degrees. It is useful to distinguish between fanatical supporters and supporters with varying levels of reservation. It seems that most practicing Catholics and urban industrial workers fell into the latter category.[25]

After 1935, reports on public opinion indicate that a particularly important factor in growing working-class support was the decline in unemployment. Official statistics in early 1933 showed that just over 6 million were out of work; in reality the figure was much higher. By 1934 the average was 2.7 million; by 1937 it was down to 912,000; and by the outbreak of war there was a serious labor shortage. To some extent these figures have to be adjusted to take account of various "voluntary" and temporary work schemes and the reintroduction of conscription. Even so, it is easy to see why many people credited the Nazis with an economic miracle.

The growth in wages seems to have been less impressive, though it is difficult to be precise, as the indexes may have been rigged. Real wages rose slowly (from an index of 92.5 in 1933, to 103 in 1937), mainly through longer working hours. Skilled workers made the biggest gains in the late 1930s, and there were clear signs of the emergence of a consumer society. On the other hand, the less well-paid category of workers may have made no gains over the period, as inflation was relatively high on basic goods.

Simply focusing on money incomes, however, ignores a variety of fringe benefits and other changes in work practice encouraged by the DAF, and its Strength through Joy (KDF) offshoot. Factories were beautified in an extensive program to reduce alienation among the workforce, which was part of a general attempt by the Nazis to value manual work more highly and to break down the divisions between manual work and white-collar work.[26] More material benefits included a substantial increase in paid leave, and the November 1939 welfare reforms announced by Ley promised significantly improved benefits—at least for those who were truly part of the racial community (*Volksgemeinschaft*)—though this proposal met with widespread opposition from more conservative elements on grounds of cost, and Hitler felt that major social reform should wait until the war was over.

The KDF organized leisure activities, including sports and subsidized holidays—helped by funds sequestered from the unions, which were dissolved in 1933. Large sums were spent on holidays for the masses. A six-story, ten-thousand-room holiday hotel was built on the island of Rügen—though the outbreak of war meant it was never used, except as a shelter for those fleeing Allied bombing and the Red Army. But by this time over seven million people had gone on other KDF holidays, together with another thirty-five million who had been on day trips. The KDF was also responsible for the construction of a People's Car, the Volkswagen, which was to be paid for by weekly subscription. Although none had been supplied by the time war broke out in 1939, working prototypes were being tested (as were militarized versions). Indeed, Hitler had taken a strong personal interest in the design details of the car that was meant to bring motoring to the masses. Secret reports to the exiled SPD indicated that this plan, and more general KDF activities, met with much approval—a point played down by those who try to argue that the working class remained a bastion of class antagonism and opposition.[27]

Paradoxically, attitudes among the farming community, which had played a major part in the rise of the Nazis, seem to have been more mixed. The Nazis had promised a great deal before coming to power and subsequent policy did little to fulfill the aspirations they had raised.[28] The creation of national marketing boards helped to raise prices initially, but did little to stop the long-term drift away from the land. Nazi attacks on the churches often caused disquiet too, for rural communities tended to be highly religious. Some Nazis, most notably Darré, who became minister of agriculture in June 1933, tried a more radical approach. His Blood and Soil ideology sought to integrate peasants by valuing their labor, in the same way the KDF sought to appeal to industrial workers. He also promoted organic farming and other changes that were in tune with nature. More technocratic Nazis, however, were suspicious about the potential impact of his proto-ecological views on production. Other opponents feared that they were based on pan-European rather than national principles.[29]

The Nazi appeal to women evoked a similarly mixed response.[30] Gregor Strasser had allowed the leader of the Nazi women's section before 1933 to claim that there would be an important place for women of talent in a Nazi state. And some Nazis in 1933 thought that the social revolution should encompass giving women military training. But the majority of Nazis sought to push women back into traditional roles, and this view dominated policy immediately after 1933.

In the public sector, married women were often dismissed to make way for men—a policy already mooted by the Brüning government. In order to encourage marriage, a system of loans was introduced: over a million were given out to happy couples between 1933 and 1938 (to be more precise, to happy Aryan couples, for all Nazi social policies were related to race). The loans could be paid off by producing offspring, each one annulling a quarter of the debt. Family allowances were introduced too, and changes were made in income tax to help larger families. As in fascist Italy, there were considerable fears about the effects, both economic and military, of Germany's declining birth rate. The policy seems to have worked, as the number of live births rose by over a half between 1933 and 1939—though this may also have reflected a response to far better male employment prospects, which meant that working-class families could afford more children.

By this time, household incomes were often rising through the contribution of women's wages. Most Nazi leaders had never been completely opposed to women working. They accepted the need for unmarried women in the labor force and saw some careers as particularly suited to women: for instance nursing or welfare services. By the mid-1930s those in charge of economic planning realized that a more general input of female labor was necessary to help expansion and keep down inflation. As a result, the number of women in paid employment outside the home was nearly fifty percent higher in 1939 than in 1933, and labor shortages meant that the gap between men's and women's wages had fallen. But while there were some prominent working women in Nazi Germany, most notably Leni Riefenstahl and the test pilot Hanna Reitsch, the vast majority of jobs taken by women tended to be menial and poorly paid. In 1938 the leader of the Nazi women's group, Gertrud Scholtz-Klink, complained to the party about the denial of opportunities to women of talent.

It is important not to think that all, or even most, women were opposed to this situation. Socialized in a man's world, many accepted their roles as housewives, mothers, and holders of lesser jobs. Some seem to have treated Hitler like a Hollywood film star, showering him with love letters. One drooled: "I kiss you on the bottom and would like to undress for you, so that you feel how dear you are to me."[31] But women in general remained relatively immune to Nazi appeals. This was partly because regular religious attendance was stronger among women. It was also to do with organization. Although the Nazis formed women's groups, few joined—least of all mothers overburdened with bringing up children. Ensuring conformism through group norms, so important to the Nazi appeal among other groups, largely failed in the case of women.

Nazi youth organizations similarly failed to attract significant numbers of female members. From the outset, the party had placed great emphasis on attracting the young (though initially the emphasis was more on those in their late teens and especially the "war generation" rather than children). Youth was radical, virile, strong, traits which were eulogized in Nazi ideology. Youth was also capable of being molded more perfectly into the new "Nazi man." To further this goal after achieving power, the Nazis made significant changes to the school syllabus, including the teaching of racial biology and a greater emphasis on sports.

Outside school hours, there was a variety of party-organized "leisure" activities. A Hitler Youth (HJ) organization had been one of the first ancillary bodies created by the party in the 1920s. After 1933 this was to become the main organization for boys. (Girls had their own body.) By 1939 these had seven million members. Important aspects of their activities were related directly to military training, such as drill. Sports also figured prominently and were especially popular. During the 1936 Berlin Olympics, which received saturation media coverage, both youth and the nation as a whole thrilled to the long list of German victories. Willy Schumann, a nine-year-old Hitler Youth who lived in the port of Brunsbüttel, could remember decades later the great enthusiasm with which children counted the gold, silver, and bronze medals won by their country's heroic athletes.[32]

Many young people became deeply impregnated with Nazi ideas. During World War II, young soldiers revealed remarkable fanaticism in destroying German's enemies on the eastern front. And studies conducted after the end of the war showed a marked longing for a strong leader among this generation.[33] However, some young people remained immune to Nazi ideology. A few even openly spurned its militaristic authority and ritual. Groups like the Edelweiss Pirates roamed the countryside in nonconformist dress, sometimes attacking Hitler Youth patrols. The Swing Kids openly aped American dress and jazz, which Nazi propaganda despised as black and decadent.

There were frequent clamp-downs on such dissent, including the imprisonment and even execution of recalcitrants, but its existence reveals that the state could not control all walks of life. In spite of the symbolic burning of books in 1933, when the works of Jewish and left-wing authors in particular met a fiery end, there was some toleration of alternative views. American films were available until the late 1930s, as was much foreign contemporary literature, but the Nazis sought a far more totalitarian control of culture than Italian fascism. Together with the movement's anti-Semitism, a significant proportion of the most talented creative artists and thinkers were driven out of Germany.

Some decided to stay, and make their own minor forms of protest. The great conductor Wilhelm Furtwängler, for instance, refused to give the Nazi salute and tried to help Jews, but his very presence lent prestige to the regime and controversy still rages about his actions and motives. Others sought internal exile, withdrawing from intellectual life, or making only the occasional metaphorical foray into the real world. Jünger was one of the most prominent to take this latter route, appalled by the amorality of the Nazi leadership. He ended up like many other such internal exiles—a dissident member of the armed forces.

Opposition to the Nazis manifested itself in a variety of other social forms. Absenteeism among workers was one way of expressing an opinion about the regime's work ethic. Political jokes, too, circulated widely. A common aphorism mocked Nazi "new men" by characterizing them as "blond like Hitler, tall like Goebbels, slim like Göring, and able to hold their drink like Ley."[34] But the climate of fear inspired by the use of informants as well as overt terror bred a tendency to mind one's own business or to immerse oneself in apparently apolitical pursuits, such as following sports or watching films—pastimes ardently sponsored by the regime as a means of social control. While the regime in many ways built a sense of community at the abstract, *Volksgemeinschaft*, level, in other ways it destroyed social bonds: paradoxically, it also in some ways created a more individualistic culture. Even friends and neighbors could not be trusted: the police seem to have obtained more information from voluntary denunciations by people seeking to curry favor, or resolve a grudge, than from paid informants.

Predictably, there was little serious overt political dissent. The forces of repression were simply too strong. Of the just over three hundred thousand Communist Party members in January 1933, over half were imprisoned or sent to concentration camps, and thirty thousand were murdered. Although communists were the main early target of the Nazis, these numbers give some idea of the extent of the post-1933 terror. Subsequently, an extensive system based on paid informers and voluntary denunciations created a widespread climate of fear, which made any kind of underground political organization difficult to maintain (though both the SPD and KPD sought to preserve cells).[35] It is, therefore, not surprising to find that the most serious attempt on Hitler's life before the July 1944 plot came when a man working totally alone set a bomb off during the Munich beer hall celebrations on November 8, 1939. Hitler survived only by making a surprise early departure. Two university students, Hans and Sophie Scholl, who bravely distributed anti-Nazi leaflets in public during early 1943, were similarly not part of a large underground political organization. They were arrested and tortured terribly, to force them to reveal other contacts, and Sophie was executed while in agony with a broken leg.

Before *Kristallnacht*, Jews were not systematically rounded up into concentration camps. If they were incarcerated, it was mainly because of "wild" actions, or because they were Marxists or some other form of designated enemy of the regime. The Nazi leadership's policy toward Jews during 1933 to 1939 was to eliminate them gradually from all walks of life and pressurize them to emigrate. As a result, between 1933 and *Kristallnacht*, two-fifths of the 562,000 people whom the regime categorized as Jews had left.

Many of those who left first had feared arrest for their political views or had talents that meant they could find work abroad—although not many countries welcomed Jewish refugees. Others who joined the early exodus came from the ranks of those pushed out, Jews in "inessential" occupations where they could easily be replaced. Some who could have left, initially chose to stay. A prominent figure in this category was Max Warburg, a member of the great banking family.[36] Like the vast majority of Jews, he felt truly German and emotionally tied to his homeland. His banking expertise enabled him to help other Jews emigrate, in particular by a remarkable arrangement made with Zionist Jews in Palestine which allowed the transfer of money from Germany through a reciprocal arrangement to buy German goods. Eventually, fifty thousand Jews were to leave by this route.

As late as January 9, 1938, Warburg could be found hammering the mezzuzah nail to dedicate a new Jewish Community Center in Hamburg. For the Jews who remained, life had to go on. But it was a leperlike life of increasing harassment and strain. After a notable lull during 1936 to coincide with the Olympics, when the regime was eager to court favorable world opinion, the Nazis had begun more systematically to take over Jewish assets at knock-down prices, and to exclude Jews from all walks of life. Against this worsening background, Warburg sailed to the United States in August 1938. He meant to return, but after agonizing with his conscience following *Kristallnacht*, he remained in North America, thus avoiding imprisonment—the fate which befell most other wealthy Jews.

The German people seem to have responded to the Jewish policy in mixed ways. There was a strong tradition of anti-Semitism, though it is wrong to see it as leading inevitably to a leader like Hitler—as some have implied.[37] During 1930 to 1932 the Nazis toned down, or dropped, their anti-Semitism in many areas because it was losing them votes. In early 1933 there was some public opposition to "wild" actions and boycotts against Jews. But the general apparatus of repression quickly made people realize the dangers of opposition. The 1935 Nuremberg Laws, which effectively withdrew citizenship from non-Aryans and banned marriage and sexual contacts between Aryan and non-Aryan, aroused little opposition, partly because some people seem to have hoped that the new laws would appease the fanatical anti-Semites and put a final end to "wild" actions.

Kristallnacht in November 1938 evoked more response. Many Germans felt sympathy for the plight of the Jews. Some even helped where they could, though this was often difficult in view of the roundups in which people were carted away. By this time, however, there seems to have been a growing sense of a new national community that did not include the Jews: they were mentally, if not physically beyond the pale. It is difficult to put figures on complex attitudes, but probably at least twenty percent of Germans could be considered serious anti-Semites, and at least another thirty percent were indifferent to the fate of the Jews.[38]

The Nazis had achieved much during six years of government. Although they came to office lacking clear plans in many areas, there was a definite desire to create a new political consciousness, especially to forge a nation united around a sense of German racial identity. Many critics have argued that the Nazis failed to create a social revolution.[39] If a revolution is understood to mean a significant shift in class relations, including a redistribution of income and wealth, then there was no Nazi revolution. But as the Bolsheviks found after 1917, it is difficult to conduct such a revolution without causing internal chaos. The Nazis, like the Italian fascists, sought to conduct a gradual revolution, which involved a degree of compromise and pragmatism. The policy toward the Jews bears this out: virulent anti-Semites collaborated with Zionists, Jews who were socially useful were initially allowed to keep their jobs, and so on. Underlying everything, however, was an ideologically driven world.

Germany: War and Death

EVEN BEFORE HITLER came to power, German governments had been moving away from the conciliatory foreign policy pursued by Stresemann during the 1920s. The arrival of Hitler on the international scene hastened the process of German self-assertion.

By 1933 Hitler's general views on foreign policy were relatively clear. At their core was a long-term goal to expand into Eastern Europe. While writing *Mein Kampf* after the Munich *putsch*, Hitler became familiar with the geopolitical ideas of Karl Haushofer. He found them congenial because they synthesized different academic disciplines and because of their basic implications for Germany.[1] Hitler had already shown that he was less interested than most radical nationalists in the restoration of Germany's colonies. Geopolitical theory furthered his belief that Germany's destiny lay in expansion eastward (*Lebensraum*), a view supported by a remarkable body of academic thought.[2] But in the short run, after 1933 Hitler's sights were focused more on rearmament and the redress of specific grievances relating to the Versailles Treaty.

During the Disarmament Conference that was held in Geneva in February 1933, the British proposed a reduction of French forces and the granting to Germany of military equality. There had always been strong doubts in British governing circles about key aspects of Versailles, and this proposal was meant to remove a major German grievance without setting in motion an arms race. Hitler welcomed the plan as offering an opportunity to achieve a long-lasting European settlement. Then, adopting a tactic he was to follow on subsequent occasions, he upped the demands. As he undoubtedly realized, fears of a German revival meant the French were unwilling to agree to any significant changes in the military balance. They therefore rejected Germany's proposals and provided the pretext for Hitler to withdraw from the negotiations. At the same time, Hitler announced that Germany was leaving the League of Nations, claiming that its legitimate grievances had been systematically ignored.[3] A subsequent referendum showed overwhelming support for these actions, which helped to legitimize Hitler's policies in foreign as well as domestic eyes.

The consolidation of Hitler's dictatorship within Germany during 1934 and the clear evidence that Germany was committed to significant rearmament led the British government to announce a program of limited rearmament. Shortly afterward, the French extended their period of conscription from twelve to eighteen months. The Germans used this as an excuse to announce the reintroduction of conscription themselves. This in turn reinforced Mussolini's fears that German eyes might turn toward union with Austria (the Anschluss), and even to the recovery of the South Tyrol (Alto Adige)—fears that were reinforced by the unsuccessful Nazi coup in Austria during 1934.

The British government still hoped to solve the problem of the reemergence of Germany as a major European power by diplomatic rather than military means. This fit in well with Hitler's plans, for he hoped he could reach some agreement with the British that would allow them to keep their empire while Germany expanded into the east. He therefore renewed a proposal for a naval agreement. The result was the the June 1935 Naval Treaty, which gave Germany the right to expand its navy to thirty-five percent of the size of the British fleet. (Germany reserved the right to parity in submarines.) Hitler afterward described it as the happiest day of his life. Further joy followed when in October Italy invaded Ethiopia. The British forced a reluctant French government to condemn the aggression with them and impose sanctions. The Germans contributed their piece to the final breakdown of the Stresa Front by secretly supplying arms to the Ethiopians, thus prolonging the war well into 1936.

In March 1936 Hitler attempted his most daring act to date. Against the advice of his leading generals, he reoccupied the demilitarized Rhineland.[4] German rearmament had not yet produced many weapons, and the number of troops involved in the action was relatively small. The French forces facing the German border were far stronger in number, but the terrible casualties suffered by France in World War I had encouraged a defensive mentality in both the military and politicians. The British, moreover, were less than lukewarm about backing France militarily. Hitler had gambled and won—a remarkable coup, for even a token show of French force would probably have led him to back down. The stakes were high, for failure might have provoked a military coup, or at least considerable restraints on his future actions. Instead, the reoccupation boosted Hitler's public standing. More importantly, it was a major factor in his growing contempt for professional advisers, and increased his belief that he was born under a lucky star.

At the outbreak of the Spanish Civil War in July 1936, German Foreign Ministry officials advised against involvement, mainly on the grounds that Spain was not central to German interests. Hitler, encouraged strongly by Göring and some sections of the military, favored intervention on behalf of General Franco's rebel troops. Göring was eager to trade arms for raw materials that were important to rearmament plans; the military saw the chance to test new weapons and tactics. The war quickly proved to have another dimension. It brought Italy, which also supplied arms and troops to Franco, closer to Germany, and heightened awareness of an impending struggle between fascism and democracy. Hitler had always admired Mussolini for the dynamic way he had led the overthrown Italian democracy, but Mussolini was initially far less impressed by the Führer, whom he found domineering and rambling. By 1936, however, he was beginning to fall under Hitler's personal spell, and the growing rapprochement between the two countries was symbolized in November 1936 by Mussolini's reference to the emergence of the Rome-Berlin Axis.

The German-Japanese Anti-Comintern Pact, agreed to the previous month, was another important development. Although not a military alliance, it clearly targeted the Soviet Union and communism as major enemies of the two regimes. It was concluded despite the opposition of both the German military and the Foreign Office. While the military leadership was strongly anticommunist, close relations had been built up with Russian counterparts as a result of secret military cooperation between the countries during the 1920s. Additionally, some military officers had worked with Chinese nationalist forces, which were threatened by Japanese expansionism. More fundamentally, there were fears particularly in the Foreign Office that the pact marked a dangerous move toward worldwide aspirations (*Weltpolitik*).

There has subsequently been much debate about whether Hitler remained true to the quest for *Lebensraum*, or whether in the late 1930s he was turning to more global goals.[5] But it is not necessary to make a crude distinction between Hitler the Central Europeanist and Hitler the World Supremacist. Hitler's primary goal was expansion to the east, but he believed that at some point conflict was likely with other power blocs, especially with the rising power of the United States—a country he despised as riddled with ethnic divisions and obsessed with individual wealth, though his feelings were tinged with fascination for its youth and dynamism.[6] In the mid-1930s Hitler was still a great admirer of the British empire and had no significant designs on it. Indeed, the Anti-Comintern Pact was partly designed to warn Britain that it had big potential enemies in the Far East and that if it were not careful it might find itself fighting on two major fronts. Hitler seems still to have hoped that Britain could be forced into some form of accommodation toward German ambitions in eastern and southeastern Europe.

Hitler's thoughts on further expansion were made clear in a meeting which he and Göring held with the foreign minister, Konstantin von Neurath, and military chiefs in November 1937. They expressed strong doubts, which encouraged the Führer to take advantage of the Blomberg-Fritsch crisis to make a series of changes to military and diplomatic personnel during early 1938. In particular Hitler swept away the conservative old guard, such as Neurath, in order to prepare for more daring initiatives.

Hitler's foreign policy has been described as largely pragmatic and reactive.[7] He was certainly quick to respond to chance, as can be seen in the moves that led to the incorporation of Austria into the Reich. The flaring up of a crisis in Austria during early 1938 encouraged Hitler to demand that the country be turned into what amounted to a German satellite. Realizing that Mussolini had withdrawn Italian protection and fearing local Nazi violence, the Austrian chancellor, Kurt von Schuschnigg, appeared to concur. But shortly afterward he announced that a referendum would take place on Austrian independence. Following a brief period of further political maneuvering between the two sides, Hitler decided to take military action, and on March 12 German troops crossed the border. The union of Austria and Germany, the Greater Germany of many nineteenth century nationalists' dreams, had at last been achieved. The Reich now encompassed seventy million Germans, almost double the population of France, though well below that of the feared and despised USSR.

An ever more confident Hitler now began to set the pace more clearly. Together with the ban on union with Austria, the territorial aspect of the peace treaties that had most angered Germans was the eastern border, which had left many German speakers outside the Reich. Even the conciliatory Stresemann had not been willing to guarantee the sanctity of these borders, though in the 1925 Locarno Treaty he had accepted Germany's new western frontier. Hitler was helped in his attempt to regain the largely German-speaking Czech Sudetenland by the presence of a local party whose leader, Konrad Henlein, was effectively under Nazi control. After the Anschluss, Henlein increasingly exploited grievances and made ever greater demands on the Czech government. The Czechs responded by bending over backward to accommodate pressures for autonomy, but by mid-September it was becoming clear that Hitler's real goal was nothing less than the destruction of the Czechoslovak state.

The situation quickly escalated into a major European crisis. The Sudetenland had a sophisticated network of defenses and considerable raw materials, which encouraged the Czechs to consider fighting rather than accepting the loss of the territory. Czech resolve was reinforced by their belief that France and the USSR were pledged by treaty to defend them. The French were again loath to fight without British support—fearing that Britain was willing to fight until the last Frenchman—and the Russians would not act unless the French did. After a piece of pioneering shuttle diplomacy by the British prime minister, Neville Chamberlain, a four-power conference was set up in Munich at the end of September. There, Chamberlain and the French prime minister, Édouard Daladier, confirmed that they would not fight for a faraway country about which they knew little, in the words of Chamberlain. Instead, they agreed to inform the hapless Czechs that they must hand over to Germany a third of their population and some of their most important industrial areas.

Chamberlain, and less certainly Daladier, had deluded themselves that Germany's relations with the Czech state were now resolved; and they also hoped that Mussolini's role in convening the Munich conference indicated that Italy was far from fully committed to the German camp. In March 1939 delusion turned to anger and apprehension when German troops marched into Prague and annexed the Czech rump state. The following month, Italian expansionist ambitions were underlined by the invasion of Albania. The British government quickly responded by guaranteeing the independence of Poland, Romania, and Greece. At last it seemed to be dawning on the British "appeasers" that the dictators had major territorial ambitions and could not be trusted to keep their word.

Hitler's eyes were already turning toward Poland. Whereas twenty percent of Czechoslovakia's population had been German, Germans in Poland accounted for only two percent. In German revanchist sentiment, however, this was minimized by the fact that Poland had gained land at German expense. Furthermore the creation of a Polish corridor to the sea meant that East Prussia was physically cut off from the rest of the Reich. Hitler now planned to resolve these remaining border issues by destroying the Polish state.

Hitler saw the main problem as diplomatic. In spite of Britain's recent guarantee to Poland, he believed the British would probably not enter the fray. He did not believe it was in Britain's interests to fight to prevent Germany expanding into Eastern Europe. Even if Germany were defeated, "victory" could only be Pyrrhic, resulting in the impoverishment of Britain and the continued growth of American and Soviet power. He was less sure, however, of the French and Soviet responses, especially as the two countries were tied by a 1935 pact aimed at countering German expansionism. The collapse of Poland could trigger a Soviet response, which in turn might finally stiffen French resolve.

Hitler's long-standing desire for an understanding with Britain was not shared by the man who had succeeded Neurath as foreign minister, Joachim von Ribbentrop.[8] Ribbentrop was a socially ambitious man, who had married well and falsely assumed his aristocratic prefix. His suave manners and linguistic ability had led to his being sent to London as ambassador in 1936 in the belief that he would be accepted by Britain's social elite. Instead, because of his arrogance and lack of basic diplomatic skills, he was virtually shunned—he was often referred to as "Ambassador Brickendrop." Ribbentrop returned to Germany convinced that the main short-term diplomatic goal was not Anglo-German but German-Russian understanding.

In 1922 Germany and the USSR—two diplomatic leper states—had signed a treaty that provided Germany with secret facilities for military training and the Soviets with German goods. The agreement had broken down when Hitler came to power, but there were groups on each side who hoped that contacts might be reestablished. Many in the German military and Foreign Office were committed to a policy of limited German expansion eastward. As a result, they believed that a realpolitik accommodation could be reached, especially as there was little love lost between the USSR and some of the buffer states, notably Poland, which had gained territory at Russian as well as German expense. Some business interests too saw great opportunities for trade. On the Soviet side, there was growing exasperation after 1935 at British and French weakness, which could all too easily be interpreted as a deliberate attempt to turn Germany eastward. The lack of urgency that the British and French accorded to military talks with the USSR after their guarantees to Poland seemed to confirm that the two countries could not be trusted to save communism. The result was the Nazi-Soviet Pact, signed by Ribbentrop in Moscow on August 23, 1939, which divided Poland into German and Soviet spheres. The USSR also agreed to supply Germany with raw materials, while the Germans agreed to furnish munitions and high-technology products in return.

There was still some opposition, both within the Nazi leadership and among military and diplomatic circles, to an imminent attack on the Poles. Göring, for instance, favored economic penetration of Eastern Europe and the use of diplomacy to gain further territorial concessions. Goebbels feared the impact of war on public opinion. But Hitler's mind was made up. Although some have argued that he was seeking to use martial glory as a way of resolving growing public discontent, there seems little doubt that his main motive was ideological: war was to mark the beginning of serious expansion into the east.[9] In the early hours of September 1, 1939, German troops invaded Poland. By September 3 the British and French were also at war with Germany—having decided to honor their guarantees, which had been made more as a deterrent than in the belief that fighting would actually begin.

ii

THE OUTBREAK OF WAR was not greeted in Germany by the scenes of jubilation that had characterized the heady days of August 1914. Propaganda told the German people that the Poles had badly mistreated their German minority. A fake attack on a German radio transmitter was even staged on August 31 to show that it was Germany which was the victim of aggression. The remarkable speed of the Germans' *Blitzkrieg* victory, however, did far more than propaganda to resolve any lingering doubts. In less than two weeks Polish resistance had collapsed, and Germany had suffered remarkably few casualties. Shortly afterward the hapless Poles suffered a second invasion, when poorly equipped Soviet troops arrived to take their share of the booty.

In the spring of 1940 the *Blitzkrieg* swept over Denmark and Norway. These had not initially formed part of Hitler's strategic vision, but Swedish iron ore was vital to the German economy. Fears that the British might occupy Norway to cut off this supply prompted a German attack northward. After a brief but heroic defense by the Norwegians and belated intervention by the British and French, further great victories were secured.

In May 1940 it was Belgium, Holland, and France's turn to face the onslaught. Attack in the west seemed to pose far more serious problems (though the agreement with the USSR meant that the Germans were able to keep only minimal forces on its new eastern frontier). The French had built a great defensive screen, stretching from the Swiss border to Belgium. Behind this Maginot Line, the French had superiority in numbers of troops and tanks, though the French air force was inferior to the Luftwaffe. But the French spread their tanks across the front and their forces lacked the confidence and élan of the victorious German armies. They also totally failed to anticipate the direction of the main thrust.

During the winter of 1939–40, Hitler and leading staff officers had separately developed the idea that the focus of the German attack should be through the supposedly impenetrable Ardennes mountains and forest, at the northern end of the Maginot Line. Having made the breakthrough, the forces would then drive for the English Channel, thus splitting the main Allied forces in two. The plan worked almost perfectly, though a decision to halt the Panzers short of the Channel in order to recoup allowed a miraculous evacuation of over three hundred thousand primarily British troops through the port of Dunkirk. The remaining French army, now in a state of shock, quickly crumbled as the German armor swept south. On June 16, the eighty-four-year-old World War I hero Marshal Pétain became French prime minister. Six days later the French signed an armistice in the same railway dining car in which German representatives had been forced to surrender at the end of World War I.

Vast crowds cheered Hitler when he appeared on the Chancellery balcony in Berlin after returning from a triumphal lightning tour of Paris. There seems little doubt that the adulation was genuine, though it was undoubtedly related to the belief that peace was now in sight.[10] Unfortunately for Hitler, the British showed no sign of negotiating. Winston Churchill, who had become prime minister in May, spoke in resonant terms of fighting on the beaches and from every ditch throughout the land (though some powerful figures pressed for an accommodation with the all-conquering Nazis). Göring responded by assuring Hitler that the Luftwaffe could bomb Britain into submission. Initially the tactic seemed to be working, but a crucial change of attack from the airfields to the cities helped to swing the balance in Britain's favor.

The remarkable solo flight to Britain in early May 1941 by Hitler's deputy, Rudolf Hess, has often been seen as a dramatic final attempt to negotiate a settlement. There is no doubt that Hess remained in contact with Karl Haushofer, who counseled the need for British friendship. And Haushofer's son, Albrecht, knew the Duke of Hamilton, whose home in Scotland Hess was trying to

find. It seems more likely, however, that Hess was mainly motivated by his increasing political marginalization. Although formally
second only to Hitler in the party hierarchy, he found that others
had built far more powerful empires within the party and state apparatus. This interpretation seems to be borne out by Hitler's anger
on hearing of the flight, which so upset him that for a time his attention was diverted from the imminent invasion of Russia.[11]

German officers who had liaised with the Red Army during the
occupation of eastern Poland believed that the recent Great Purges
had left the Red Army emasculated. The image was reinforced by
its poor showing during the subsequent winter war with Finland.
Given Hitler's sweeping ambitions in the east it was therefore inevitable that his thoughts would turn to an attack on the homeland
of the hated communism. Although some have argued that the
Nazi attack on Russia was a preemptive strike, ideology was inevitably driving Hitler eastward.[12] Indeed, Hitler first mooted an invasion as early as July 1940, but the undertaking required a major
military refit and extensive planning.

The initial goal was to attack in May 1941, but preparations
were delayed while sufficient supplies were built up. Some delay
may also have resulted from the Germans once again bailing out the
Italians. (An army under General Rommel had already been sent to
prop up their resistance to the British in Libya.) After belatedly entering the war in June 1940, Mussolini had been rewarded with few
spoils. He was troubled by growing German economic and political
influence in southeastern Europe, where the Soviet Union also had
ambitions, especially after its occupation of part of Romania. Mussolini's response was to order an attack on Greece. This proved a
disaster, as the Greeks, backed by British troops, drove the Italians
back into Albania. The Germans decided it was necessary to secure
the Balkan flank by invading Greece and also Yugoslavia, where a
coup had just brought to power an antifascist government.

Operation Barbarossa, the attack on the Soviet Union, finally
commenced on June 22, 1941. The Germans committed 187 divisions, backed by Finnish and Romanian troops. In spite of warnings
from several sources, the Soviet leadership was caught totally unprepared. In the opening hours of the campaign most Soviet planes
were destroyed on the ground. Only 444 of the 3,648 German

tanks used were the latest type of Panzer IVs, compared to the Soviet complement of 1,861 of the roughly made but excellent T34
and other heavy tanks, plus thousands of obsolete models. But with
the Russians lacking air cover and their High Command in disarray, the Germans quickly made vast gains and took huge numbers
of prisoners.

By early December the story was very different. General Winter had struck with a vengeance. The Germans were ill equipped
for fighting in the desperately cold Russian weather, where tem-
peratures could drop to forty degrees below freezing, at which
point machines and humans ceased to function efficiently—if at all.
Soon a hundred thousand men were suffering from frostbite, and
desperate appeals were being made in Germany for the public to
donate winter clothing.

Part of the reason for the German reverse was an inability to organize war production efficiently, but there was an underlying ideological difficulty too, relating to the basic *Blitzkrieg* philosophy.
Some critics have argued that this strategy was developed because
the Nazis feared public opinion in the event of a drawn-out war:
memories of revolution after 1918 were still strong. Others have
stressed the fact that Germany's resources did not allow for a long
war against opponents capable of mobilizing large numbers of
troops and reserves of economic wealth[13] There is no doubt that
both factors, the second especially, played their part. But it is also
important to note the Blitzkrieg's more ideological appeal to Nazis.
It combined high technology with a traditional view of individual
valor: the pilot and the tank commander were the surrogate knights
of old. The emphasis on the sudden strike, the decisive moment,
elevated the importance of leadership and will: central facets in
Hitler's thinking.

Hitler's views also played a more specific part during late 1941.
The victory in France had convinced him that he was a military genius, a view encouraged by obsequious political and military sub-
ordinates, like Keitel—who called him the "Greatest War Lord of
All Times." The result was that Hitler played down the contribution made by professional soldiers to past victories, and increasingly
ignored their judgments. In the summer of 1941 this may have led
to a crucial error. Much of the High Command sought to push di-

rectly ahead toward Moscow. Instead, Hitler turned the German armies north and south in great pincer movements, thus capturing vast numbers of prisoners. These had proved good tactics when the lines of communication were short. Now the German forces were logistically stretched even before the onset of winter, a danger that Hitler played down in his tendency to treat war like a giant board game. Had the Germans pushed on to the gates of Moscow, the Soviets might have been tempted into one final great battle. Even if the Soviets had continued to retreat, the capture of the capital would have been a grave psychological blow.[14]

Instead, on December 6 the Germans were surprised by a major counterattack. Information from the Soviet master spy Richard Sorge indicated that Japan was preparing a strike against the United States—a telling comment on the failure of the Nazis to coordinate a world strategy, for the Japanese only needed to maintain a serious threat of invasion in order to tie up large numbers of Soviet troops. Freed from the fear of a Japanese attack, crack and experienced Soviet troops equipped for winter fighting were moved from the Siberian front. Soviet fighting resolve was further reinforced by draconian discipline, imposed by political commissars—who themselves faced sanctions against their families in the event of being captured. "Comrade, kill your German" (or be killed) was now the universal catchphrase. Defense of "Mother Russia," rather than "International Brotherhood," became the metaphor.

The German forces had helped to sow this whirlwind of hate. They could have come as liberators, exploiting anticommunist sentiment, especially among the non-Russian nationalities. The diversion away from Moscow to swing into the Ukraine would have made sense if a "liberationist" philosophy had been part of the grand design. Instead, little was made initially of such possibilities. Although peasants were sometimes promised land, the need for immediate agricultural production meant that collectives were often taken over and run as Nazi concerns. Even more damagingly, racial theory relegated the Slavs to the role of Germany's future slaves. The appalling treatment of prisoners and local populations encouraged military resistance and the creation of partisan units. The army lived off the land, a euphemism for taking from the poorest of peasants. Prisoners were often shot out of hand or left to starve: approximately 2.25 million were never to return. Whole villages were massacred, often as reprisal for guerrilla attacks—but the excessiveness of the German response encouraged yet more Russians to seek safety, and revenge, among the partisans in the forests and marshes.[15]

Faced at the beginning of December 1941 by a powerful and ruthless Soviet onslaught, most of the High Command recommended a tactical retreat. Hitler responded by ordering his commanders to stand their ground, fearing the psychological effect of a retreat from Moscow in winter, which would have evoked powerful visions of Napoleon's fateful retreat in 1812, when vast numbers of troops had been lost. On this occasion, Hitler was undoubtedly right. But defense in such conditions was no easy option. It was a bloody, grim affair, with the weather adding to the troops' woes and taking its own toll.

iii

BETWEEN THE SIGNING of the Nazi-Soviet Pact and the commencement of Barbarossa, Goebbels had allowed anticommunism largely to disappear from German propaganda. In the days immediately following the invasion, a new wave of propaganda portrayed the Germans as striking preemptively in order to prevent a Soviet attack. As the Panzers rolled ever deeper into the Russian steppes, however, old stereotypes began to reemerge in German propaganda. In particular, communism was portrayed as an alien Jewish creed, imposed on the simple Slavs by fanatical and ruthless political commissars. Propaganda of this kind was designed to do far more than bolster support for the war effort. It was aimed at nothing less than preparing opinion for a new Germanic racial order in Eastern Europe.

Hitler's plans for change in Eastern Europe were not conditioned simply by the desire for treaty revision or by an economically driven quest for land and raw materials. They were based on an utter contempt for the indigenous peoples, whom he likened to the Indians of North America: primitive peoples whose lands needed to be taken by the more dynamic and virile race—a German version of American "manifest destiny." If anything, during the 1930s this racism was reinforced by growing interest in Japan, the most ethnically pure of the major powers, and a country that was following a policy of brutal suppression and murder in conquered China and Korea.

To complete the extinction of Poland, Hitler had made Himmler—as head of the SS, which from the outset had been based on strict racial selection and indoctrination—Reich Commissar for the Consolidation of Ethnic Germandom, a new office endowed with sweeping powers in the conquered territories.[16] A major task given to the SS, whom Himmler sometimes compared to Japanese Samurai, was the clearing of tracts of *Lebensraum*, where German settlers could begin a new life, unpolluted by the racially inferior. As a result, many Poles were sent wandering from their homes with nothing but a small suitcase, a blanket, and a handful of food and cash. The less fortunate were taken to Germany, where they were kept in pitiful conditions, to become forced labor. Jews suffered an even worse fate. SS and military units sometimes massacred Jews on the spot, though in general Jews were herded into cramped and unsanitary ghettos, where they were kept in near starvation. Gypsies too, as carriers of alien and degenerate blood, were singled out for special treatment.

In September 1939 just under two hundred thousand Jews were still living in the German Reich. Officially the policy for Jews remained one of forced emigration. A special office of Himmler's Security Division of the SS had even been set up to speed emigration—a body which had been especially active in terrorizing Jews out of Austria after the Anschluss. In practice, the presence of over three million Jews in Poland changed the nature of the problem. No country was willing to accept so large a number—and Israel did not yet exist. Besides, Polish Jews were in the main relatively poor, unable to fund their passage, let alone to pay the leaving "tax" that was often levied by extortionate Nazi administrators, many of whom became rich through such practices within Germany.

At the time of the attack on the USSR, a definite decision on the fate of Europe's Jews had still not been reached. Within a matter of weeks, the issue quickly became one of the utmost urgency, for over six million Jews lived in the Soviet Union. The invading German armies had been issued with orders to shoot communist political commissars and officials who fell into their hands. Given the Nazi equation between Jews and communism, this encouraged the targeting of Jews, regardless of their political positions. Initially this mainly involved Germans killing Jews, but increasingly the task was left to the many anti-Semites who were to be found among Eastern Europe's population, and who had a strong tradition of engaging in pogroms.

At first, the main method of execution was shooting, but this program put considerable psychological strains on the troops involved. Some of the troops were formed into specially chosen killer units (*Einsatzgruppen*), but others were less homogeneous in their ideological and psychological bonding. A glimmer of the almost unimaginable horror of racial war can be gained by considering the killing of the Jews from the village of Józefów. The officer in charge was Major Wilhelm Trapp, a fifty-three-year-old policeman. Although he had joined the Nazis in 1932, he was no racial fanatic. When ordered to kill everyone in the village—except young males, who were to be kept for forced labor—he allowed those under his command who did not wish to participate to step out of line. Witnesses later in the day saw Trapp weeping, and justifying himself by saying that orders were orders. The troops involved paired up with Jews on trucks that took them just outside the village. There the Jews were shot—a task which often required several bullets to finish the job, as nerves and alcohol led to unsteady hands. At the end of a long day, fifteen hundred Jews lay dead in a mass grave.[17]

During 1941 a major change of policy took place concerning the fate of Jews and Gypsies throughout Europe. The exact timing of the decision to remove them to concentration camps and kill them systematically remains shrouded in fog. Some have argued that the autumn and early winter of 1941 were the crucial period. The main reason usually cited is frustration over the *Blitzkrieg*'s failure to destroy communism, the resulting tension encouraging Nazism to lash out at its most fundamental ideological enemies: the Jews.[18] Others have suggested late summer was the crucial date—a time when the Nazis seemed on top of the world and at last capable of realizing their racial fantasy of making Europe truly "Jew free." It was also a time when the Nazi leadership was becoming increasingly concerned by American support for the war effort, a commitment which they believed was driven by a Jewish desire to destroy Germany. It was during this period that preparations were made to gas the first prisoners at the Auschwitz concentration camp, which had been built in 1940 primarily for Polish political prisoners.[19]

Questions of timing are related to more fundamental issues about Nazi decision making. Those who view the Nazi state as a "polyocracy," or Hitler as a "weak" dictator, are often led to the conclusion that he played little or no part in the decisions that led to the systematic killing of Europe's Jews and others. Sometimes this is used to point the finger of guilt at Himmler and the SS, who provided some of the troops for the *Einsatzgruppen* and ran the concentration camps.[20] The camps were sometimes more than just prisons: they were a growing source of production. A pool of slave Jewish labor offered the prospect of massively expanding this empire and providing the SS with a source of income independent of party or state. When faced with vast numbers of Jews in the conquered territories, SS leaders like Reinhard Heydrich calmly but ruthlessly plotted to kill all but those who could work—and they would soon die of exhaustion or be thrown to the flames to make way for fresh recruits. Aided by countless functionaries such as Adolf Eichmann, the epitome of the "banality of evil," and by an army of doctors and other experts, ever more efficient forms of killing were sought out and implemented. (Some of the expertise came from practioners in the euthanasia program.)[21]

These arguments offer important perspectives, especially on the process by which a modern state could launch a program of mass murder—though even here they play down the role of Nazi ideology and the German tradition of racial thought in conditioning beliefs and action even among the more educated and scientific personnel involved.[22] It is virtually inconceivable, however, that the Final Solution could have taken place without Hitler, a man who believed that "all who were not racially pure were mere chaff." *Mein Kampf* and other statements by Hitler clearly reveal his obsession with Jews. It is true that he made few major speeches relating to the Jews in the years immediately after 1933, but this was a reflection of his desire to court moderate domestic and international opinion—and the fact that his priorities lay elsewhere. As war approached, clear intimations of his underlying anti-Semitism began to reappear: for instance in a speech to the Reichstag in January 1939, Hitler warned "International Jewry" that in the event of another major European war, this time the victims would be the Jews, not the Germans. Although this was not a major theme in his speeches and it should not be equated with the formulation of a genocidal plan, there is evidence that by July 1941 Hitler had either given direct verbal orders for the killing of the Jews or had made it clear to leading Nazis—especially the loyal and bureaucratically efficient Himmler—that this was his aspiration.[23]

The ensuing Holocaust became a modern version of hell. Camps were built, trains were chartered, even Jewish community officials were drawn into the bureaucracy to help provide priority lists of those to be taken. (They were obviously deceived about the true nature of "resettlement.") It was, in a cruelly perverse way, remarkable evidence of German efficiency and the power of the state. But it was also an inferno of chaos and torture, both mental and physical. Sometimes the deportations went smoothly, but on other occasions people committed suicide or resisted. Children were often separated from parents; families were divided. A railway service that charged excursion fares for the trip began by providing a foretaste of what was to come. Carriages were too good for Jews; instead, they were herded into cattle trucks for journeys that sometimes took days.

Some of the concentration camps had major war production, as well as killing, facilities—for instance, IG Farben's works beside Auschwitz-Birkenau. At these camps new arrivals were separated into those who could work and those who could not be exploited. Those spared rapid death eked out an existence in which death by disease, or on the whim of a guard, was an ever-present reality. Perhaps predictably, the best descriptions can only come from those who experienced such horrors, men like Primo Levi, who has written of his Auschwitz experience: "You who live safe In your warm houses . . . Consider if this is a man, Who works in the mud Who does not know peace Who fights for a scrap of bread Who dies because of a yes or a no."[24] It is difficult for those who live in the warm even to begin to imagine what it is like to be frozen to death in cold water in experiments to test the best way of reviving hypothermia victims. Yet that is how some victims died—in the name of science, and of German survival.

Considerable debate surrounds the question of how much the

German people knew about the Final Solution. Many Germans were later to claim they comprehended nothing of such horrors, but others have argued that awareness of the camps was widespread, and that by 1943 the use of poison gas as the means of killing was well known.[25] The claim needs probing very carefully; in particular it is necessary to distinguish between knowledge and belief.[26] Many may have heard rumors, but during World War I the British had spread the most outlandish stories about Germans, including claims that they boiled up bodies behind the front lines to provide necessary fats. It must have been easy to discount such stories as new propaganda, or simply to have considered them unbelievable. Certainly Speer, who by this time held ministerial office, which meant that he was ultimately responsible for the war production carried out in the camps, was later to claim that he was unaware of the program (though he had good reason to deny knowledge after 1945 and seems unquestionably to have understood the outlines of the Final Solution).[27]

It is also important to distinguish between *Einsatzgruppen*-type killings in the field and murder in the camps. Relatively few Germans worked in the main killing centers, like Auschwitz or Treblinka, all of which were outside Germany. (Concentration camps within the old German boundaries, like Dachau or Bergen–Belsen, were never used for mass killing, though thousands died in these camps from the appalling conditions near the end of the war.) It seems likely that far more information came back about shootings than gassings. It was easy, however, to interpret these as something other than genocide, especially as the occupying forces operated a ruthless policy of mass reprisals on civilians for partisan attacks, regardless of whether or not they were Jews. Public opinion surveys show an increase in anti-Semitism after the attack on the USSR, but the typical German citizen almost certainly lacked detailed knowledge about the killings. There were unquestionably rumors about mass racial murder, and by 1943 all the remaining Jews had been deported from Germany. (Approximately five thousand remained in hiding with German help.) But the predominant sentiment seems to have been one of indifference—the fate of the Jews was simply not a central concern.

During 1942–3 most Germans became increasingly preoccupied with the course of the war and with the fate of their loved ones. The euphoria following the early days of Barbarossa had given way to serious doubts as the attack was halted. The declaration of war against the United States after the Japanese attack at Pearl Harbor in December 1941 caused further apprehension. A rise in optimism can be charted during much of 1942, with new territorial gains being made in the USSR, with Rommel's army sweeping all before it in Africa, and with the U-boat campaign in the North Atlantic beginning to strangle Britain. By the summer of 1943 the military situation took a major turn for the worse. In February German troops around Stalingrad surrendered, a battle Hitler had sworn never to lose. By May Rommel had been chased out of Africa. In July the great tank engagement that raged around Kursk was lost. Shortly afterward, it became clear that the tide had turned in the U-boat war. And during the autumn it became necessary to withdraw thirty-five divisions from the eastern front in order to prop up Italian resistance, after an Allied landing in Sicily had led to the overthrow of Mussolini and Italy's withdrawal from the war.

Everyday life at home was getting worse too. There were growing shortages of goods, and prices were rising—partly fueled by the printing of money to pay for the war. Allied bombing of German cities was beginning to inflict serious damage and casualties. Before the war was over, more than three hundred thousand Germans were to lose their lives through bombing attacks—which sometimes went on night and day over the same target—and almost a million had been seriously wounded. Sometimes the result of bombing was like a scene from Armageddon. The firebombing attack on Hamburg during late July 1943 killed as many as forty thousand people, after horrifying hurricane-force winds swept people living near the epicenter into the inferno. Even canals and rivers caught fire because of the fuel that spilled from boats; many were burned to death while seeking refuge in the water. Another firebomb attack on the historic city of Dresden in February 1945 killed a similar number, though some have claimed far higher figures. Overall, the Allies dropped 650,000 tons of bombs in 1944, and another 500,000 tons during the first four months of 1945.

The raids were the source of great anger at the time and have been the source of much controversy since. But it is difficult to judge them a war crime, as some—especially Germans—have done. Initially, the main rationale was to boost British morale, to strike back in the only way possible and repay the German mass raids on cities like London and Coventry. Later, the attacks were justified by the damage they would inflict on morale and production. The fact that they do not seem to have had a great effect—though it is impossible to measure exactly what morale and production would otherwise have been—does not necessarily undermine the rationale. Perhaps by the time of Dresden the case for continuing was less clear, but at this time German resistance was still strong, and a rain of the new V2 rockets was falling on London.[28]

The main escalation of "strategic bombing" came at a time when the Germans were trying to increase war production substantially. The *Blitzkrieg* philosophy was linked to an economy that even in 1941 was not geared to fight an extended war. Various forms of inessential production and services, such as luxury goods shops, were still operating—mainly because the Nazis, fearing adverse public opinion, had tried to conduct the war without demanding undue sacrifices on the home front. Within the industrial sector, ideological opposition meant that no serious effort had been made to recruit female labor to free men for service at the front. By late 1941 Goebbels in particular wanted to change the tone of propaganda and emulate Churchill's entreaties to "blood, toil, tears, and sweat." But it was to be February 1943, in the traumatic aftermath of the Stalingrad defeat, before such propaganda got into full swing, though with the characteristic Nazi affinity for the past, Goebbels chose as his key phrase words immortalized by the German states' resistance to Napoleon in 1812: "Now Folk Rise Up and Storm Break Loose."[29] Behind this "total war" commitment lay a new economic reality. In February 1942 Speer had been appointed minister of armamaments and war production, a shrewd decision by Hitler, who realized that Speer had far more organizational talent than most of the other leading Nazis. He quickly helped bring about a remarkable increase in the supply of war matériel. In January 1942 the index of arms production had stood at 100; by July 1943 it was 229 and by July 1944 it had reached 322.[30]

Speer was a technocrat rather than an ideologue, and he was certainly no believer in racial utopias. He had been attracted to the

Nazis in the first place mainly by Hitler's charisma and a sense of grievance about Germany's condition. Yet he became corrupted by the general climate of opinion, which treated the peoples of Eastern Europe as subhumans, mere cogs in a process. Although the program began in 1939, under Speer the employment of foreign and slave labor reached new peaks. Some workers came of their own free will; others were prisoners of war who were not returned; many more were forced laborers, often rounded up from the streets like the victims of the press gangs of old. By the summer of 1944 approximately 2.8 million Russians, 1.7 million Poles, 1.3 million French, and approaching 2 million others were slaving for the Reich—often in appalling conditions even outside the concentration camps.

Germany's armed forces too were coming to rely more on a "European" input. A significant change had taken place on the eastern front, where the military leadership and at least part of the Nazi hierarchy had increasingly come to realize the advantage of recruiting locals. The new policy was not simply a question of taking locals on as auxiliaries, or to help hunt down Jews and run camps. By 1944 members of ex-Soviet nationalities, such as Ukrainians and Georgians, fought alongside Germans. Indeed, in some cases, they were better represented in the Wehrmacht than in the Red Army.[31] There was even some change in Nazi racial theory to accommodate such multinational forces, though the issue predictably caused divisions within the party. Some people in Eastern Europe, especially the Ukrainians, were portrayed as warrior peasants of old and thus capable of being assimilated into the Aryan tradition.

There had always been a strand in Nazism that was European rather than national, though in some sense the antithesis is false because many Nazis saw Germany as the natural leader of Europe.[32] But there was a more genuine side to Nazi Europeanism. The 1931 marriage order for the SS noted that it was "a union of Germans of Nordic characteristics." Even the purest of the pure had traits that extended beyond national boundaries, or likely future ones. During World War II this was consciously articulated into a Europeanist ideal in SS publications, and Nietzsche and others were conjured up as suitably prestigious founders of the cause. But it was probably more anticommunism that attracted volunteers from across Europe to the ranks of the Waffen SS—men like Léon Degrelle, the prewar leader of the Belgian Rexist Party. (Twenty-five hundred other Belgians fought with him on the eastern front.)[33] It is interesting to note that Hitler once told Degrelle that if he had ever had a son, he would have liked him to grow up like Degrelle, who chose the SS rather than his own country, and who fought with great valor.

iv

BY EARLY 1943 Hitler was showing clear signs of strain. His left arm was beginning to shake, and he was suffering from periods of dizziness, possibly symptoms of Parkinson's disease. Such was his general physical degeneration that the Führer had aged dramatically since the beginning of the war. His quack doctor, Theodor Morell, fed him no fewer than ninety separate patent medicines and injections. Always a faddish and erratic eater, Hitler now usually ate quickly alone. For relaxation, he would sometimes take his German shepherd bitch Blondi for a short walk. The view must have been uninspiring, for by this time Hitler had largely forsaken Berlin and the Berghof—which had been built in his beloved Obersalzberg at immense expense—to spend much of his time ensconced in his military headquarters in the east. This situation often exasperated Goebbels, who felt that the Führer's presence could have contributed significantly to morale after heavy bombing raids on German cities, or at some of the many Wagner concerts which were held for seriously wounded troops.

Hitler's dealings with military leaders became even more fraught. Occasionally, there were major disputes over tactics. More frequently Hitler gave a theatrical performance, which left many bemused, even angry. Typical of the latter reaction was Field Marshal Erich von Manstein's when he met Hitler shortly before the Kursk battle. Manstein had sometimes managed to persuade Hitler to take his advice. Yet at this crucial juncture, with Germany set to fight what was to be the greatest tank battle of all time, Hitler completely ignored issues of strategy and tactics. The meeting ended with Hitler staring von Manstein in the eye and calling on God to bless the offensive.

Although the Kursk battle was lost, there were still hopes in late 1943 that Germany could win the war, or at least not lose it.[34] One reason for this optimism was the colossal attrition rate of Soviet troops. The Soviet leadership valued life cheaply: attacks were sometimes led by convict battalions, followed by political commissars with orders to shoot anyone who retreated. Even so, it seemed hard to believe that the USSR could sustain such high losses. Another reason for optimism about the future focused on dreams of a quarrel among the Allies, which would allow Germany to make peace with the Western Allies and to concentrate on the war with the USSR—Hitler was particularly fond of alluding to the breakup of the alliance against Frederick the Great. Although the Allies were committed to a policy of unconditional surrender, many believed that the prospect of the Soviet Union rolling up much of Eastern Europe would cause increasing consternation in London and Washington. Yet another reason for optimism among the Nazi political and military leadership was the great faith they placed in the development of new weapons. These included the V1 and V2 rockets, which were to open a bombing offensive on Britain, and the jet-propelled Messerschmitt Me262, which was to prove far faster than any Allied combat plane (though this was initially vitiated by Hitler's insistence that it should be deployed as a bomber!).

Such hopes began to fade rapidly after the successful Allied landings in Normandy during June 1944. In retrospect, it is easy to see the opening of a second front as inevitable, a reflection of the greater economic and military power of the Allies. (The Americans alone produced 256,000 planes during the war compared to the Germans' 92,650.) At the time it was close. Hitler, rejecting the advice of Rommel to fight on the beaches, kept significant forces in reserve. Allied deception—helped by the fact that the Germans had not cracked their codes, whereas the Allies had penetrated Enigma—encouraged the belief that a more important attack was to be made across the Pas de Calais: the ruse caused further delays in the commitment of the reserve troops. The result was that by July, the Allies had firmly established a bridgehead and were expanding eastward.

For some time there had been growing talk of the need to prepare for a new German regime among a section of the officer class and a group of primarily conservative members of the Establishment (people who had little contact with the "masses" who in general remained remarkably loyal to Hitler). One notable source of such planning was the Kreisau Circle, which often gathered at Helmuth von Moltke's estate in Lower Silesia. Moltke's opposition to Nazism was essentially moral, however, and he shied away from thoughts of assassinating Hitler, though this did not stop him from being arrested as a dissident in early 1944. It was therefore left to others in the days after the Normandy landings to mount the last fateful attack on Hitler's life.[35]

By June 1944 a group of plotters had decided that it was vital to kill Hitler and form a new government, though what they planned as a replacement would still have had a distinctly nationalist hue. The chosen assassin was Claus Schenk von Stauffenberg. Although a monarchist and deeply religious, Stauffenberg believed fervently in the need for the rebirth of Germany and had accepted the Nazis coming to power as a means to achieving this. By the time of *Kristallnacht*, he was beginning to have serious doubts, for he was never a Nazi in any serious ideological sense. The treatment of prisoners and Jews after the attack on the USSR culminated in his total disillusionment. After being seriously wounded in Tunisia, injuries which included the loss of his left eye and right hand, he was appointed chief of staff to the commander of the Reserve Army, a post which gave him access to Hitler's headquarters. On July 20, 1944, he attended a conference where Hitler was to discuss the military situation. In his briefcase was a bomb.

Stauffenberg made an excuse to leave the meeting early and immediately flew back to Berlin, convinced that the Führer had been assassinated. But the bomb had been placed under a heavy table, which muffled part of the blast. Although four people were killed and seven seriously injured, Hitler survived. As the plotters had failed to destroy the communications center at Hitler's headquarters, this information was quickly transmitted to Berlin. There, poor planning and fatal hesitation further ensured that all was lost. Stauffenberg and several other plotters were arrested that very day and shot after a drumhead court martial. Thousands of arrests followed. Many of the principal plotters were subsequently brought before the People's Court, whose president, Roland Freisler, had been a Bolshevik in Russia briefly after 1918. In a manner reminiscent of the Moscow show trials during the 1930s, Freisler repeatedly harangued the accused: when Count von Schwanenfeld tried to defend his opposition by talking of the horrors perpetrated by the Nazis in Poland, Freisler described him as "you miserable scum." Worse was to come. Many of the accused were subsequently executed by garrotting from meat hooks. A film of their excruciating death throes was made for the Führer's enjoyment. When the bloodletting was over, around five thousand "conspirators" were dead, including some, like Rommel, who had not been directly implicated in the July Plot: in "gratitude" for past services Rommel was allowed to commit suicide, and subsequently given a war hero's state funeral so that Germans were kept in the dark as to the true reason for his death.

The main result of the assassination attempt was a further increase in the formal power of Himmler and his SS empire, which had done much to hunt down the plotters. Although Himmler's snobbery meant that he had recruited many aristocrats into the SS, Hitler believed that here lay the core of the new Nazi revolution. Hitler's confidence in his "true Himmler," and contempt for the old professionals, is clearly revealed in the new posts he gave to Himmler: that of commander-in-chief of the Reserve Army and supreme commander of the Army Group Vistula. The ex-chicken farmer was thus given the primary task of defending the homeland against the hordes from the east.

Another Nazi who benefited from the July Plot was Martin Bormann, Hess's deputy from 1933 to 1941 and subsequently head of the Reich Chancellery. Increasingly after 1941 the cunning Bormann controlled who saw Hitler, and plotted against party rivals. Indeed, other leading Nazis grew to fear the small and stocky latter-day Machiavelli, suspecting that he was perfectly capable of poisoning them given half a chance. After the July Plot, Himmler became the main target of Bormann's plotting and venom, a task made easier by the fact that the Reichsführer SS quickly proved to be signally lacking in the military skills to match his new tasks. Indeed, by March 1945 Himmler had come to despair of the military situation and had begun to send out peace feelers to the Allies in the remarkable belief that they might find him an acceptable postwar leader. By late April, Göring too was seeking to conduct peace negotiations, though he believed that Hitler had effectively handed control over to him—a confusion which Bormann probably helped to sow.

As the Soviet armies approached, a physically drained Hitler decided to remain in his bunker in Berlin and to take his own life.[36] Two hundred feet below ground, he whiled away the final hours, sometimes talking with Bormann and Goebbels about what might have been. Historians would later argue about whether the Nazis had conducted a social revolution. Hitler would have sided with those who believed that the Nazis brought about only limited changes. He now believed that war had come too early, before he could bring about a fundamental change in the nature of Germans and create a new elite—though his post-July 1944 bloodletting did much to destroy an old one.[37] He still believed that Britain had made a mistake in not coming to terms with Germany. Now the result would be the decline of Britain and rise of an American-Soviet hegemony.

Among the small band who chose to stay with Hitler in the bunker was Eva Braun, who had been his mistress since the early 1930s. Braun had little interest in politics, being devoted more to dancing and films, but she was totally loyal to her Führer. Her decision to remain gained her the only kiss on the lips in public from Hitler, who decided to reward her by marriage. At a civil ceremony that took place during the early hours of Sunday, April 29, both bride and groom swore that they were "of pure Aryan descent." Two upright models of Aryan manhood, Bormann and Goebbels, were witnesses.

While the small band of guests were sipping champagne and talking nostalgically of the old days, Hitler slipped away to dictate his final testament and will. In the latter, he gave virtually all his possessions to the party or, in the event of this ceasing to exist, to the state. He specifically noted that the art collection he had built up had always been intended for a new gallery he planned to build in his hometown of Linz.

In Hitler's final testament, there was not a word of regret, not even for the 6.8 million Germans who had lost their lives as a direct result of the war. In many ways, Hitler never really idealized the Germans: he sought a new European order rather than the rebirth of Germany—an Aryan Europe that would be capable of overcoming the twin evils of Soviet communism and American capitalism. Indeed, as the end approached, his obsession with race and the Jews seems to have become even greater. In this vein, he recommended to future leaders of the nation the "scrupulous observance of the laws of race and . . . a merciless resistance against the poisoner of all peoples—international Jewry." On the question of his immediate succession, Hitler stripped the disloyal Göring and Himmler of all party and state posts. The new Reich president and supreme commander of the armed forces was to be Admiral Dönitz, a pointed insult to the army leaders, whom Hitler held largely to blame for the military defeats. Goebbels was appointed chancellor, and Bormann party secretary.

On April 30 Hitler had his dog, Blondi, poisoned, and made his farewells to the dwindling band who were left behind in the bunker. He then committed suicide with his bride around three-thirty P.M. Following prior orders, the Führer's and Eva Braun's bodies were laid out in a shallow pit and their bodies burned, though a shortage of gas meant that the Russians would recover the remains. The next day Goebbels and his wife took their lives, having previously poisoned their six children. Bormann probably died the following day attempting to break out past the encircling Russians.

Initially Dönitz planned to fight on. He was convinced that the Allies planned to dismember Germany, and was embittered by the fact that he had lost his two sons in the U-boat campaign and his brother in an air raid on Berlin. But after further rear-guard actions—which allowed perhaps three million more Germans to escape the Red Army in the east—he accepted that the die was cast. On May 7, German representatives signed an order of unconditional surrender in Reims. The following day, on Soviet insistence, Keitel signed a formal surrender, with all the Allies in Berlin. The war in Europe was over.

9

France: From Failure
to the Firing Squad

i

IN 1919 the Bloc National government proceeded to wrap itself in the Tricolor. Symbolically it made the feast day of Joan of Arc into a public holiday and turned the memory of the Maid of Orléans into a cult. Although France had lost proportionately more men than any of the other major combatants, the humiliating defeat of 1870 had at last been avenged. Popular nationalism was no longer a virulent revanchist sentiment, which posed a threat to mainstream politics. Rather, it had again become a prop on which the republic was founded.

Even the highly anti-Republican Action Française was almost silenced by the war. In the years immediately before 1914 it had managed to rally a small but talented group of intellectuals, like Charles Maurras, to the cause of monarchism and reactionary conservatism via its claim that the divisive and weak republic could never restore France's former glories. In the red, white, and blue light of victorious dawn, such arguments seemed anachronistic. Nor could the Action Française hope to benefit from widespread fear of the left. Although the 1919 elections showed that socialism was continuing to grow as a parliamentary force, there was never the panic about revolution that gripped sections of the Establishment in Italy after 1918. France was troubled by industrial unrest, but it was relatively low key and there was no equivalent of the widespread unrest in the Italian countryside.

It was, therefore, hardly surprising that the sudden rise of Italian fascism during 1920–22 provoked considerable interest within the ranks of the stagnant AF. Did fascism offer lessons for its own salvation? Was it a kindred movement, or was it something radically different? Answers to these questions were often conditioned by the

foreign policy implications of fascism. The consolidation of the
Bolshevik regime in 1918–20 seemed to imply that it would no
longer be possible to count on the Russian "steamroller" to tie up
German troops in the event of renewed aggression. The United
States' return to isolationism and Britain's imperial preoccupations
further heightened French fears about the dangers of a revived Germany in years to come. Italy thus took on the role of a potentially
important ally. The interest was mutual because the Italians feared
German desire for unity with Austria, and the implications this
would have for the German-speaking regions gained from Austria-
Hungary at the end of World War I. However, there were areas
where French and Italian interests and ambitions clashed, most notably in North Africa. The AF's interpretation of fascism, therefore,
was to go through a variety of phases that were influenced by
France's immediate foreign policy aspirations and fears.[2]

But immediately after 1922 the basic AF line was to see Italian
fascism as a fraternal movement. Maurras perceived differences: in
particular, he saw fascism as more statist and centralizing. He believed, nevertheless, that the new Italian nationalism that underlay
fascism owed much to French thought, including his own. Maurras
was especially interested in the way that Mussolini had come to
power. There had always been ambiguity in the AF over whether its
main short-term goal was to achieve a relatively widespread conversion to monarchism or whether it should first seek to influence elite
opinion. Fascism in Italy had clearly come to power through elite
connivance at a time when many people were opposed to, or unaware of, the fascist message. As a result, the March on Rome gave
new hope to the AF in that it seemed to point to the crucial role
elites could play in politics. There had also been a long-standing tension within the AF between its more intellectual and activist sides.
Although Maurras did not fully understand the nature of fascist
squad discipline and violence, he did perceive that it had played a
role both in terms of intimidating opponents and in attracting elite
attention. Such beliefs led to an increase in activity by the AF's "defense" wing, the Camelots du Roi. During 1923 the group's actions
included an attack on several leading members of the moderate left
as they made their way to a rally against "fascism."

The attack had a far greater impact than Maurras intended. Although the left's main focus was on fascism in Italy, even in 1923 parallels were being drawn between the French and Italian situations. Many on the left realized how quickly fascist violence had destroyed powerful working-class organizations. Understandably, this meant that AF violence was greeted with considerable apprehension. Many on the left also equated fascism and business interests. While the AF had never been a major beneficiary of business support, it undoubtedly enjoyed the patronage of some entrepreneurs. It was, therefore, almost inevitable that the AF would become branded as fascist by left-wing opponents who were quickly finding a practical benefit to antifascism—namely, the power of the cause to rally together the forces of the center-left.

During 1923 and 1924, the fear of fascism played its part in the forging of a center-left Cartel des Gauches, which won the 1924 legislative elections. This, in turn, had a significant effect on the right. In the four years after Clemenceau's resignation as premier in 1920, France had witnessed seven governments quickly come and go. The result of the 1924 elections threatened yet further executive weakness, for the loyalty to the government among center-left deputies seemed fragile. The Cartel's victory sent a shiver down the spines of the propertied classes. There was a general loss of economic confidence, and fears were especially strong among businessmen who thought that they might be targets for nationalization or excess profits tax.

Further fears were aroused after 1924 by new directions in foreign policy. During 1923 the government of Raymond Poincaré had ordered French troops to occupy the Ruhr, as Germany was in default on reparations payments. This forceful action was greeted with enthusiasm by a broad section of French opinion, but by 1924 the French troops had been withdrawn. There was strong pressure from countries like Britain to take a more conciliatory line, and a new German government showed a clear desire to improve Franco-German relations. The outcome was that between 1924 and 1926 Germany moved away from diplomatic isolation and joined key aspects of the postwar security system, like the League of Nations. Although this was accepted by sections of French opinion, others feared the wrath of a powerful Germany that seemed to be re-emerging only shortly after total defeat.

ii

AGAINST THIS BACKGROUND, a set of new radical nationalist groups began to emerge. The first organization of note was the Jeunesses Patriotes (JP), created shortly after the victory of the Cartel. The key figure in this group was Pierre Taittinger, who had been elected in 1919 as part of the conservative Republican Federation on a Bonapartist ticket (namely, a revival of the strong executive, headed by the directly elected president). Taittinger was fascinated by the appeal that fascism in Italy seemed to have for the young. He was worried by the growing strength of the French left and particularly concerned for the future of the electoral right. Groups like the Republican Federation were based on local personalities, who employed influence more than ideology or organization to ensure election. They seemed, therefore, vulnerable to the new mass politics that were emerging in Italy and elsewhere.[3]

The Jeunesses Patriotes were intended to attract young supporters through a mixture of fervent French nationalism, anticommunism, and a defense of traditional Catholic values. By 1926 the group had acquired perhaps sixty-five thousand members, some of whom were attracted by the possibilities for violence. Taittinger claimed that membership soared after a clash with communists during 1925, which left four of his blue-bereted followers dead and thirty wounded. But while left-wing opponents and some subsequent historians have seen the Jeunesses Patriotes as fascist, it is more accurately classed as an ex-serviceman's league than a political party.[4] To the extent that it had an ideology, the JP was essentially a form of paternalist populism. It had no commitment to radical social change, nor did it focus on the cathartic side of violence or on foreign expansion, both characteristics of Italian and German fascism.

Critics at the time cruelly, though not entirely unfairly, described the leadership of the Jeunesses Patriotes as a group of dandies in gaiters, trying to defend their daddies' dividends. This jibe could not have been applied to the Faisceau, which was formed in 1925. Its founder was George Valois (a literary pseudonym). Brought up in great poverty by strict grandparents, Valois was initially inclined to anarchism. But during his twenties he turned to the AF, attracted by his hatred of money-dominated society and his belief in the need for firm leadership and discipline. Valois had become a Social Darwinist who reversed Rousseau: man was born idle and lacking goals until forced to higher forms of civilization by strong leaders. Hostility to materialist bourgeois culture did not mean that Valois shared Maurras's indifference to economic growth, which he saw as vital to underpin both defense and welfare programs. Shortly before 1914, Valois helped found the Cercle Proudhon, which brought together several like-minded members of the AF and key syndicalists like Sorel. But at this time his nationalism was still stronger than his "socialism," and nothing specific came of these meetings.

After the war the emphasis on economic dynamism and a heightened desire to help the masses—who had given so much for their country—widened a rift between Valois and the AF. A further source of division was Vilfredo Pareto's influence on Valois, who had come to believe that the AF's elitism was too backward-looking: the crucial point was to produce a new, young, dynamic elite that was not tainted by either the aristocratic or bourgeois past. In pursuit of this goal, in 1923 Valois visited Italy and was impressed by the new fascist experiment. Yet in spite of the clear allusion in the Faisceau's name, Valois argued that the movement's key ideas were based on French traditions: he cited as particularly seminal influences Barrès's nationalism and the socialism of Sorel. This reflected a further important point about the party's ideology. While its program did not move much beyond vague commitments to corporatism and economic dynamism, it was clearly intended to appeal across the political spectrum—to both left and right.

Critics at the time—and since—have claimed that it is important not to take Valois's left-wing aspect at face value.[5] Certainly he received considerable funds from some industrialists, including the maverick cosmetics manufacturer, François Coty. (Further funds probably came from Mussolini.) But these subsidies do not prove that Valois lacked a socialist side—unless socialism is defined as necessarily involving the extensive ownership of the means of production. Valois was genuinely critical of the way in which Mussolini had pandered to business interests, and sought to keep the Faisceau more independent. He also tried hard to attract left-wing supporters, including communists. One notable early convert from this quarter was Marcel Delagrange, a former mayor of Périgueux (though it should be added that it is not clear how important ideology was in this conversion: Delagrange's actions were also conditioned by his admiring mistress, the Comtesse de Chasteigner, and the fact that Valois paid him two hundred francs a month).[6]

By 1926 the Faisceau had attracted thirty thousand or so primarily middle-class members, a relatively large number in a country where parties tended to be based on local notables. The party was capable of mounting large rallies, though Valois was a competent rather than inspiring speaker, which may explain the absence of a leader cult within the Faisceau. Success, however, attracted a growing band of critics. The left saw the Faisceau as yet further evidence of the rise of fascism, and violently attacked its meetings. (Little violence was directly initiated by the Faisceau's blue-shirted Légions.)[7] On the right several key members of the AF were incensed by Valois's disloyalty and probably more than a little jealous of his movement's sudden rise. Maurras claimed that Valois was a traitor in the pay of Italy, and exerted influence on industrialists to cut off the supply of funds. By 1928 most had done so, though AF influence was less important than Valois's socially radical rhetoric. Thus by 1929 the Faisceau was dead and Valois had begun a remarkable intellectual journey, which would lead him to the nonconformist left during the 1930s, then into the Resistance against the Nazis, and finally to death in the Nazi Bergen-Belsen concentration camp in 1945.[8]

A further nail in the coffin of the Faisceau had been struck by Raymond Poincaré, when he returned to government in 1926 in the face of a mounting economic crisis. Poincaré managed to stabilize the franc and restore business confidence. These factors helped France to ride out the great world depression that struck after 1929. When the bottom of the depression was reached in 1936, notably later than in other countries, the Gross Domestic Product had fallen from an index of 100 in 1929 to 91. At the same time, unemployment had risen to approximately sixteen percent of the labor force, with women suffering a particularly large loss of jobs and many men on short-time working hours. The ensuing poverty and misery undoubtedly heightened social tensions, though the overall impact of depression was less intense than in Germany. Similar points could be made about the rural sector, which accounted for forty percent of the labor force in the 1930s. Agricultural incomes fell significantly, yet there was never the impending sense of doom that overcame many German rural areas, or the sense of imminent revolution that was so crucial in Italy. France's large number of small businessmen and artisans also suffered relatively large drops in income, but they had never formed the backbone of alienated nationalist groups, like the *völkisch* movement in Germany.

Relative economic stability was not accompanied by governmental stability. Poincaré was to remain premier for just over three years, but by January 31, 1933—the day after Hitler became chancellor—France was witnessing the creation of its twenty-eighth administration since the resignation of Clemenceau in 1919. To some extent, instability was an illusion: ministers often played musical chairs with their offices, while policies remained largely unchanged. But the unsavory process of breaking and forming ministries reinforced a long-held impression that parliamentary politics was a game, or worse, a system based on a gigantic web of spoils.

The image of corruption was abetted by the periodic financial scandals that rocked the Third Republic virtually from its outset. During late 1933 a new scandal emerged which was perfectly designed to inflame the extremist right. Alexandre Stavisky, a flamboyant Ukrainian Jew and naturalized Frenchman, disappeared leaving massive debts—and several politicians and officials implicated in bribe-taking. When the police eventually tracked the fugitive down to a Chamonix hideout, he took his own life. Or at least that was the police story, for the more scurrilous sections of the right were only too happy to claim that Stavisky had been killed to keep him from naming a galaxy of accomplices. Various politicians and officials had already been found to be in his pay, and these were widely thought to have been the tip of the iceberg.

Throughout January 1934 radical nationalist groups, including the Action Française, called their supporters on to the streets of Paris to protest—a kind of Boulangist outburst, but without a general. The AF's membership had continued to dwindle, especially after the Pope had put the party on the proscribed list in 1926 because Maurras was an atheist, but it could still bring several thousand supporters out in the capital. Other key groups that became involved in organizing the demonstrations were the Jeunesses Patri-otes and the Solidarité Française, which had been founded in 1933 by Coty as part of his continuing quest to promote an authoritarian government.

These increasingly large and rowdy demonstrations met with a muted response from the police, a situation which quickly added a further dimension to the affair. Left-wingers suspected the Paris po-lice chief, Jean Chiappe, of sympathizing with the right. To appease such critics and support a new administration, the Radical politician Edouard Daladier decided to shunt Chiappe out to Morocco as governor. The radical nationalist groups responded by claiming that Paris was being made safe for a left-wing revolution, and called a mass rally to coincide with the investiture of Daladier's government on February 6. Around twenty-five thousand people gathered near the Chamber of Deputies, and in the ensuing riot fifteen people were killed and more than two thousand were wounded.[9]

Another of the radical nationalist groups involved was the Croix de Feu, which was subsequently accused by many of the more fanatical members of the right of failing to press home the at-tack against the republic, a charge that was sometimes accompanied by the claim—not without some evidence—that its leader was in the pay of the government. These accusations illustrate the ambiva-lent nature of the organization. In spite of its name (the French for "swastika" is *croix gammée*), the early Croix de Feu was not an at-tempt to copy fascism. At the time of its foundation in 1927 it was a movement for ex-servicemen who had been decorated. By 1933 membership had been extended to include all citizens, and the movement had acquired a new leader, the aristocratic and rather colorless Colonel de la Rocque. In many ways he was like Tait-tinger, a middle-aged man—both were born in the late 1880s—worried about the threat to the mainstream right and seeking to create a new organization that would revive the community he had found in the armed forces. It is this side of the Croix de Feu that is stressed by most historians, who do not see it as truly fascist.[10]

But there was a more radical side to la Rocque that was largely absent in Taittinger. Although la Rocque was no serious thinker, his views extended well beyond the conventional nationalism and anticommunism of the right to include, in particular, some criticism of capitalist society. While aspects of this, for instance attacks on banks, can be read as a form of anti-Semitism, there seems little doubt that la Rocque was genuinely concerned to improve the material and spiritual situation of the working class. During 1934–5, moreover, he built up a significant paramilitary organization— though in keeping with his enigmatic face, this engaged in symbolic acts such as giant motorcades rather than systematic attacks on opponents or the state. This proved a heady package, and Croix de Feu membership expanded dramatically from around thirty thousand in 1933 to a claimed five hundred thousand by 1936.

These developments had a major impact on the left in France. During the 1920s there had been an element of shadowboxing in the "antifascist" campaign. Although there were genuine fears about the growth of fascism, there was no movement in France that came anywhere near the same size and power of Italian fascism just before the March on Rome, or even the Nazis in the late 1920s when they were beginning to emerge as a true mass movement. The events of February 1934 changed all this. Most leaders of the left believed that France had been close to a coup d'état. And the subsequent rise of the Croix de Feu—together with the formation of new groups, like Marcel Bucard's openly fascist Francistes—were viewed with considerable alarm.

A particularly important development took place within the French Communist Party (PCF). During 1933 to 1935, the Moscow-dominated Communist International ordered parties to drop their revolutionary line and create Popular Fronts of all antifascists, a line determined primarily by Moscow's fears of Nazism and desire to create a broad international pact against Nazi expansionism eastward. The new tactic paved the way for a growing agreement between France's center-left parties during 1935 and 1936.

The victory of the Popular Front in the 1936 elections aroused considerable fears across the right. It marked the emergence for the first time of the PCF as a significant electoral force, for the communists nearly doubled their vote and PCF representation in the Chamber rose from ten to seventy-one seats. Their total was well behind the socialists and radicals, but it seemed to mark an ominous trend. Worse was to follow. A wave of sit-in strikes hit the factories. While the main causes were related to wage demands and recognition for union rights, the new militancy inevitably raised fears of working-class revolution. The Popular Front government quickly confirmed the fears of the owning classes, for it began to implement a program of social reforms. Rational judgments of the merits of its reforms gave way to panic.

Shortly before the elections, the socialist leader Léon Blum had been attacked by a former member of the Action Française. The incident marked the end of right-wing paramilitary groups, for one of the first acts of the subsequent Blum government was to ban combat groups and private militias, which had burgeoned during the 1930s. There was now no question of allowing the kind of major paramilitary movements that had characterized the rise of fascism in both Italy and Germany. Large demonstrations, however, continued and often provoked violence—most spectacularly at Clichy in 1937 when an antifascist counterdemonstration led to seven people being killed and several hundred wounded.

The right responded to this ban in a variety of ways. A few turned to terrorism. The main perpetrator of the attack on Blum was Eugène Deloncle, a well-known marine engineer who had become disillusioned with Maurras and the "Inaction Française." During 1936–7 he set about organising a Comité Secret d'Action Révolutionnaire, which was to become more commonly known as the Cagoule. Deloncle's shadowy and well-connected organization carried out the assassination of two leading Italian antifascist exiles, probably on the instructions of Mussolini's secret service and in exchange for arms. Other activities included placing a bomb outside the employers' federation headquarters in the apparent hope that this would be taken as a communist attack. But while the organization seems to have attracted a small number of converts in the army, the forces of law and order in general remained loyal to the republic and during 1937–8 the Cagoule was effectively broken up.[11]

La Rocque responded to the Popular Front by turning the Croix de Feu into a political party, the Parti Social Français (PSF).[12] To some of the more extreme nationalists, this was further proof that la Rocque's real game was to prevent the emergence of a truly radical movement. La Rocque and several leading supporters, however, seem genuinely to have believed that the conditions existed to launch a major new party. And while the program of the PSF remained vague, this reflected a realization that excessive social radicalism was likely to lose important backers and alienate the middle class, which had made up the bulk of the Croix de Feu's membership.

La Rocque had found in the early 1930s that his socially radical side frightened some wealthy potential supporters. He had also experienced opposition from sections of the Catholic hierarchy, which ordered priests not to join the Croix de Feu. The fear of losing conservative support led him to tone down his statement and to concentrate more on alleviatory measures for the poor, such as setting up soup kitchens. After 1936 he sought to appeal to the working class without antagonizing potential patrons. He set up PSF unions in order to exploit the anticommunist sentiment of many workers, though in reality these were often mini-corporations, including workers and employers. He also established local social organizations, such as sports and holiday clubs, in order to build loyalty in a largely nonpolitical, communal way. He tried to exploit both socialist and Catholic internationalism by talking of the need to establish a European federation.

The potency of this package can be seen by the dramatic rise in support for the PSF. By 1937 it claimed to have approaching one million members, and three million by 1939. Even allowing for exaggeration and fluid loyalties, it had quickly become the largest party in France in terms of membership. Many historians have claimed that PSF support was primarily middle class. Certainly the bulk of the party's early members came from the upper middle class and white-collar workers. By the late 1930s, however, the PSF was making gains among the workers and peasants.[13] Rural workers especially were beginning to desert old loyalties under the pressure of growing social change and new forms of organization. Had war not broken out in 1939, the PSF might well have gone on to become a major force in parliamentary politics, though whether it could have maintained its momentum is another matter.

The PSF was not the only new party created at this time. Another was the Parti Populaire Français (PPF), whose leader, Jacques Doriot, was a charismatic figure who presents an especially interesting case study in ideological metamorphosis.[14] Doriot's father was a blacksmith and Doriot himself held a variety of working-class occupations during his early life. After fighting as a raw teenager in the closing stages of World War I, he joined the Socialist Party and quickly sided with the group that went on to form the Communists. Tall, physically impressive, and a good speaker, he rose quickly in the party: by 1924 he headed its youth section and was a member of the Chamber of Deputies. A bright future seemed to lie ahead for Doriot, who epitomized the young revolutionary armed with a dagger between his teeth.

But Doriot was a man who favored action over doctrine, the deed over the careful building of bureaucratic structures, and he soon found himself in growing conflict with those within the party who were rising more by doctrinal sophistry and stealth. After 1928, he chafed against the adoption by the Communist International of the "Social Fascist" line—the ban on cooperation with more moderate socialists in the fight against fascism. Doriot retreated into his personal fiefdom of Paris Saint-Denis, where he was elected mayor in 1931. After the Paris riots of February 1934, he formed an action committee that included socialists as well as communists, and called for an understanding with the Socialists. The PCF denounced him for sinking into "social democratic vomit" and expelled him—an ironic twist of fate, for the Moscow line was soon to change to encompass the Popular Front tactic.

For Doriot there was no going back. The break had led to considerable bitterness on both sides: Doriot was especially contemptuous of the PCF's slavish adherence to foreign directives and sectarianism—and the way in which it seemed to be pushing France toward a war that he now thought was mainly in the Soviet Union's interests. Doriot had, moreover, begun to build up his own machine in Saint-Denis, and many leading local communists broke with the PCF at the same time. By 1935 there were increasing contacts between this group, sections of the Action Française who were critical of their party's inability to attract a mass following, and certain business interests who were interested in sponsoring an anticommunist party. Doriot's break with the left was completed during the election campaign of 1936. Attempting to hold his Saint-Denis seat, he found that his main support now came from the right.

The narrowness of his victory convinced Doriot that, if he were to remain in politics, he needed a new party vehicle to organize support. The result was the PPF, which was highly critical of the current economic and political system as socially divisive and incapable of decisive action.

In its place the PPF advocated a more authoritarian government based on corporatism. Doriot's underlying ideology seems to have become a variant of Third Way thinking, but his reliance on money from business sources—including some Jewish ones—meant that he had to tone down the more radical side of the program. (Funds also came from fascist Italy.) This side of the PPF helps explain why Doriot often relied on charisma and symbolism rather than clear program: for instance, he combined images of Joan of Arc, whom some on the left rejected as a nationalist and Catholic saint, with allusions to the 1871 Paris Commune, one of the key defining acts of left-wing rebellion. In the field of foreign policy, Doriot advocated the appeasement of Germany on the grounds that France should try to turn Hitler's attentions eastward rather than seek to contain him—a "France first" policy. This was linked to his advocacy of nonintervention on behalf of the Spanish Popular Front in its civil war against General Franco's rebels: Doriot believed that participation in the conflict could only worsen relations between France and the fascist dictators.

By 1938 the PPF claimed three hundred thousand members: while the true figure was probably at most sixty thousand, this still made it by far the largest of the truly fascist interwar movements in France. There was little real prospect, however, that it could have developed into a major mass movement. While Doriot was willing to encourage strike-breaking and to foster anticommunist unions, the collapse of the Popular Front during 1937–8 meant that most businessmen lost interest in the new movements, especially ones that had a potentially radical social hue. Doriot also found it difficult to find a popular rallying cry. Opinion polls showed that most French people were reluctantly coming to believe that it would be necessary to make a stand against Nazi Germany. Doriot's support for appeasement, therefore, largely fell on stony ground. Indeed, it contributed to significant defections after the Munich conference in September 1938—including some of the party's more notable intellectual supporters, like Bertrand de Jouvenel. (De Jouvenel, whose mother was Jewish, was also worried by the anti-Semitic views of some of those attracted to the PPF.)

There were opportunities for the emergence of new parties, as was demonstrated by the rise of the PSF, or the sudden rise of Henri Dorgères's violent Front Paysan, with its green-shirted youth movement. These parties, however, had to be able to penetrate local communities or to make deals with existing notables. Doriot was aware of this, and during 1937 he had tried to create a reverse Popular Front with the PSF, the conservative Republican Federation and the Parti Républicain et Social (the successor to the Jeunesses Patriotes). But most other party leaders had no intention of helping Doriot to establish himself. Besides, by 1937 the fear of left extremism was beginning to fade, and with it went Doriot's trump card—his charismatic appeal to a section of the working class.

The PPF was left as a party that played a significant role in only a small number of areas where it had managed to establish a local organization. Even in areas of relative strength, the nature of the party's support could be remarkably pragmatic and tenuous, as can be seen in Marseilles. Here the PPF was run by Simon Sabiani, a Corsican former communist who had created a clientelist political machine based on a section of the Marseilles working class who were attracted by Sabiani's judicious distribution of favors. By 1936 he found his position threatened on the one hand by the rise of the local communists, and on the other by the growing influence of la Rocque's movement. Although Sabiani made a genuine movement from class-based to nationalist politics at this time, his motives in joining the PPF were unquestionably related to the maintenance of his local political influence. Predictably, many of those who turned to the PPF in Marseilles were attracted either because of past favors or in the hope of future ones. Fascism in Marseilles, therefore, owed more to interest than ideology.[15]

iii

IT IS EASY to see why French legend holds that fascism was a marginal movement in France during the interwar years. It is far more difficult to understand the counterclaim that France was riddled with fascist ideology.[16] To understand the latter argument, it is necessary to turn from the world of concrete politics to the arena of ideas—an important one in a country that takes intellectuals seriously. Whereas few politicians were willing openly to proclaim themselves fascist, more intellectuals were willing to embrace the ideology—or to exhibit aspects of thought that had strong affinities with fascism, and that more generally contributed to the critique of parliamentary democracy. While this may not have produced a fascist mass movement during the 1930s, it undoubtedly helped to condition attitudes after France's defeat in 1940.

During the early 1930s a group of young writers and artists emerged, many of whom were collectively known as the Jeune Droite. They recognized Maurras as a major source of nationalist inspiration and were often associated with Action Française publications, which continued to attract a small but able group of intellectuals. They shared common concerns about decadence and the communist menace, but had noticeable philosophical differences. There was a general desire for spiritual rebirth, but some saw this mainly in religious terms while for others it had a more Nietzschean side, stressing the need for leadership and will. Another major division was between those more concerned with program and those more interested in developing a kind of Sorelian myth that could rejuvenate either the masses or an elite. In general, those who represented the religious or programmatic tendencies were more hostile to fascism—though there was no rigid division. The novelist Alphonse de Chateaubriand was attracted to Nazism precisely because he saw it as the incarnation of religious spiritual rebirth (thus managing to ignore its clear pagan side).

The differences over fascism can be seen even more clearly by comparing two leading members of Jeune Droite, Thierry Maulnier, and Robert Brasillach. Maulnier was particularly worried by the Nazis, whom he found vulgar and addicted to a dangerous suppression of cultural diversity. He was also concerned that their "new man" was essentially German rather than European. Brasillach too was worried about the Germanic side of Nazism, believing that there was a collectivism and conformity in German culture that did not exist among the more individualistic French. He was attracted all the same by other aspects of the Nazi "new man," especially his youth and his dynamism. He held vague Third Way views which interested him in Nazi social experiments, like the KDF organization. Unlike Maulnier, Brasillach was an aesthete more than a serious thinker, a man who sought an art that would fuse force and form. Details of program mattered less than images. Symptomatically, he described fascism as "poetry" rather than doctrine—it was about feeling, rhythm, and spirit rather than rational thought.[17]

Arguably the most important thinker among the literary fascists was Pierre Drieu la Rochelle.[18] Unlike Brasillach and Maulnier, who were born in 1909, Drieu was a World War I veteran, but he was not one of those who returned from the war seeking to create a new community of the trenches—or believing that war and violence were cathartic experiences. He was more an intellectual gadfly, dabbling with surrealism and other fads. By the early 1930s he was becoming concerned with what he saw as the decadence of France and of European culture in general. He came to believe that some form of United States of Europe was necessary, which would abandon liberal capitalism and parliamentary democracy. By 1934 he had published a book entitled *Fascist Socialism*, which clearly revealed his move toward Third Way thinking. It also revealed that Drieu was no conformist seeking to lose himself in a mass movement. In fact, he retained a strong individualist streak, and his fascism was more of the elite than the mass kind: it was based on a Nietzschean belief that the few could will a new form of politics. He believed that an individual could find fresh psychic force in an ideal or movement, a key theme of his seminal novel *Gilles* (1939).

In the early 1930s Drieu had written disapprovingly of the way that Hitler and Mussolini had made too many concessions to the wealthy, and he had heaped scorn on biological ideas of race. After 1935 his attitudes toward the fascist dictators became more confused. He came to support the appeasement of Hitler, but not because he wanted German aggrandizement. Rather, he feared French defeat in a war that he believed would mainly serve Soviet interests. Drieu was moving toward a form of conspiracy theory, which almost inevitably led him to anti-Semitism. He came to believe that powerful Jewish interests sought war, a view that attracted growing support among radical nationalists in the late 1930s—partly because Blum and several leading members of the Popular Front were Jewish.[19]

Drieu joined the PPF in 1936, helping to give the party intellectual prestige. He subsequently eulogized Doriot for his realism, and for not being taken in by liberal and left-wing "claptrap" about the goodness of man or the rationality of behavior. Drieu was a Social Darwinist, who saw history as cyclical and regularly punctuated by wars. By late 1938, however, Drieu had become disillusioned with Doriot's attempts to attract wealthy supporters and with his failings as a thinker. He was also worried about the growing menace of Nazi Germany. He broke with the PPF, though his writings showed that his underlying fascist views remained essentially unchanged.

A few leading intellectuals moved even further toward fascism and anti-Semitism. Ferdinand-Louis Céline had been seriously injured in World War I and was determined to prevent future wars.[20] Like Drieu, he came to see communism as the main threat to the peace and to European culture. Far more than Drieu, Céline became obsessed with the allegedly virulent influence of the Jewish bacillus on France. (Céline was a doctor who liked medical metaphors.) Céline saw the Jews as the source of both materialism and left-wing class war. By the late 1930s, he had come to admire the Nazis for their anti-Semitism and for their attempt to create a new community founded on social unity. Indeed, by 1939 Céline had effectively transferred his loyalty from France to Germany, holding that the land of his birth was irretrievably lost to decadence and Jewish influence.

Such views were strongly attacked by Brasillach and other leading radical nationalists, who realized that support for the appeasement of Germany—and especially pro-German views—were losing rather than gaining them support. But there was a sense in which Céline anticipated the future all too clearly. What if you had to choose sides? How would people respond if Germany did defeat France?

iv

DURING 1940 the nightmare became reality. In May the Germans attacked, bypassing the great defensive Maginot Line. For the most part, the French troops fought bravely—120,000 were to be killed and nearly a quarter of a million wounded in the space of just four weeks—but the brilliance of the German strategy and quality of its battle-hardened troops proved decisive against an often incompetent French military leadership. Within days the Panzers had driven nearly to the Channel coast, splitting the Allied armies in two. The French government responded by firing their supreme commander, General Gamelin (who had played an important role in easing civil-military tensions after his appointment in 1935, and thus minimizing support for groups like the Cagoule).[21] His replacement, General Weygand, proved no more successful in the face of the German second thrust, which pushed into central France. On one day alone—June 16—General Rommel's Panzer group advanced 150 miles without firing a shot.

The French government had already appointed as vice-premier the aging Marshal Pétain, in the hope that he would rally French resistance, as he had done at Verdun in 1916. Now, with France facing total and humiliating defeat, Pétain became head of government.[22] North of the Loire, France was one giant sea of refugees—though the response of inhabitants to the invading Boche could vary dramatically even within small areas. In the village of Tichey, for instance, only 4 people out of 220 left; a few miles away, all 150 inhabitants of Bousselange took flight, with the exception of one family who committed collective suicide.[23]

Faced with the breakdown of military and civil authority, Pétain and the majority of the government decided on an armistice; among the minority was a junior minister named General de Gaulle, a rare example of someone who chose to organize resistance from abroad rather than accept defeat. Although some Germans sought to impose humiliating terms, Hitler decided that pending a full peace treaty it was in Germany's interests to secure the collaboration of the French government. He was particularly anxious that the French fleet should not sail to join the British. Furthermore, full occupation of France would tie up considerable manpower. The armistice that came into effect on June 25, therefore, allowed the French government to retain sovereignty over French territory, though this provision was heavily constrained by the fact that the Germans occupied a large section of France, stretching from the Swiss border west toward Tours and then south toward the Spanish border near Hendaye.

During June the French politicians set out on their own Tour de France, before finally descending from the saddle in the sleepy spa town of Vichy. Here, the general sense of France's failure played into the hands of those who sought a formal end to the Third Republic. Prominent among this group was Pierre Laval—an ambitious former prime minister, and the archetypal scheming intriguer of the old parliamentary system.[24] On July 10 there was an overwhelming vote to grant "full powers" to Pétain, who had long dreamed of the day when a crisis might bring him to power. France had effectively become a dictatorship.

The ensuing Vichy government has become the subject of much controversy, not least over the question of whether it should be classified as fascist.[25] Pétain himself presents few serious problems of categorization. Although he had cleverly portrayed himself during the interwar years as being above politics, his basic views were reactionary. It was no accident that he was to send to Maurras a copy of his speeches with the inscription: "To Charles Maurras, the most French of Frenchmen." While Vichy propaganda talked of the need for a "National Revolution," Pétain's eyes were set on restoration more than radicalism. He wanted France to be born again, once more to become a land of Catholicism and natural values, such as the family or the village. However, he did not accept Maurras's arguments in favor of a return to the monarchy, which he thought was more likely to divide than unite a people in whom the republican myth was strong.

The Vichy government, rather than Pétain personally, presents more tricky problems of classification, especially as it went through markedly different phases. The early Vichy period saw an attempt to rally support by Pétainist homilies on "Work, Family and Country," accompanied by relatively minor policy changes—such as further attempts to improve the birth rate, which had been a source of concern since defeat in 1870. The program was more symptomatic of authoritarian conservatism than fascism.

Vichy, however, was no simple dictatorship. In several areas of life it sought to institute a form of totalitarian state, complete with an extensive propaganda network and mechanisms of social control. Many Vichy leaders identified decadence as beginning during youth, a view they shared with German and Italian fascist leaders.

Youth was also seen as the leaders of the future. As a result, more physical education was introduced into the school syllabus, and manual work was introduced for older children. As a replacement for military service, young men were sent to do useful public works, or to engage in activities to beautify the countryside. A college was even established at Uriage to help train the new elites who would lead the "National Revolution."[26]

In the socioeconomic sphere, the regime attempted to create a corporate state. The effort did not amount to much, except perhaps in the peasant sector—where Pétain's eulogies to simple, rural life struck a chord (and where Dorgères initially helped in the propaganda campaign). The basic problem, as in Italy, was the excessive power wielded by employers in a system in which free unions had been banned. But many Vichy leaders genuinely wanted to overcome the employer-employee division and to coordinate industry and state needs. The desire for social reconciliation can be seen by another, and initially less marked, aspect of Vichy economic policy—the appointment of technocrats to key positions. The technocrats tended to be hostile to liberal economics and sought to develop a form of state planning that, while leaving most industry in private hands, would coordinate the private and public spheres. Some analysts of French development have claimed that this aspect of the Vichy program laid an important basis for the dynamic postwar French economic growth.[27]

The Vichy regime, therefore, was an unholy amalgam of different ideologies and motives—both reactionary and modernizing. Such a mixture in itself would not prevent it from being labeled fascist, as both the Nazi and Italian fascist states exhibited many similar features. The crucial point is that none of the key figures in the Vichy government sought the social revolution which is a defining characteristic of fascist Third Way thinking. Mussolini and Hitler, for all their tactical concessions to conservative forces, were ultimately radicals. Vichy was more a form of authoritarian populism, an attempt to revive the true France of the past, though in its more progressive guises this took the form of marrying the French past to the needs of the modern industrial state.

The true fascists in France were under no illusion that Vichy was fascist.[28] During 1941 a new party was created which ridiculed the Vichy "National Revolution." This was the Rassemblement National Populaire (RNP), set up by the ascetic Marcel Déat. Déat is especially interesting because he underlines that the route to fascism in the 1930s did not lie solely on the right. He was a well-educated former Socialist Party deputy, who in the early 1930s had come to believe that class was too narrow a basis on which to form a party that could launch a true revolution. A major source of inspiration was the cosmopolitan Belgian socialist theorist Henri De Man, especially in his seminal book *Beyond Marxism* (1926), which Mussolini praised highly. In this, De Man attacked the psychological basis of Marxism: he was concerned by the way in which World War I had shown that the nation rather than class, or socialism, was the great idea for which men would fight. By the early 1930s Déat too had come to see the nation as the great idea that would integrate the working class into the community. Like De Man, he linked this to the need for a plan, which effectively meant accepting that much of industry would remain in private hands as long as it produced dynamic growth and operated in the interests of the nation. He also became an advocate of social and political systems based on corporations, which would institutionalize social unity.

These views alone would not have made Déat a fascist, but, like De Man, there were seeds in his thoughts that pushed him toward fascism rather than the left. One was the fact that his conception of the plan was not purely technocratic: there was a Sorelian side too, an acceptance that manipulation was necessary to "manage" the masses. Like Hitler and Mussolini, he saw the need for a "vanguard" party to lead this revolution—though following most French fascists he preferred to portray his view as part of the French political tradition, namely the Jacobin legacy. Déat's emphasis on leadership was linked to a growing concern about decadence and the health of society, views inspired by Nietzschean and eugenicist thought. He sought the forging of a more spartan France, more virile and determined to reverse France's decline. Even before 1939, his thought had effectively become fascist in ideological form: defeat produced the circumstances where he could "come out," and more openly identify with the great ideological—and military—force that seemed to be sweeping Europe and destroying both democracy and old conservative elites before it.

Pétain and most of his advisers, however, had no interest in setting up a single-party state—or indeed any party within Vichy-controlled France. Déat was, therefore, forced to concentrate his efforts on Paris, and in the German-occupied zone. Here he initially attracted a variety of supporters, including the German ambassador, Otto Abetz. Abetz, agreeing that the Vichy regime was not fascist, was looking for a vehicle that would use radical ideas, including anti-Semitism, to pressure Vichy—even to break through traditional Catholic culture and French individualism. Unfortunately for his plans, the RNP proved a weak vehicle. Like many fascist groups, it was plagued by chronic division between those attracted by its more left-wing ideas and those attracted by its right-wing side and anti-Semitism. Ideological division led to a major split between Déat and another leading figure, Deloncle. (There was even talk of murder plots.) By 1942 Déat was leading a rump party that had at most twenty-five thousand adherents, who came mainly from the middle class, including a smattering of teachers and the educated.

By this time Doriot's PPF was making a notable comeback. During the late 1930s his party had declined rapidly. The former Bolshevik monk acquired a taste for wine, women, and song, which fueled stories of his being in the pay of rich industrialists and bankers, and after the Munich conference the party had suffered a serious split over support for German appeasement. But the German attack on the USSR in 1941 gave Doriot new life. (He portrayed the attack as ideological, rather like the one launched by the French army after the Revolution.) It would have been sensible to pool resources with Déat, but there was little love lost between the two men. For Doriot, Déat was too ascetic and cerebral, the very epitome of the bureaucratic teacher. Déat responded by seeing the "Grand Jacques" as too carried away with himself, too prone to sell out doctrine to other interests.

Doriot's self-confidence and charisma seemed undimmed: his powerful speeches were soon attracting thousands, and party membership revived to perhaps fifty thousand, slightly less than its 1930s peak. Anticommunism came easily to the former communist. "Rather Hitler than Stalin" replaced the anti-Popular Front rallying cry of "Rather Hitler than Blum." The creation of a new Europe rather than national grandeur was the dominant theme. Rhetoric was backed up by action, for Doriot became involved in the attempt to recruit volunteers to fight communism, and spent some time himself on the eastern front. Between 1941 and 1944, ten thousand Frenchmen were to volunteer to fight against "Bolshevism," a crusade portrayed on recruitment posters as part of the battle for social reform and to create a "new socialist Europe." Located initially within the German armed forces, the volunteers were later grouped into a special French Charlemagne Division of the Waffen SS, which went on to help defend Hitler's bunker during the bloody last days in Berlin. Many of these recruits came through the PPF, though some—like the aristocratic Christian de la Nazière—were not fascists. They were more authoritarian conservatives, who sought personal and social rebirth through battle against the communist enemy.[29]

The failure of these groups to attract significant support left the Germans with little choice other than to stick with the Vichy regime. After the Allied landings in North Africa in the autumn of 1942, however, the Germans annexed the "Free Zone" and began to make increasing demands on Vichy to conform to German wishes. The Vichy government found itself under pressure from another sphere—growing public opposition. In 1940–1 most French people rallied around Pétain—though as in Germany and Italy, there was more support for the leader than for the regime.[30] But as the tide of war began to turn against Germany, opposition to Vichy mounted. German demands for labor to work in German factories were a particular source of discontent and led many to join the growing Resistance rather than face industrial "conscription," especially given the growing stories of the poor conditions in which such workers often toiled.

In July 1940 Pétain had rewarded Laval by appointing him deputy prime minister, but by December Laval had been fired, mainly because he seemed too ready to collaborate with the Germans. Laval, however, remained politically active, encouraging the formation of the RNP as a means of putting pressure on the Vichy government. By 1942 he had been reinstated as head of government, and during the closing phase of the Vichy regime he was perhaps its key figure in terms of decision making. Defenders of Pétain were later to point the finger at Laval as the true collaborator, arguing that the marshal had done no more than rally France in her hour of need, or had pursued collaboration in an attempt to gain specific concessions from the Germans—especially the return of the large number of prisoners of war whom the Germans used as a source of virtual slave labor for their war machine.[31]

There were almost as many forms of collaboration as there were collaborators, but Laval managed to combine several of these in one person. He came from a small-business background, and his views were initially a form of moderate socialism. During the 1920s he moved increasingly to the right, but this did not stem from any ideological belief in nationalism as a force capable of ensuring social regeneration. Laval was essentially uninterested in ideas. He was a pragmatist who understood men and believed in the primacy of base motives. He was also extremely ambitious politically, though the fascination seems to have been with power rather than money, for he lived simply.

Laval saw French defeat in 1940 as a chance for personal advancement. He believed that he understood the Germans and that they did not seek to dismember and weaken France. Indeed, he believed that by accommodating German demands, France could become a major partner in the creation of a new Europe once communism had been eliminated. Laval's Jewish wife warned him not to take Hitler at his word, and a shrewder appreciation of the situation might have led him to realize that the Nazis were divided over how to treat France in the long run. By 1942 he should have been more aware of the possibility of German defeat. But overweening belief in his own judgment meant that he did not ask the right questions until too late. By then, he was far too tainted to retract—unlike lesser figures, such as François Mitterrand, whose own ambition and judgment were to take him from right to left and to the summit of French politics in the postwar era.[32]

Probably in no area has the record of Laval and Vichy been more attacked than in its dealings with the Jews.[33] There is no doubt that Vichy rallied many anti-Semites, including literary figures like Brasillach and Drieu, whose support helped to give the regime cultural prestige. The first discriminatory measures against Jews, including their banning from political office and various occupations, were taken by the Vichy regime with no prompting from the Nazis. But except in some pockets, for instance among haut-bourgeois Catholics, anti-Semitic and racist views were far less deeply entrenched than in German society. In rural areas there was usually no patois word for *Jew* before the occupation. In urban areas reports show that wide sections of French opinion were shocked by news of prewar Nazi atrocities, especially at the time of Kristallnacht in 1938. Even fascist and proto-fascist groups before 1939 had tended not to focus on anti-Semitism in the way Nazism did, though they usually stressed opposition to further Jewish immigration from Germany and elsewhere.

In 1940 three hundred thousand Jews lived in France, a significant number of whom were not French citizens; seventy-six thousand—men, women, and children—died in Nazi concentration camps or were otherwise killed during the war. Most of those who died were transported in 1942 before the Germans moved into the Vichy zone. Often they were rounded up by French policemen and then kept briefly in French transit camps, like the one at Drancy. Even the Vélodrome d'Hiver cycle stadium was roped in to house thirteen thousand, including four thousand children, after one notorious roundup.

These policies caused great suffering. Drancy was an unfinished housing block, almost totally lacking in facilities. Over a hundred suicides were reported at the time of the Vélodrome d'Hiver *rafle*. Vichy's basic policy, however, was a complex game of making concessions to the Germans over non-French Jews, in an attempt to provide a shelter for its own citizens. As it became increasingly clear from late 1942 onward that deportation meant death rather than work in labor camps, Laval withstood considerable German pressure to sign what amounted to permission to deport Jews who were French citizens. This was hardly a high moral position, but outright rejection of German demands risked direct German intervention and the possibility of total deportation.

Toward the end of the war, rounding up Jews became a task increasingly undertaken by the Germans, often eagerly aided by a new Vichy paramilitary organization known as the Milice. The formation of this group at the turn of 1943 has widely been seen as marking the beginning of a final phase of Vichy, the stage during which it fell heavily under German control. Certainly there was German pressure to set up such a group, though Laval hoped that by complying he would keep down German action within the Vichy zone. He also believed that forming a Vichy paramilitary group would preempt the RNP and PPF setting up their own anti-Resistance forces, bands which were likely to be controlled more by the Germans than the French state.

While the Milice was initially placed under Laval, effective control quickly passed to Joseph Darnand, a man who by 1944 had taken an oath of personal loyalty to the Führer. Here lies another of the strange paradoxes of collaboration, for this ex-Action Française and Cagoule member was a fervent nationalist who had been violently anti-German. Indeed he was decorated for bravery during World War I and had become a front-page national hero in 1940 when he had made a valiant attempt to rescue another former Cagoule member during a commando raid on the Germans. But his right-wing views, and childlike devotion to Pétain, led him to become active in an ex-serviceman's organization which took on an increasingly paramilitary air. It was out of this body that the Milice grew.

The Milice, whose membership numbered at most thirty thousand, became a particular target for the growing forces of the Resistance, which encouraged its ever closer links with the Germans.[34] The attacks met with a bloody response: members of the Resistance who were captured were often tortured in ways that must have caused unimaginable suffering. A leading figure in a communist Resistance group, Colonel "Gilles," had his face crushed to pulp by the Gestapo, who kept a specially made leather mask just for this purpose. Amazingly, he yielded no names before he died—like most captured members of the Resistance. Ordinary citizens too increasingly suffered in reprisals, or at the hands of German troops brutalized by war in the east—most notoriously, in the massacre of almost every villager in Oradour-sur-Glane during June 1944, a carnage which involved deliberately burning the women and children to death in the local church.

The troops involved at Oradour, the SS Das Reich Division, were journeying north to face the Allied invasion of the Normandy beaches. But it was a losing battle. By the end of 1944 the Allied armies had swept across much of France. As the Germans retreated, the decision was taken to carry with them the two leaders who had most come to personify the Vichy regime: Pétain and Laval. Eventually they arrived in Germany, whence the collaborationist leaders Doriot and Déat had already fled. It was here that Doriot was killed in February 1945 when his car was strafed by an Allied plane. Near the end Déat managed to slip over the Swiss border and disappear, dying of natural causes in 1955.

Most of the other leading survivors of collaboration were not so lucky. Brought back to France, they were to be put on trial with thousands of others who had committed crimes or shown undue support for the enemy. Justice—and revenge—were at hand.

10

Britain: From Farce to Failure

i

IN THE YEARS after 1918 a new strand entered British stereotypes of Italy and her people. During the nineteenth century, Italians had frequently been portrayed in popular culture as organ grinders or ice-cream salesmen, occupations often filled by Britain's small number of Italian immigrants. Now a new volume was added (unjustly) to the list of the world's shortest books: *The Italian War Hero*. World War I did not simply reinforce British self-images; it also underlined the sense of us and them, a geographical world in which Europe curiously did not include Britain. Britain was exceptional, endowed by God with the English Channel, which cut it off from comic opera and, more dangerous, foreigners.

Perhaps predictably, the leader of the first party in Britain that bore the name "fascist" could hardly have been more eccentric. The British Fascisti was founded in May 1923 by Rotha Linton Orman, a young woman who came from a long line of military forebears. Finding it difficult to adjust to life in rural Somerset after driving an ambulance in wartime Serbia, Orman placed an advertisement in a small right-wing journal. She appealed to those who shared her view that the country was about to be overrun by Bolsheviks to join together and fight back.[1]

Her clarion call was made against a background of considerable postwar industrial unrest, which had prompted fears of a general strike. There were fears too that a socialist government was imminent, for the Labor Party had grown rapidly after the war. Social and political conditions in Britain, however, were very different from those that had spawned a fascist mass movement in Italy and that were later to breed one in Germany. Economically, times were hard, but there was not mass destitution of the type that afflicted

Germany after 1929. Politically, British trade unions and the Labor Party were clearly more moderate than their Italian and German counterparts. More importantly still, while the British Conservative Party had been badly divided during the early part of the twentieth century, by 1923 it was largely reunited under the shrewd leadership of Stanley Baldwin. Unlike in Italy and Germany, few perceived the usefulness of a new right-wing party.

In a country like Britain, where coalition government was the exception rather than the norm, this was particularly true of a reactionary party that had no hope of attracting a mass base. Although Orman called her party fascist, she seems to have known almost nothing about Italian fascism and had few ideas about policy, other than a vague defense of king and country, which was understood essentially in terms of rural England. It is symptomatic that one of her more constructive ideas was a proposal to cut taxes on gentlefolk, so they could employ more servants and thus ease unemployment.

Similar points could be made about the few thousand members that the party attracted. Mostly these were retired military officers and obscure peers, though the party included a smattering of upper-middle-class youths too. Predictably, there was little if anything about these supporters that could reasonably be termed fascist other than a vague desire for dictatorship and a willingness to use violence against the dangerous "left." The term embraced the Labor Party as well as the small British Communist Party, for within the British Fascisti's ranks were many who thought that Labor planned little short of Red Revolution, a myth that the relatively moderate record of Labor's fist minority administration during 1924 did nothing to dispel.

How to pronounce the party's name seemed to occupy more time than substantive issues. The inner core preferred the British-sounding "fassisti," whereas others said "fashisti." This dispute was linked to fears that the foreign origin of the word *fascist* was a disadvantage for a party that was nothing if not intensely nationalistic. As a result, in 1924 it was decided to adopt the name "British Fascists," hardly a major change. To make matters worse, party members, and especially opponents, often abbreviated this to "BFs," an unfortunate acronym, as in slang terminology it denoted "bloody fools."

Fools can be dangerous, but BF activism was low-key stuff in comparison to the *squadristi* or SA. The party set up "flying squads" with cars and motorcycles, though poor young members made do with bicycles. These squads were relatively few in number, and typical actions involved attacks on the vendors of left-wing newspapers. The BF's most spectacular action smacked more of a student stunt than serious violence: the kidnapping in March 1925 of the leader of the British Communist Party, Harry Pollitt. Five members of the BF were subsequently charged by the police, though they were acquitted after they claimed that they had intended to take Pollitt away for a pleasant weekend. They added that Pollitt had accepted five pounds when released to cover his trouble and expenses.

The court's judgment illustrates that, as in Germany, there was a leniency toward the patriotic right that was not usually extended to the left. But there was basically little sympathy within the forces of law and order or the government for the British Fascists. Although the immediate postwar period with its strikes and social unrest had aroused fears, the vast majority of leading politicians and officials had not panicked. Commitment to the basic democratic process remained strong, partly because of the common belief that the British working man was essentially patriotic.[2]

In the time preceding the 1926 General Strike, the home secretary, William Joynson-Hicks, had sponsored various organizations to help maintain order and preserve the delivery of essential supplies in the event of mass working-class action. Yet when the British Fascists offered their services, Hicks—who was perhaps the most reactionary cabinet minister of the interwar era—threatened to resign if the BFs were allowed to work with the government. He was strongly opposed to the BF's rejection of parliamentary government and the rule of law, though this view was clearly related to the fact that the Conservatives had a majority in the House of Commons and could therefore determine policy and change the law.

Some members of the BFs helped to run essential services during the brief period that the General Strike lasted, including one who was killed when he put his head out of a railway engine while approaching a bridge, thus becoming British "fascism's" first interwar martyr. The government's rebuff of formal BF participation, however, set in motion the first of several breakaways that were to take place between 1925 and the death of Orman in 1935—by which time the BFs had effectively ceased to exist.

The loss of a few more clearly conservative members at the time of the General Strike made it easier for the British Fascists to take on some of the overt trappings of a fascist ideology and style. Surprisingly for a party led by someone with a taste for military apparel, the BFs had no prescribed formal dress before 1926. Subsequently a blue-shirted uniform was adopted. There was some discussion of corporatism and economic policy, but the party was never really to break away from its reactionary roots—though it had a curious strand of conservative feminism within it, including an all-woman patrol group that roamed the streets of London looking for prostitutes and communists to save.

By 1929 the BFs faced a challenge from another self-proclaimed fascist group: the Imperial Fascist League, set up by a fifty-one-year-old veterinary surgeon named Arnold Leese. After a period of colonial travels, Leese had settled in Stamford, where he joined the BFs, thus becoming their leading expert on camels. But he quickly became disillusioned with an organization that he was to describe as "Conservatism with knobs on."[3] During the 1920s Leese became increasingly hostile toward the aristocracy, whom he saw as undynamic, and toward the nouveaux riches, whom he viewed as too individualistic and materialist. Although Leese's views were often ill thought out and hardly constituted a serious ideology, he was clearly influenced by eugenicist thought—by a belief in the need to produce a society led by the purest and the best.

Leese was also a virulent anti-Semite. His racism may have been connected with his eugenicist views, though the intellectual connection is not a necessary one, as some turn-of-the-century British eugenicists had welcomed Jewish immigration as a way of improving the British stock. The origins of Leese's anti-Semitism seem rather to have lain in a belief that the Jewish form of ritual slaughter was inherently cruel. But the development of a more systematic anti-Semitism almost certainly stemmed from his contact with Henry Hamilton Beamish.[4]

Beamish was the son of an admiral who had been an aide-de-camp to Queen Victoria. He had traveled widely in the colonies before settling in South Africa, where a great revelation began to dawn on him: that behind the facade of government and business lay the hidden hand of the Jew. Returning to England, Beamish sought to launch himself on a political career as an extreme nationalist. In 1918 he came within just over a thousand votes of being elected to Parliament in a by-election that he fought on a strong anti-German and anti-Semitic platform. By 1919, however, he had come to see that anti-Germanism could not form the basis of a long-term political movement, especially as he had come to believe that the Germans too were the victims of Jewish machinations. By 1919 he was also in trouble with the law for slandering a leading Jewish industrialist, Sir Alfred Mond.

Beamish chose to flee the country, but not before setting up an organization called "the Britons." It was essentially a publishing house, which sought to educate the British to the Jewish menace. In the early 1920s its most famous product was the notorious forgery, *The Protocols of the Elders of Zion*, which purported to show that there was a Jewish conspiracy to achieve world domination. Belief in the existence of a dangerous Jewish plot was linked to the espousal of radical views on the Jewish "problem." Britons' publications argued that only expulsion or even extermination could eliminate the menace— extermination was justified by claiming that the Jews had used this tactic on the natives when they first arrived in Palestine. But unlike in Germany, no extensive network of *völkisch* and anti-Semitic groups existed to help disseminate such views, for British anti-Semitism was based more on diffuse stereotyping than on organized movements. The main role of the Britons, therefore, was to influence a limited number of individuals, like Leese, who came into contact with its leaders and publications.

Leese was conscious that his Imperial Fascist League had to be more than an anti-Semitic pressure group if it was to make a significant political impact. The possibilities of an all-embracing creed was one of the reasons why he was attracted to fascism. Fascism seemed to have the dynamism of youth; its corporatist side seemed to offer the prospect of creating a more united society; and its statism appealed to the eugenicist belief in the need to plan a better race. Even so, while the Imperial Fascist League was more truly fascist than the BFs, especially in its attack on existing elites and espousal of vague Third Way ideas, it had much in common with its rival.

It never attracted more than a few thousand primarily middle-class, mostly self-employed people. Although grouped into "Legions," the Imperial Fascist League was no street-fighting organization. It was essentially a talking shop for cranks, who were more concerned with Jews than with developing a serious doctrine. Leese found it difficult to hide his central obsession. Eventually his repeated and bizarre claims, most notably that Jews engaged in ritual murder of Christians, led to prosecution and six months' imprisonment after refusing to pay a fine. He was released in 1937, when he launched a campaign against fighting a war with Nazi Germany, a conflict whose main effect would be to defend "Jewish" communism in the Soviet Union. The impact was minimal, for it had long since been clear that the Imperial Fascist League had joined the lengthy list of one-man-and-his-dog fringe British political parties.

ii

BY THE MID-1930s the fascist torch in Britain had been passed on to a new organization, the British Union of Fascists (BUF). Its leader was Sir Oswald Mosley, a man judged by some historians to have been one of the great lost talents of British politics.[5] Born into considerable wealth, Mosley showed little interest in politics before 1914. Wartime service led to a dramatic change, which culminated in his adoption as a Conservative candidate for Harrow. In the 1918 "Hang the Kaiser" general election, when politicians fell over themselves to prove their anti-German sentiments, the twenty-one-year-old was duly elected. Mosley quickly began to make a name for himself as a backbencher. He was tall and handsome, and although a somewhat contrived orator—he took voice lessons and practiced gestures in front of a mirror—he could speak forcefully.

Unfortunately for his career as a Conservative, Mosley quickly aroused the wrath of his local party association. He exhibited little of the deference to the party leadership that characterized most Conservatives. Instead Mosley was independent and at times highly critical, most notably over the failure to fulfill the wartime promises to create a "land fit for heroes." Although a third of the Conservative vote normally came from the working class and the party was willing on occasion to put up working men for Parliament, it was essentially dominated by men of money. Meritocratic new wealth was increasingly taking the place of the aristocracy, but for Mosley this still left the Conservatives as the party of the "haves," who at most were willing to make limited and gradual concessions to the ordinary man and woman.

A radical young man in a hurry, Mosley left the Conservatives and by 1926 was Labor MP for Smethwick. Once again, Mosley soon proved that he was a troublesome colleague. His sense of dynamism meant that he felt contempt for much of Labor's quiescent leadership, which tended to sit back and blame social ills on "capitalism." After entering the cabinet of the 1929 second Labor minority government, he came in particular to despise the man supposedly in charge of alleviating unemployment. This was the hard-drinking J. R. Thomas, a former railway-union leader who told the queen that Britain was the greatest country on earth, as it allowed men like him to rise from a being a "Carriage Councillor to a Privy Cleaner." Such deference (and blurred vision) had done much in the early 1920s to assuage Conservative fears about Labor, but it did nothing to placate Mosley's impatient ambition.

Mosley proposed that the government should immediately stimulate the economy with a Keynesian package of measures, such as reducing the retirement age to sixty, and a scheme of public works. Rejected by both the cabinet and the Labor Party annual conference, Mosley chose early in 1931 to form his own grouping, the New Party, which would pioneer a "third solution." Some have argued that with more patience he might have converted the Labor Party and gone on to be its leader, but this reveals an ignorance of Labor politics almost equal to Mosley's own blindness. There was a strong aversion within Labor circles to charismatic leadership, especially when it came from educated or wealthy "intellectuals," a term applied liberally to anyone with ideas. Mosley was especially distrusted by the leaders of most of the unions, which largely funded the party, and who were beginning to reassert their influence over the political wing.

Mosley never really understood that the Labor Party placed loyalty to the organization far above devotion to ideas. His son was later to portray Mosley as a man who broke the "rules of the game."[6] It might be more accurate to say that Mosley never understood the rules, nor their meaning for others. This point is underlined by his private life, where his philandering shocked conventional opinion. It also caused great sorrow to his first wife, Cimmie (a daughter of Lord Curzon), when he eventually decided shortly before her death in the 1930s to confess to a long list of conquests. Mosley subsequently confided to one of his best friends that he had luckily not told Cimmie about her stepmother and her sister. Baldwin, who was prime minister from 1924 to 1929 and again from 1934 to 1937, spoke for many in the Establishment when he concluded that Mosley was a "cad" and a "wrong 'un."

Mosley's break with the Labor Party was not simply based on egomania, or his tendency to sudden flare-ups; once when disturbed by his children's dog while working, he leaned out of his study window and shot the exuberant animal. He believed that he had built a strong political base in the Midlands, but he failed to anticipate the wrath that would fall on him when he established his New Party after leaving the Labor Party, an anger that frequently spilled over into physical attacks. Mosley responded by setting up a "Biff Boys" protection group, which inevitably became involved in violent confrontations. Some leading supporters began to drift away, and by the summer of 1931 this and other issues were causing serious divisions within the New Party, which had always been an unstable alliance of relatively young people eager to adopt positive measures to fight economic depression. The final blow came with the snap election that followed the breakup of the Labor government during late August. In a highly polarized and vituperative campaign, Mosley and the twenty-three other New Party candidates went down to humiliating defeat.

Shortly before the election, Mosley had held talks with David Lloyd George, Winston Churchill, and other relatively independent backbenchers about the possibility of forming a transparty opposition. Former Labor Prime Minister Ramsay MacDonald and several leading colleagues had just formed a National Government including Conservatives and Liberals, so new groupings were in the air. There were intellectual signs of novel directions too, especially the growth of "Middle Way" thinking, which sought to combine the best aspects of capitalism and socialism within a democratic framework (though economic depression was soon to lead Lloyd George and some others to flirt with dictatorship).[7] The prospect of

significant agreement between these three egotistical political rene-
gades was never great, and the talks petered out. Churchill in particular seems to have realized that the best hope of a comeback was
to remain within the Conservative Party, which had actually gained
votes in 1931 after the dramatic and bitter collapse of the Labor
government.

Failure to come to an agreement with Churchill and Lloyd
George reflected a more fundamental development in Mosley's
thought. He was moving toward a break with parliamentary
democracy, which he felt was incapable of providing the decisive
leadership necessary to solve the growing economic problem. Certainly economic problems were mounting fast. Unemployment had
never fallen below 1 million after 1918; by 1931 it was approaching
2.5 million. Although various forms of welfare kept most people
out of ultimate distress, the rapid increase in unemployment after
1929 began to produce whole towns, even regions, which were
pitifully depressed—especially in the old industrial areas. (Parts of
southern England remained relatively prosperous.)

A further crucial development in Mosley's thought during 1931
concerned his attitude to the working class. He had always been an
atypical socialist in the sense that he had never seen the proletariat
as a vanguard or fount of wisdom. After the collapse of the New
Party, his view of the "masses" became even more condescending.
At one point he thought that a marigold might be an appropriate
badge for the followers of his next movement. He told a close
friend that this would add color to the drab lives of the working
class, who besides had no sense of the ridiculous.

Searching for a new cause, Mosley decided to undertake a fateful journey of discovery to Italy. During the 1920s he had not taken
much interest in Mussolini's government. To the extent that he
had any views on fascism, they seem to have been more typical of
Conservative responses rather than Labor ones. Mosley admired the
way in which Mussolini had created order in a nation characterized
by divisive tendencies, but he saw fascism as a doctrine that was
more suited to the "theatrical" Italians than to the British.[8] Yet during January 1932 Mosley saw the future—and he knew it worked.
He returned to Britain convinced that only dictatorship could se-

cure dynamic action and sure that the Italian corporate state was laying the basis for a new form of social unity and welfare.

iii

THE OFFICIAL FORMATION of the British Union of Fascists was announced in October 1932. It was accompanied by a statement of policy entitled *The Greater Britain*. Together with subsequent expansions, most notably A. Raven Thomson's *The Coming Corporate State* (1935) and Mosley's *Tomorrow We Live* (1938), the BUF program represents one of the clearest statements of policy ever to be put forward by a fascist group.[9] Here was fascism with a rational-constructive rather than mythical-populist face, though from the outset the charismatic Mosley was well aware of the power of a more emotive appeal, especially at mass meetings.

Mosley's writings portrayed a world in which Britain would have ever more industrial competitors and in which science and technology would mean fewer and fewer workers were needed. He suggested that imperial autarchy was necessary, because a largely closed market allowed for increased living standards without cheap imports being sucked in. Within this system, society would be organized on the basis of corporatism, which was portrayed rather unconvincingly as an old English idea deriving from the medieval guilds: for most people the Tudor period conjured up images of imperial expansion rather than social peace. Although the economy would still be based largely on private enterprise, the new corporations would have the legal power to enforce the compliance of banks and industry with their decisions. The trade-union side of the corporations was also faced with a drastic curtailment of traditional rights. Mosley claimed that the unions' ability to influence the decisions of the corporations, and the prosperity that the system would bring, would make strikes "unnecessary."

An economic program of this kind would not have made Mosley a fascist, though it exhibits clear parallels with much continental Third Way thinking. More explicitly fascist was Mosley's mixture of the belief that people were necessarily unequal with a desire to destroy class differences. The first led him to stress the vital importance of leadership. Among the conclusions he derived from the second belief was the necessity for all schools to be controlled by the state in order to create a true meritocracy. Even more clearly fascist was the general attempt to synthesize key aspects of the old with the new, especially in the quest to produce a new fascist man.

The program was accompanied by a dual political strategy: the desire to create a trans-class mass movement and an attempt to court sections of Establishment opinion. Popular conceptions of Mosley have focused on the former side of his activities, but during the early phase of the BUF he put considerable emphasis upon the latter. Mosley was very conscious that fascism in both Italy and Germany had come to power in part through elite connivance, and he saw Establishment support as the key to creating a mass movement, which in turn would help produce the political conditions necessary for him to come to power.

During the New Party phase, Mosley had learned that his emphasis on economic regeneration could appeal to some businessmen. Lord Nuffield, the founder of the Morris car company, had been an important financial benefactor at this time. With the creation of the BUF, considerable emphasis was placed on maintaining and increasing such donations as the New Party spent lavishly on a large "Black House" headquarters in Chelsea. The employment of several hundred full-time officials, and payments to some blackshirt activists, were further major expenses.

Another lesson from New Party days was the potential for attracting the support of Britain's maverick press barons. British people bought more newspapers per capita than any other nation in the world. Usually the owners of these great press empires were Conservatives, but they tended to be highly critical of what they saw as the moderate and undynamic leadership of the party during the interwar period. As a result, by late 1933 Lord Rothermere had decided to use his papers to back the BUF—a decision trumpeted on the front page of the mass-circulation *Daily Mail* during January 1934 with the headline HURRAH FOR THE BLACKSHIRTS.

There was another, more diffuse aspect to Mosley's elite strategy. It involved a number of discreet dinners and other meetings designed to attract dissident Conservatives and members of the Establishment who saw the fascist dictators as a bastion against communism, but who would almost certainly never have dreamed of openly attending a BUF meeting.[10] Particular targets of this propaganda were friends of the Prince of Wales. Mosley seems to have believed, not without reason, that the soon-to-be Edward VIII harbored sympathies for fascism, or at least hankered after a more authoritarian form of government. Indeed, Mosley seems to have envisaged that it would be the next king who would invite him to form an administration.[11]

During early 1934 Mosley was especially optimistic that his dual strategy was working, for the BUF was beginning to experience a dramatic increase in membership, almost certainly as a result of the publicity in Rothermere's papers. From around ten thousand to fifteen thousand members during 1932–3, the BUF had grown to approximately fifty thousand by June 1934. Initially its membership was based primarily on the remnants of the New Party and converts from the British Fascists and the Imperial Fascist League. Such a base meant that the membership had a strong military, middle-class, and self-employed bias, though the working class were notable among the more activist blackshirt membership and in specific areas.[12] There was a strong geographical base to membership too. Much of it was heavily concentrated in London and a small number of other urban centers like the Midlands, Leeds, and parts of Lancashire, though the BUF had pockets of support in some rural areas, which in Britain were politically far less important than in Germany and Italy, given the small size of the rural workforce.[13]

Many women joined the BUF. Fascism is normally portrayed as highly antifeminist, and female supporters tend to be ignored by critics or seen as ciphers of male partners. In fact, Mosley's and the BUF's line on women was relatively positive, although there were strong divisions within the party over this. Raven Thomson, the party's leading ideologue, advocated a variety of "progressive" policies, including no dismissal as a result of marriage (a common policy in occupations such as teaching) and paid maternity leave.[14] At least twenty percent of the BUF's membership was female, though it is not clear to what extent this can be explained by the BUF's program. Some were attracted by its promises to women, but others were undoubtedly attracted more by Mosley's charisma. And some, like Nellie Driver, seem to have found in the BUF a surrogate religion. Born into poverty in Lancashire, Driver was apolitical until attracted by the BUF's campaign to exploit distress in the cotton industry. In 1937 she became female district leader, finding a self-respect and sense of mission in the movement which she had never previously found in the church.[15]

While Driver was discovering her soul, the BUF was falling from grace nationally. Mosley's elite-oriented political strategy had always been rash. Although there were divisions within the Conservative Party, it still enjoyed the support of most of the Establishment. The economic crisis from 1929 to 1933 had never been catastrophic, and there was no serious threat from the radical left. Mosley's attempt to create a mass political movement, moreover, ran up against a strong fear of "demagogues," "populism," and the sanctioning of political violence—a fear that was colored by personal loathing in Mosley's case, as many Conservatives saw him as an egocentric and amoral turncoat.

Over the summer of 1934, dislike and suspicion of Mosley were heightened by a mass rally held in London's Olympia Hall on June 8, the greatest BUF gathering to date. Part of the problem was its style: the uniformed Mosley was surrounded by banners and spotlights, the deification of the great leader. It smacked all too clearly of foreign influence. Mosley had tried to counter the impression by stressing British antecedents for the BUF, most notably the prewar Ulster Volunteers. But here again his quest for historical legitimacy lacked feel, for the Volunteers meant little to most British people, though stereotypes of the Irish as drunken and troublesome were strong. Such connotations of disorder were doubly unfortunate, for the Olympia meeting was accompanied by considerable violence. Although the immediate cause of the disturbances was organized antifascist protest, the force used by blackshirt stewards in dealing with it shocked many people. The events were extensively, and sensationally, covered in the media.

Olympia was a disaster for the BUF, but it was quickly followed by a second body blow—the brutal Nazi Night of the Long Knives, which again received widespread publicity in the British media. It reinforced images of fascist lawlessness and bloodletting, and associated Mosley even more clearly with alien powers. The BUF was about to move completely beyond the pale.

iv

SOON AFTER the Night of the Long Knives, the government sent covert instructions to the media requesting that they starve the BUF of publicity. Rothermere needed no prompting to announce that he was withdrawing the support of his newspapers for the BUF. He was never a fascist and was mainly interested in using the BUF to put pressure on the government to adopt a more nationalist and dynamic policy. The combination of Olympia and the Night of the Long Knives undermined this strategy, for together they had clearly antagonized a broad section of opinion.

Mosley did not see the matter in this light and argued that Rothermere had been pressured into dropping the BUF by powerful Jewish advertisers. Mosley had a point: various Jewish individuals and groups inevitably were highly concerned at the rise of Nazism. There was, however, no coherent and organized Jewish lobby in Britain. The main organs of Jewish opinion, the Board of Deputies and the *Jewish Chronicle*, tended to take a rather optimistic view of British tolerance and commitment to liberal values. As a result, they tried not to panic or seem to be exercising undue pressure—though there is no doubt that opinions were offered behind the scenes to ministers and officials.

Before 1934 Mosley cannot be considered anti-Semitic in any deep-rooted sense. His New Party "Biff Boys" had been trained by a Jewish boxer, Kid Lewis, who was also a New Party candidate in the 1931 general election. The BUF in its early days included Jewish members, which led the truly anti-Semitic Leese to refer to it as the "British Jewnion of Fascists." But Mosley's increasing belief in the existence of a Jewish conspiracy was pushing him toward overt anti-Semitism. Further pressure came from virulent anti-Semites within BUF ranks, most notably from two of its most dynamic recruits, William Joyce and John Beckett.[16]

Anti-Semites are often portrayed in a simplistic manner, usually in terms of various psychological failings. Mosley, Joyce, and Beckett serve to illustrate the different routes that can lead to anti-Semitism. Mosley was essentially the amoral opportunist, driven by his quest for an issue that could rally the foolish masses. Joyce was more complex. Of Irish-American extraction, he became a member of the British Fascisti shortly after their formation in 1923. However, he was not one of the more mindless conservatives within their ranks. In 1927 he was to obtain a first-class degree in English from London University. Although there was a strongly Romantic streak of hero-worship in his makeup, he seems to have been one of those anti-Semites whose views were largely based on widespread reading and thought. Beckett's anti-Semitism was even more curious. He was a former left-wing MP and had a Jewish mother to whom he was devoted. The fact that she had been disowned by her relatives for marrying a non-Jew almost certainly played a major part in Beckett becoming a scourge of alleged financial and other misdeeds by prominent Jews even while he was in the Labor Party.

By 1936 Joyce and Beckett were trying to persuade Mosley that the BUF should pursue a highly antagonistic and violent campaign against the Jews, even courting imprisonment as a way of radicalizing the situation. During 1935–6, the BUF had begun to focus its activities on London's slum-ridden East End, the center of the Jewish population in Britain, and probably the only area of Britain in which a significant anti-Semitic tradition already existed. The main themes of BUF speakers were the staple old canards, particularly the depiction of the Jews as the hidden power in Britain, though a new strand emerged with the claim that the Jews were pushing Britain toward an unnecessary war. The BUF campaign quickly struck a chord among a section of the relatively poor and ununionized non-Jewish population, who often led a hopeless existence, surviving from hand to mouth. It was also helped by the fact that a relatively large number of Jews, and Irish Catholics, were active in the local Labor and Communist parties, which enabled the BUF to portray itself as the true "British Party."

But even in so economically bleak an area, people did not automatically turn to anti-Semitism or fascism. The father of John Gorman was so desperate that he sold his son's prized cigarette-card collection for a mere threepence to buy two sausages and some potatoes—a meal for a hungry family of four. The trauma for both father and son was immense, but it did not make them fascists.[17] There were strong civic and left-wing traditions in the East End too, which provided people with a political barrier to the fascist message. There were also highly active Jewish groups, which often overlapped with the left wing. By 1936, the latter were cooperating increasingly at the local level under an anti-fascist "Popular Front" banner.

Although BUF marches and speeches could be highly provocative, violent incidents often began with antifascist attacks.[18] Such a pattern was very much the case during the so-called Battle of Cable Street in October 1936, when as many as a hundred thousand anti-fascists rallied in the East End to the cry of "They shall not pass"— a phrase that echoed the Republican defenders of the Spanish Civil War, which was beginning to have a dramatic effect on sections of public opinion. Although six thousand police had been drafted in, it quickly became clear that a serious riot would ensue if the BUF continued with its plan to march into the East End. Orders were therefore given to Mosley to disperse the BUF contingent, and the bulk of them set off westward along the Embankment—thus following their normal practice of obeying specific police instructions (though there were numerous violent incidents).

It is not clear why Mosley decided to adopt this essentially law-abiding line. Perhaps the reason lay at the very core of his ideology, for Mosley's fascism was not based on the Romantic conception of violence as a form of transcendence that characterized many continental fascists. Possibly he still hoped that he had not burned his bridges with at least a section of the Establishment, particularly after the accession to the throne of Edward VIII in January 1936. More likely, he realized correctly that the BUF was being carefully monitored by the relatively efficient British intelligence and police services: Mosley was almost certainly aware that the party had been penetrated by several agents, though he probably did not know that the man in charge of the operation was a former member of the British Fascists. As a result, Mosley seems to have feared that if the BUF decided to adopt more violent tactics, the result would be bans or changes in the law.

Although many left-wing critics at the time, and since, have held that the forces of law and order sympathized with the BUF, in reality they contained few true fascists. Instead, there was a widespread desire within the higher levels of both the police and Home Office to balance freedom of speech with the maintenance of public order, a policy very much in keeping with the traditions of British government.[19] It was this feeling that led shortly after the Battle of Cable Street to the passing of the Public Order Act, which gave the police additional powers in dealing with marches and demonstrations, and which banned the wearing of political uniforms. Never again were the blackshirts to sally forth en masse, though by this time the party's support had dwindled outside a handful of areas.

A few days after the Battle of Cable Street, Mosley visited Germany, where he married his second aristocratic wife, Diana Mitford—whose Hitler-infatuated sister Unity was to try to commit suicide in Germany shortly after the beginning of World War II. Among those present at the marriage were Goebbels and his wife.[20] The marriage was initially kept secret, but Mosley's trip was public knowledge. It was ill-timed, coming as it did after a recent decision to change the party's name to British Union of Fascists and National Socialists. Although this was often shortened to "British Union," the change inevitably heightened the impression that the movement at best was foreign-inspired—and at worst was treacherous.

Such suspicions were further inspired by the line Mosley took on foreign affairs, an increasingly important concern after 1935. The BUF's foreign policy was essentially based on an attempt to maintain the imperial status quo. Given Britain's relative world decline, there was clearly no question of major expansion. Mosley was, therefore, willing to approve German and Italian aspirations as long as they did not conflict with British interests. As a result, his line on the Italian invasion of Ethiopia was one of noninvolvement. From 1936 on he similarly advocated neutrality toward Germany. Mosley not only argued that Germany posed no major threat to British interests, but added that even if Britain were to fight and defeat Germany, the main beneficiary would be communism rather than the British Empire, which would be denuded by the war effort—a line that has been echoed by some recent "revisionist" historians.[21]

Mosley's mounting "peace campaign" after 1935–6 made some converts, most notably the eccentric proto-ecological author of *Tarka the Otter* and other works, Henry Williamson.[22] Williamson is an archetypal example of the fascist who provides a field day for those with a bent for the psychological approach to politics. He had been a lonely child, a boy out of place at school, and a man left terribly scarred mentally by fighting in World War I. He was left with a burning desire to prevent Britain from ever again fighting a major war, and sought to promote Anglo-German friendship. Such pacifism, together with his strong tendency toward hero worship, led him to believe that Hitler's main aim was to rectify grievances stemming from the Versailles Treaty. In the spring of 1935 Williamson approached another hero, Lawrence of Arabia, with the suggestion that he should make direct contact with Hitler in order to promote a British peace movement. Tragically Lawrence was killed while riding his motorbike back from the post office where he had just telegraphed Williamson expressing his interest in the idea. Subsequently Williamson became a disciple of Mosley's, in spite of the fact that Mosley's rationalistic economic doctrine was somewhat at odds with his more romantic creed of social rebirth.

Williamson finally joined the party in 1937, a significant year for the BUF, as Mosley had decided to test public opinion for the first time by contesting a small number of London local elections. Although the best-placed BUF candidate won only twenty-three percent of the vote in Bethnal Green, Mosley sought to portray the results as a triumph given that the ratepayer franchise in local elections excluded some of his younger supporters. Yet the East End proved to be the epicenter of BUF support. Elsewhere the BUF had little organization, for by 1936 its membership had dropped to around five thousand. It also had few supporters, for the Conservatives remained a powerful electoral force on the right, and Labor had quickly recovered from its traumas of 1931. The absence of any serious electoral base for the BUF was clearly revealed in other local elections it fought during 1937. Even in Leeds, which had a large Jewish population, the two candidates could not muster two hundred votes between them.

During 1937 Mosley was forced to take action to resolve a serious financial crisis. Donations from business had largely dried up by late 1934. Subsequently the BUF relied on three main sources for funds: Mosley himself, Mussolini, and the party's generally highly active members. (The Nazis do not appear to have supplied money, probably realizing that the BUF was not a serious force.) With funds from the Duce and the dwindling membership drying up,

Mosley decided to launch a series of commercial radio stations. The plan was that they would both be profitable and provide a way to break the media silence that made it difficult for the BUF to disseminate its point of view outside a handful of areas. But this did not solve the short-term financial problem, and it became necessary to make economies by sharp cutbacks in the number of officials employed by the party. Among those affected were Beckett, who at the time was director of publications, and Joyce, who was director of propaganda.

Both had become key figures in their own right within the BUF, and their posts were important. It is, therefore, hard to avoid the conclusion that an element of personality as well as financial necessity came into this decision. Beckett in particular was all too prone to give advice, something Mosley was rarely inclined to take. He was also irreverent, witty, and suspicious of authority, the very opposite of the stereotypical fascist. Certainly, Joyce and Beckett saw their firings as unnecessary, and responded by leaving the BUF. Together they set up a rival National Socialist League, though Beckett soon broke away from this minuscule faction over Joyce's increasingly pro-German views. Beckett subsequently became involved with the Duke of Bedford's grossly misnamed British People's Party, which sought to promote friendship with Germany and to avoid a new European war, a cause that had attracted a small but active following among sections of the Establishment.[23]

Conciliation of Hitler was a message that was falling on increasingly stony ground. Although many historians have sought to show that there was widespread public support for the appeasement of the dictators, in reality there was significant opposition to the Italian conquest of Ethiopia and a growing distaste for Nazi expansionism after 1936, by which time the most humiliating aspects of the Versailles Treaty had been rectified.[24] Opposition to appeasement emerged particularly after the occupation of the Sudetenland in October 1938. Prime Minister Neville Chamberlain came home to a rapturous welcome after signing the Munich agreement, but the cinema hoardings that proclaimed "Chamberlain the Peacemaker: for One Week Only" contained an inadvertent core of truth. Relief quickly turned to hostility, which was reinforced in November 1938 by Kristallnacht: this torment of the Jews was reported even by the normally cautious local press with main headlines such as REIGN OF TERROR FOR JEWS THROUGHOUT GERMANY. The new opinion polls that emerged in the late 1930s show consistently high levels of opposition to Nazism. Antifascist sentiment did not necessarily mean that people wanted war, but most people seem to have sensed the essentially amoral nature of fascism, and especially the dangers of basing British foreign policy on the most favorable reading of Hitler's plans. (These views would have made it difficult for Britain to have come to a compromise peace with the Nazis after the fall of France in 1940, a policy advocated by some revisionist historians who have a kind of accountants' view of history without people.)[25]

When war eventually broke out in September 1939, Mosley proclaimed his patriotic fervor—though he reserved the right to criticize what he saw as an unnecessary war. Membership of the BUF was rising shortly before the war, and Mosley still believed that he could lead a popular peace movement. After the German Blitzkrieg against France, however, the government decided to intern most of the BUF's leading members. Also arrested were many of the leaders of the various pro-German groups that had sprung up during the 1930s, often with covert German support. Largely they were anticommunist rather than pro-Nazi, but at times the dividing line was thin—a point that can be seen clearly in the case of the Right Club, which was set up by a Conservative MP, William Maule Ramsay. Even after the outbreak of war the club was issuing anti-Semitic propaganda, such as a verse entitled "Land of Dope and Jewry."

In all, about fifteen hundred people were detained for fascist or pro-German sympathies. Although rumors have persisted concerning Ramsay, most were undoubtedly loyal citizens. Indeed, one BUF member was arrested while planning to sail to save men from Dunkirk, and another was arrested on his return from the brave rescue operation. By the end of 1941 only about two hundred remained in custody. These included Mosley and his wife, though there were no serious fears that Mosley was anything other than patriotic. Eventually in November 1943 he was released from jail into what amounted to house arrest on grounds of illness, a decision met by a vociferous campaign from some members of the left, especially communists and crypto-communists. In 1940, government panic was understandable, but later Mosley was undoubtedly imprisoned largely because of his views rather than for what he might do. But British civility and the rule of law meant that he, and other internees, were kept in relatively good condition and well treated.[26]

The rule of law was applied far more dubiously to another former member of the BUF. Just before the start of the war, Joyce had slipped out of Britain and traveled to Germany, where he was recruited to work in English-language radio broadcasting.[27] His magnetic quest for heroes had drawn him ultimately to the most Nordic pole and he became a total defender of Nazi policy. In Britain Joyce quickly became known as "Lord Haw-Haw"—a name coined for his ex-guards officer news-reading predecessor. His strangely accented daily dose of "Jairmany calling, Jairmany calling" made him a household name and the subject of great notoriety. After being arrested by British troops in May 1945, he was tried for treason. Although born an American and legally naturalized a German in 1939, it was decided that he had traveled to Germany on a British passport, thus accepting the protection of the Crown. On this legal nicety, he was condemned to be hanged. In spite of a surprising number of appeals for clemency, the sentence was carried out in Wandsworth jail during January 1946, where an unrepentant Joyce announced: "I am proud to die for my ideals and I am sorry for the sons of Britain who have died without knowing why."

Thus ended the final chapter of British fascism, or so it seemed at the time. In 1946 few noticed that there was a darker, more social-imperialist, side to British culture that Mosley had failed to tap. Britain's economic crisis was unquestionably less serious than Germany's, but other crucial factors in Mosley's failure included the way in which the Conservatives effectively portrayed themselves as *the* patriotic party, and Mosley's error of dressing himself in foreign garb, thus undermining any hope of legitimacy.

PART THREE

Fascism Since 1945

Neofascism in Italy

i

THE PALACE COUP that overthrew Mussolini during July 1943 did not mark the beginning of a smooth transition from dictatorship to democracy. After his daring rescue by Otto Skorzeny's SS commandos, the Duce founded the Salò Republic, which nominally still controlled most of Italy. In reality his masters were the Germans, whose armies rushed south in an attempt to stem the advance of the Allies from their Sicilian bridgehead. Confronted with this German move, the king and Marshal Badoglio's new government fled from Rome to avoid capture and probable trial by the Germans.[1]

The political vacuum created by this ignominious flight brought to prominence the opposition groups that had begun to form even before Mussolini's fall. These tended to be based on the growing Communist Party, which had maintained a skeleton underground organization; but they usually included a broad spectrum of opinion, including remnants from the old Catholic Popular Party, which were soon to coalesce into a new Christian Democratic Party (DC). The National Liberation Committees formed a remarkable popular front, out of which a broadly based coalition government emerged toward the end of the war.

Behind this facade of national solidarity lay significant social and political divisions. In the south, liberation had come in the wake of the invading Allied armies, with little help from the locals, who had remained remarkably unchanged by twenty years of fascist government. Even fascism's limited achievement in imprisoning some Mafia leaders was undone by the liberating Americans, who appointed various *mafiosi* to positions of authority in the belief that they were good antifascists (Previously, a deal had been made with the American Mafia to provide information and support.) Quickly the hidden hands of crime and influential local conservatives began to reassert themselves.

The situation was very different north of Rome. Here anti-fascists had to remain underground after the July 1943 coup. In these areas the Resistance played an active part in helping to liberate Italy, though the main fighting was done by the Allied armies. Numbering over one hundred thousand regulars by early 1945, the partisans launched a series of attacks on the Germans and supporters of the Salò Republic. The communists especially fought a brutal war with Mussolini's remaining followers, which almost certainly increased the ferocity of the fascist response. Killing fascists continued even after liberation. Estimates vary considerably, but probably at least fifteen thousand fascists died in this blood purge. Many former fascists were imprisoned too, often without being formally charged. More frequently fascists were roughed up or humiliated. Old scores were settled. One Turin left-winger, for instance, had carefully bottled the excrement that resulted after he was purged with castor oil; on liberation, he forced his fascist tormentor to drink the "wine."[2]

The division between northern and southern Italy was clearly underlined in the referendum that took place in 1946 on the future of the monarchy. The king's role in bringing Mussolini to power and supporting him at crucial moments had led to a strong desire to abolish the monarchy among the center and left-wing parties. Shortly before the referendum, however, Vittorio Emanuele abdicated in favor of his son, Umberto. The fresh appeal of the new monarch, and the widespread support for the monarchy among voters in the more conservative south, meant that the creation of a republic was approved by only fifty-four percent of Italian voters.

At the same time, Italians voted for a Constituent Assembly, which went on to approve a new constitution. The document clearly reflected a reaction against the fascist form of government: the president was to be a weak figurehead elected by Parliament, and the adoption of a list form of proportional representation meant that it was unlikely that a single party could ever again control the Chamber of Deputies. Rather than government by one party, headed by a strong leader, the intention was to encourage consensual multiparty administrations, which would be strictly answerable to the Chamber of Deputies. A commitment to regional government marked a further break with fascism, which had been highly centralized. As an additional safeguard, a ban on the reformation of the Fascist Party was incorporated into the constitution.

Behind the facade of government much remained unchanged. The absence of a major purge helps to explain the relatively benign treatment of former leading fascists by the courts or tribunals. (The smaller fry who had been kept in jail were released in 1946, when the government passed an amnesty as an act of reconciliation.) The trial of Valerio Borghese, a charismatic and much-decorated hero of the naval war against the British, was typical. He had become the leader of one of the Salò Republic's most notorious military units, which engaged in torture and reprisals against villages in the battle against the Resistance. Yet he was put on trial in Rome, well away from the scene of most of his crimes. And although sentenced to a long term of imprisonment, he was shortly afterward set free on grounds of extenuating circumstances.

By the late 1940s a further reason had emerged for leniency toward former fascists: the decision taken in 1947 by the Christian Democrat prime minister, Alceste De Gasperi, to push the communists out of his government (the socialists followed too). In effect this made former fascists potential allies, even supporters, of the DC in an anticommunist crusade.

An important section of Vatican opinion had never liked the alliance with the communists and by 1946 growing pressure was being put on De Gasperi. The rapid onset of the Cold War between East and West and the general rise of anticommunism was another factor, especially as it led to further pressures from the Americans to dump the communists. De Gasperi was in no position to resist. The DC relied heavily on the support of the Catholic church, and Italy was highly dependent on American aid in her quest to rebuild the economy. Besides, a formal peace treaty had not been signed, and De Gasperi was eager to maximize American sympathy. The government was resigned to the loss of most of Italy's former colonies, but hoped for a favorable settlement of the dispute with Yugoslavia over the northeastern border.

Hostility to communism went on to play a major part in the

1948 general elections, the first to be held under the new republican constitution. Although the communists were led by the
conciliatory Palmiro Togliatti, the power of the anticommunist
platform—underpinned by Vatican and covert American support—meant that the Christian Democrats won a remarkable
48.5 percent of the vote, which was translated into a small overall majority of seats in the Chamber of Deputies. The communists and socialists, however, remained a relatively strong force,
and the far-from-united DC still chose to form a center-right
coalition government—thus setting the pattern for postwar Italian administrations.

ii

AFTER THE WAR many fascists who wished to stay politically active
decided that their best course of action was to join one of the mainstream parties, especially the Christian Democrats. But others devoted their energies to two new parties that emerged during
1945–6.

The first was called the Party of the Common Man (UQ).³ Its
founder was Guglielmo Giannini, a writer of popular police stories.
In 1944 he started a newspaper of the same name (*L'Uomo
Qualunque*), which quickly attracted a readership of several hundred
thousand, primarily on a diet of gossip and scandal. Giannini later
claimed that it was pressure from readers that led him to form a
party during 1945. The paper sold mainly in the south, where there
was growing discontent over the political wind blowing from the
north. Considerable impetus, however, came from local ex-fascists
who were seeking a vehicle to reenter politics, and from others
who felt that a political party was useful as a means of organizing
patronage and influence. In the latter group were several landowners
and industrialists, including Achille Lauro, a Neapolitan shipowner
who had wanted to join the DC, which would not have him because of his support for Mussolini.⁴

The party's logo was a little man being crushed—by the parties,
bureaucracy, and the occupying forces. Its policy was a demagogic
collection of populist measures, such as protection for the ordinary
taxpayer from the rapacious state. On this largely negative platform,
the Party of the Common Man attracted considerable support dur-

ing 1946—twenty percent of the vote in Rome and Naples, and more in alliance with other parties elsewhere in the south. Yet the party's days were numbered: it had little sense of internal coherence, and more importantly the Christian Democrats feared that it could undermine their moves to build support in the south. Great efforts were therefore made to detach patrons such as Lauro.

A further problem was that during 1947–8, some fascist supporters of the UQ turned to another new party. This was the Italian Social Movement (MSI), which won two percent of the vote in the 1948 elections, mainly in the former UQ strongholds around Rome and in the south: antifascist activity made it difficult for the party to organize in the north, though its main weakness here stemmed from the general hostility aroused by the closing phase of the Salò Republic.[5] Although hardly a sign of mass support, the Italian election system meant that the MSI was rewarded with six seats in the Chamber of Deputies, thus establishing a presence it was never to lose.

The MSI had been founded at a small meeting in Rome on December 26, 1946. The majority of those present came from the radical wing of fascism and had been supporters of the Salò Republic. One of the key figures was Giorgio Pini, a university graduate, a journalist by profession, who had held the post of undersecretary of the interior in the Social Republic, though he tempered support for Mussolini with opposition to the Germans and the growing lawlessness within the state. Another was Giorgio Almirante, significantly younger than Pini, at thirty-two, but sharing Pini's educational background and profession.[6] He worked for a time on the main fascist racist organ, *La Difesa della Razza*, and supported the Social Republic, having been chief of cabinet to the minister of popular culture (i.e., propaganda). At the end of the war Almirante had been forced into hiding, but after the 1946 amnesty he had become active in one of the many small neofascist groups that were set up, bands engaged in painting wall slogans or occasionally attacking left-wingers.

A forceful and theatrical speaker (his father had been an actor), Almirante became the first leader of the MSI. In many ways, he led the party into an open defense of both fascist ideology and style. Its name—especially in the form *Missini,* referring to its members—

sounded like "Mussolini." Its symbol was the Italian tricolor in the
shape of a flame above a funeral bier—the phoenix rising from Mussolini's ashes. Its ideological stock in trade was anticommunism and
nationalism, which conveniently combined over strong opposition
to the territorial gains Yugoslavia had made from Italy in the 1947
peace treaty. Its social policies were a clear extension of the Salò Republic's attempt to create a more effective corporate state, and included commitments to worker participation in management and
a willingness to consider state ownership where this was in the
nation's interest. Overall, the party was to sum up its policies in the
slogan: "There are three solutions—Russia, the United States, or
the MSI."

Yet in other ways the MSI's program represented more of a
break with the past. For instance, it advocated a directly elected
presidency as a means of strengthening the executive, and the use of
frequent referenda to test public opinion—rather like the new
Gaullist Party in France, to which the MSI sometimes alluded. It is
not clear what is the main factor in explaining these changes. Unquestionably there were fears that legal suppression would follow if
the MSI appeared to endorse fascism. Possibly Almirante and other
MSI leaders genuinely perceived problems with classic fascism
(which would have been consistent with some of Mussolini's statements after his overthrow in 1943). The most likely explanation,
though not inconsistent with the previous points, is that the MSI
included a significant moderate wing, which had never been fully
fascist in a radical ideological sense.

The key member of this group was Arturo Michelini, a thirty-
seven-year-old accountant. He had been secretary of the Rome
Fascist Party, and had fought in the Spanish Civil War, but had held
no office during the Salò Republic. Another important member of
the moderate wing of the MSI was Augusto De Marsanich, an
older-generation fascist who had stayed loyal to Mussolini after the
king's coup and held various offices in the Social Republic. This
wing of the party believed that the way forward was to turn the
MSI into a clearly right-wing party—though the term "right wing"
was rarely used, as in the Italian context it conjured up images of
backwardness or extremism and alienated radical elements within
the party who claimed they were not right wing. Their strategy in-

cluded a willingness to form alliances with at least some of the "Resistance" parties in an anticommunist front.

During 1949–50, friction between these two wings grew. One major argument was about whether Italy should join NATO, which had just been formed on the initiative of two recent enemies, Britain and the United States. Almirante and the radicals were opposed, stressing the need for a European Third Force (a policy which was linked to cooperation with other European neofascist parties, though little came of this). The moderate wing, on the other hand, was willing to accept NATO as part of the defense against communism, a course that was carried by the party congress. The upshot of these wrangles was that Almirante was replaced as leader by De Marsanich in 1950.

Shortly afterward, an electoral alliance with the Monarchist Party was announced, another source of friction within the MSI, as the monarchy symbolized the betrayal of Mussolini in 1943. In the 1953 general election, the agreement worked well and it helped the MSI to win 5.9 percent of the national vote. This gave it twenty-nine seats in the lower chamber and eighteen in the Senate, which was elected on a slightly different franchise. The party's vote had a strong regional bias, with its best results coming in Sicily and Lazio, where it polled just over 11 percent. Socially it was strong among small businessmen and sections of the young, but it also had wealthier members and some working-class supporters. It seems that most of these voters were motivated by the politics of local "influence," or protest, rather than by ideology.

Many on the moderate wing of the party believed that the best way to further electoral gains was to come to some form of arrangement with the Christian Democrats. There had already been local arrangements between the parties, but the official DC line remained hostile. De Gasperi in particular believed that it was wrong to give the MSI any form of legitimacy. But there were others in the Christian Democrats, and in the Vatican, who were more sympathetic if such an alliance would keep out the left.

In 1954 De Marsanich was replaced as leader by Michelini, who was committed to the importance of an understanding. Sections of the DC responded encouragingly. In 1957 the government even authorized the relocation of Mussolini's remains to a family plot and granted a pension to his widow. Yet no formal agreement emerged and for the next general election in 1958 the MSI was forced to fight alone, the alliance with the Monarchists having collapsed: the result was a slight drop in both votes and seats. The election was clearly a setback for Michelini's strategy, but there were signs that an agreement with the DC might still be possible. The Christian Democrats were finding it increasingly difficult to forge a stable center-right parliamentary coalition without the MSI. As a result, some were talking of the need for an understanding with the socialists, a policy strongly opposed by groups within the Vatican and by the American administration.

In 1960 the situation led to a major political crisis. The president appointed a new government under Ferdinando Tambroni, a member of the DC, and the appointment was ratified in the Chamber of Deputies by a majority of just seven votes. The MSI had voted for Tambroni, so its support was crucial to his confirmation. Several ministers stated that they would resign rather than serve in a government that relied on fascist support. Tambroni therefore reconstructed his government with more compliant ministers. The new administration was provocation enough, but shortly afterward the government authorized the MSI to hold its national congress in Genoa.

Genoa had been a center of Resistance activity, and allowing the conference to take place there was clearly ill advised, given that wartime memories remained strong. Many locals had been deported to work in Germany and others killed, events that led the local prefect to be convicted of war crimes. An antifascist front, led by the communists, took to the streets in protest. The Tambroni government had already condoned considerable police force in dealing with a wave of industrial unrest. The same muscle was now turned on the antifascist protesters. The result was a near revolt in the city. Quickly, serious troubles spread to other parts of Italy. The ensuing riots left several people dead, and there was fighting in the Chamber of Deputies itself.

Michelini's strategy had failed, though he survived as leader until 1969. The MSI struggled on as an electoral grouping, occasionally gaining a new recruit. The most colorful was Ernesto "Last Shot" Brivio, who at the very end of the war had attacked left-wing workers. He was captured and tortured, but was released in 1947 and went on to make his fortune in South America. Returning to Italy, he spent a considerable sum on gaining election to Rome's city council in 1962—and on becoming chairman of Rome's Lazio soccer club.[7] But the MSI in general was signally failing to progress—and Brivio's hour in the limelight was short-lived, for it was not long before he disappeared again under mysterious circumstances.

iii

AT THE 1956 MSI National Congress a group of dissidents had chanted, "Fewer double-breasted suits—more brass-knuckles." The attack illustrates another problem that plagued the De Marsanich–Michelini plan to present the MSI as a respectable element of the right: the group of neofascists who were strongly, even violently, opposed to courting the DC.

As the MSI had moved rightward, Almirante had resigned from the National Committee in order to launch an attack on the leadership. He claimed that the party was essentially proletarian, a clear reference to fascism's more left-wing roots. He also spoke of replacing a "quantitative democracy" with a "qualitative one," underlining his continued contempt for the masses and commitment to elitist thought. Pini also attacked the rightward drift, arguing that the MSI was a reactionary party without a future. Pini left the party and formed a Turin-based rival group, one of several minor sects that sought to remain true to the Verona program. Almirante, however, decided to remain and work within the MSI. By the mid-1950s, the party had built up a relatively strong organization, including its own press, youth groups, and trade union—the Italian Confederation of National Workers Union. Given that fascism was a minority strand in Italian postwar culture, it would clearly have been difficult to build a major rival organization.

Almirante's views were increasingly being influenced by the writings of Julius Evola. Evola, who was born in 1898 into an aristocratic family, began his career as a Futurist and Dadaist painter and poet—early signs of hostility of the dominant "bourgeois" culture. He subsequently turned to fascism, though he never joined the Fascist Party. As an artist and thinker he saw himself standing above politics. Besides, his contempt for the masses and his strongly pagan views clearly differentiated him from the more populist and conservative side of Mussolini's regime. Evola had more in common with Nazism than fascism though his racism was based on cultural rather than biological traits, a point recognized by Mussolini when he endorsed Evola's book *Synthesis of the Doctrine of Race* (1941) as the official statement of fascism's "spiritualist" racism.

In 1944 while staying in Vienna, Evola was permanently crippled by a Russian bomb. The injury reinforced his leaning toward thought rather than action, and after the war he remained aloof from party politics until his death in 1974. Instead he devoted himself mainly to writing, producing a voluminous output to add to his prewar works. The result has been described as the most original and creative body of thought to come from an Italian fascist.[8] In fact, much of the doctrine was secondhand and Evola's writings are often obscure, but this has not stopped him from becoming a seminal source of reference for neofascists, in Italy and elsewhere.

Evola's thought was the quintessential fascist blend of rationality and myth. His central idea, which he developed in *The Revolt Against the Modern World* (1934), was that Western society was in terminal decline because it had moved away from the hierarchical, warrior-priest society which he saw as central to successful previous civilizations.[9] Like many intellectuals who turned to fascism in the early twentieth century, Evola was interested in other cultures. Japan particularly influenced him, especially its Samurai code (*bushido*), though he was also interested in the Islamic notion of Holy War (*jihad*) and Hindu martial models. Evola contrasted such codes with the materialist decadence he saw as lying at the heart of Western society. He believed this was leading to a rootless society, which would soon succumb to the challenge from a more martial opponent. Predictably, during World War II his views led him to admire the Waffen SS as the embodiment of the defense of European culture against the alien hordes.

Evola's contempt for bourgeois society and nonlinear view of history owed much to Nietzsche, Spengler, and the German conservative revolutionaries. Their influence can also be seen in the immediate political conclusion he drew from his thought: the need to withdraw from the day-to-day issues of politics and to concentrate on creating a new elite class that would be imbued with the ethic of the warrior-priest, men who could unite society around a new secular religion and provide it with a sense of purpose worth defending. This aspect of mental preparation and waiting under-pinned Almirante's patient opposition within the MSI.[10]

The immediate political implications of Evola's thought, how-ever, could be read another way. Evola wrote of the need to create "Political Soldiers," who would lead the new revolution against capitalist decadence. Evola may have used the term simply to under-line the martial attributes necessary for his new elite, but it was easy to deduce that he was really advocating a policy of terrorist violence, actions that would serve both to develop the consciousness and mental discipline of the Political Soldier, and to destabilize the hated democratic state.

These ambiguities in Evola's thought were reflected in the views of a group of dissidents in the MSI. A key figure in his fac-tion was Giuseppe (Pino) Rauti. Born in 1926, he had volunteered to fight in the Social Republic's militia. After a period of exile in the Spanish Foreign Legion, he returned to Italy and joined the MSI in 1948. Subsequently, he was one of the founders of an Evo-lian study group named New Order. This group more openly pro-claimed its hostility to liberal democracy, and some within it were clearly attracted to violence. In 1956 the New Order became an autonomous organization when Rauti left the MSI, disgusted with its conservatism. By the late 1950s the group had attracted nearly ten thousand recruits.

One of those who joined the New Order was Stefano Delle Chiaie, another admirer of Evola. Delle Chiaie, who became known as the "Black Bombardier" or "Shorty" (a term rarely used to his face because he was a martial arts expert), was in many ways typical of the emerging generation of neofascist terrorists. He was young (born in 1936), and had been a student, though he did not finish his studies. Politically active in the MSI from an early age, he had come to despair of its moderation. He tired of the New Order too, which he thought was mainly a talking shop. During 1960, therefore, he formed the National Vanguard, which quickly at-tracted about two thousand members, especially in Rome, Milan, and Turin. Most were young males, usually from the lower-middle or professional classes. Initially, its main activities were attacks against left-wingers, though it was also probably behind a small number of assaults on Jews.

By the mid-1960s Delle Chiaie and others were beginning to develop a more refined theory of political violence. They realized that there was no prospect in the foreseeable future of conducting another March on Rome, as Mussolini had done in 1922. It was not simply a result of the small number of radical neofascists compared to the *squadrista* forces Mussolini was able to mobilize in 1922. They also realized that the left was willing to resist—as it had in Genoa at the time of the Tambroni affair. Their thoughts, therefore, turned more to the need for a military coup. In order to prepare the way, they decided that it was necessary to condition public opinion by committing acts of violence that could be blamed on the left.

There were groups within the Italian Establishment who held similar views about a takeover, though mostly they sought to establish an authoritarian conservative regime rather than a socially radical fascist one. Some were strongly opposed to the entry of the socialists into the governing coalition that had taken place during 1963. Even more ominously, the continued growth of the PCI, which won twenty-seven percent of the vote in 1963, was viewed with considerable dismay in many quarters—especially as some believed that the communists were only waiting for an opportune moment to launch their own coup.

Against this background, a still mysterious plot was hatched during the early 1960s by the commander-in-chief of the Carabinieri (militarized police), General Giovanni De Lorenzo.[11] De Lorenzo was a burly but athletic man, the very image of the right-wing dictator, complete with monocle and mustache. Politically, his track record was enigmatic, for after 1943 he had helped train partisans, which was an unusual course of action among professional officers, who tended to remain aloof from the mainly communist-controlled Resistance. After the war he became a head of intelligence, which brought him into contact with Americans who were unhappy about the communist threat. De Lorenzo had built up dossiers on politicians, trade-union leaders, journalists, and others whom he believed to be politically dangerous. He planned to use this material to convince the other armed services that a left-wing coup d'état was imminent unless he struck first.

When the socialists brought down the government in 1964 as a result of its failure to implement various reforms, De Lorenzo was given the pretext to set the wheels in motion. The plot began to come unstuck, however, when he failed to gain the cooperation of the other services, partly as a result of their personal antagonism toward him. Another crucial factor was that key members of the interim administration, especially Aldo Moro, got wind of what was afoot and ordered loyal army units into Rome. Remarkably, it was two years before news leaked out to the public: predictably, given De Lorenzo's expertise in covert operations, the resulting parliamentary committee of investigation proved inconclusive, though an indication of the nature of De Lorenzo's politics later emerged when he became an MSI deputy.

The failure of this plot did not put an end to what the violent neofascists called the "strategy of tension." The successful coup in Greece carried out by a group of authoritarian conservative colonels in 1967 seemed to show that a small body of men could overthrow a democratic government. Moreover, 1967–9 was a time of considerable social and political discontent in Italy. This included the emergence of left-wing terrorism in the form of the Red Brigades, who were to launch a series of violent attacks on individuals and the state. (Among their victims was to be Moro, who had helped to defuse the De Lorenzo coup.) Another major trend that worried conservatives during the late 1960s was the rise of a more militant trade unionism, as workers sought to benefit from the rapid economic growth that was taking place especially in the north. More generally, the late 1960s saw an explosion of youth culture and radical views, including opposition to American involvement in the Vietnam War and to American economic and cultural "imperialism." It was an age of long hair, loud music, sexual revolution, and protest, all of which often shocked the more staid and prudish.

With fears of the left and social disorder growing, a bomb exploded outside the Agricultural Bank in Milan's Piazza Fontana on

December 12, 1969. Sixteen people were killed and over ninety were injured. Police quickly arrested two left-wingers, one of whom died shortly afterward following a mysterious fall from a window at police headquarters. A variety of other attacks and bombings during the ensuing months were similarly blamed on the left.[12]

One man who may not have ordered the attacks, but who almost certainly saw them as preparing the ground for a coup, was Borghese. After his early release from postwar imprisonment, Borghese had joined the MSI, but in the early 1960s he had broken with the party and founded the National Front. Tall and imposing, Borghese envisaged himself as a new Duce, and used his group to rally a hard core of violent activists. Although the exact details remain unclear, it seems that Borghese sought to launch his coup on the night of December 7–8, 1970.

A group of National Front supporters, together with members of Delle Chiaie's National Vanguard and other groups, gathered in Rome. The plan was to occupy key government buildings and to capture the state radio and television network, thus gaining control of the main source of information, which would be crucial immediately after the coup. But drama soon turned to farce as torrential rain damped the spirits of the stormtroopers, who were waiting for an order that mysteriously never came. Shortly afterward, Borghese fled to Spain, and the attempted coup was hushed up initially. A series of revelations during 1971 to 1973, however, made it clear that there had been a conspiracy in which neofascists were implicated. Further evidence revealed that Borghese had devised another scheme, which involved the assassination of fifteen hundred people, including leading members of the government.

New charges were now made concerning the 1969 Milan bombing and other terrorist incidents. The main neofascist activist charged with the Milan carnage was Franco (Giorgio) Freda, who was a member of Rauti's shadowy New Order. After a lengthy process, Freda and two other people were sentenced to life imprisonment, though the fact that they might have been framed meant they went for retrial in the 1980s and were acquitted. It is interesting to note that Freda did not conform to the stereotype of the terrorist as the mindless psychopath: he was a lawyer by training, and was particularly able to develop a sophisticated defense of the use of political radicalism in the pursuit of what he termed a "Nazi-Maoist" strategy.

The government went on to ban New Order, together with Delle Chiaie's National Vanguard. But the bombings did not end. Old groups reformed, while new ones, like the Armed Revolutionary Nuclei (NAR) emerged to continue the slaughter. Three attacks in particular indicate the indiscriminate nature of this violence. In Brescia on May 28, 1974, eight people were killed and seventy-nine injured following a bombing aimed at a political meeting that had been organized jointly by the left and Christian Democrats to protest against neofascist violence.[13] On August 4, 1974, a bomb exploded on the Italicus express train as it passed through a tunnel outside Bologna, a prominent municipality controlled by the communists: twelve people were killed and forty-eight injured. Almost six years to the day later, on August 1, 1980, Bologna was the scene of Europe's worst neofascist massacre. In peak holiday season a bomb was planted in the railway-station waiting room: its explosion left eighty-five people dead or dying, and another two hundred injured.

Up until the mid-1970s, elements within the Italian state had often turned a blind eye to neofascist terrorism. Their myopia had begun to diminish even before the 1980 Bologna massacre, as the banning of some groups shows. But the combination of Bologna and the assassination of a judge who was investigating neofascist terrorism led to a more systematic pursuit of the guilty. Picked up in the process was a remarkable collection of characters, many of whom belonged to a Masonic Lodge known as P2.[14] P2 was a long-established lodge for those in delicate or important positions, and it seems to have been a center for plotting among leading right-wing members of the political, business, and military Establishment during the late 1960s. Interest in some form of coup was revived during the late 1970s by fears that an important wing in the Christian Democrats, including Moro, were willing to come to a "historic compromise" with the PCI. Under the leadership of Enrico Berlinguer, the communists had moved toward a highly moderate line, accompanied by continued electoral growth: it seemed that it would be only a short matter of time before the PCI replaced the Christian Democrats as the largest party.

The key figure in P2 plotting seems to have been its grand master, Licio Gelli. A man who had volunteered to fight with the fascist forces beside General Franco during the Spanish Civil War, Gelli had managed to change sides after the Allied invasion of Italy. Subsequently, he maintained murky relations with a variety of interests, including Italian and foreign intelligence services. His main contact among the neofascist radicals was Delle Chiaie. When the pair eventually came to court in 1988, they were cleared of participation in terrorist activities, though they were convicted of perjury in connection with the multifarious cover-ups that surrounded various bombings and plots. The full truth about who was involved in the strategy of tension, even the exact role of P2, never came out.

iv

AT THE TIME of the first major neofascist bombings in 1969, the MSI had been languishing as a parliamentary force. It had lost votes in three general elections running and seemed to have no serious prospects. But in 1969 Michelini died and Almirante returned as leader of the party. His stated goal was to lead the MSI in a new direction, though one that did not lose sight of the past, a policy he summed up with the enigmatic phrase "Back to the Future" (*Nostalgia dell'Avvenire*).

Almirante believed that the antifascists had won the postwar battle of images and words. He tried, therefore, to persuade activists to drop their symbols, such as the black shirts and the one-armed salute, which most Italians saw as embodying an alien past. To appease hard-core MSI members, party propaganda often contained hidden messages relating to the past, images that activists could "decode."[15] To extend the party's appeal beyond a dwindling band of nostalgics and its southern clienteles, Almirante began to pay more attention to the styles and themes of the left, focusing on youth culture, ecology, and women's issues.[16] He was well aware, however, that most MSI voters were conservative rather than radical, and this new emphasis on left-wing symbolism was countered by the use of more traditional Catholic imagery, such as the Madonna. For similar reasons, the MSI continued to stress issues that were dear to the heart of most Catholics, like opposition to abortion and divorce—themes that coexisted at best uneasily with the attempt to portray the party as "modern."

"Back to the Future" was not so much a break with the past as an attempt to make the MSI a broader church, more capable of attracting a variety of supporters. The strategy was quickly rewarded as a growing number of former Christian Democrats showed themselves willing to appear on the platform at MSI rallies, and even on their electoral lists. And although Almirante had been critical of the alliance with the Monarchists in the 1950s, in 1972 he signed a new agreement. Monarchist support had shrunk to 1 percent of the vote, but it retained some important backers and helped to underline the MSI's respectability as an alternative to the Christian Democrats. In the 1972 general election, this policy reaped rewards when the new alliance, fighting under the revealing name "National Right" (*Destra Nazionale*), gained 8.7 percent of the vote, nearly double the 1968 figure.[17]

These gains were largely lost during the 1976 and 1979 general elections, though the party obtained a minor consolation in 1979 by winning a toehold in the first direct elections to the European Parliament. Sensing the danger, the Christian Democrats had launched a strong attack on the MSI, claiming that it was linked to the wave of terrorist bombings and other violence. The view was shared by some within the moderate wing of the MSI, which was an important factor in the major breakaway led by the party's spokesman in the Chamber of Deputies. As a result, by the end of the 1970s, the MSI found itself as isolated as ever, and still tarred with the extremist, even terrorist, brush.

Paradoxically, the situation began to take a turn for the better after the 1980 Bologna bombing. The revelations surrounding the P2 lodge had implicated various leading politicians, which led to the fall of the Christian Democrat–dominated government and the appointment of Italy's first postwar prime minister who did not come from the DC. The realization was growing that Italian politics had become dangerously polarized and that alienation from the system was on the increase. Awareness of the latter problem set in train a search for new ideas about the structure of government, which heightened the profile of the MSI, since its official line had always stressed the need for a stronger executive and other constitutional changes.

The quest for reconciliation can be seen in the remarkable decision taken by Berlinguer to send condolences on behalf of the PCI to the parents of an MSI youth who had been mortally attacked while putting up posters. When Berlinguer suffered a brain hemorrhage during the 1984 European election campaign, Almirante returned the goodwill by sending a note expressing his hopes that the communist leader would make a speedy recovery. The possibility that the MSI might have something to contribute to public debate about constitutional reform was underlined when Almirante was accorded for the first time an official meeting with the president of the Republic. This trend was continued during the late 1980s and early 1990s by the new president, Francesco Cossiga. (Cynics claimed that he ardently promoted reform to divert attention from his alleged past role in setting up the secret Gladio network to resist a communist takeover, news of which broke in the late 1980s.)

At the same time a slow but sure reassessment of the fascist past was taking place. During the mid-1970s, Italy's leading academic specialist on Mussolini, Renzo De Felice, had caused a major stir when he argued that up until the late 1930s the Duce had enjoyed widespread support.[18] His argument contrasted markedly with the almost consensual Resistance view that fascism had been imposed and maintained by violence, a view superbly captured at this time by Bernardo Bertolucci's epic left-wing film *1900* (1976).[19] When the smoke died down, a growing understanding began to emerge that—while the nature of support needed accurate probing—fascism did have strong roots in Italy. The understanding that fascism was not a bolt from the blue was accompanied by an appreciation of the more positive aspects of the regime, such as its attempt to curb the Mafia, or its social policies. There were even signs of revisionism relating to the brutal closing phase of the Social Republic. The popular image, depicted in an extreme form in Paolo Pasolini's film *Salò: One Hundred and Twenty Days of Sodom* (1975), was that this was a period when the brutality of fascism reached its most appalling peak. New work began to show that sometimes fascist violence was a response to communist provocation.[20]

At the 1987 MSI Congress, Almirante pointed to the collapse of old certainties and argued that there were increasing signs that people were searching for an alternative to Marxism and liberal capitalism. He highlighted the new emphasis on national identity and the growth of worker cooperation with management as signs of this change in the political climate. Almirante had previously announced his decision to stand down from the leadership, and this speech was unquestionably a swan song, defending a life dedicated to fascist politics. But there is no doubt that he captured a widespread feeling when he argued that fascism was at last emerging from Purgatory.

Almirante's resignation meant that the 1987 Congress became a battle for the succession, which turned into a two-horse race.[21] One major contender was Rauti, who had rejoined the party in 1969 and been elected to the Chamber of Deputies in 1972, and who had become a prominent figure in the European Parliament in the 1980s. The other main challenger was Gianfranco Fini, who at the tender age of thirty-five was twenty-six years Rauti's junior. Since 1983 he too had been a deputy, having previously risen rapidly through the party's youth movement.

Rauti remained a disciple of Evola: he rejected the growing Americanization of European values and stressed the need for spiritual over monetary values.[22] Another key influence on Rauti by the late 1980s were the Italian disciples of the French New Right.[23] Their influence can be seen in a variety of other policies, such as the acceptance of Third World nationalism and the espousal of "differentialism": the belief that Western culture was a form of racism in the sense that it obliterated all cultural distinctions. This was linked to an appeal to the left, especially by linking the process of Americanization to the allegedly rapacious activities of multinational companies, which were beginning to destroy jobs in Italy as they transferred their activities to the more easily exploited Third World. Many of these views found a strong echo, especially among the MSI's younger members, who were often very different from the archetypal, mindlessly authoritarian right-winger. The youth wing of the party had focused increasingly on issues that were often similar to those stressed by left-wing youth, including ecological issues, support for greater equality in gender relationships, and pro-Palestinian views on the Middle East.

Fini was a protégé of Almirante, which reveals much, and yet little. It clearly meant that Fini believed the MSI could become a significant electoral force, especially by playing down the more radical side of fascism. It also indicated that he would support further contacts with other parties as a way of underlining respectability. But it was unclear whether there was a hidden agenda behind such views, for Almirante's conversion to a more moderate line was largely pragmatic. Nor was it clear whether Fini intended to follow Almirante in turning a blind eye to the violent element in the party, and those who continued to deck themselves in fascist regalia. Even so, Fini clearly appealed to the less radical wing of the party and to others who thought that Rauti was too compromised by the past. As a result, Fini emerged the winner by 727 votes to 608.

Shortly after this narrow victory, Fini made a series of philosophical and policy statements designed to appease the radical wing of the party. They acknowledged that fascism was not a right-wing doctrine and supported more worker control over large enterprises. Strong tensions remained between the Rauti and Fini factions, however, and a dispute flared up over immigration. Before the late 1980s this had not been a significant issue, as relatively few immigrants lived in Italy.[24] A combination of growing numbers and the sudden rise of the anti-immigrant Front National in France encouraged Fini to think that here lay an issue that could broaden the MSI's base. Rauti responded by stressing the need to solve the problems of Third World poverty, which was caused by the capitalist system. Although this tendency to portray immigrants as victims rather than a menace failed to strike a major chord among the activists, there was widespread fear that Fini was seeking to make the MSI a populist rather than a fascist party, in much the same way that Le Pen had played down the fascist side of the Front National.[25] Such fears were to play a major part in Rauti replacing Fini as leader during 1990.

Splits within the party, continuing revelations about past terrorism, and the fact that fascism's rehabilitation was far from complete all help explain why the MSI's electoral position remained relatively weak at this time. In the 1987 general elections it had dropped back to 5.7 percent of the vote; in 1992 the figure fell slightly again. The 1992 result was particularly disappointing for the

MSI, as the elections had been fought against a background of mounting economic problems, most notably serious unemployment and a massive public debt. Also growing was public disillusion with the governing parties, which were increasingly being viewed as an incompetent and corrupt *partitocrazia*. Widespread concern had inspired the use in 1991 of the popularly initiated referendum to change the electoral system in order to minimize the possibility of fraud. The system, however, remained based on proportional representation, which helped a variety of new parties, including an anti-Mafia one set up by a brave core of activists, to gain representation in the Chamber of Deputies.

The most significant new party was the Northern League.[26] Its leader was the charismatic Umberto Bossi, a middle-aged electrical technician by trade, who had played a major role in building the party from scratch during the 1980s. Bossi was erratic and prone to gaffes: when judges were rumored to be about to implicate the League in financial scandals, he had responded provocatively. More generally his approach was based on an antisystem attack rather than a clear and detailed program. But he also was a master of manipulating the media, not least through his ability to furnish a catchy sound bite: one of the more salacious proclaimed that "The League's got a hard one," which might have backfired in Anglo-Saxon countries but which struck a ready appeal in a country whose soccer programs on television are sometimes hosted by scantily dressed bimbos. Bossi proved particularly adept at exploiting a sense of historical difference between the "productive" north and the "African" south. Belief in northern supremacy had the advantage of seeming to legitimize anti-immigrant politics. Immigrants did not simply take jobs or become involved in crime—they posed a danger to the very soul of the "Lombard" nation. Bossi even talked of multicultural society as being like Hell.[27]

Bossi's forceful leadership, his ethnocentric policies, and the support the League attracted from northern Italy's many small-business owners, inevitably led some commentators to class the party as fascist.[28] There were, however, crucial ideological differences. Although at times vague about policy, the League basically advocated a free market economy, anathema to all true fascists. The League's hostility to strong central government was also quite alien to the fas-

cist tradition, which sought to complete the Risorgimento by re-
making the Italian people. The League is better seen as a form of
populism, fueled largely by growing discontent with the political
class—an alienation that was reinforced in the north by the belief
that large parts of the state system had been colonized by nepotistic
southerners.

As the MSI was largely a southern-based party, it had not been
able to exploit this sentiment, though it had made gains in some
northern areas where there was hostility to demands for autonomy
from German speakers. But a wave of scandals throughout 1992–3
prepared the way for a major breakthrough on the electoral front.
A series of revelations showed extensive fraud and corruption, particularly among members of the governing parties, who had often
taken payment from private business in return for favors. At one
point 221 deputies in the 1992 parliament, five ex-party leaders,
four ex-prime ministers, and three thousand others were under investigation in a process that culminated in 1995 in the charging of
seven-times Prime Minister Giulio Andreotti with collaboration
with the Mafia. The main party affected was the Christian Democrats, and the way seemed open for an MSI breakthrough, since the
party was left notably untouched by these scandals.

During 1993 the MSI made a series of gains in elections. Among
its more spectacular performances in the first half of the year was its
takeover of the municipal council of Latina, a fascist new town built
in the 1930s that had been controlled by the Christian Democrats
since 1948. The new mayor was an unrepentant seventy-two-year-
old former supporter of the Salò Republic who had spent four years
in jail after being condemned to death in 1945: he portrayed Mussolini as a man who had conquered sickness, poverty, and misery.
During the December municipal elections, two campaigns in particular attracted attention. Mussolini's granddaughter, Alessandra, came
close to being elected mayor of Naples, where this young and attractive former minor film star had been elected to the Chamber of
Deputies in the previous general election. In Rome, Fini came even
nearer to winning when he gained forty-seven percent of the vote
in the runoff ballot.

By this time Fini's more moderate policies had helped him to
regain the leadership of the party from Rauti. Fini had also attracted

the support of the private television networks of the maverick conservative business mogul Silvio Berlusconi. The result was an increasingly high public profile of the MSI leader, which differed significantly from the image of the archetypal fascist. Slim, wearing glasses, and normally dressed in well-cut and sober double-breasted suits, Fini looked more like a middle-aged conservative academic than a political extremist. An ardent supporter of Rome's Lazio soccer team, there was a more popular side to his image too. His attractive wife, Daniela, added further gloss to the image of the happy, clean-cut family man: the media frequently described her as a model of elegance.

Berlusconi, whose media empire helped launch Fini as a major public figure, was no fascist: he was a strong defender of the free market, but he was also ardently anticommunist. Although in 1989 the Communist Party had reformed itself into the Party of Democratic Socialism (PDS), apparently committed to extremely moderate policies, this did not end anticommunism among a section of the right. The December 1993 municipal elections seemed to indicate that a PDS–led alliance would win Italy's next national elections. These elections even raised the specter of the destruction of much of the parliamentary center and right, for a further referendum in 1993 had led to the introduction of a new electoral system in which three-quarters of the seats would be won by the first-past-the-post system. Such a system could produce a grossly disproportional result, particularly if a largely united center-left faced a divided right. As a result, Berlusconi launched his own political party in January 1994, which was named Forza Italia ("Come on Italy"). A combination of Berlusconi's financial resources and the extensive network of AC Milan's supporters' clubs (Italy's most famous soccer club was part of Berlusconi's empire) quickly provided the new party with the basis of a national organization.

The MSI too gained a new label for these elections. In January 1994 Fini announced the creation of the National Alliance (AN), which included some former Christian Democrat members.[29] Fini accompanied this by openly avowing that the AN was a right-wing grouping: one 1994 election poster showed a confident-looking Fini above the words: "A right ready to govern. At last. To rebuild Italy."[30] The party's policy stressed the less radical side of the MSI program. Key elements included a package of institutional reforms that the party had pushed for some time, notably a French-style strong presidential executive and the greater use of referenda. Economically Fini proposed to temper the free market by giving the state a guiding role, but anticapitalism and corporatism were kept under careful wraps. Socially, old Catholic values were stressed, including the fight against abortion and the defense of the family as an institution. Foreign policy figured prominently. The AN proposed a federation of independent European states rather than a truly federal one. The issue of border revision with the former Yugoslavia was also featured.[31]

Under Berlusconi's leadership, Forza Italia, the AN, and the Northern League formed a Freedom Alliance for the forthcoming national elections. Backed heavily by his media network, Berlusconi (known as *"Sua Emittenza"* or "his broadcastship") went on to emerge as the leader of the largest party. His party's policies were at times vague, especially on foreign policy, but the elegantly dressed and confident Berlusconi quickly proved that he had the demagogue's touch when it came to exploiting popular grievances, and his own dynamic image. He subsequently became the first prime minister of what many dubbed Italy's Second Republic. The AN gained 13.5 percent of the vote and 107 deputies, the vast majority of whom came from within the ranks of the MSI—far higher than any previous MSI vote. It was rewarded with five seats in the new ministry, the first fascists to hold government posts since 1945.

There was a wave of international protests about fascist participation in government, but the result did not shock most Italians. Nor did reports that Fini had referred to Mussolini as the greatest statesman of the century. (Fini claimed he was misreported: he had really said that the Duce was one of the men who most encapsulated the century, and sought to make it clear that he referred to the pre-1938 period.) In the June 1994 elections the AN confirmed its new respectability, gaining eleven seats in the European Parliament, compared to four in 1989. By the autumn, the MSI leader found himself attracting growing respect, even from opponents—a fact reflected in a series of polls which showed that Fini had become Italy's most popular politician, a man whose appeal was increasingly cutting across age and class barriers.

Fini was more than ever convinced that the way forward was to turn the MSI into a "post-fascist," moderate right-wing party, modeled loosely on the lines of French Gaullism. In pursuit of this goal, he announced that the main item on the agenda of the party's January 1995 Congress would be the creation of a formal "National Alliance" party, which would not necessarily accept all of the two hundred thousand former MSI members. The Congress turned out to be historic in several ways. With the exception of one lone dissenting voice, it agreed to the change of title and proclaimed itself committed to "freedom, justice and democracy" and opposed to "all forms of racism and totalitarianism." Equally remarkably, the PDS sent an official delegate (no PCI delegate ever attended an MSI Congress), a man who had actually fought against fascism in the Resistance. The only black spot was the fact that Rauti and his faction abstained on the crucial vote, though Fini may have welcomed this, as it was clearly his intention to exclude the old hardliners from the new party.

At this point a series of problems for the AN begin to emerge. One problem concerns the likely loss of support of many MSI activists, for it is clear from the leadership struggles from 1987 to 1992 that the MSI has a major radical wing. Although the MSI-AN has recruited a considerable number of new activists, some of these lack experience in important areas—such as running elections. It is less clear how many former MSI voters were ideologically radical, but MSI voting cannot entirely be explained by protest factors. Fini hopes that losses among radicals will be more than made up for by new recruits, but here lies the central enigma of the new AN. There are still strong fears that behind the moderate right-wing facade lies a radical soul.[32] Fini has not so much disowned the fascist past as written off the parts that are indefensible—especially the anti-Semitism and the stifling dictatorship.

In December 1994 Fini tried to portray the party as having roots deep in Italian culture, stretching back to Dante and Machiavelli; but his simultaneous reference to the key fascist theorist Gentile and the communist theorist Antonio Gramsci seemed to indicate that the core fascist tendency toward syncretic thought was far from dead. Critical references to the problems of the public sector and need for more emphasis on markets must also be examined closely. State enterprise in Italy is relatively large scale and often inefficient. Classic fascism had not been highly statist in its early days: rather it had stressed the importance of private property. Its main goal was to change values, to end bourgeois individualism and greed. It is interesting in this context to note that at the 1995 Congress, the works of Evola figured prominently in book displays and reportedly sold well. Nor can the 1995 commitment to antiracism, apparently inspired by the New Right, necessarily be taken at face value. While this rejects the notion of a hierarchy of races and accepts nationalism as natural for others, the underlying message is that blacks (or whoever) are fine—as long as they remain in their own countries. It is a form of "antiracism" that is perfectly consistent with anti-immigrant politics.

Such views would probably be popular with a significant element of the Italian electorate, which has become even more sensitive to immigration after the breakup of Yugoslavia and has growing fears about North African Islamic fundamentalism. But the issue will need to be handled carefully if it is not to arouse fears that there is a hidden racist agenda. Groups that in the past have been associated with the MSI could also damage its new "clean" image: these include the growing number of "Naziskins," who in 1994 staged a dramatic rally in the city of Vicenza. Fini subsequently disowned them, but the more radical wing of the MSI has been more sympathetic to skinheads: for instance, during October 1994 this wing allowed neo-Nazi "Naziskins" to be present at a mass for Mussolini and his wife that took place in Predappio, the Duce's birthplace and now a shrine to fascism. Should there be an escalation in skinhead, or other, attacks on immigrants, the new AN might find itself in a difficult position.

In the same month that the MSI was changing its title, a magistrate in Verona was opening proceedings against a neofascist activist who was accused of running the New Order, which had been widely linked with the post-1969 bombing campaign. The Italian state now seems far more committed to dealing with the problem of terrorism. Even so, it could take only one or two bombs to raise fears that an important wing of fascism remains addicted to old practices. "Postfascism's" new men in double-breasted suits must be sitting with their fingers crossed that those who still sport the bomber jacket or the razor-cropped hair do not spoil their strategy now that power at last beckons.

A month before the historic 1995 MSI Congress, the Berlusconi government collapsed, leaving the MSI out of office. A series of wrangles with Bossi, and accusations that *Sua Emittenza* was implicated in scandals and unable to distinguish between his personal and the public good, finally proved too much for the unstable coalition and its troubled leader. It was followed by a largely technocratic government of bankers and experts formed in January 1995, an administration that had no strong party base. Such governments are vulnerable to economic downturns, when they are likely to lose both public and parliamentary support. Given Italy's fundamental economic problems, not least the budget deficit and the continuing issue of the south, it seems hard to believe that technocratic government can provide the basis for a long-term administration. Although the AN failed to make further major gains in the 1995 local elections, its prospects during the late 1990s seem to be good, especially as the declining fortunes of the Northern League— racked by internal disputes, not least over its erratic leader—open the way for further electoral penetration of the AN into regions where it had previously been weak. Berlusconi's troubles too mean that the center-right could soon be in need of a new leader.

Indeed, by early 1996 Fini's popularity rating in opinion polls had soared to over sixty percent (though the AN lagged well behind). As his agenda for a stronger, directly elected president has moved even closer to center stage, Fini may soon achieve something Mussolini never did—a genuine democratic popular mandate.

12

Neofascism in Germany

i

WHEN HITLER committed suicide on April 30, 1945, he knew that Germany had suffered total defeat. The Russians were in Berlin, while the Western Allied armies had advanced far beyond the Rhine. This pattern of occupation was later to form the basis for the division of Germany into two states. In 1945, however, an uneasy truce existed among the wartime Allies, who were faced with the task of rebuilding life in a country that had been severely ravaged by war.

Well before the surrender, various plans had been drawn up to determine the postwar fate of Germany. In their more extreme versions they had involved returning the country to a state of virtual deindustrialization, or breaking it up into a series of small states rather as it had been in the early nineteenth century, though with Poland and Russia taking significant chunks of territory from what had once been Prussia. But the rapid onset of the Cold War pushed both the Western powers and the USSR toward less ambitious plans to prevent Germany from ever again threatening the peace of Europe.

The Americans especially were convinced that German national identity was based on core values that had helped to underpin Nazism, qualities such as respect for authority, admiration for strong leaders, and a conception of citizenship that was based on blood. The belief that there was a German affinity with extreme nationalism led to the construction of detailed programs to help reshape German political culture, including the provision of new school texts and curricula to ensure that the next generation would be inoculated against the German virus. The belief was also widespread among the Allies that Hitler had been helped to power by the army and large-scale business. So they too became targets for reform. The guiding principles of this remarkable attempt to re-shape a national identity were known as the Four Ds: "Denazify, Demilitarize, Decartelize, and Democratize."

An important aspect of the policy was the attempt to make Germans come to terms with their own immediate past. In the weeks immediately after defeat, many ordinary Germans were taken to the concentration camps that were dotted around the country, although the main killing camps lay in Poland. Exhibitions were put on and films were made to demonstrate the degradation and horrors that had been inflicted on millions of innocent victims. Most spectacularly of all, at the end of October 1945 it was an-nounced that a group of leading Nazis were to be prosecuted at Nuremberg as war criminals.

The choice of Nuremberg was symbolic, for it was here that the great Nazi annual rallies had been held since the late 1920s. It was also in Nuremberg that the main body of anti-Jewish laws had been promulgated in 1935. The trials took several months and were unsatisfactory from a legal point of view. The Russians were them-selves clearly guilty under Charge One (conspiracy to wage aggres-sive war), for they had invaded Finland and Poland in 1939–40. Germans particularly complained at the fact that there was no ques-tion of judgment being passed on the Russians for their extensive killing of civilians on the eastern front, or on the morality of the later stages of British and American "strategic bombing." In spite of these problems, the trial produced extensive documentation con-cerning the evil at the heart of Nazism and proved an important part of the reeducation program.[1]

In terms of judgment, the result of the trial was that three of the accused were acquitted, including former economics minister Hjal-mar Schacht; four were sentenced to long fixed terms, most notably former Munitions Minister Albert Speer; three were sentenced to life imprisonment, including Party Secretary Rudolf Hess, who had been in British custody since his flight in 1941; and twelve were sentenced to death. Among those hanged were Wilhelm Frick (minister of the interior), Wilhelm Keitel (chief of the High Com-mand), Joachim von Ribbentrop (foreign minister), and Alfred Rosenberg (racist ideologue who later had ministerial responsibility

for part of the conquered territories). Hermann Göring, nominally
Hitler's heir apparent, committed suicide shortly before his ren-
dezvous with the hangman, following in the steps of SS chief Heinrich Himmler, who had taken his own life shortly after the war
ended.

The judgments were accompanied by further trials of lesser figures, and a purge of former Nazis from public life. Anticipating the
worst, many leading Nazis had already fled, and an elaborate network was set up to help others who remained. The best known of
these was the ODESSA organization, which helped high-ranking SS
officials in particular. A key figure in establishing ODESSA was
Otto Skorzeny, who had rescued Mussolini from his Italian captors
in 1943 and who had played a key part organizing behind-the-lines
activity during the German Ardennes offensive in December 1944.
Skorzeny fled to Spain before he could be brought before a court,
and from there arranged the finances that supported an array of
helpers from Bremen to Bari. Some fugitives traveled to Spain and
Portugal, others to the middle East, and yet more to South America,
especially Argentina—where the close season on Nazi hunting lasted
for 365 days a year. Among the most notorious Nazis to flee this
way was Adolf Eichmann, one of the main bureaucratic organizers
of the Final Solution.

To deal with the large number of remaining Nazi Party members, the Americans required people in their zone of occupation to
undergo an extensive form of political checkup, which involved
providing written life histories and supplying testimonials that confirmed the suspect's good character. Predictably the process often
led to one former Nazi exonerating the other and it quickly became discredited for handing out "Persil certificates" (they washed
whiter than white). The system also involved much rough justice,
especially as some who had committed crimes had never been in
the party.

The Americans used the latest techniques of opinion polling
and psychological research to test the general state of German opinion, though the problems for the researchers were considerable.
Many of those polled had good reasons for not admitting to Nazi
support in the past: on the other hand, many did not want to appear to be unpatriotic or treacherous. Polling took place against a

background of dislocation caused by the war, including considerable unemployment and shortages, which contrasted markedly with the relative prosperity and full employment of the late 1930s. Even so, a relatively clear picture comes through from these extensive studies.

Although only about ten to fifteen percent of the population were classified as hard-core Nazi, the researchers found that there was a strong lingering sense of racism. In 1946, forty-eight percent of Germans thought that some races were more fit to rule than others; even more remarkably, in 1949, fifty-nine percent were willing to say that Nazism was a good idea badly carried out. Nazism's main positive points were seen as: good job opportunities, the high standard of living, and the welfare programs. While most regretted the war, few claimed to be have been opponents of the regime. Allied analysts thought that about fifteen percent of the population had been passive opponents and ten percent more committed anti-Nazis.[2]

Such attitudes led the Allies to fear that a new Nazi movement might emerge. They therefore exercised a supervisory role over the drafting of the "Basic Law," which effectively established the West German Federal Republic in May 1949. Particular attention was paid to redressing the institutional weaknesses that many identified in the Weimar Republic's constitution. One major change adopted in 1949 concerned the powers of the president, who was to be mainly a figurehead, elected by the parliament, and with no powers to use emergency decrees. The chancellor was also appointed by parliament and could only be removed by a "constructive vote of no confidence," which required that a successor had to be elected at the same time. Another crucial change concerned the election system, which was based on a split first-past-the-post and proportional system, with parties receiving less than five percent of the vote or three seats in one of the federal *Länder* ("regions") being eliminated. As a final safeguard, the Constitutional Court was given the power to ban nonconstitutional parties, a provision that underlined the attempt to redefine the citizens' loyalty to a civic set of institutions rather than the nation.

The main work on drafting the Basic Law had been done by politicians from various German parties that the Allies had allowed to form during 1945 and 1946. In August 1949 these parties presented themselves to the West German people for the first time in statewide elections. Immediately after the Nazis' defeat, many had thought that the left would emerge as the main force, given its relative strength prior to 1933. The communists, however, were harmed by the onset of the Cold War, which underlined their foreign allegiance, while the socialists retained their old failing of ignoring the impact of their radical rhetoric. Although they emerged as a far more important force than the communists, by 1949 they had effectively antagonized a considerable swath of middle-class and Catholic opinion—together with some important figures in the occupying authorities, especially the Americans, who had no time for talk of nationalization and other left-wing plans.

Problems on the left contributed to the emergence of the primarily Catholic Christian Democrats (CDU) and their much smaller Bavarian allies, the Christian Social Union (CSU), as the largest party grouping in the 1949 elections. After 1945 political Catholicism was given a further boost by territorial changes, for the new West German state included a significantly greater percentage of Catholics than the old Germany. The CDU quickly found that it had another asset: a leader by the name of Konrad Adenauer. Adenauer, a member of the old Catholic Center Party, had been the mayor of Cologne in 1933, but had been dismissed by the Nazis. Coming out of retirement in 1945 at the age of sixty-nine, his remarkable drive and shrewdness had taken him to the top of the new CDU. Although Adenauer's personal contribution to the 1949 victory was not great, his role was critical to the form of government that duly emerged.

The CDU-CSU had only come out just ahead of the SPD in terms of seats in the Bundestag. Adenauer lacked an overall majority because a variety of other parties had gained representation too, including a relatively strong liberal-conservative grouping known as the Free Democratic Party (FDP). The result encouraged a widespread feeling (including within the more left-wing faction of the CDU-CSU) that the best form of administration would be some form of "Grand Coalition," which would help underline the need for political reconciliation. Adenauer was strongly opposed to this. He bitterly disliked the SPD leader, Kurt Schumacher, and had no desire to work closely with him—antisocialist rhetoric was to be a significant feature of Adenauer's formidable political armory. He also believed that a center-right coalition would be in a better position to cut the ground from under a Nazi or radical nationalist revival. After considerable maneuvering, he built a coalition in which the main partner was the FDP. For the next sixteen years this was to form the basis of West German government—which symbolically chose as its new home the small town of Bonn, in the Catholic Rhineland.

ii

ADENAUER'S FEARS were understandable. A remarkable variety of conservative and nationalist groups had contested the 1949 elections, gaining a total of 10.5 percent of the vote. By far the most important of these groups was the German Conservative Party–German Right Party (DKP-DRP), which had been formed in 1946 (it adopted one or the other name in different *Länder*). Initially based on part of Alfred Hugenberg's old authoritarian-conservative German People's Nationalist Party (DNVP), it had quickly attracted many former Nazis. Its fervent nationalism and anticommunism provided a far more congenial home than was to be found in the other new parties, and by 1949 the DKP-DRP was campaigning in some areas on a blatantly Nazi program.[3] It was rewarded with five seats in the Bundestag.

After the 1949 Bundestag elections, the Allied system of licensing parties ended. The new German government ran down the denazification program, which was already losing impetus as the Cold War led to changing Allied perspectives (including the need to rearm West Germany as part of the Western front line). This new climate provided the opportunity to create a more truly neo-Nazi party.

The result was the Socialist Reich Party (SRP), founded in October 1949 as a result of a break away from the DKP-DRP. The party's chairman was Dr. Fritz Dorls, who had been a member of the Nazi Party since 1929 and a CDU member in the immediate postwar era, like many other former lower-ranking Nazis. Other leading members included Fritz Rössler, a Nazi Party member since 1930 and a man who even after the war retained a marked preference for jackboots and breeches. (Until 1952 he operated under the false name of Dr. Franz Richter.) The party program was clearly neo-Nazi. Germans who had now adopted the anti-Nazi cause were seen as traitors, and it was claimed that the gas chambers had been built after the war. Indeed, the whole postwar political edifice was seen as nothing less than an Allied creation—a "freshly painted Coca-Cola" stall, totally lacking in legitimacy. According to the SRP, Admiral Dönitz, who had been nominated as head of state by Hitler in his final will and testament, was still the legitimate ruler of Germany, though Dönitz had been sentenced to ten years' imprisonment at Nuremberg. Exactly what the SRP wished to put in place of the West German state remained vague. It talked of "German" or "Peoples' Socialism," which seemed to mean a form of authoritarian, leader-oriented system, which would—allegedly—restore German unity, both socially and politically.

On this program, the SRP quickly attracted around ten thousand members. In Lower Saxony it attracted a particularly strong electoral following, eleven percent of the vote in the 1951 *Länder* elections, and it also did well in Bremen. As with the Nazi Party, its support came essentially from Protestants, particularly people who lived in smaller towns and who were not active in trade unions. It was also heavily male-biased, not a feature of later Nazi voting. Polls showed that a greater than average number of SRP supporters thought that there was more good than evil in Nazism, although many of them tended to explain their choice of party primarily in economic terms.[4] This has generally been explained by arguing that the SRP vote came from the more economically aggrieved sector of the electorate: as such, it could be seen largely as a protest vote.[5] There is some truth in this, but there were strong Nazi traditions in these areas, and the sudden rise of the SRP provides further evidence of the sensitivity of a section of the German electorate to economic prosperity.

Whatever the motives of SRP voters, there is no doubt that most of its gains came at the expense of the CDU and its allies, thus underlining Adenauer's fears of radical nationalism. As a result, he asked the Constitutional Court to investigate the SRP under the clause in the Basic Law that banned nondemocratic parties. The court came to its decision the following year and the SRP was duly banned, but the party's leaders and local activists soon reemerged in a variety of other organizations, including the CDU.

The breakaway of the SRP in 1949 did not mean the collapse of the DKP-DRP. During 1950 the rump of this party had merged with some smaller groups to create the German Reich Party (DRP). Many of its leading members had links with the Nazi past, but they tended to come from the more conservative wing of Nazism or to have a military background. Perhaps the most colorful of the leading figures who emerged in the party during the 1950s was the one-legged Hans-Ulrich Rudel. Rudel was the most highly decorated member of the German armed services during the war. A pilot popularly known as the "Eagle of the Eastern Front," he had been credited with a vast number of "kills," including 519 Russian tanks. Imprisoned for a year by the Americans at the end of the war, he subsequently left for Argentina, where he worked with the ODESSA organization. Returning to Germany in the early 1950s, Rudel published a series of memoirs and was a frequent speaker at the blossoming number of ex-combatants' meetings. He also joined the DRP and was perhaps its most popular lecturer.

In view of the fate of the SRP, the DRP paid lip service to the Basic Law, though behind this facade it had clear links with the past. It advocated a *Volksgemeinschaft*-based society, stressed that there had been many good points of the Third Reich, and called for the end of the persecution of "war criminals." A significant wing of the party exhibited its hostility to the Western Allies by advocating the adoption of a neutral foreign policy. (It was hoped that this might encourage the USSR to leave East Germany, thus allowing reunification.) Although aspects of this policy, especially the dream of a reunited Reich, exerted some appeal, in the 1953 Bundestag elections the DRP managed to attract a mere one percent of the vote.

An important reason for the DRP's failure was the fact that it faced another challenger for the nationalist vote. This was the Union of Expellees (BHE), which had been formed in 1950. As its name implies, this appealed to the several million Germans who had been forced out of, or chosen to leave, Eastern Europe. Now the Germans found themselves the victims of often brutal ethnic cleansing: for instance, in the Czech Sudetenland three million were forced out or fled. Although the BHE included former Nazis, the focus of its program related more to specific grievances concerning housing, compensation, and other social issues. These struck a ready chord in the 1953 general election and the BHE won 5.9 percent of the vote and representation in the Bundestag. The government responded by meeting many of the expellees' demands and, more generally, appeasing other right-wing interest groups, most notably ex-combatants.[6]

By the beginning of the 1960s, radical nationalist groups seemed to be slipping into oblivion. One major reason for this was the German economic miracle. Helped by American aid, the Western rearmament boom, and the influx of new labor, the German economy in little more than a decade moved from chaos to being Europe's strongest. Another factor in the decline of extremism was the way in which Adenauer diverted attention from the impossible dream of reunification toward Franco-German rapprochement and the furthering of Western European unity (a policy partly linked to its economic benefits). Last but by no means least, Adenauer increasingly emerged with the persona of the strong leader, guiding his people out of the wilderness: surveys of CDU supporters often found that they put this leader-factor before economic reasons in explaining their vote.

In 1964 the Ministry of the Interior's official report on neo-Nazism and radical nationalism put forward further reasons for the electoral collapse of this fringe: the growing awareness of the evils of the past, weak radical leadership, personal differences between the leaders, and a strong tendency toward factionalism which made it difficult for one major organization to emerge.[7] But hardly was the ink dry on the report than a new organization was formed, which within a short space of time was to shatter this complacency. This was the National Democratic Party (NPD), formed in 1964 by remnants of the DRP, BHE, and several other small groups. The NPD's first chairman was Friedrich Thielen, a respectable concrete manufacturer from Bremen who had previously played a leading role in fringe conservative politics in northern Germany.

The cochairman was Adolf von Thadden. Born in 1921 into a relatively wealthy background, Thadden was slightly younger than most of those who emerged to lead neo-Nazi groups after 1945. His stepsister was executed by the Nazis for treason and defeatism, but Thadden fought in the war—though he does not seem to have been an ardent Nazi. At the end of the war he tried to rescue his mother from communist-occupied territory, was captured by the Poles and apparently tortured. This confirmed his strong anti-communist leanings, and on returning to West Germany, Thadden became active in the DRP, becoming the youngest deputy elected to the Bundestag in 1949. He subsequently became a leading light in the DRP, where he was a representative of the more moderate, pro-Western faction. A brilliant orator and good organizer, he was the force behind the NPD, and in 1967 he formally became leader of the party.

Initially, the party's program was vague. It was clearest in the sphere of foreign policy, where it presented itself as the successor to the Adenauer tradition of hostility to détente. This did not make it Atlanticist, for it was highly critical of continued American influence over Germany and called for all foreign troops to be sent home. These policies increasingly became linked to the call for an end to the feeling of collective guilt, and the reestablishment of a self-confident German identity based on reunification. Turning to domestic policy, the NPD advocated the expulsion of the growing number of foreign workers (*Gastarbeiter*) who had been attracted by West Germany's economic miracle. Little was said about the basic structure of government or economic policy, but the image created was that the NPD supported a far stronger, directive state that would end class division; it was ambiguous about whether the desired state was to be dictatorial or democratic.[8] As such, it was too conservative to be classed as truly neo-Nazi, though like many groups in the postwar era, it needs understanding at different levels, for locally it sometimes disseminated a far more clearly Nazi message.

In the 1965 Bundestag elections the NPD gave little indication of gains to come. But from 1966 onward it fought a series of elections in the *Länder,* which by 1968 had brought it representatives in seven *Land* parliaments, with a best result of 9.8 percent of the vote in Baden-Württemberg in April 1968. At the same time party membership began to grow rapidly, reaching perhaps twenty-eight thousand by 1968, thus making the NPD a far larger organization than any previous neo-Nazi or radical nationalist group. The sudden rise was prompted largely by a mini-recession in the German economy during 1965: growth rates slackened and unemployment began to rise, developments which raised the specter of the great crash after 1929. Fears about the impact of a new depression encouraged the creation in December 1966 of a Grand Coalition, including the SPD, to deal with the problems. The new government included Willy Brandt, the leader of the SPD, as foreign minister. Brandt quickly showed a much greater willingness than his predecessors to come to some form of understanding with the East German regime—a red flag to nationalist extremists, who were already critical of the fact that he had spent the period 1933 to 1945 in exile, where he took Norwegian citizenship.

Sociological studies of NPD voting have often stressed that it included a large element of protest and that support should not be confused with ideological affinity. The party undoubtedly attracted some voters for negative reasons, but over half had voted for previous extremist parties and this was a strong feature among the party's male and older voters. There were also some geographical parallels with the Nazi vote—for instance, the NPD's relative strength in Schleswig-Holstein.[9] This meant that it mainly appealed in Protestant areas, but its foothold in some Catholic areas indicates the decline of politically induced religious allegiance. More generally, the NPD was especially strong among small farmers and artisans, by now a much smaller force than in Weimar days, and the middle class, though the party had a sizable working-class following in smaller towns.

These voting trends raised major fears that the NPD would gain representation in the Bundestag, but in the 1969 elections the party received just 4.3 percent of the vote, failing to cross the crucial 5 percent hurdle. Probably the main reason for this was the revival of the economy and resulting decline in protest voting. The fact that the elections threatened to bring about an SPD-based government also brought supporters back to the CDU-CSU. Such fears particularly affected the more moderate NPD supporters, who seem to have been shocked by the growing violence that accompanied the rise of the NPD. Student groups especially had challenged the NPD in a series of demonstrations and confrontations, which peaked during the 1969 election campaign. Although these sometimes reinforced fears of youth and left-wing rebellion—this was a time when left-wing terrorism began to emerge as a notable force—there seems little doubt that the activities of the NPD's thuggish security force in responding to the challenge revealed a violent side to the NPD that its leadership was desperately trying to hide.

iii

THE MAIN REASON behind the creation of the NPD was the belief that the formation of an extremist coalition would quickly lead to tangible electoral results. The 1969 vote was a serious blow to this strategy, and it was followed by a yet more dismal performance in 1972. Even during the mini-recession that followed the 1973 Middle Eastern War, the NPD proved incapable of making any kind of comeback. The collapse inevitably led to schisms within the NPD.

After the 1969 elections, an SPD FDP coalition was formed under Brandt. This pursued an understanding with the East German government (Ostpolitik). The NPD's leadership decided to resort to public demonstrations to halt the rapprochement, but it was badly divided over whether this action should be peaceful. Splits also emerged over Thadden's desire to stay basically committed to a parliamentary strategy. The upshot of this discontent was Thadden's replacement as leader in 1972. During the next ten years the NPD moved toward a more radical stance, which involved a clear break with the old line on defense. The new policy was accompanied by the demand that West Germany should leave NATO and that East Germany should withdraw from the Warsaw Pact as a prelude to reunification. Domestically, the NPD adopted a more clearly anticapitalist "Third Way" line. The new radicalism was sometimes overtly connected to the defense of "Strasserite" Nazism: the belief that Nazism was truly socialist, but that Hitler had steered the party away from this route (which had been mapped out most notably by Gregor and Otto Strasser) in order to court support among conservative sections of the army and business. Predictably, a more genuine Nazi-socialism frightened off much of the NPD's conservative support. By the mid-1980s the party had at most a few thousand members, who were mainly concerned with ideological debate and issuing propaganda—though the party still contested the occasional election.

The mid-1960s marks the first important turning point in postwar neofascism, in the sense that the period witnessed the rise of a new generation of activists.[10] But in other ways the early NPD was a continuation of the old DRP, and the major growth in a new generation of youth who were attracted to neofascism came during the 1970s. This can be seen by examining internal developments within the NPD, which were often driven by the party's radical youth wing. It can be seen even more clearly by turning to the burgeoning of more violent forms of neo-Nazism during the 1970s.

One of the first new groups to be formed illustrates that this was a strangely mixed demiworld of ideologues, Walter Mittys, and psychopaths. It underlines too that not all of those involved in violent activity were young. The organization in question was the War Sport Group, formed in 1973 by Karl-Heinz Hoffmann, a middle-aged man with notable talents in the fields of languages and fine arts. Among the weapons this group managed to collect were twenty-five trucks and cross-country vehicles; a twelve-ton armored personnel carrier (in need of repair); an armored tracked vehicle; military motorcycles; and a two-centimeter antiaircraft gun. The four hundred or so primarily young members the group attracted seem to have used these as adult toys. There was, however, a far more dangerous side to the movement, which led to its being banned by the federal authorities in 1980. Hoffmann, who had links with Palestinian organizations, was subsequently charged with the murder of a Jewish publisher and his friend. Although acquitted, he was later charged successfully with a variety of other offenses, including wrongful imprisonment and grievous bodily harm. Another former member of the group blew himself up while placing a bomb at the 1980 Munich Beer Festival, killing another 12 people and injuring 211.[11]

A second significant group was the National Socialist Action Front (ANS), formed in 1977. Its leader, Michael Kühnen, was a twenty-two-year-old from a middle-class Catholic background. Kühnen is remarkable because he managed to combine fanaticism with a certain charm and openness of mind, thus providing a good example of the different types of personality that can be attracted by fascism.[12] Politically committed from youth, Kühnen was influenced by a strange mixture of Marxism and Nietzsche. From the latter he learned his elitism, and he openly advocated the re-creation of a society led by a radical SA-type vanguard. From Marx, Kühnen learned more the necessity of violence in order to overthrow the state. He built around him a small group willing to engage in terrorism until his plans were curtailed by his arrest and imprisonment in 1979 and the proscription of the ANS in the 1980s. Curiously for a man who portrayed homosexuality as a bane on society, the gay Kühnen was to die of AIDS in 1991, though not before helping to induct yet more youngsters into neo-Nazi activity.

With the ban on the ANS, the key focus of the more violent neo-Nazi youth became the Free German Workers' Party (FAP), which was founded in 1978.[13] This group had little by the way of serious ideology: in many ways it was the stereotypical neo-Nazi group, characterized more by alienation than a serious political strategy. There seems little doubt, however, that his organization sought to promote political violence, though this was aimed at political opponents and foreign workers, rather than the state. The FAP recruited particularly from among the growing bands of skinheads and soccer hooligans: male youths with low levels of formal education and an addiction to alcohol (and stronger substances) rather than ideology. The numbers involved at this time were small, but the attacks marked the beginning of a trend that was soon to lead many foreign workers, especially Turks, to live in fear of assault and harassment.

By no means all neofascist activity at this time focused on violence or recruiting alienated youths. Another major organizational axis was publishing and propaganda. This was not an entirely new development. Various journals and discussion groups had sprung up in the past, especially after 1949 with the relaxing of de-Nazification. Among the first wave was the monthly journal *Nation Europa*, which was active in developing the strand in Nazi ideology that had stressed a shared European destiny, a strand to be found most notably in Waffen SS propaganda. *Nation Europa* sought to promote trans-European links with groups such as the MSI in Italy and with Sir Oswald Mosley in Britain, and to distribute books that advocated "Europeanist" ideas, for example, those written by the former Belgian fascist and Waffen SS general, Léon Degrelle.[14] These efforts were largely unsuccessful in the 1950s and 1960s, but by the 1970s there were growing links between various European neofascist activists at an unofficial level.

One crucial area where European neofascists have co-operated in terms of publications is the so-called "Holocaust Denial." (Its practitioners prefer to call themselves "Historical Revisionists.")[15] Since 1945 there had always been a strand in neo-Nazism which claimed that there had been no policy of systematic genocide and that the gas chambers had been built by the Allies after the war. During the early 1970s these arguments began to gain wider currency. One reason for this lay in the activities of Thies Christophersen, who set up a publishing house in 1971 primarily to distribute neo-Nazi views. Christophersen had worked for a time as an agricultural expert in the Auschwitz camp, and in 1973 wrote a booklet entitled *The Auschwitz Lie*, which argued that he had seen no evidence of genocide and that the presence of crematoria were explained by the fact that this was a large camp, which frequently suffered typhus and other epidemics.[16]

Various bans on neo-Nazi publications, culminating in the criminalization of the Holocaust Denial in 1985, have meant that most of this literature has been circulated covertly, although it is sometimes printed in Britain and the United States, where such arguments are not banned.[17] But a more cautious version can be discerned in the publications of Gerhard Frey. Born shortly after Hitler came to power, Frey gained a doctoral degree in politics and then turned his talents to publishing. He began by founding a newspaper in 1958 that survived mainly on a diet of radical German nationalism and attacks on Allied "war crimes," plus strong criticism of the presence of foreign workers in Germany. During the late 1960s Frey gave some support to the NPD (though he was on bad terms with Thadden), but by the early 1970s he realized that a new strategy was necessary, one aimed more at conditioning the general climate of opinion rather than promoting a specific party.

The result was the creation in 1971 of the German Peoples' Union (DVU). Among its publications was the weekly *Deutsche National Zeitung*, whose circulation by the 1980s was approaching a hundred thousand. The DVU also ran a major book club and arranged talks. A favorite speaker was Rudel, who retained strong links with ex-combatant groups. Later a favored speaker was the British historian David Irving, who as a young researcher in the early 1960s had published a book damning as a war crime the Anglo-American firebombing of Dresden in February 1945. During the late 1970s Irving argued in another book that there were absolutely no documents in which Hitler revealed any knowledge of the Final Solution, though tons of documents relating to the concentration camps existed—he even offered a $1,000 dollar cash prize to anyone who could produce a document showing that Hitler had ordered, or was aware of, the extermination policy. Irving argued that the Final Solution was largely organized at the lower level by Himmler and the SS.[18]

In the early 1980s Irving was awarded a prize funded by Frey, yet by the 1990s he found himself banned from speaking in Germany after claiming that Auschwitz's gas chambers were constructed after the war. Irving had changed his line on the Holocaust during the late 1980s to argue it was the "Hoax of the Century" (to adopt the title of one of the key Holocaust Denial books). In 1989 he wrote that this conversion resulted from the emergence of scientific evidence that no traces of hydro-cyanic gas could be found in the walls of the surviving "gas chambers" (though there were elements in the walls of small delousing chambers) and proof that the gassings, at least of large numbers of people, were technically impossible.[19] Irving accepts that there were concentration camps but holds that there was no policy of deliberate genocide.

Irving is able to develop a highly sophisticated level of argument, as are some of the other leading figures involved in this campaign. This helps explain why opinion polls in several countries have shown a surprising number of people willing to believe that there were no systematic killings. Legal proscription still hampers the campaign in Germany, but in his journal *Action Report* during 1995 Irving argued that there were signs that times were changing. In this he wrote that a leading German historian had advocated in a newspaper that there should be a public debate on whether there was a deliberate Nazi policy to exterminate Europe's Jews. Although the paper had responded by telling the historian that his services would no longer be needed, Irving pointed to signs of an increasing willingness to debate aspects of the Holocaust.

Most people with affinities toward neofascism have chosen a rather different form of historical revisionism: one that focuses on intellectual history and philosophy rather than the reinterpretation of great events. The central thrust of this effort has been to revive key thinkers who, while clearly related to the fascist tradition, can be separated from its most awful aspects. Particularly important here are "conservative revolutionaries," such as the writer Ernst Jünger, or Oswald Spengler, whose works were widely read during the 1920s. The conservative revolutionaries celebrated the importance of national identity, community, and authority, but tended to despise the mass mobilization and immorality of Nazism. Another key source is Carl Schmitt, the academic lawyer who for a brief time after 1933 was the "Crown Jurist" of the Third Reich, before he fell foul of more radical and racist elements in the Nazi Party.[20] As well as the importance of leadership and a strong state as a means of uniting society and overcoming dangerous liberal individualism, Schmitt stressed particularly the importance of a clear friend-enemy distinction in order to mold identity. Conservative revolutionary ideas became central to the German New Right that emerged during the 1970s, a group that had many parallels with the French intellectual movement of the same name.[21]

Initially, these developments took place on the political fringe, the arguments being put forward by people—like Irving—who held no academic post. Increasingly during the 1980s some of these arguments began to find an echo in the university community and among mainstream politicians. The trend first became clear in the late 1970s. The charismatic leader of the CSU, Franz-Josef Strauss, was particularly important in using nationalist rhetoric to attack the SPD-FDP coalition government's regularization of relations with East Germany and in arguing that the time had come for Germany to "emerge from the shadow of Hitler" and become a "normal nation" again. His attempts to lead the CDU-CSU to electoral victory in 1980 failed, but rivals within the party recognized the potential potency of the message, especially if it could be packaged less stridently.

Helmut Kohl, who became chancellor in 1982, seems to have decided that the time had come to bury the past and to develop a more clear-cut German identity, which was linked to a more assertive role for Germany within Europe. Kohl, an ex-history student, had as one of his key advisers a professional historian, Michael Stürmer, who believed that shaping the past was vital to controlling the future: among the more overt signs of this new concern was the opening of a German History Museum in Berlin and another in Bonn. The desire to "normalize" the past was almost certainly the motivation behind Kohl's controversial decision to invite President Ronald Reagan to attend a ceremony at the Bitburg military cemetery to commemorate the fortieth anniversary of the end of World War II. Among the graves were forty-five for members of the Waffen SS, a name that still provoked shock and horror among many, partly because the Waffen SS, which was primarily a fighting unit, was confused with the security SS—though no neat line can be drawn between the two groups.

At the same time, a growing number of academics and intellectuals picked up on the issue of national identity and of coming to terms with the past. It was a sign of the times that in 1982 Jünger was awarded the prestigious Goethe Prize, and that even his 1920s writings were accorded belated recognition for their literary and intellectual content. In the same year a group of fifteen professors from leading universities wrote a manifesto that appeared in the press expressing their worries about the subversion of the German people caused by the influx of foreigners. Others wrote of the need to rediscover self-pride and not to wallow in guilt, and opinion polls picked up an increasing unease.[22]

The most dramatic aspect of this academic revisionism broke out in 1986. The key figure was Ernst Nolte, a former philosophy student of Heidegger's and a historian who had made an important contribution to the study of comparative fascism during the 1960s, when he argued that fascism was an "epochal" movement that would not return as a significant force in the postwar era. In 1986 Nolte asked whether Hitler and the German people had enacted the "Asiatic deed" of the Holocaust because they saw themselves as potential victims of such horrors. In other words, fear of communism—of its mass killings of "undesirable classes" and establishment of gulags—was a major factor in explaining why many Germans held strong fears about the left and the Jews, who were often identified with communism. To add insult to injury, Nolte added that the World Jewish Agency had virtually declared war on Germany in 1939, which further explained why Jews were rounded up into concentration camps.

Some other German academics endorsed these arguments, or raised the more general question of why Germany was so damned when Soviet communism had undoubtedly killed more people, often in the most appalling ways, a discussion that spilled over into arguments about Soviet "atrocities" during World War II. The suicide in 1987 of the ninety-three-year-old Rudolf Hess, who had never been released from Spandau prison, added further fuel to the fire, particularly among radical nationalist circles. It revived old issues about Allied justice at the Nuremberg trials, though for some it also raised the possibility that Hitler really had sought a compromise peace after the great victories in France. Predictably the whole affair, which became known as the "Historians' Battle" (Historikerstreit), aroused massive controversy and great public interest. For many Germans, particularly on the left, the controversy smacked of a deliberate attempt to rehabilitate Nazism, or at least to make nationalism an acceptable part of contemporary political discourse.[23]

iv

IN 1989, thirty-eight percent of West Germans thought that, but for the persecution of the Jews, Hitler could be counted among the country's top statesmen. This was ten percent fewer than twenty-five years before, but marked an increase on figures for the 1960s and 1970s. There seems little doubt that intellectual and political moves during the 1970s and more especially the 1980s had helped to rehabilitate aspects of Nazism and had set an agenda that asked central questions about national identity.

It was a sign of the times that in 1987 Frey decided to take the DVU into the electoral arena. The NPD too showed an increased interest in electoral activity and began to attract more votes (though like the DVU much of its activity remained focused on propaganda). There was even growing cooperation between the two groups, which in the past had tended to act more like enemies than ideological cousins. But it was a relatively new party that attracted the most spectacular rise in support at the turn of the 1990s. This was the Republikaner Party (REP), which had been set up in 1983 by two former CSU Bundestag Deputies, Franz Handlos and Ekkehard Voigt, together with Franz Schönhuber, a man with a grudge against some of the leading lights in the CSU.

Schönhuber was a most interesting character. Born in 1923, he was the son of a butcher who was a member of the Nazi Party. Schönhuber joined the Waffen SS during the war. He subsequently became a journalist and was generally considered to be left wing— his wife was a leading local light in the SPD. But during the 1970s he turned more to the CSU, partly, it appears, to help his career, which had now taken him into Bavarian television. In 1981 Schönhuber published his war memoirs, *I Was There*.[24] Although at times critical, they were widely seen as too apologetic for the Nazi past and as implying the need for a new German consciousness. As a result Schönhuber found himself deserted by former friends and political allies and hounded out of his job. The book became a bestseller and attracted much publicity for the charismatic Schönhuber. After the formation of the REP, he was to turn this renown to good effect, though some of the publicity the party received may have been motivated by left-wing journalists trying to promote a party that could harm the mainstream right.[25]

Schönhuber's early policy statements concentrated on issues such as the defense of the family, and the need to limit the number of foreign workers and asylum seekers coming to Germany. (The Basic Law, in atonement for the Nazi past, welcomed those seeking political asylum.) By the late 1980s it was becoming more clearly a radical nationalist party, though its preferred self-definition was "patriotic." It called stridently for German reunification, based on Germany's prewar boundaries. Its 1987 program denied the "singular guilt" of Hitler's Germany for the outbreak of World War II, and talked coyly of the exaggerations and falsifications that are "mostly believed by our youth." But it did not openly defend Nazism, nor did it call for dictatorship. Rather, it seemed to advocate a more authoritarian government, which would restore order and national pride.

The party's first electoral breakthrough came in the West Berlin local elections during January 1989. Boosted by an aggressive media advertising campaign, which focused on images of Turks, drug addicts, and anarchists, it won six percent of the vote and representation in the local parliament. This was followed by success in the 1989 European elections. The Republikaners' main theme was strong hostility to Euro-federalism; it was the only party to adopt this policy, as by 1989 the previously hostile Greens had toned down their position. The result was that the Republikaner won 7.1 percent of the vote, which took Schönhuber and five others to the Strasburg parliament.

In the mid-1980s Republikaner supporters had been relatively old and middle class. But by 1989, it had attracted a remarkably diverse cross-section. In Berlin it had made gains among both young people and the working class, who often lived in closest proximity to the guest-workers. In the European elections its voter profile was similar to that of the CDU-CSU, which meant that it managed to attract Catholic as well as Protestant voters. Its two main distinguishing features were that it appealed to males particularly, and that it was especially strong in southern Germany, where the death of Franz-Josef Strauss in 1988 had deprived the CSU of its most charismatic and nationalist leader. The main motive for voting REP seems to have been policy rather than protest. Its voters were not the most disadvantaged groups economically: they seem to have liked the more strident attacks on foreign workers, the call for German reunification, and the creation of a new national pride.

The 1989 elections brought the party significant income through the system of state financing of parties. Membership tripled to around twenty-five-thousand in early 1990, bringing in further funds and helping hands. But the party's hope of a major breakthrough in the Bundestag were dashed when in the December 1990 elections it gained only 2.1 percent of the national vote. The REP was undoubtedly harmed by divisions that had emerged—a split led to Schönhuber briefly standing down as leader. Animosity was particularly strong in the European parliamentary group, which by 1991 consisted solely of Schönhuber, the others having been expelled or having left the party amid allegations of corruption and incompetence. Another problem was the growing charge that the party was really Nazi. The charge was strengthened by the fact the

REP had attracted a neo-Nazi wing, especially former members of the NPD. The party tried to counter these charges by adopting a new program that seemed to commit it more clearly to the constitution, but by then the damage to its image had been done.

A further problem for the REP was that the December 1990 Bundestag elections were the first to be held since the remarkably swift events that had led to the collapse of the East German regime and Eastern European communism in general. A significant part of the party's program had thus been achieved by the Kohl government, for, after dithering, Kohl issued a guarantee that Germany accepted her post-1945 eastern boundaries. While the extremists continued to call for a return to the prewar boundaries, most Germans seem to have been delighted with the sudden turn of affairs: reunification, which only shortly before had seemed beyond their wildest dreams, was now a reality.

Euphoria was quickly followed by shock, for during 1991–2 a major wave of neo-Nazi violence swept the country, particularly in the so-called "new" *Länder*. The first major incident began on November 17, 1991, in Hoyerswerda, a bleak high-rise town built in the 1950s. Here a gang of skinheads decided to make the town "foreigner free"—an echo of the 1930s Nazi policy of making Germany "Jew free"—by attacking the homes of foreign workers and asylum seekers, and burning them out. The local population seemed indifferent or even supported the attackers, while the police appeared powerless in the face of violent protest, for which they were unprepared. More serious rioting took place elsewhere, especially at Rostock during August 1992. Here a gang of over a thousand neo-Nazis attacked immigrants and asylum seekers. Media reports of the riots brought in further supporters, together with radical-left opponents who fought the "Nazis" in the street.

The violence more commonly involved a handful of people, usually young males, often under the influence of alcohol, but it seemed to be escalating at a remarkable pace. According to the Federal Office for the Protection of the Constitution, during 1992 alone there were over 2,500 attacks on foreigners across Germany, 697 cases of arson, and 17 people were left dead.[26] It was a remarkable change compared to 1989, when the number of militant neo-

Nazis had slumped to around 1,500, and the Office for the Protection of the Constitution was reporting relatively low levels of serious attacks on foreigners.

The changing nature of Germany's foreign population offers a key to this sudden outburst. During the 1950s guest-workers had primarily been Western European young males, some of whom returned home with their newfound earnings. But during the 1960s and 1970s new arrivals came increasingly from Turkey. More importantly, *Gastarbeiter* began to stay and set up families, posing a potentially serious problem concerning citizenship, for German nationality was essentially defined in terms of "blood." The crucial issue was line of descent, rather than place of birth or length of residence. The number of people seeking asylum under Germany's liberal laws also increased suddenly, the figure rising more than tenfold between 1983 and 1992 (438,000 arrived in 1992). Many of those who came, for instance the particularly disliked Romanian Gypsies, seemed to be economic migrants rather than political refugees.

The nature of East German society itself contributed further to the sudden explosion of violence. People in the new *Länder* went remarkably quickly from a society with full employment to a new Germany where unemployment and insecurity were more the norm; most industries in the new *Länder* suffered from chronic inefficiency and had survived in the past largely by trading with even more inefficient communist countries in Eastern Europe. Years of communist conditioning played their part too. Communism had tended to stress leader worship, social homogeneity, and a clear friend-enemy distinction. After 1990 it was easy to transfer these values to the neo-Nazi cause, or at least to sympathize with its broad aims. Even before 1990 there had been deep alienation among a section of the young: witness the fact that there were more skinheads in the much smaller new *Länder* than in the old (three thousand, compared to twelve hundred, though not all were neo-Nazis). Communism, far from creating a new society, had created a time bomb.

Some of the most significant incidents in the violence after 1990 appear to have been fomented by people who had become neo-Nazis while the East German communist regime still existed.

(It is possible that some were agents provocateurs and the possibility cannot be ruled out that some "neo-Nazi" violence was instigated by others who felt they could exploit the issue.) A key figure was Frank Hübner, who had been imprisoned for his activities, but was bought out by the West German government as part of its program to help "political prisoners." On the surface, Hübner was the antithesis of the archetypal neo-Nazi: good-looking, in his twenties, he seemed more at home keying information into computer networks than putting in the boot. In person, he was another of those neofascists who at times could appear charming and reasonable. Yet behind the facade was a fanatical ideologue. He was a key figure in setting up the German Alternative (DA) in 1989, whose program bore marked similarities to Nazism. The new group quickly attracted around four hundred supporters and spread into former East Germany after unification, where it played an important part in the violence in 1992. Its members, unlike Hübner, formed an unsophisticated rabble, motivated by economic grievances or by their alienation from family and society, which attracted them to the close bonds that often grew up among these small neo-Nazi groups.[27]

In December 1992 the government decided to ban the German Alternative, as part of a belated response to the sudden upsurge of violence. (By 1995 ten organizations had been banned, including the FAP.) The attacks had caused a wave of international concern. Strong antifascist protests in Germany included a mass candlelit vigil after a firebomb attack at Mölln in former West Germany had killed a Turkish woman with her young granddaughter and niece. The government was clearly concerned that appearing to take a lax attitude could lose vital center-ground support, for there is no doubt that the attacks caused widespread revulsion. Before the Mölln murders only forty-three percent of the population were definitely against the slogan "foreigners out"; immediately after the firebombing, the figure rose to sixty percent.

Other polls, however, revealed a lingering anti-Semitism. They indicated that around ten to fifteen percent of Germans could be classed as anti-Semitic and that negative stereotypes, such as the belief that Jews were cunning, were increasing—trends that help to explain why Jews too became a target after 1991, though Germany's Jewish population had dropped from just over five hundred thousand in 1933 to around twenty thousand in the 1990s.[28] More generally, polls showed that the majority of Germans thought there were too many foreigners in the country. Many people clearly disliked the ethnic minorities, but they rejected neo-Nazi criminal violence even more. As a result, there was little public opposition to a change in the Asylum Law during 1993, which sought to restrict entry. Left-wing critics, however, bitterly attacked the government for exploiting the 1991–2 violence to secure this change in the Basic Law and gain party advantage.

The rise in violence after 1990 did not immediately tarnish the electoral prospects of the Republikaner Party and other fringe radical-nationalist groups. Their association with strident anti-immigrant politics helped to differentiate them from the more sanitized statements of the CDU-CSU. The post-1990 period, moreover, was one of growing public discontent with the mainstream parties and politicians. *Politikverdrossenheit* ("being fed up with the lot of them") was the mood of the hour as a wave of scandals mostly involving corruption, the mounting cost of reunification, growing unemployment, and a series of other problems followed in quick succession.

By late 1993, nevertheless, there were growing signs that the wave of violence was beginning to damage the electoral prospects of the radical nationalists. Sections of the media were particularly assiduous in highlighting links between violence and members of the NPD and REP, both of which had tried to distance themselves from the militant neo-Nazis during 1991 and 1992, especially the Republikaner. This downward electoral trend was confirmed by the Republikaner vote in the 1994 European elections, when they won 3.5 percent of the vote, less than half their total in 1989. Schönhuber was well aware that this augured badly for the federal elections, which were due in October 1994. Not only were they tarred with extremism, but opinion polls indicated that the SPD was likely to emerge as the largest party and return to government, having been out of national office since 1982. This prospect was likely to minimize the protest vote and encourage a rallying around the CDU-CSU.

In August 1994, Schönhuber announced the creation of a "defensive force" with Frey's DVU against the "leftist popular front."

(There was talk of an SPD–Green coalition.) In the past Schönhuber had tried to keep his distance from the DVU, which was an organization formally monitored by the Office for the Protection of the Constitution, and thus officially labeled a potential threat to democracy. This lack of cooperation had even led the two parties to contest the same election on occasion, thus splitting the radical-nationalist vote. After 1992, however, the REP had also been added to the list of nationally monitored organizations. There was, therefore, less reason for caution than in the past.

The decision was highly controversial within the Republikaner Party, as the DVU remained more clearly an extremist organization, especially after the REP had shed some of its former NPD members during 1990 to 1992. In December 1993 the DVU had even invited the unstable Russian "fascist" Vladimir Zhirinovksy to a rally, hardly the action of a responsible political party. The moderate wing of the REP, therefore, saw the pact with the DVU as a disaster, which would make it impossible to appeal to more respectable voters in the future. The result was that Schönhuber was deposed shortly before the election, though he responded by taking legal action to reverse this decision. The party entered the elections effectively leaderless and hopelessly divided.

Predictably, the Republikaner did even worse than in 1990—gaining just 1.9 percent of the vote. Most former REP voters seem to have turned to the CDU, whose leader Helmut Kohl had managed to transform himself from a political corpse into the reincarnation of Adenauer: the epitome of the strong and successful leader, a change of image helped by a sudden upturn in the economy and a distinctly uncharismatic SPD leader. Most of these converts from the REP seem to have been suspicious of Kohl's commitment to further European integration, but Kohl pandered to more nationalistic sentiment by clearly implying that Germany would now increasingly provide the lead within the European Union, and on a broader stage. (In 1994, the Constitutional Court was to give permission for German troops to be deployed beyond NATO frontiers.) Even in Bavaria, the Republikaner only won just over 3 percent of the vote, though here it faced a rather different challenge in the shape of a rejuvenated CSU which had forged its own powerful matrix of regional-nationalism and Euroscepticism.

The decline of both the REP and racially motivated violence since 1992–3 seems to provide strong evidence that Germany is not about to become the Fourth Reich.[29] Only the historically ignorant make glib parallels between politics in the 1990s and Weimar Germany. The great bogey of the past—communism—is dead (though its successor party in East Germany has shown growing signs of vitality). The neo-Nazis remain small in number and can in no way be compared to the mass Nazi Party after 1930, which regularly battled in the streets with the left. Nor is there an important section of the Establishment that dreams of overthrowing democracy. In particular, there are no disaffected army, agricultural, or business interests that seek the creation of an authoritarian nationalist state, though some left-wing antifascists would question the army's commitment to a limited, democratic role.[30] Nor should the power of antifascism be neglected, including the rise of a women's movement willing to challenge neofacism and the exceptionally strong criticism of Nazism and racism made by church leaders during January 1995 (thus criticizing their own past too).

Society is different now. The Nazis gained their greatest success among voters in rural areas, who now account for a far smaller section of the electorate. The same point can be made about small-business people. In the towns and cities, the Nazis made their greatest leap forward against a background of catastrophic depression, which meant that as much as forty percent of the workforce was unemployed. Germany is no longer a country of full employment, especially in the new *Länder,* but unemployment today stands at less than a third of this level. Besides, German unemployment and welfare benefits are among the most generous in the world—a marked change from the desperate situation of those without work in the interwar years.

Yet there are worrying continuities and parallels that should not be glossed over. Germany may have been reunited politically, but it is still divided in the head between "Ossis" and "Wessis"—whose understanding of each other may have diminished since 1990. Certainly since 1990 there have been few signs of the "blossoming landscapes" that Kohl promised to the Ossis. Indeed, German-based companies like Mercedes have been making ominous noises that the levels of taxation and social security payments are such that they may not be able to maintain production in the land of their birth. Politically, former East Germany may have been Kohlonized, but economically horizons seem to be moving farther east.

The possibility of companies moving eastward, or into developing countries outside Europe, raises a more general problem for Germany. Throughout modern history German elites have sought to unite the country by promising economic prosperity or social benefits. During the 1950s there were considerable fears among Anglo-American social scientists that polls revealing increased West German support for democracy were really picking up a "feel-good" factor associated with the economic miracle. During the 1960s and 1970s there was more widespread acceptance that a new West German democratic culture had been created.[31] Even so, doubts have to remain about the country's ability to survive a significant economic downturn, though in the new *Länder* this could benefit the Communist Party's successor more than the radical right.

Beneath the apparent stability of the German party system, epitomized by Kohl's reelection as chancellor in 1994, lies the potential for considerable change. Interestingly, this seems to be the view of Wolfgang Schäuble, the CDU leader in the Bundestag and Kohl's possible successor as chancellor, who is confined to a wheelchair after being attacked in 1990. Even more than Kohl, Schäuble has been willing to use nationalism to rally support to the CDU, which is now much less firmly rooted in the Catholic community and whose supporters in general are less strongly committed than during the 1950s. Schäuble's main purpose seems to be to build a new coalition on the right which will not allow political space for parties such as the Republikaner. He also seems to hope that nationalism can even appeal to some of those who have not traditionally supported the right. A few years ago this would have seemed an impossible dream, given the antipathy of the left to any hint of nationalist revival. But recently there has been a notable trend among intellectuals away from the left toward a position where the quest for national identity has become central.

A major figure in this trend has been Botho Strauss, Germany's best-known playwright. His characters are often hopeless and introspective, floating in the vacuum of materialist German society. Perhaps here lies the clue to his conversion: he has become convinced that the left offers only another form of materialism, where nationalism offers a chance to "return to basic values," to commune with nature and create a more truly united and meaningful society. It is easy to dismiss such figures as marginal, especially as Strauss often writes in a literary German which is inaccessible to the average citizen. But his "coming out" in an article in the leading weekly *Der Spiegel* during 1993 has attracted significant publicity. There is more concrete opinion-poll data which shows that attitudes are changing: for instance, in January 1995, the newspaper *Süddeutsche Zeitung* reported that twenty-five percent of older Bremen school pupils supported extreme right-wing views. In subsequent local elections this was not converted into support for the extremist nationalist parties, but the sudden rise of a new populist party in Bremen illustrated the weakening of the old party ties. Perhaps the central question is not so much whether there is a nationalist revival as who will be the main beneficiaries politically—the radical groups or the CDU?

The question is also linked to the issue of who will succeed Kohl as leader of the CDU. Kohl, although wishing to normalize Germany's past, has been eager to follow Adenauer's tradition of tying Germany to Europe: hence his strong support for European Monetary Union in 1995–6. But polls in 1996 show such union to be unpopular. Moreover, in early 1996 the German unemployment rate crept up to over ten percent and is now higher than at any time since the 1930s. There will be strong temptations for the next German chancellor to pursue an economic policy that is more clearly nationalist. However, even this may not be enough. There are signs that the globalization of the economy threatens doom for German's postwar high-wage high-welfare economy. Against this background, the mainstream parties may not be able to hold back the floodgates of mounting discontent, especially as increasing anti-European, nationalistic attitudes within the mainstream parties could legitimize more extreme positions.

13

Neofascism in France

i

As the Allied armies drove through France after D-Day, a bloody and bitter settling of accounts followed in their wake as the Resistance wreaked retribution.[1] The small fry, like the women who had practiced "horizontal collaboration," were usually roughed up and socially humiliated and ostracized. Others paid more dearly for their errors. Françoise Armagnac, who lived near Excideuil, was taken by a marauding group of the Resistance as she left her wedding in the summer of 1944. She was led to her large house nearby, where the wedding breakfast awaited. There the members of the Resistance found a diary which showed that she had briefly been in the Milice. She was shot, still wearing her wedding dress, in the garden of the house, at sunset next day.[2] Probably at least ten thousand people were killed during this process of "Purification" (*l'Épuration*), and over a hundred thousand were arrested.

There was much rough justice in postliberation France: the communists especially paid off old scores in those areas controlled by the major communist wing of the Resistance. Partly as a result, the story of the purge could vary notably from area to area. In Peyranne, for instance, when the local chief of the Resistance received orders from the regional purification committee to arrest various local supporters of the Vichy government, he tore up the telegram.[3] Some local communities were able to demonstrate remarkable powers of collective amnesia: at times this was because local bonding was particularly close, but the more perceptive local leaders also looked to the future. They realized that with Liberation would come the need to forge a new national consensus, which would remove the stain of Vichy.

An important part of this process was the series of trials that began in late 1944. Thousands of people were arraigned before the courts, and many others would have been had they not gone into hiding. The two main defendants were Pétain and Pierre Laval. The eighty-nine-year-old marshal was duly sentenced to death, though this was later commuted to life imprisonment. (He died in 1951.) Laval did not have age and a World War I record to protect him, and after a travesty of a trial, he was executed in 1945. Among the other leading figures executed was Darnand, whose murderous collaborationist activities offered no hope of a defense. Several key intellectuals too were targets of postliberation wrath, reflecting the importance accorded to intellectuals in French life. Robert Brasillach was executed in 1945 after another mockery of a trial, despite a petition for clemency signed by numerous intellectuals who did not sympathize with his views. Drieu La Rochelle committed suicide after penning a defense in which he seemed to welcome death, perhaps realizing that fascism needed to die to be born again, and that he was a microcosm of this process, a martyr to the cause. The aging Charles Maurras was condemned to life imprisonment: his pre-1940 writings had undoubtedly condemned him in the eyes of many, but he had sealed his fate by approving the Milice and the brutal suppression of "terrorists." On hearing the verdict, he cried, "This is the revenge of Dreyfus." The revenge of the left, and of a French people anxious to place most of the blame on a few dangerous "teachers" and politicians, would perhaps be a more accurate epitaph.[4]

The experience of war and "Purification" helped to make antifascism a central part of national identity. (Remarkably large numbers of French people managed mentally to backdate their membership of the Resistance to before the liberation.) Antifascism also provided the basis of the government headed by General de Gaulle, who had triumphantly returned to Paris in August 1944 at the head of the Free French forces. De Gaulle's desire to portray himself as standing above politics meant that he resisted the temptation to form his own party. Instead, he formed an administration comprised mainly of the groups and parties that had cooperated uneasily in the closing stages of the Resistance, namely the Communists (though elements in the party advocated a coup), the socialists, and a new Christian Democrat–style party called the Popular Republican Movement (MRP).

One major postwar task was the choice of France's form of government, for the new administration rested on no formal authority. Before this could be done, however, de Gaulle suddenly resigned in January 1946, announcing that the party leaders were showing their time-honored tendency to squabble and to make sectional demands. The new constitution of the Fourth Republic, narrowly endorsed by referendum later in 1946, did nothing to allay these fears. It adopted a list system of proportional representation, which guaranteed that several major parties would gain representation. More importantly, it provided for only a figurehead president and accorded considerable powers to parliament rather than the executive. As such, it seemed a perfect recipe for a rapid return to the old ways of the Third Republic.

De Gaulle certainly saw it this way. In 1947 he responded by announcing the formation of the Rally of the French People (RPF), effectively a Gaullist party, which proceeded to organize a series of mass rallies. De Gaulle's charisma and belief in himself as a man of destiny, his calls for a strong presidency, Third Way socioeconomic views, and his growing anticommunism, quickly attracted the tag of "fascist" from opponents on the left. The fact that some neofascist parties, most notably the Italian Social Movement, showed an interest in Gaullism illustrates that there were some interesting parallels, although the RPF was clearly not truly fascist in terms of social radicalism. (This was especially true of the miscellaneous groups of adaptable conservatives who coalesced around Gaullism as a way of reentering politics after the traumas of Vichy.)[5] Certainly most French people did not see the party as fascist. Indeed, it began to attract support rapidly, and in the 1951 elections it became the largest party in the National Assembly. But it was well short of an overall majority, and de Gaulle soon slipped back into retirement, leaving the RPF a divided but troublesome opposition group within the Chamber of Deputies.

Because the third largest party, the Communists, had retreated into Cold War isolation during 1947, governments had to be constructed from the remaining parties, who were bitterly divided over many issues. The result was the continuation of the old pattern of ministerial turnover, and between the 1951 and 1956 elections, France was governed by eleven ministries. Parallels with the Third Republic were heightened by the fact that the whiff of corruption and scandal was again in the air. *Plus ça change, plus c'est la même chose* increasingly seemed the order of the day.

ii

WHILE MAINSTREAM political life was reviving, former fascists and leading supporters of the Vichy government were initially forced to live a more precarious existence. But enthusiasm for the purge died quickly after 1945. It had served its purpose; besides, by 1947 the onset of the Cold War had turned the spotlight on to the communists as the new enemy. One sign of the times was the reemergence in 1947 of an Action Française periodical, *Aspects de France*, edited by Xavier Vallat, who was a former commissioner of Jewish affairs in the Vichy government. By the early 1950s a variety of other journals and groups had been formed, such as Jeune Nation, which was set up by Pierre Sidos, whose father had been executed at the end of the war for being a leading member of Milice. (Jeune Nation adopted as its emblem the Celtic cross, a symbol previously carried by the French Waffen SS Charlemagne division.) Although these groups and journals had small memberships, they actively kept alive noncomformist traditions and sought new supporters.[6]

The most important figure in the reemergence of radical nationalism was Maurice Bardèche, one of the few significant people outside the ranks of violent extremism who was willing after 1945 to proclaim openly: "I am a fascist." Bardèche, who married Brasillach's sister, was an academic who had been fired from his post and briefly imprisoned at the end of the war: his crime was writing for extremist publications. Ostracized from academic life, though he went on to write some notable works on French literature, Bardèche turned to polemics and ideology. In 1947 he published a strong defense of collaboration and an attack on the Resistance myth; he followed this with works challenging the validity of the Nuremberg trials and various points about evidence relating to the Holocaust.

Nineteen fifty-one found Bardèche traveling abroad to meet Sir Oswald Mosley, members of the Italian Social Movement, and other neofascists in an attempt to found a European neofascist "International." Like most intellectual fascists, Bardèche sought to defend European as well as French civilization, though in keeping with the French political tradition he tended to equate the two. Later that year he set up a monthly journal, appropriately named *Défense de l'Occident*, which over the next two decades was to be a particularly important source for more serious European neofascist thought. Bardèche portrayed fascism as an attempt to synthesize nationalism and socialism in order to achieve a gradual revolution in values. As such, he held that Hitler had departed significantly from the model, and saw no significant connection between fascism and alleged contemporary examples, like Franco's Spain. Rather, he argued that the fascist ideal was most clearly encapsulated in the theory—if not always the practice—of the Salò Republic, the closing phase of Italian fascism when Mussolini had sought to return to his radical roots.[7]

Bardèche's main concern was to fight the battle at the level of ideas. By 1951 other supporters of Vichy were reemerging on the electoral front. They rallied in particular behind a new grouping called the Union of National and Independent Republicans (UNIR), which contested a limited number of seats—mainly those where there was a tradition of extremist voting—and returned four Deputies to the National Assembly. Among those returned were Jacques Isorni, Pétain's former defense counsel and the man who led the campaign to rehabilitate the marshal. Subsequently UNIR became absorbed into the peasant parliamentary group, which itself contained former supporters of Vichy.

The presence of such a group in the Chamber of Deputies illustrates that France was in many ways still a rural country. But economic development, spearheaded by a set of talented state planners, was taking place rapidly after 1945. Although change affected all sectors of society, it particularly hit small farmers and businesses—groups that had done well during the war and in the immediate postwar period. With the growth of competition, times became much harder for small producers and retailers. Many were forced to close down or eke out an existence on the margins of survival while they watched the professional middle class and much of the working class become relatively richer.

These developments set the scene for the sudden explosion of a new political movement. In 1953, a thirty-three-year-old small shopkeeper named Pierre Poujade helped to organize a demonstration to prevent the hated tax inspector from visiting a neighbor's business. The tactic spread to other villages and towns. Soon Poujade found himself at the head of a pressure group, the Union for the Defense of Shopkeepers and Artisans (UDCA), which railed against the alleged iniquities of the tax system and the uncaring and corrupt nature of the Deputies in Paris. This quickly built up a national organization backed by a variety of newspapers, often specially founded by small-scale printers who rallied to the cause. By 1955 this organization had spawned a political party, the French Union and Fraternity (UFF), which trumpeted even more stridently the Poujadist assault on the "system."[8]

Poujade depicted himself as the typical ordinary man (*petit gars*), brought into politics by an unjust and rotten system. Most historians have accepted this self-image, portraying Poujadism either as lacking a clear ideological character or as a form of populism.[9] The truth was rather different. Poujade was brought up in a middle-class family that despised the Republic. In his teens he had been involved with Doriot's PPF. In 1940 he had initially supported the Vichy government, but had fled to Spain as the government's collaborationism became ever greater; from Spain he traveled to Britain, where he joined the air force. After 1945 Poujade initially kept out of politics, but this instinctively political animal soon reemerged as an activist in the Gaullist party. With the Gaullists' demise, by 1953 Poujade was looking for a new political vehicle.

Tall and physically impressive, Poujade traveled throughout France addressing rapturous large meetings. Often speaking in shirtsleeves, he cleverly used the Republican myth to suggest radical policies. The "small man" was eulogized as the very epitome of "Liberty, Equality and Fraternity." (The real target was capitalism, which was to be replaced by an ill-defined corporatist system.) By 1955 Poujade was calling for the summoning of an Estates General to produce a new constitution. (Here the target was parliamentary democracy.) Behind the calls to defend France's interests, especially her colonies, was a strong sense of the threat from the enemy within (namely Jews, who were behind both capitalism and parliament). Although the message appeared to be a classic form of negative populism, there was more than an element of truth in the nickname given to Poujade by left-wing critics—"Poujadolf."

The UFF's main slogan for the January 1956 elections to the National Assembly was: "Kick the Old Gang Out" (*Sortez les Sortants*). In his television broadcast before the election, the leader of the Poujadist peasant group concluded that for the next Revolution they would not need the guillotine, as a rope was cheaper and faster and Paris had plenty of lampposts. Amazingly, the UFF won 11.6 percent of the vote and fifty-two seats in the elections.[10] An important part of the vote came from artisans, small-business owners, and farmers, who were experiencing hard times or who felt threatened by change. There was a major protest element too, people who even in the towns and cities felt some form of hostility toward the "them" who ran the system. Interestingly, in terms of region, Poujadism was often strong in traditionally left-wing areas. This was almost certainly a reflection of the way in which he had adopted the rhetoric of the Revolution, rather than attack it in the way of old right-wing groups like the Action Française.

The problem for Poujade was that it is hard to found a durable movement on charisma, rhetoric, and protest—especially in a country where the diffuse forces of conservatism had strong roots. There were still economic grievances to exploit, but it was difficult to keep together a movement whose activists and deputies held a remarkable variety of views. As well as left-right splits, there was a notable group within the UDCA that had opposed the move into party politics, either on the grounds that it was bad for business or fearing that it was a personal vehicle for Poujade's ambitions. Another problem was that Poujade was becoming increasingly involved in the campaign to preserve France's beleaguered empire. While the issue struck a chord with many voters, it was a tune other parties could play only too well. The result was a rapid loss of support for Poujadism, and by the 1958 elections it had slumped to under three percent of the vote.

These elections were the result of a dramatic turn of events.

The immediate cause of the crisis was a revolt in Algiers. In 1954 the French army had suffered a humiliating defeat at Dien Bien Phu, which had led to the loss of French Indochina (Vietnam). In the same year a nationalist rising had begun in Algeria, which was formally part of "Metropolitan" France and which had a significant French minority among its population. (In this sense, Algeria was a very atypical "colony.") Soon France had committed nearly four hundred thousand troops to Algeria and was engaged in a bloody and torturous war.

In May 1958 many army leaders and settlers in Algeria had become convinced that yet another ministerial crisis in Paris was about to lead to the appointment of a government of "scuttle." Although there was a strong body of opinion in France, especially on the left, that sought to end France's sovereignty over Algeria, the cause of *Algérie française* had many supporters too. Predictably in Algeria the French *colons* were almost universally in favor of continuing French control. Most settlers were motivated essentially by economic factors; an independent Algeria seemed to threaten their basic way of life and they might even be forced to leave. Economic factors, however, cannot be separated totally from political ones. Many saw Algerian nationalism as atavistic and in danger of falling prey to Islamic conservatism, traits that ran counter to the French view of "progress" and of their "civilizing mission." Algerian nationalism could be seen as the forerunner of colonial revolution that threatened French and, more generally, European interests and values. Predictably, these doom-laden messages were preached in particular by a small but active group of neofascists and extremist civilian leaders who were violently opposed to any form of hand-over.

The culmination of these developments was a revolt in Algiers during May 1958 and the appointment of a Committee of Public Safety. Shortly afterward General Salan publicly appealed to de Gaulle to emerge from retirement and lead the nation out of its crisis and divisions. (It is not clear whether de Gaulle or key supporters encouraged these events.) The next couple weeks were full of plot and maneuver. Fears of a military coup were heightened when Corsica was occupied by rebellious paratroops. The government responded by holding talks with the transport workers about a strike in the event of a coup (though paratroops did not travel much by train or bus). But by late May it had become widely accepted among political leaders and deputies that de Gaulle should return as prime minister.[11]

Duly voted into office, de Gaulle proceeded to draft a new constitution. Later in 1958 the French people overwhelmingly voted in a referendum to ratify the creation of the Fifth Republic. Among the main provisions of the new constitution was a change in the electoral system from proportional representation to two ballots in single-member constituencies, which favored parties capable of making alliances for the second ballot, and which was aimed at weakening the communists—though it also harmed right-wing extremist prospects. Far greater powers were accorded to the president, a position filled by de Gaulle after the lawmaking was done. Shortly afterward, elections to the National Assembly took place. A newly formed Gaullist party emerged as the largest grouping.

It quickly became clear that, far from pursuing the war more vigorously, de Gaulle was willing to contemplate withdrawal. Fears of government "betrayal" led to further settler unrest, which culminated in the Week of Barricades in Algiers during January 1960. Led by a variety of extremists like the charismatic student, Pierre Lagaillarde, a group of *colons* again challenged the French government. After a period of violent resistance, when Frenchman fired on Frenchman, the revolt was suppressed. But the plotting continued. In April 1961 Generals Challe, Salan, and others attempted a *putsch* in Algiers. It was a powerful statement of the extent to which disaffection had spread among the army leadership, backed by much of the settler population. The generals, however, were divided over what they sought to achieve and could not rely on the loyalty of their conscript troops, or even some fellow officers. De Gaulle shrewdly used the radio to broadcast over the heads of the plotters, contemptuously dismissing them and calling on the army to be loyal. The revolt fizzled out almost as suddenly as it had emerged.

Shortly before, Lagaillarde and other Algiers plotters had played a crucial role in forming the Secret Army Organization (OAS). Some of those who became involved in this new organization were neofascists, men like Jean-Jacques Susini, a student leader who later explained at his trial for insurrection that his true goal was to forge a movement that could synthesize the two great movements of the twentieth century—nationalism and social reform. Others who helped set up the OAS came more from an authoritarian military background, men such as General Salan, who sought to defend the honor of the army. The result of this terrorist coalition's formation was a wave of bombings on the French mainland, which injured many innocent people; a wave of terror also broke out in Algeria. De Gaulle miraculously survived a series of assassination attempts. If anything, this increased his resolve to achieve a settlement, and in 1962 France signed an accord with the Algerian nationalists.[12]

Some neofascists were later to rue the Algerian War as a great lost opportunity to forge a new mass movement.[13] De Gaulle, however, had appreciated that many French people opposed the continuation of the war and that others had come to accept the inevitable. He was careful to guard his nationalist flank. Under his leadership, France had quickly become the dominant force in the European Economic Community (later European Union), which had come into existence in 1958. Most dramatically, de Gaulle played the crucial role in blocking British membership in 1961–3. His vision of European unity, unlike that of the federalist visionaries, was based on retaining the sovereignty of nation states. Indeed, the continuing independent aspect of French policy was forcefully underlined by de Gaulle's decision to produce an independent French nuclear strike capability—although he sometimes linked this to a Europeanist position, which would involve a significant decline in American influence in Europe.

The lack of any serious support for a rival nationalist movement is illustrated by the result of the 1965 presidential election, the first to be held since de Gaulle had used a referendum to change the system to direct election by popular vote. De Gaulle's main opponent was the socialist François Mitterrand, but another of his rivals was Jean-Louis Tixier-Vignancourt, a man who had supported the AF in his youth. Tixier was a lawyer by profession, who had been elected as a right-wing deputy in 1936 and for a time had headed the radio network in the Vichy regime. After the Purification, he became active in various small extremist groups and publishing activities, including Jeune Nation and *Défense de l'Occident*. In 1956, he reemerged as a right-wing deputy and was particularly active in trying to mold the disparate Poujadists into a more effective parliamentary grouping. Having lost his seat in 1958, Tixier returned to his legal practice and defended some of the most notorious members of the OAS (including Salan and Colonel Bastien-Thiry, who had led one of the assassination attempts on de Gaulle). But his real goal was to form an umbrella group that could gather together the disparate and often hostile forces on the extreme right.[14]

His main aim in running for the 1965 presidential elections was to put down a marker for such a grouping. Given his former experience in propaganda and skills as a lawyer, "TV"—as he was commonly known—tried to exploit the media to gain coverage. He realized that the days of mass rallies were passing and that favorable press, radio, and especially television coverage were crucial to political success. The French broadcasting networks, however, were effectively controlled by the government, and while TV gained some publicity, he notably failed to carry his message to most voters. Besides, the mainstays of his campaign, support for *Algérie française* and criticism of de Gaulle, were simply not what people wanted to hear. Therefore the result was a bitterly disppointing one for TV and the others who had hoped to found a new movement on the back of a good showing. He obtained a mere 5.3 percent of the vote on the first ballot. In the second ballot, much of his support transferred not to de Gaulle, but to Mitterrand: one prominent Tixier supporter, Isorni, rationalized this decision by saying that he had never heard Mitterrand say a bad word about Vichy. Such was the gulf between the extremists and the Gaullist mainstream, though a few knew more about Mitterrand than he was letting on in public, where he stressed his Resistance credentials.

iii

THE ALGERIAN WAR had failed to create the conditions for the rise of a radical nationalist mass movement. But by heightening a sense of external threat, internal divisions, and hostility toward the left, the war provided a fertile climate in which to attract a fresh generation to the cause of violent extremism. Many activists joined new groupings, which were constantly springing up, mainly to get around government bans, though ideological differences encouraged factionalism. The most prominent of the new sects was Occident, which was founded in 1964: its best-known leader was a young *Algérie française* activist named François Duprat.[15] Although Duprat was an advocate of radical Third Way views and most of Occident's two thousand or so members were university students, its activities focused on confrontations with the left rather than the development of doctrine. By the end of 1968 the resulting violence had led to its disbandment by the government, though it was quickly succeeded by an array of smaller student groups, most notably the Group Union Law (GUD).

Nineteen sixty-eight was an important year for many on the radical right. For a time during May and June, left-wing student riots and a wave of sit-in strikes by workers had appeared to be on the verge of toppling the government. At one point panic spread through government circles when it was thought that de Gaulle had fled, though in reality he had traveled to the military command in Germany, where he seems to have made a deal by which the army guaranteed to support him in return for the release from prison of leading OAS plotters, including General Salan. The departure of de Gaulle would have aroused little sorrow among the extremists, but the fear that the country had been on the verge of left-wing revolution helped give impetus to two important developments.

The first was the emergence of what was to become known as the New Right (ND), a loose grouping that in no way should be confused with the Anglo-American free-market New Right. The basic idea behind the ND was not to engage in Occident-type street confrontations with the left. Nor did it seek to attract "notables," like Tixier-Vignancourt, and engage in major election campaigns that could only end in humiliation, at least in the foreseeable future. Rather, the New Right sought nothing less than to change the basis of political culture and language.[16]

Its leading strategist was Alain de Benoist, a graduate of Paris University. From youth, de Benoist had been involved in a variety of right-wing extremist groups that came and went during the late 1950s and 1960s. Unlike most radical right-wing intellectuals, de Benoist was interested in left-wing theory and practice. He was particularly fascinated by the writings of Antonio Gramsci, a founding member of the Italian Communist Party who had died in a fascist jail. Gramsci had been critical of the crude Marxist line that power in capitalist society stemmed simply from the ownership of capital. He believed that the social system was heavily reinforced by the activities of a host of people who were not necessarily wealthy, including journalists, academics, teachers, and the clergy. Gramsci argued that in order for a revolution to be successful, it was necessary to counter the "hegemony" of ideas created by these groups: in other words, the way in which they helped to define what was consensual, what was "normal." De Benoist adopted this theory to his own ends, for he believed that since 1945, the left had come to dominate culture in France. His answer was an attempt to create a "Gramsciism of the Right."[17]

In an interview during the 1970s, de Benoist was to endorse the old aphorism that France had "the most stupid right in the world."[18] In a country that saw itself as the fount of modernity, France had produced a long line of right-wing dinosaurs addicted to lost causes—like the monarchy—or ruled by a predilection to admire foreign countries and their dictatorial rulers. De Benoist sought to change all this: he wanted to create a right that was both intellectual and modern. His adoption of the term *right* was interesting, given its connotations with reactionary and fascist views: he seems to have been unhappy about using the term, but accepted that *right* was a necessary shorthand for activists and journalists—and for situating the movement as hostile to the organized left.

The main vehicles for the New Right were high-quality publications and related small discussion groups. During 1968–9, the first two key forums in this strategy were formed. One was the quarterly journal *Nouvelle École*, which by the 1970s had an impressive list of patrons, including many from academic life in France and abroad: the French patrons included Louis Rougier and Julien Freund, while foreign ones encompassed Mircea Eliade and Hans Eysenck, all people of considerable renown. The second was the Group for the Research and Study of European Civilization, which became better known by its clever acronym GRECE, a name replete with images of heritage and learning. Subsequently, other journals and groups became part of the New Right network, most notably the more "popular" *Éléments* monthly journal and the Club de l'Horloge—though this grouping of higher civil servants was linked through personnel rather than formal structures.

Seminal influences on New Right thought were Nietzsche and Julius Evola. Their ideas can be seen in the starting point of its philosophy, which held that the root of Europe's problems was its adoption of "Judeo-Christian" values rather than indigenous pagan ones.[19] The Judeo-Christian tradition was seen as stressing monotheism and monoculturalism, which for the ND marked the origins of totalitarianism. The Judeo-Christian culture was also attacked for its egalitarianism, which was seen as spawning secular ethics like Marxism. In its place, the New Right sought to substitute a more hierarchical philosophy, pointing to scientific evidence that people were not equal. But such was the power of this Judeo-Christian conditioning, according to the ND, that it would be necessary to build "man" again from scratch.

From this sweeping starting point, the New Right argued that it was necessary to rediscover Europe's true identity. The roots of this community, it was alleged, were to be found in neither of the two dominant world systems—communism and capitalism. The former was ultimately based on coercion; the latter was based on a divisive and alienating pursuit of money. These antipathies were important to the ND because, following the key theorist of the early Nazi regime, Carl Schmitt, it realized that pinpointing the enemy was crucial to the development of identity. Somewhat surprisingly, de Benoist picked on American individualism and materialism as a greater danger than communism (an echo of 1920s "National Bolshevik" thinking that he was to develop more fully during the 1990s when he sought to promote a "Brown-Red" alliance).

The New Right was far less clear when it came to fleshing out what the substance of its political system would be. There were echoes of Ernst Jünger and the German conservative revolutionaries in its references to the need to make work more spiritual and less concerned with the purely economic, but its goal of a "directed organic community" seemed little more than a verbal formula. It was unclear what implications the new system would have for other peoples, especially those living within Europe. De Benoist claimed that the ND was perfectly happy to accept the identity of others: he argued that the real racism was that of the left, which sought to make all cultures the same, and which demonized those—Europeans at least—who sought the roots of their own cultures. The ND was, therefore, "anti-anti-racist": it was "differentialist," the supporter of the birthright of each cultural group to be different and to retain its identity.

Some critics responded by arguing that the New Right represented a new form of fascism, pointing to its ideological mentors and to the way in which it was clearly trying to legitimate a series of ideas that had underpinned fascism. They also argued that the attack on "Judeo-Christian" values was really a means of dressing up anti-Semitism in a semi-respectable guise. Other critics argued that the ND was not truly fascist, highlighting its form and style—the way in which it made no effort to become a mass movement or to encourage violence as a cathartic force.[20] But there was widespread agreement among all critics that it was racist: for all its talk of cultural diversity, the New Right clearly did not envisage a multicultural France or Europe. "Immigrants are not wanted here" could easily have been its motto had it not been involved in a sophisticated attempt to legitimize extremist politics.

Anti-immigrant politics were central to another organization that emerged in the aftermath of 1968, a movement that reflected the second new strategic direction taken by the extremists at this time. The group, which had its roots in a series of meetings that took place during late 1969, was called New Order (ON).[21] Unlike the ND, which was a small and relatively homogeneous group, the ON was meant to link different types of nationalists, both fascist and nonfascist. From the former category, it attracted François Duprat, who in the late 1960s had written a sympathetic history of the SS for Bardèche's publishing house, and who was beginning to show a marked interest in Holocaust Denial arguments. Among the leading nonfascists was François Brigneau, who had served with the Milice under the Vichy government, and who was editor of the extreme-right weekly *Minute*.

New Order wanted to model itself on the Italian Social Movement, which managed to combine within one organization violent activists and those who sought a more respectable electoral strategy. Although the leaders of the ON were eager to develop the latter side, they were well aware that they could not ignore the former: most of the two thousand or so members who joined during 1969 and 1970 came from violent extremist organizations—and in some cases held joint membership with street-fighting units like GUD. Any overtly right-wing extremist party, moreover, was likely to attract the attentions of left-wing extremist groups. As there were more of these, the nationalist extremists were often the victims rather than the perpetrators of violence, though they tried to give as good as they got and would certainly have been more aggressive had their numbers been greater.

The ON leadership believed that it had found an important new electoral issue: opposition to immigration. About eight percent of France's population was foreign, a figure that had remained unchanged throughout the twentieth century. But within these figures, there had been a marked rise during the 1960s of immigrants from North Africa, especially Algeria. North Africans were not only more visible; they were anathema to the supporters of *Algérie française*. (The only exception were the Harkis, Algerians who had fought for France and been forced to flee for their lives in 1962.) The ON line was that having pushed the French out of Algeria, Arabs were now set to take over the rest of France. Immigration, therefore, seemed the ideal topic, combining economic fears, racist sentiment, and pandering to the obsessions of an important part of the party's hard core.

When the ON tested the water in local elections after 1970, however, the results were highly disappointing. Although de Gaulle had resigned from the presidency in 1969, his support had largely been transferred to his former prime minister, Georges Pompidou, who easily won the ensuing presidential election. The Gaullist party too survived the departure of its leader, which dented the optimistic view that de Gaulle's support was personal and that Gaullism would disappear with his retirement. Few voters showed any inclination to transfer their loyalties to a party that was clearly tainted with the extremist brush.

ON leaders like Duprat and Brigneau came to accept that to attract a significant electoral following they needed to set up another organization that was totally separate. The resulting group was formed in 1972 and took the name Front National (FN); its title was an indication that it brought together a coalition of forces on the extremist and nationalist right: genuine fascists, monarchists, Catholic fundamentalists, nostalgics for *Algérie française,* and others. At the time of the formation of the ON, its leadership was agreed that it should not become a vehicle for a personality like Tixier-Vignancourt. They wanted a party driven by a clearer sense of ideological purpose, even if there was some disagreement over exactly what this ideology was. But when it came to choosing a leader for the FN, they agreed to accept another of the notables they had so suspected in 1969–70, Jean-Marie Le Pen.

Le Pen came from Brittany, where he had been orphaned during the war after his father's fishing boat hit a German mine.[22] It is not clear whether he played any part in the Resistance at the end of the war. It seems most likely that he became politically active after communist attempts to dominate the Resistance aroused his antagonism. Certainly by the late 1940s he was active in extreme right-wing politics in Paris, where he was studying for a law degree. During the 1950s Le Pen turned from street fighting, in which he lost an eye, to fighting with the paratroops in Algeria. In between times he managed to be elected to the Chamber of Deputies in 1956 as a Poujadist, before returning to Algeria, where he was accused of using torture on suspects. In 1958 he was reelected under the Independent Peasant banner, but he lost the seat in the Gaullist landslide of 1962. In the wake of the Algerian War, Le Pen was one of many who dreamed of setting up a major new organization, and he was active helping the Tixier-Vignancourt campaign, but this ended in a clash between these two strong personalities. During much of the 1960s and early 1970s Le Pen largely dropped out of active politics, becoming involved in a variety of business adventures, which included setting up a publishing company that sold, among other things, Nazi speeches and German marching songs—an activity that brought him before the courts charged with promoting sympathy for war crimes.

The choice of Le Pen as leader of the Front National reflected hopes that his charisma and contacts could help gain the party wider media coverage and support. Pompidou's premature death in 1974 provided him with an early opportunity to underline his leadership by putting up a good performance. Hopes ran particularly high as the Gaullists were divided, and a new center-right challenger had emerged in the shape of former Finance Minister Valéry Giscard d'Estaing, who went on to win. Le Pen's campaign focused on a variety of themes, including a vague Atlanticism and hostility to the big state—exactly the sort of views that had made him unpopular with many hard-line neofascists. He talked of the urgent need for national rebirth, but it was not entirely clear what this involved other than boosting the birth rate and cutting the immigrant population. Although there were growing signs of hostility toward immigrants, this program fell on largely deaf ears: Le Pen won a mere 0.7 percent of the vote on the first ballot.

This poor showing increased friction within the FN. A section of the ON had never been happy with Le Pen, seeing him as a careerist willing to set aside ideology for advancement. This was a major reason why the ON had not dissolved itself at the time of the formation of the Front National. But in 1973 the ON had been banned by the government after a series of violent incidents. As a result, after the 1974 elections (in which some supported Giscard), some of its members decided to set up a rival organization called the Parti des Forces Nouvelles (PFN): among the leaders who went over to this grouping was Brigneau. There ensued a period of bitter relations on the right, during which Le Pen's house was bombed in 1976 and Duprat, who remained loyal to the FN, was killed by a car bomb in 1978, though it was never clear exactly who perpetrated these attacks.

Electorally the FN continued to do badly. In the 1979 European elections, the first direct elections to the European Parliament, the FN did not even run candidates, though a PFN list won 1.3 percent of the vote. Further humiliation for Le Pen followed as the 1981 presidential elections approached: he could not collect the five hundred signatures necessary from various local officials to allow him to run. If further proof were needed of the failure of the FN, this came in the ensuing legislative elections, when it gained a mere 0.4 percent of the vote. Oblivion beckoned.

iv

REMARKABLY, within the space of little over a year, there were growing signs that Le Pen and the Front National might be able to achieve a miraculous comeback from the dead. The election of Mitterrand as president, accompanied by the victory in the ensuing legislative elections of a left-wing coalition that included communists, led to a radical change in economic policy, which quickly fueled a crisis. Government popularity began to slump dramatically. The two main parties of the moderate right had their problems too, especially the Gaullists, who under Jacques Chirac had moved away from the nationalistic, vaguely Third Way policies of the general. In their place came a more technocratic style and interest in Anglo-American New Right policies. Although the more free-market views had their attractions given the socialists' problems, they opened a space for a more nationalistic appeal. They also encouraged a drift of activists from the moderate parties to the FN, a move that brought several people with significant intellectual and organizational skills into the party—including a small but important group from the Club de l'Horloge, most notably Bruno Mégret, later a deputy leader of the FN.

Le Pen's immigration theme was also showing signs of striking a chord, as polls registered increasing levels of concern with this, and related issues such as law and order (*l'insécurité*).[23] The development was clearly related to growing unemployment, but the Front National's agenda had also been highlighted by a remarkable wave of publicity the ND had attracted during and after 1979. During 1978, Louis Pauwels, the editor of the leading daily newspaper, *Le Figaro*, had appointed some key members of the ND, including de Benoist, to his staff. (Pauwels during the 1950s had held some views that were similar to Evola's, most notably an interest in the occult.) The appointments helped to spread ND ideas beyond the narrow circles in which they had previously been disseminated. The immediate result was an outcry in some other sections of the media and on the left, but the response helped give the ideas even further publicity. By the early 1980s, the theme of the need to rediscover national identity was increasingly becoming the focus of much media reporting, thus helping to give legitimacy to these ideas.

Television in France was still heavily controlled by the state and was more cautious in following this line. Possibly in an attempt to weaken the mainstream right, Mitterrand seems to have played a part in instructing the state television network to give the fringe parties more access. Le Pen quickly began to exploit his limited opportunities, proving himself to be an excellent speaker on television as well as at mass rallies (very different techniques, for the "cool" medium of television requires a more restrained approach). Given the importance of television to modern political campaigning and legitimacy, this was a major breakthrough. It also particularly suited a party whose leader had a strong charismatic appeal, for Le Pen's image tended to affect people more than his policy statements. In turn Le Pen's charisma attracted a media that liked to feature "personalities."

The first major evidence of an FN breakthrough came in 1983, when the FN won 16.7 percent of the vote in local elections in Dreux, a town where there was a large immigrant population and where the FN had been particularly well organized by a husband-and-wife team, Jean-Pierre and Marie-France Stirbois, who had met while active in Tixier-Vignancourt's 1965 campaign. The Dreux vote alone would have boosted the FN's confidence, both locally and nationally, but the elections were fought over two ballots—and for the second ballot the two mainstream right parties formed an alliance with the FN. The result was that the FN gained representation on the local council, with Jean-Pierre Stirbois as deputy mayor.

These results encouraged hopes that the FN could put up a creditable performance in the 1984 European elections, expectations that were further raised by the demise of the PFN after the 1981 elections. The party had always been an unstable coalition, but Brigneau's conversion back to the FN reveals the importance of Le Pen in the rise of the FN. Brigneau was one of those who in the early 1970s had accused Le Pen of personal ambition: after 1981 he used his media columns to praise the "inspired prophet" and the "Breton genius." For all the failures of the FN during the 1970s, Brigneau had come to realize that only Le Pen had the charisma and political skills to forge a united party and extend its appeal outside the traditional extreme right.

In the 1984 European elections the FN won almost 11 percent of the vote and was rewarded with ten seats in the European Parliament. The fact that the moderate right had put up as their leading candidate Simone Veil, a Jew and a Europhile, undoubtedly helped the FN, not least as she was associated with introducing an abortion law in the 1970s that had been strongly opposed by many Catholics. Even so, the FN had made a dramatic breakthrough that augured well for the next parliamentary elections. FN hopes were further raised when Mitterrand announced that there would be a change to the party list electoral system, the arrangement used in the Fourth Republic and for the 1984 European elections. Once again, Mitterrand seemed to be seeking to split the right-wing vote. The tactic failed to prevent the moderate right from duly winning these elections and returning to government in cohabitation with a socialist president (who was elected for seven years). But the new electoral system meant that the FN's 9.9 percent of the vote gave it thirty-five seats in the Chamber of Deputies.

There was an element of protest voting in FN support, but there was also a more positive side to allegiance.[24] The Front was especially strong among *pieds noirs,* settlers who had returned from Algeria and who made up a particularly important constituency in some parts of southern France. (Their total numbers, including descendants, probably approached a million.) The FN also appealed to some voters who lived in close proximity to immigrant communities, especially around Paris. In socioeconomic terms, its voters tended to be male, middle-aged, and middle class, with small-business owners especially well represented. But the FN gained converts among most groups, including disillusioned younger voters. Perhaps not typical but symptomatic was a teenager named Arnaud Dubreuil, who was fascinated when he saw Le Pen on television. He went on to start reading radical publications like *Éléments* and was soon to become a disciple of Evola: rapidly he had moved from alienation to being an ideologue.[25]

The sudden rise of the FN led to an inevitable counterattack, especially from antifascist and antiracist groups. They were becoming increasingly worried because opinion polls were indicating that Le Pen's claim that he said what others thought was dangerously true. A typical poll in 1984 found that twenty-five percent of respondents wanted most immigrants to go home; another poll found that sixty-six percent of French people thought that there were "far too many" North Africans in France. By the mid-1980s, polls showed that immigration and related themes were central to the electorate's concerns. Even unemployment, the most commonly

cited issue of concern, was linked in the sense that the Front cam-
paigned strongly on the theme "Two million unemployed is two
million immigrants too many."

After the 1983–4 FN breakthroughs, stories of Le Pen's involvement in torture during the Algerian War and his sales of Nazi
memorabilia during the 1960s resurfaced. To this growing wave of
criticism was added the claim that at the local level the FN dealt in
Hitler nostalgia, and other forms of extremism.[26] Even Le Pen's es-
tranged wife joined in the damning chorus, saying that Le Pen
wanted her to act like a servant: in 1987 she appeared in the French
edition of *Playboy*, dressed scantily in just a maid's apron. In the
same year Le Pen added fuel to the fire when in a television program he referred to the Holocaust as a "detail of history." This
seemed to offer guarded support for the thesis that there had been
no systematic policy of Nazi genocide—an argument that had attracted notable attention in France after the 1970s as a result of the
writings of a number of academics and a group of their supporters,
some of whom came from the "anti-Zionist" left.[27] It was a highly
sensitive claim, given that France's Jewish population of six hundred thousand was the largest in Western Europe and had been the
object of increasing attacks, both physical and verbal, since the
1970s.[28] Even some of the more moderate members of the FN were
shocked by Le Pen's "detail" comment, and a few left the party as a
result, including one of FN's members of the European Parliament.

Le Pen quickly tried to repair the damage by stressing that he
was not endorsing Nazism or anti-Semitic views. Perhaps he had
just been caught out by an unfortunate slip of words, but suspicion
remained that the formula may have been deliberate: perhaps he
was testing the water for the resonance of more radical views. More
probably he was sending a signal to the party's extreme supporters
that their voices were not being forgotten. As the party had begun
to grow during the 1980s, it had sought to encourage support by
setting up special sections for different interests: young people, doctors, lawyers, and so on. These helped to establish a national organization and brought people into the party who might not have
joined otherwise. (By 1985 the FN was claiming sixty thousand
members.) But this diffusion of membership worried many of the

hard-liners, who felt that Le Pen was watering down doctrine too much in order to give the FN a broad-based appeal.

By the 1980s Le Pen's political discourse was remarkably sophisticated in its appeal to different strands of French opinion.[29] He probably learned some of this technique from Poujade, who had cleverly exploited the Republican tradition to appeal across the political spectrum. Le Pen likewise used the language of the Revolution (such as "fraternity" and "freedom") to sell his message (France needed to rebuild her shattered community and free herself from foreign and dangerous influences). He also seems to have learned from the New Right and its attempt to defuse charges that it was racist or fascist. He did not portray opposition to immigrants in terms of their inferiority; rather he talked in aphorisms—"I love my daughters more than my cousins, my cousins more than my neighbors," and so on—which implied that there was no universal humankind for which he felt equal liking. He was very conscious of the use of symbolism: an important day in the FN calendar is the *Fête de Jeanne d'Arc,* for Joan of Arc symbolizes both the revival of the nation and resistance to the enemy within.

This ability to present a complex mask almost certainly helped Le Pen to overcome some of the damage caused by his "detail" comment, and the general antifascist attack. Indeed in the 1988 presidential election he won over fourteen percent of the vote on the first ballot, only five points behind Jacques Chirac, who went on to lose the second ballot to Mitterrand. But in the ensuing legislative elections, the FN managed to elect only one deputy. The post-1986 mainstream-right government had reverted to the old two-ballot electoral system, which made it difficult for the FN to win seats, given the reluctance of most in the mainstream right to form local alliances for the second ballot.

The unwillingness of much of the mainstream right to make pacts did not mean that it had jumped on the antifascist bandwagon. Although Le Pen was often denounced for extremism, the mainstream parties were increasingly borrowing crucial parts of his program and rhetoric.[30] In the second ballot of the 1988 presidentials, Chirac clearly bid for the Le Pen vote. By the early 1990s this tendency was becoming even stronger: Chirac talked of understanding why people disliked the smell of immigrants, while Giscard d'Estaing spoke of the need to base citizenship on "blood." Even the socialist prime minister could talk in terms of chartering planes to take home illegal immigrants. Although the socialists had taken a strong line against any form of cooperation with Le Pen, they could see that the immigration issue had been an important factor in the growing working-class support he attracted through the 1980s. Some aspects of immigration also worried the Socialist Party in more fundamental ideological terms, especially the extent to which immigrants had to drop their identity and become "French": an issue highlighted dramatically in 1989 by Muslim girls whose parents insisted that they wore the traditional headscarf to school, a symbol for many people of Islam's suppression of women.

The headscarf issue was particularly useful to the FN. Polls showed widespread opposition to allowing the practice, a feeling that encouraged Le Pen to call for a referendum on the issue. The issue highlighted FN arguments that French identity was threatened, that a new wave of immigrants were arriving who did not want to become French, especially the three million to five million Muslims who lived in France by the early 1990s. They had engaged in an extensive program of mosque building during the 1980s, hardly a sign that they intended to return "home" someday. This in turn heightened fears of a further wave of immigration, driven by North Africa's rapidly increasing population, or perhaps by people fleeing from an Islamic government. (Algeria only avoided such a government in 1992 by the military stopping elections.)

Elections during 1990–4, however, showed that the FN vote had stabilized at around ten to fourteen percent. This plateau and the adoption of many of the FN's policies by mainstream parties began to push the party toward a more radical program. For much of the 1980s Le Pen had defended almost Thatcherite economic policies, stressing the individual and expressing hostility to much state action. In the 1990s a significant change has taken place. A more clearly corporatist strand has emerged, and during the 1994 European election campaign Le Pen even described free-market economics as an evil (*néfaste*) ideology, arguing that it was vital to achieve "balance," a synthesis of the state and private markets. For his 1995 presidential campaign, he stressed the importance of "national preference," which was not simply a case of putting the French first in terms of jobs or housing. It was also linked to a more restrictive view of trade, a reflection of growing fears that a vast number of jobs, particularly for the unskilled, were being "exported" to foreign countries.

During the 1980s an academic boom industry developed in France, and elsewhere, dealing with the question of whether the FN could reasonably be termed "fascist" or "neofascist." Most French academics tended to reject the tag, in part a reflection of a long-running tendency to play down the importance of fascism in France: instead they preferred "Poujadist," "Bonapartist," and especially "National Populist."[31] What these arguments glossed over was that, in a sense, the FN was all of these things. It was deliberately vague about its core: Le Pen specifically denied that it had an ideology, portraying it more as the defense of common sense, a good populist theme. Recent developments within the FN, however, tend to indicate that there always was a core and its name is fascism. This is not to argue that Le Pen, or leading members of the FN, like Mégret, are closet Nazis—though the party clearly has this side at the local level.[32] The point is related to a more fundamental ideology, to an attempt to create a new holistic community, to achieve a radical change in the nature of socioeconomic organization.

Le Pen, however, remained a master of disguises and his 1995 presidential election campaign cleverly combined a commitment to change with more populist themes—especially the promise to expel three million immigrants. It proved a highly appealing package, and Le Pen saw his vote rise to an unprecedented fifteen percent on the first ballot—including further significant gains in working-class areas. In local elections later in 1995 the FN did even better, winning control of three large towns—and it would have won more had there not been a concerted media and antifascist campaign.

Whether the FN can maintain this new impetus is another matter: Le Pen's career is coming to an end, and before the next presidential election it will have to choose a new leader. His successor may not have the skills to keep the party together, or may simply find the task impossible. On the other hand, a new leader may be less tainted by the past than Le Pen. The man who was elected secretary general of the FN in late 1995, Bruno Gollnisch, is a former university teacher whose wife is Japanese. The party could also benefit from sudden shocks to the system. Perhaps the most dramatic event that could help it would be an Islamic takeover in Algeria, or in the longer term a significantly greater military threat from Islamic forces. There is also growing evidence that the French public has become highly alienated by stories of corruption among the political class. While it is true that these trends may benefit other political outsiders, the FN has established a major presence in French politics. Its main themes—national identity, hostility to immigrants, even fears about long-run economic prospects—have never been more central to the political agenda. President Chirac will have his work cut out to defuse these problems—especially if the terrorist bombings of 1995 continue and radical groups begin to attract large numbers of disaffected French Muslims.

The demonstrations of 1995–6 against government attempts to cut expenditure and welfare, partly in order to meet European Monetary Union requirements, point to another major source of problems. European integration is increasingly producing a nationalist backlash. Moreover, France—like Italy—has a major problem financing public expenditure, but electoral pressures make it difficult to cut. The situation may not be Weimar in 1929, but there are ominous signs that the postwar west European political consensus built upon democracy, full employment, and welfare is coming under major strains.

Neofascism in Britain

DURING THE 1930s fascism was increasingly perceived in Britain as an alien, menacing creed. World War II helped to make antifascism a key aspect of British national identity and served to reinforce central aspects of Britishness. The disaster of the evacuation from the French beaches in 1940 brought out the indomitable "Dunkirk Spirit" in the ordinary man and woman. It was followed by the Battle of Britain; the Blitz showed that "Britain could take it," that a deep-rooted sense of national unity was able to overcome all adversity. Together these episodes formed part of a defiant story of democratic Britain standing alone, the only country (together with the Dominions) that fought from beginning to end against fascism. In the resonant words of Winston Churchill, this was Britain's "finest hour." Thus while Britain was never occupied, there were myths of antifascist resistance, just as there were French and Italian myths of the Resistance.[1]

World War II strengthened British self-images of decency and tolerance. It also laid down an agenda of social reform, for propaganda had told the British people that they were fighting not simply to defeat the Nazis but to create a new Britain: remarkably little was made of Nazi atrocities, even in the closing stages of the war. These were major factors in the landslide victory of the Labor Party in the general election that followed shortly after the victory in Europe. Although Winston Churchill had been considered a great wartime leader, British suspicion of demagogic leadership counted against him in 1945, and the Conservatives went down to a surprise electoral defeat. Six years of Labor government followed, marked by full employment and a historic program of social reform.

ii

THE FACT THAT the leader of the interwar British Union of Fascists, Sir Oswald Mosley, planned a comeback in such a hostile climate reveals much about the man. When Mosley had eventually been released from internment in late 1943, he was still convinced that fascist ideology provided the key to the future, but government restrictions meant that he had to wait until the end of the war before he could take the first tentative steps to relaunch his career.[2]

Initially Mosley contented himself with publishing activities and organizing a book club in order to keep contact with his old supporters. During 1947, however, he became increasingly convinced that the new order was at hand. The Labor government found itself faced by a mounting economic crisis: a shortage of foreign currency led to bread rationing—something that had never happened during the war—and to the banning of "luxury" imports like canned fruits. Such a dramatic turn of affairs reinforced Mosley's belief that the economic crisis he had forecast in the 1930s had only been avoided by rearmament and war. During 1947 he came to believe that cataclysmic collapse could not be postponed much longer.

Mosley's response was to create the Union Movement in February 1948, a rather grandiose title for a small coterie of fanatical Mosleyites.[3] The eight thousand or so who rallied to the cause were concentrated primarily in areas of former BUF strength, notably London's depressed East End. Although the guerrilla war that had been fought against Britain by some Palestinian Jews heightened anti-Semitism in 1945–8, the Union Movement was unable to capitalize on this to make new recruits. It seems that outside the fascist ranks anti-Semites shunned Mosley, seeing him as a lost cause.[4] Mosley alienated many more people than he attracted. From youth he had been a loner, a man who resented criticism. Internment during the war, if anything, had increased his messianic tendencies and his unwillingness to listen. His closest supporters after 1945, Jeffrey Hamm for instance, tended to be loyal rather than critical, yes men who did not force Mosley to stand back and consider his actions more carefully.

Hamm, a Welsh schoolmaster by profession, was a brave street speaker, often facing physical opposition from the Jewish and left-wing groups that inevitably emerged to counter a revival of fascism and its provocative activities.[5] But here was part of the problem: the street politics of the Union Movement made it impossible for Mosley to break free from his 1930s image. In the early 1950s he moved to Ireland for a time, largely forsaking active politics in order to write and to launch a cultural journal, *The European*. Although it attracted contributions from writers such as Henry Williamson, Ezra Pound, and Roy Campbell, its clear links with Mosley left it with no hope of appealing to the vast bulk of the intelligentsia. Mosley was, moreover, trapped by his own activist ideology: while he perceived the growing importance of the media in political campaigning, he never lost faith in the powers of his own oratory.

Mosley's best hope after 1945, albeit a slender one, would have been to remain above everyday politics and portray himself as a kind of philosopher-king. Mosley had read widely during the war and his post-1945 writings constitute an important statement of fascist philosophy.[6] Mosley was not a major original thinker: some of his ideas can be traced back to the program of the Salò Republic, or Drieu la Rochelle, and his proposals were sometimes ill thought out, even contradictory. But the main thrust of Mosley's postwar thinking was concerned with rational debate, with leading rather than following public opinion, just as it had been during the early days of the BUF.

Mosley's first postwar book, *My Answer* (1946), defended the correctness of BUF policies and attacked the iniquities of his imprisonment, given that he was a true British patriot. In a bitter aside he noted that those who had admired the Soviet Union were not considered traitors, but weakened the force of this argument by his rose-tinted view of the fascist regimes and their leaders. He was later to argue that if Hitler had resigned or been assassinated in 1939 or 1940, he would have gone down as a great leader.

Mosley's defense of fascism was more than simply an attempt to justify his prewar policies. It reflected fundamental philosophical continuities in his postwar thought. In particular, a strong emphasis on leadership and will remained, traits that Mosley believed could produce a synthesis of what others saw as opposites. It also contained the same criticism of materialist, capitalist society, and the continuing search for a movement that could move men's souls and help to transform human nature. Mosley's main biographer has argued that he employed a Marxist-like economic logic that took little account of spiritual, moral, and ideological factors.[7] Mosley certainly focused on economic issues, but he also placed considerable emphasis on the idea of synthesis. He wanted to create both a more prosperous economy and a new form of "man." He sought to synthesise "classic philosophy and Christian teaching": taking from the former the ideas of heroism, of leadership, and from the latter the concepts of service, self-sacrifice to the cause and the fusion of the individual into a greater whole. The resulting creed would be "both a religion and a science," which would require a "union of intellect and will." Its values would combine syndicalism and individualism, "action with liberty."

Mosley remained highly critical of liberal democracy. He believed that as a form of government, democracy encouraged inaction, and that parliamentary control of the executive was a farce, and dismissed "popular sovereignty" as a sham: "Tell them they run the world, and, then, give them the films, the 'dogs' and the Press to stop them thinking about anything," was his damning description. Instead, he sought to combine two goals: a strong executive that could take difficult decisions, and the means to change it quickly if it failed or abused power. The people would be invited at regular intervals to approve or reject the government by referendum. In the event of an adverse vote, a new administration would be chosen by a judicial panel. To counter the charge that a government might prolong its life indefinitely or abuse the legal system, Mosley argued that judicial independence would be guaranteed and the state generally was accorded a weaker role than he had envisaged before 1945.

Mosley believed that interwar fascism had been too nationalist. He argued that national economies were now too small in a world dominated by two superpowers. What was needed as a counterweight was a greater Europe, which Mosley initially linked to the retention of part of Africa as Europe's natural sphere of influence. Europeanism had always been latent in fascist thought, and as early as 1937 Mosley had advocated European union. However, he made "Europe a Nation" a central feature of his postwar thought and actively pressed this vision of a Third Force Europe on fellow European fascists, most notably at a Venice summit in 1962. He envisaged full integration rather than a "miserable federal compromise," a vision that proved far too sweeping for most other fascist groups.

Mosley's views differed notably from those of most activists in the Union Movement. These were men who were nothing if not rabid nationalists, who knew that "wogs" started at Dover. Mosley tried to get around this problem by operating a dual strategy: he courted the mantle of the responsible thinker, while his lower-level activists pandered to the crudest common denominator of street racism. But in such a leader-oriented movement, it was difficult to separate the leader from popular concerns, and Mosley was always the activist, magnetically drawn back to the crowd.

By the late 1950s Mosley believed he had found the populist issue that would lead him triumphantly back to center stage: the growing number of nonwhite immigrants who were arriving from Britain's Commonwealth. In 1945 Britain was essentially a white country, though there were small pockets of ethnic minorities in London and seaports such as Liverpool. Postwar full employment and the absence of immigration controls on British Commonwealth citizens meant that after 1947 a trickle turned into a stream. By 1954–5, twenty thousand immigrants were arriving yearly, mainly from the West Indies. By the early 1960s this figure had risen to nearly sixty thousand, with a growing number now coming from the Indian subcontinent.

The new immigrants quickly found that British tolerance and fair play were partly mythical. A revealing insight into people's views on racial issues is provided by a 1948 government survey, which found a widespread belief that "colored" people were characterized by headhunting, black magic, polygamy, and enormous sexual appetites. Although these views did not immediately translate into organized political action against immigrants, during 1954–5 leading members of the Conservative government considered making opposition to significant further immigration a major plank in their next general election program.[8] They seem to have been deterred mainly by fears of an adverse response from some Commonwealth governments, by a continued aversion to populist politics, and by genuinely liberal attitudes among an important section of the party's elite.

Mosley had no such qualms, particularly after the 1958 "race riots" in London's Notting Hill had underlined the hostility to immigrants that existed in a section of the white population. The disturbances encouraged him to stand for West Kensington, which included Notting Hill, in the 1959 general election. Mosley's campaign was based on a high and a low road, which underlined the split between his philosophical flights and the grubby street life of the Union Movement. The high road talked of colored repatriation, accompanied by loans to the receiving countries for economic development, and long-term contracts to buy their produce. The low road wandered through the swamps of black crime, sexual innuendo, and claims that immigrants lived on Kit-E-Kat pet food. Mosley's eldest son, Nicholas, strongly rebuked his father over this, later noting that the right hand dealt with great ideas, but the left let the rats out of the sewer.[9]

This was the Union Movement's first foray into parliamentary elections. It had previously contested some local elections in London, usually attracting a minimal vote, but Mosley believed he had a serious chance of winning. In the final count, he received only 8.1 percent of the vote and lost his electoral deposit for the first time in his career. Buoyed up, nevertheless, by the belief that immigration was about to transform the political horizon, he launched a new round of political rallies, which inevitably attracted antifascist counterprotests. In the early 1960s Mosley pulled bigger crowds than at any time since the war, and the Union Movement's membership revived to perhaps five thousand. But when Mosley again tested the electoral climate in the 1966 general election, he met even less success than in 1959. (The only other Union Movement candidate, Hamm, did worse still.)[10]

Mosley concluded that electoral breakthrough was not imminent and reluctantly announced his retirement from "party warfare" (though the Union Movement lingered on in some localities into the 1970s). He believed that he had underestimated the hold that the two major parties exerted over the electorate. He had also underestimated their adaptability, which at the local level included Conservatives pandering to racist sentiments. In Mosley's former constituency of Smethwick some local activists adopted the slogan: "If you want a nigger for a neighbor, vote Labor." At a national level, the Conservative government's 1961 act limiting immigration from the nonwhite Commonwealth defused more overt forms of racist politics. Although much criticized by the opposition parties in Parliament, the Labor governments after 1964 made no effort to return to free immigration. (Labor consciences were partly salved by the passing of the 1965 Race Relations Act, which sought among other things to prohibit inflammatory rhetoric.)

For Mosley retirement did not mean loss of hope. He still believed that he could make a political comeback. The 1964–70 Labor governments were racked by economic crises, which Mosley took as confirmation of his view that economic meltdown in the late 1940s had only been staved off by a massive Western rearmament program to counter the Soviet menace. Mosley's "retirement" was, therefore, not so much an admission of failure as a final attempt to rise above politics and portray himself as the natural leader of a government of national union. For a time he believed this strategy was working, as he suddenly regained access to the mass media. He was hailed by some leading historians, most notably the maverick A. J. P. Taylor, who had always had a taste for academic mischief, as the great lost talent of British politics. However, Mosley died in 1980 still waiting for the call to kiss the monarch's hand and be given the commission to form a government. The mold had not been broken.

iii

MOSLEY'S VIEWS, if not the day-to-day politics of the Union Movement, stood in sharp contrast to another strand in British fascism. There had always been an element that tended to have little interest in developing a serious program of economic and social reform, and was based more on a virulent form of racism and nationalism. During the late 1940s and early 1950s this radical nationalist-racist strand was nurtured by Arnold Leese and A. K. Chesterton.

Leese, who had spent much of the war in internment, celebrated Victory in Europe Day by publishing a short book entitled *The Jewish War of Survival*. As its title implies, this claimed that Britain had been duped into fighting a war that was primarily for the benefit of international Jewish interests. Leese offered to give evidence on "the Jewish issue" in defense of the Nazi leaders who stood accused at the Nuremberg trials. He believed that the rounding up and killing of Jews were explained by the fact that Jews had been at the core of the partisan resistance to the Nazis.

Leese realized that he was too old to form a new political movement. Until his death in 1956 he helped to induct a new generation of anti-Semites into politics, a task helped by the money he inherited in 1948 from the founder of the Britons publishing house, Hamilton Beamish. One of the most significant figures whom Leese helped was a young Cambridge University history graduate, Colin Jordan, who later formed a variety of small, openly neo-Nazi groups. Of these the most notable was the National Socialist Movement, founded in 1962, complete with its own paramilitary organization named Spearhead.

Chesterton was a more active and complex character than Leese, though he has often been portrayed as the archetypal fascist "authoritarian personality."[11] He was a second cousin of the Catholic writer G. K. Chesterton, and followed in the family tradition both in his gift for writing and his penchant for radical politics. During the 1930s he had joined the BUF, where he became director of publicity and propaganda. His main desire seems to have been to reconcile the classes and to re-create the community that he had found so consoling while serving in World War I. He was also attracted by the BUF's growing anti-Semitism, for he was addicted to conspiracy theory, but he was not a pathological anti-Semite driven by personal unhappiness. Nor was he pro-Nazi. He had a socialist wife whom he loved, and in 1938 broke with Mosley over his increasingly pro-German policy.

Chesterton served in the British forces during World War II, then found himself drawn back to anti-Semitism, though he managed to maintain relatively friendly relations with some Jews. He returned to active politics, and in 1954 helped to set up the League of Empire Loyalists, which proved another important vehicle for inducting and training a new coterie of anti-Semites. Most of its two thousand to three thousand active members were Colonel Blimpish rather than fascist: in fact, many members saw it as a Conservative ginger group rather than a radical rival, an attempt to keep the Conservatives true to the imperial way. In spite of Chesterton's anti-Semitism, he shared Mosley's ability to develop a rational argument. His opposition to the European Community, for example, was not simply based on crude nationalism but involved arguments concerning the bureaucratic nature of the emerging community and the problems of achieving democracy in large units that lacked any real sense of communal allegiance.

Relative moderation of this kind led to Chesterton's selection as the first chairman of the National Front (NF), which was founded in 1967 through the amalgamation of the Loyalists and some smaller extreme right-wing groups.[12] By 1971 Chesterton had been pushed out and quickly slipped into obscurity. The problem was partly one of age, for Chesterton was over seventy and spent the winter in the warmer climes of South Africa. More fundamentally, policy was a source of conflict. Chesterton saw the Front as a pressure group, but others were impressed by its rapidly growing membership—which peaked at approximately fifteen thousand in 1972. Such numbers held out the prospect that the NF could become a serious player in the electoral game.

The main opposition to Chesterton came from within a group that had not initially been allowed to join the NF, the Greater Britain Movement, which emerged after breaking with Jordan's National Socialist Movement. The leader of the Greater Britain Movement was John Tyndall, who seems to have held that Jordan's overt Nazism would be counterproductive, and who sought a radical movement that would stress more distinctly British roots. There was also considerable personal antipathy between these two would-be Führers, not least over Jordan's marriage in 1963 to Françoise Dior, the niece of the famous couturier and a former flame of Tyndall's. (The couple's party marriage ceremony was reported to involve swearing that they were of pure Aryan blood, which they followed by mingling drops of their blood over a virgin copy of Hitler's *Mein Kampf.*)

Although Tyndall had not been particularly academic at school, he could develop a relatively serious argument when he chose. His main work, *Six Principles of Nationalism* (1966), made a considerable impression on Chesterton and did much to encourage him to allow the Greater Britain Movement to join the NF. In it Tyndall argued that there might be a democratic way to create a new state based on racialism and nationalism. He thus moved away from the fantasy-*putschist* world of the lunatic neo-Nazis, turning his attention to the potential of the ballot box to establish a government based on a corporate state and guided by strong leadership. Tyndall claimed that this would use regular referenda to ratify decisions, so the system would not be a dictatorship.

With fellow former Greater Britain Movement member Martin Webster, Tyndall was to dominate National Front politics during much of the 1970s. Their pedigree underlines the importance of understanding the NF at several levels, for on the surface the party was the epitome of populist racial nationalism, which has led some historians and journalists to argue that the party was not fascist.[13] The Front's best-known policy was its advocacy of the repatriation by "the most humane means possible" of Britain's nonwhite population, which the NF numbered at five million to six million, though under two million was the official figure. Other major themes included hostility to Britain's membership of the European Community, which was highly unpopular with a broad section of British opinion. Among more hard-core members, however, the message seems to have been very different. Here a pure brand of Nazism often held sway, typified by the growing claim that the Holocaust of the Jews was the hoax of the century.[14] The Front's unwillingness to make a complete break with the past is underlined by the fact that Tyndall's political journal was named *Spearhead*, recalling the National Socialist Movement's paramilitary activities, which had led to Tyndall, Jordan, and others being prosecuted for offenses against the 1936 Public Order Act.[15]

Under Tyndall's leadership the NF tried hard to hide its neo-Nazism from public view, fearing it might damage popular support. By the early 1970s a majority of the NF leadership had come to believe that the impact of immigration opened the possibility of winning elections, though there were differences of opinion about who were the most likely converts. Initially there was a tendency to look to disillusioned, largely middle-class Conservatives. Growing links with the reactionary Conservative Monday Club reinforced this approach.[16] Others, however, believed that the NF's best hopes lay within the working class—a belief encouraged by the popular reception given to a much-publicized speech made by Conservative MP Enoch Powell in April 1968.

Powell's speech was the first time a leading politician referred to the impact of the new ethnic communities in a highly inflammatory way. He argued that the immigrant population should immediately be reduced to negligible proportions by reemigration. A former university professor of classics, he backed up his argument with a vivid turn of phrase: "Like the Roman, I seem to see the River Tiber foaming with much blood." Powell had previously been known as an apostle of liberal free-market views, and it is not clear why he now turned to racial disharmony. There seems little doubt that he was genuinely concerned by what he saw as the threat to British society posed by immigration, but he was probably also courting a popular constituency to boost his position within the party.

If this was the motive, Powell had struck the right chord. Opinion polls taken immediately after the "River of Blood" speech showed that three-quarters of British people agreed with his prophecies, and many clearly agreed with his remedy. Two speeches on similar themes during the 1970 general election campaign attracted major media attention. They played a significant part in detaching a section of Labor's traditional working-class support and contributed more generally to the growing image of the Conservatives as the "tough" party on immigration.[17] But while Powell struck the right note, he was playing in the wrong orchestra. Deep-rooted Conservative aversion to populist politics, and a genuine fear that his views would harm race relations, led to him being fired from the Shadow Cabinet after the speech. Nor was there to be a reconciliation after the surprise Conservative victory in 1970: Powell went on to become a troublesome critic of the administration, bitterly attacking its decision to allow into Britain the expelled Ugandan Asians and to enter into the European Community. His opposition finally led him to break with the increasingly divided Conservatives in the next election.

The NF went into the February 1974 general election with high hopes. At the local level during 1968 to 1973, its candidates had begun to show signs that they could pick up significant support, and in a parliamentary election at West Bromwich in 1973 Webster had polled a surprising 16 percent. Shortly afterward, a substantial sum of money seems to have arrived in the party coffers from sources rumored to be close to the Tory right, which may have been looking for ways of pressuring the liberal leadership of Edward Heath. The money helped to fund a substantial increase in the number of NF candidates in the ensuing general election, who went on to average only 3.2 percent of the poll. The result was bitterly disappointing for a party that shortly before had believed that it was on the verge of electoral breakthrough, especially as the Liberal Party made a great leap forward partly on the basis of Powellite protest votes.

Many sociologists have argued that the NF vote at this time was a form of protest, rather than support for radical nationalism, let alone fascism.[18] On this interpretation, protest voters preferred to vote Liberal rather than for "illegitimate" parties such as the NF. Undoubtedly NF electoral support had a strong protest element, but there is evidence that some voters believed that the Liberals were "hard" on immigration issues. The NF vote was to pick up again during 1976–7, when there were considerable fears about a new wave of immigration into Britain after Malawi expelled its Asians, anxieties fanned by a tabloid media that for many years reinforced racial stereotypes.[19] On several occasions during 1976–7, the NF pushed the Liberals into fourth place in parliamentary by-elections, and in the 1977 Greater London Council elections the NF polled a total of 119,000 votes. The NF won no seats (though the breakaway National Party won two in Blackburn local elections in 1976), but its anti-immigrant politics were clearly striking a chord with a section of the electorate. Although in some areas, such as London's East End, NF support was built on a long tradition of fascist activity, it could also establish a strong presence in new areas, such as parts of Leicester, which felt a threat of "invasion" from immigrants.[20] The NF's appeal seems to have been especially strong among small businessmen, and the semi- and unskilled male working class (though it had some female activists and supporters).[21] These were the people most directly threatened by growing unemployment, or by more diffuse changes in the labor market that were creating "knicker" jobs in service industries while "men's" jobs such as docking or steel making were in free fall; though in areas where there was a tradition of unionism and Labor voting, such as the mining valleys of South Wales, the NF exerted little appeal. It did best where it could gain a foothold in local organizations, such as housing associations, or even within pub culture—sometimes an oasis of "community" in a sea of change and urban blight.

During 1976–7, many journalists and sociologists believed the NF was on the verge of breaking out of the extremist electoral ghetto. Although this grossly overstated the strength of the NF outside a handful of urban areas, it was a belief that had important consequences. Fear of the NF encouraged antifascist opposition, particularly in the form of the so-called Anti-Nazi League, a radical-left-inspired group that attracted a broad church of support, including some personality endorsements. Although formed after the NF vote had peaked, it helped disseminate the view that "The National Front is a Nazi Front," a task made easier by the NF's decision to engage in a series of provocative marches through or near areas with large ethnic minorities. This message was further reinforced by sections of the media, which after 1976 began to show more responsibility in reporting on the NF, though not always in terms of focusing on issues that might help it, such as drug-related crime. Labor and the trade unions too became more actively involved in "antiracist" programs, especially with their members.

Even more important was the attention the NF attracted within the Conservative Party leadership. In 1978 Margaret Thatcher appeared on a popular radio show and told listeners that she understood why some British people feared their culture was being swamped by immigrants and why some were turning to the NF. The same themes were heard in a series of other speeches, proving an excellent example of what some have termed the "new racism," in which arguments are put in terms of people's "natural" feelings rather than in terms of damning ethnic groups as inferior.[22] Conservative strategists seem to have been well aware that almost a third of British voters were willing to tell pollsters they supported the compulsory repatriation of immigrants. Polls further revealed that more voters feared extensive race riots than economic collapse.[23] Running into the 1979 elections, therefore, the Conservatives shrewdly played on the electorate's fears by promising yet more curbs on immigration and by stressing the need for more law and order.

Buoyed by its gains in 1976–7, the NF put up 303 candidates for the 1979 general election, the largest number by an insurgent party since Labor in 1918. They managed to average only 1.4 percent of the poll. Probably with some form of proportional representation the party would have done slightly better. But there can be no doubt that the 1979 result reflected widespread perceptions of the National Front's lack of legitimacy and the belief that many of its more moderate proposals would be better cared for by the new Conservative government. A decade that had started with high hopes within the Front ended in shattered dreams.

iv

THE LEADERSHIP of the NF was badly divided even before the 1979 general election humiliation. There had been a major split in 1975, which led to the breakaway of a group who formed the National Party. Although this quickly disappeared, it had rallied various cliques who were opposed to the Tyndall-Webster leadership: in particular, the racial-populists, who saw Tyndall and Webster as closet Nazis and therefore an electoral liability, and those who disliked Tyndall and Webster on personal grounds. Tyndall was widely seen as bombastic and pompous, whereas Webster's main "crime" was his alleged predilection for members of the same sex.

In the aftermath of the 1979 election debacle, a similar coalition of forces came together and led to the departure of first Tyndall and then Webster. The shedding of the old guard was accompanied by a general ideological fervor among the remaining leadership. Indeed, there was a widespread belief in the need for greater education of activists and for the development of a far more detailed and structured ideology. During the early 1980s this led to an amazingly eclectic set of developments, with NF leaders turning to various sources for inspiration, including Strasserism, which advocated a radical appeal to the working class on an anticapitalist program, and the French New Right, which advocated a more long-term cultural strategy. By the mid-1980s two strands were beginning to emerge within the NF leadership—both radically different.

One group, numbering at most a few hundred supporters, adopted a fanatical position seeking to found an elite movement with full membership only for a selected few who had undergone rigorous cadre training. Its supporters became known as the "Political Soldiers," after the idealized, dedicated activists it sought to recruit. Its leaders in the late 1980s were young and often held college degrees. Judging by its surprisingly theoretical publications, the inspiration behind this group came largely from continental neofascism. One major source seems to have been members of the Armed Revolutionary Nuclei (NAR), who had fled to London to escape arrest for bombings in Italy, and who helped to disseminate the ideas of Julius Evola. It is not clear to what extent NF leaders were aware of Evola's thought, which is obscure and largely unavailable in English, but there are clear links—to the extent that the NF came to eulogize some of the relatively obscure European groups Evola had admired, like Corneliu Codreanu's 1930s Romanian Iron Guard.[24] The most important connection was the shared emphasis on the re-creation of a more simple but united form of society. The Political Soldiers argued that the fundamental failure of the NF in the 1970s was its concentration on elections and rallies. Instead, the key task was portrayed as the building of a fresh ethos, a fanatical, nonmaterialist, quasi-religious "New Man." It seems that this would have required the destruction of urban life and rebirth in the purer countryside, a form of British Pol Potism.

The New Right's influence can be seen in the Political Soldiers' adoption of a form of Europeanism, rather than the crude British nationalism that was so central to the old NF's appeal. The new line involved a rejection of a hierarchical racism, though this did not mean an acceptance of multiculturalism. *National Front News* covers in the late 1980s even featured pictures of black separatists meeting NF activists. Most remarkably of all, one issue included front-cover pictures of Colonel Gaddafi, the Ayatollah Khomeini, and the American black separatist leader Louis Farrakhan, who were eulogized as great leaders of their people. The fact that all just happened to be anti-Semitic—and in the case of the first two, potential suppliers of funds—strongly points to a hidden agenda. There seems little doubt, however, that most of the Political Soldiers were sincere in their highly radical views.

These developments were viewed with derision within the second main NF faction that emerged after 1979, which was essentially a continuation of the racial-populist tradition. Although there were some educated or middle-class people in this group, it tended to include the more working-class side of the NF leadership. Predictably it bitterly attacked the Political Soldiers as a group of intellectuals indulgently following foreign ideological fads. Such esoteric appeals were seen as harming the Front at precisely the time when socioeconomic factors, especially rapidly growing unemployment and worsening inner-city race relations, were turning in its favor.

The rise of the new Social Democratic Party after 1981 was taken as a sign that the party system was at last on the verge of cracking, a development that encouraged the NF to put up sixty candidates in the 1983 general election, a large number for a party whose membership had slumped since the late 1970s to at most a few thousand. They averaged only 1.1 percent of the vote. Although opposition to further immigration had faded as a major Conservative theme, the party's nationalist credentials were strengthened by the growing image of Thatcher as the "Iron Lady." The successful 1982 Falklands War in particular raised the Conservatives, and their leader, to new peaks of popularity. Bad quickly turned to worse for the NF during the late 1980s and early 1990s. The divisions within the party, and especially the ideology of the Political Soldiers, were well publicized and exploited by antifascists, in the magazine *Searchlight*, for example.[25] Membership slumped yet further and the party virtually disappeared from the electoral scene.

As the NF declined during the 1980s, white racial violence in Britain grew significantly, as did violence aimed at antifascists and homosexuals. Racial violence did not begin in the 1980s: even before World War II, there had been occasional troubles between white and ethnic communities in the small number of localities where they came together. During the 1970s, however, racial attacks began to take on a more serious dimension, with some members of the ethnic communities living in virtual siege conditions.[26]

The political origins of the latest wave of racial attacks need tracing back to the formation in 1968 of the British Movement as a successor to the National Socialist Movement. Some of its members had realized that there was little hope of creating a major paramilitary force without some dramatic change in events. As a result, the British Movement encouraged attacks on the ethnic communities almost certainly in the hope of promoting a race war. There was also a wing in the NF that was interested in attracting violent youths, though here the focus initially tended to be more on soccer hooligans. During the 1970s the NF specifically courted such support with publications that listed the soccer grounds that were most likely to be the scenes of violence; there were "League Tables" of the clubs that had the most Jewish directors too. The NF strategy seems to have been to induct supporters through immediate concerns, and then to introduce them to a wider ideology of nationalism and race, though there were some in the lower levels of the party who were only interested in creating mayhem.

The exact relationship between racial violence and extremist parties is unclear. It is possible to produce a good Identi-Kit picture of the typical assailant: male, under the age of twenty-five, probably under the influence of alcohol and acting in a group. But, surprisingly, most attackers are not members of any political group, nor have they been in the past. The absence of clear political roots might be taken to imply that the main cause of racial violence is a more diffuse sense of frustration about socioeconomic change and the bleak prospects for youths in many inner-city areas. But an area in London that exhibited an increase in such crime surrounded the headquarters of a racist group—a fact which many have used to argue that its propaganda is an important factor in conditioning such attacks.[27]

The group in question was the British National Party (BNP), set up during the early 1980s by Tyndall after his break with the National Front. In many ways the BNP was an extension of the 1970s NF, though Tyndall came to believe that a mistake had been made in recruiting violent and alienated youths, and in engaging in provocative mass rallies. Tyndall's initial aim seems to have been to make the BNP attractive to what he believed would be a flood of disillusioned Conservatives. The problem with this strategy was that, although the Conservatives could not deliver repatriation, they were well protected on their nationalist flank. Tyndall's overt fascist past did not help either, especially as his journal *Spearhead* continued to provide ample fare for antifascists and journalists to exploit. Another problem concerned organization, for the BNP only operated in a handful of areas, mainly where it had managed to exploit local issues—such as fears in some northern cities about British Muslim support for the *fatwa* imposed by the Ayatollah Khomeini on the "blasphemous" novelist Salman Rushdie, or for Saddam Hussein during the 1990–1 Gulf War (though in general the war reinforced antifascist myths, with its portrayal of Hussein as a new Hitler).

As the NF's collapse became clearer, the BNP began to pick up many of the human pieces, but here yet another problem set in. In and around the NF were a variety of alienated and violent groups. These included several "Oi" pop groups, sometimes characterized by drunken behavior and racist lyrics. The best known was Skrewdriver, led by Ian Stuart Donaldson; a typical lyric ended: "Europe awake, for the white man's sake, Europe awake, before it's too late, Europe awake, Europe awake now." Donaldson went on to form his own small group, Blood and Honour, but others in the late 1980s and early 1990s were left lacking a political home as the NF imploded. The BNP, which by the early 1990s had perhaps two thousand to three thousand members, was in no position to turn away such recruits unless there was a very good reason, especially as the BNP had always contained a violent minority of its own. It became, therefore, a rather strange mix. On the one hand were Tyndall and other leaders who tried to stress the party's relative respectability, a task hampered by their collection of convictions, mainly under race relations laws. On the other hand, the BNP had an increasing street presence that was characterized more by young toughs, though most of these seem to have passed through the party rather quickly. They were certainly not the type of recruit who could mount a serious election campaign, let alone present a respectable face to most voters.

The BNP's performance in the 1992 general election seemed to confirm the party's failure to break out of the extremist ghetto. Its best result in the thirteen constituencies it contested was 3.6 percent of the poll. Fringe parties, however, have always tended to do better in local elections and by-elections, when protest voting is stronger and they can concentrate organizational resources. This tendency was dramatically illustrated when in September 1993 the

BNP won a narrow local election victory over Labor, whose campaign had helped the BNP's credibility by stressing its local strength. The scene was the Isle of Dogs, part of London's East End which has a significant ethnic community and which was polarized between an economically threatened white working class and new yuppy interlopers: conditions that had encouraged the local Liberal Democrats to pander to anti-immigrant sentiments in their own effort to win votes. The BNP's winning candidate was Derek Beackon, a rather gray middle-aged man who had been active in anti-immigrant politics for some time. His share of the vote was only 34 percent, but it was a dramatic victory nonetheless, for Beackon was the first BNP candidate ever to win a local election.

Beackon lost the seat in 1994 after a strong antifascist and media campaign had helped to raise turnout, though he managed to increase his total vote. The BNP's subsequent failure to put up any candidates in the 1994 European elections, and a further failure by Beackon to win an East End seat, underline the fact that the BNP is not on the verge of a major electoral breakthrough. Indeed, doubts about its electoral prospects and unhappiness with its "moderate" leadership have encouraged growing support for the violent Combat 18 group, and the linked National Socialist Alliance, which seems to be a more organized version of earlier tendencies within the NF and British Movement. (Another important similarity is the strong evidence that some leading members are working for the state, which in Britain since the 1920s has effectively maintained surveillance in this area.) But it is important not to confuse voting for a particular group with potential for a racist-populist breakthrough in some urban areas, particularly if race relations deteriorate (a trend that could stem from extremist developments within the ethnic as well as the white community).

The Conservative Party in particular has reason to fear a rising potential for racial populism. Historically, the Conservatives have been the party that has wrapped itself in the Union Jack. Since the 1960s they have managed to combine their classic nationalist appeal with Britain's ever deeper commitment to the European Union, a remarkable feat in view of the strong popular animosity to integration. One crucial factor in this delicate balancing act was Thatcher's ability to play the nationalist card: in the 1987 election, the first

Conservative television advertisement began with images of the Battle of Britain and the fight for "freedom," set to strains of "I Vow to Thee, My Country." Another has been the continuing perception of the Conservatives as the party that is tough on race and immigration: a little-noted aspect of the 1992 general election was the way in which some Conservative leaders, such as Kenneth Baker, exploited fears about Labor being soft on asylum seekers and other immigrants, a theme highlighted by Conservative tabloid newspapers with headlines such as BAKER'S MIGRANT FLOOD WARNING.

Radical left-wing critics often portray the Conservative Party, and its partisan press, as a major reason for the persistence of British racism.[28] In truth, the relationship between the Conservatives and racial traditions has been complex. The Conservatives have unquestionably pandered to a racist constituency on occasion, but their basic role has been to manage racism rather than to cause it. While this has undoubtedly helped reinforce racial stereotypes and simplistic conclusions, such as immigration being a major cause of unemployment, an important effect of this tactic has been to minimize support for fringe parties. The crucial issue for the future is whether they can keep doing this: can they manage both to play the nationalist card and take Britain into ever closer union with "Europe"? Will the issue of greater integration break the party, or will a "European" Conservative party open space for a new nationalist force?

The importance of national identity seems clear, but the British nation has changed. A variety of groups now vie for their own institutions and rights—Scottish parliaments, halal-killed meat on school menus, and so on. More than at any time since the emergence of mass democracy, society is divided, not least between rich and poor. The world has changed too, as the rise of multinational companies, European transnational government, and Pacific Rim economic power clearly shows. Historically, British identity was forged around civic symbols like the monarchy and Parliament, or by a sense of what Britain was not: namely part of a continental Europe, characterized by Catholicism, rationalism, autocracy, and other "un-British" traits. The power of these symbols has waned, while the sense of the enemy is now largely missing. So too is the leadership necessary to create new symbols, a new sense of direction. Indeed, the Conservatives recently have seemed tempted by the use of a referendum on Europe to get them off the hook, a populist device that tends to follow rather than lead opinion.

In place of the old myths, many Conservatives had substituted a more economically based ideology. Even in the 1992 election, when the economy was performing relatively poorly, they chose to take Labor on in terms of economic management and personal income gains. Given the electorate's fears about Labor's competence, this proved a winning strategy. The same point applies to the way in which the European Union is primarily presented. For Conservatives, there is little attempt to portray it as a real or mythical ideal. Rather, it is an economic club to which Britain necessarily has to belong in order to stay a member of the first division. The argument has its uses when it comes to underlining that some form of European cooperation is a necessity: there is no alternative. Yet these essentially economic appeals pose major problems in the event of an economic downturn or a lengthy period of minimal growth.

The Conservatives need to make a crucial decision: either they must attempt to reforge national unity, while delineating a viable relationship with Europe, or they must adopt a more forceful vision of Europe. Both paths are fraught with electoral and social dangers. The potential for a new force was demonstrated in 1995 when an opinion poll showed that nine percent of British people would vote for a Le Pen–type (more "respectable") party, and another seventeen percent would seriously consider doing so. Not surprisingly, in the queen's speech for the 1995–6 Parliament, the government announced new tough measures to control asylum seekers: anti-immigrant politics again reared their head.

Given the disarray in the BNP and the growing support on the extremist fringe for a policy of "leaderless resistance" (a cell-based violent strategy aimed mainly at ethnic groups), the Conservatives have little to fear in the short run in terms of a nationalist electoral challenge. But the internal dynamics of the party pose longer-term problems, and the possibility of increasing racial tensions could have major implications for party politics in general. A more legitimate nationalist party, resulting from a split in the Conservatives, could have a significant potential.

15

Götterdämmerung?

i

"NEVER BEFORE was the relationship between masters and slaves so consciously aestheticized. Sade had to make up his theatre of punishment and delight from scratch. Now there is a master scenario available to everyone. The color is black, the material is leather . . . the aim is ecstasy, the fantasy is death." These words, written by the American cultural critic Susan Sontag at the turn of the 1970s, superbly capture the way in which popular images of fascism came in the postwar era to combine elements of the bestial horror story and sadomasochistic pornography. Fascism had become the ultimate trip into the beyond, where the pleasures of an immoral elite ruled everyday life, while violence and destruction reigned supreme.

What was true in the 1970s remains largely the case more than twenty years later. Popular films like *Schindler's List* (1993) constantly update memories of genocide and the horror at the heart of Nazism. The media unquestionably retain a fascination with fascist iconography. The racial attacks that took place in Germany during 1991–2 attracted so much attention because they conformed to media "paradigms," ways of ordering the news for popular consumption. They not only provided dramatic pictures to arouse the viewers' and readers' interest, but clearly identified who were the villains: young males, dressed in Nazi regalia and shouting "Sieg Heil!" while the boot went in.

The power of the label "fascist" to brand a political movement as outside the realms of civilized politics remains strong—a point well understood by antifascist and antiracist groups, with investigations into the revival of extremism growing dramatically during the 1980s and 1990s. Particularly active have been groups representing the interests of minorities, especially the Jewish community, which has increasingly sponsored serious research that can be used to brief journalists, politicians, and other interested parties. The European Parliament has produced well-documented studies of neofascism and racism on two separate occasions. Encouraged initially by the sudden breakthrough of Le Pen's Front National in 1984, the reports went on to reveal a remarkably broad range of extremist activities throughout Europe: both attracted considerable publicity. But there are growing signs, especially among young people, that this is a past that is fast fading into ancient history. In 1995 a third of British teenagers did not know what VE day stood for or who Churchill was, and more than sixty percent did not know what the Holocaust was.

In spite of the efforts of those like David Irving who seek to claim that there were no Nazi gas chambers, that the Holocaust was the "Hoax of the Century," it is unlikely that Nazism can ever be seriously rehabilitated. No civilized state can wage racial war or view vast tracts of land as populated by subhumans fit only to form a pool of slave labor—or to be exterminated. Only a regime run by sadists could execute people by dangling them on piano wire strung from meathooks. Only contemporary neo-Nazis, or those who ignore vast tracts of evidence, can fail to see that brutality and racism were the essence of the Nazi regime.

Nazism, however, can be relativized by more respectable revisionist historians as "simply" one of many examples of genocide—a controversial point made by the leading German historian, Ernst Nolte, during the *Historikerstreit* of the late 1980s. It can be seen as an understandable response to the fears aroused by the menace of "Asiatic" communism, a system that had already introduced an extensive concentration camp system in which vast numbers perished. The figure of the six million Jews who died in the Holocaust is well known; few realize that the number of Ukrainians who died in the famine that was deliberately induced by the Stalinist government at the turn of the 1930s was closer to eight million. Similar arguments can be used to explain the invasion of the USSR in 1941 and the remarkable brutality of German fighting on the eastern front. But the extent to which an overwhelming fear of communism influenced Nazi policy remains a moot point among historians: Nolte has undoubtedly lost most of the arguments with his critics since the 1980s, especially with those who pointed to Hitler's personal role and to the biological basis of Nazi ideology.

Aspects of Nazi domestic policy, such as its full employment and welfare policies, provide more fertile ground for a favorable revisionist gloss, though this requires painting over awkward questions about what these programs meant for women, let alone for Jews and other "undesirables." Less controversially, some revisionist historians have sought to point out serious intellectual roots to Nazism. The rehabilitation process has gone furthest with the "conservative revolutionaries." Ernst Jünger is now accepted as one of the greatest German writers of the century. Other serious thinkers linked to the Nazis who have attracted significant attention recently are Carl Schmitt and Martin Heidegger, both now widely ranked among the century's greatest thinkers.

Italian fascism too will probably never be fully rehabilitated, though there is far more scope for revisionist historians to portray it in a favorable light. Although fascism engaged in a brutal war in Ethiopia and the regime subsequently established there was based on a form of apartheid, this was not accompanied by a Nazi-style body of racial doctrine. Until Mussolini fell increasingly under Hitler's influence in the late 1930s and introduced a set of anti-Semitic laws, most fascists held biological racial theory in contempt. For all its horrors, Italian colonialism had more in common with British and French expansionism than with German. There was an element of "civilizing mission" in its purpose, a desire to help the "natives": while ethnocentric, it was very different from the supremacist racism of Nazism.

The fascist dictatorship in Italy was less brutal than its German equivalent. Long-term political prisoners were relatively few in number, though many were sent into internal exile and dissidents risked losing their jobs. And while "totalitarianism" was Mussolini's stated goal, this did not necessarily mean the long-run physical suppression of opponents or the people in general. It was consistent with the extensive use of propaganda, backed by economic development, to encourage conformity. (Interestingly, the Bolsheviks held very similar views.) A few leading fascists, like Bottai, do not even seem to have sought a dictatorship: they appear to have wanted to synthesize authoritarianism and democracy, though the fascist tendency to stress action over blueprints makes it difficult to be certain what was planned, and it would be misleading to portray this as a major strand of fascism.

As with Nazism, it is possible to single out concrete aspects of the fascist regime that can be presented in a sympathetic light. Most frequently, the attempt to create full employment and the extensive welfare system are emphasized. Interest is also growing in the way that the regime tried to control the Mafia, as is acceptance that some of the corruption that came to surround fascist rule reveals more about Italian political traditions than about the inherent nature of fascism: in particular, Italy's lack of a civic tradition and extended sense of community, traits that help to explain fascism's desire to create "new" Italians. It is no surprise, therefore, to find that an increasing number of Italians accept the arguments of their leading historian of fascism, Renzo De Felice, who has long claimed that there was a more positive side to Mussolini's regime—at least before the introduction of the anti-Semitic laws in 1938.

The history of French and British interwar fascism has been revised in many ways since the early 1970s. New work on French fascism has shown that it was not a minor foreign import, but that proto-fascist ideology was an important strand in the French political tradition stretching back through Sorel into the prewar era. The leading Israeli historian Zeev Sternhell has even argued that fascist ideology reached its most advanced state in interwar France, representing a serious synthesis of nationalism and socialism. This argument is overstated and focuses too much on fascism's left-wing roots, but it underlines the growing willingness to accept fascism as being based on a serious body of doctrine. The last point could also be made about Britain, for Mosley's main academic biographer, Robert Skidelsky, has portrayed his subject as capable of developing a serious program concerned with Britain's long-run economic decline. He has also argued that the BUF were the victims more than the perpetrators of violence, a line that has been taken up by some other historians. While the claim plays down the provocative nature of local fascist activities, it highlights the fact that some on the left—especially the communists—were happy to use violence and believed that they could gain support by adopting an antifascist mantle.

There is unquestionably a lag between academic developments and their widespread diffusion among the public, especially as in the case of fascism there are powerful forces countering revisionism. There are growing signs, however, that within the next ten to twenty years significant aspects of fascism will be viewed in a more favorable light. At the turn of the twentieth century, a new set of ideas emerged to challenge the dominant ideas of liberalism and socialism. The emerging partial rehabilitation of fascism could help to contribute to a similar *fin de siècle* stirring. Fascism is still an ideology that dare not speak its name in polite company, but central tenets—such as the quest for community, the desire to rediscover national identity, and the belief that a new socioeconomic order is required—seem to be reemerging on the European mental landscape. Fascism is not about to revive as a mass movement in its classic form, typified by jackboots and paramilitary rallies. But a new strand is emerging, which is learning to repackage fascism for the twenty-first century—a process that is being helped by important intellectual, economic, and political trends.

ii

ALTHOUGH HISTORY may not repeat itself in a precise sense, there are lessons to be learned by extrapolating from past developments. Fascism did not become a mass movement simply because of ideological developments, though these may have inspired some activists. Rather, fascism emerged as a significant force (or failed to, as the case may be) as a result of a complex interrelationship between national traditions, the actions of key leaders—both fascist and nonfascist—and socioeconomic developments, especially crisis.

These factors also help provide an important guide as to why fascism has failed to become a mass force in Western Europe since 1945. Fascism has not simply been identified with bestiality and terror: antifascism has become a central part of national identity. In Italy and France powerful myths emerged about the growth of widespread Resistance movements that helped to overthrow a fascist clique. The absence of major resistance in Germany produced a somewhat different result—a tendency to play down nationalism and to identify the new (West) German state in terms that were antithetical to Nazism: constitutional, tolerant, internationalist. Even Britain has its myths of resistance with its celebration of the "Dunkirk spirit," and the ultimate triumph of the decency of the common man and woman over continental despotism.

Postwar political leadership has in general been confident, and not characterized by the dangerous hostility to democracy that proved so fatal to Italian parliamentary democracy after 1918 and to the Weimar Republic especially, which had never been accepted by a large part of the German Establishment. At crucial moments the hour has found the great leader. Adenauer played a vital role in steering Germans away from reunification and toward a Franco-German rapprochement, while his strong-man personality appealed to many who had been brought up on even harder stuff. The return of de Gaulle in 1958 helped to resolve an apparently intractable colonial war and rallied most French people behind his form of Europeanist-nationalism.

Adenauer and de Gaulle were both helped in their task by rapid economic growth in their respective countries. West Germany witnessed an economic miracle that took her from the destruction and dislocation of Hour Zero to the largest gross domestic product in Western Europe by the early 1960s. France went from being a highly rural country in 1945 to having the second largest economy in Western Europe by the early 1970s. Across Western Europe the period since 1945 has in general been one of remarkable economic growth and optimism, while extensive social benefits have mitigated the worst of remaining deprivation. It has only really been in the 1990s that serious doubts have begun to emerge about the future.

Today Western Europe is changing in an economically and socially complex way. "Hyperchange" at the global level seems difficult to fathom, but it has produced two broad sets of views about the future. Optimists hold that this process will mean a new round of European prosperity, based on high-tech industries that will sell into an ever-expanding global market. This will produce temporary social problems, such as the shedding of many less skilled jobs and the need to adjust to the fact that in a rapidly changing world, jobs may not last for life. But the future is essentially viewed with rose-tinted glasses.

Prophets of doom fear that European prosperity is about to be eclipsed by the power of the rising Pacific Rim countries and low-cost producers throughout the world. The impact will not simply be felt by the less skilled, who are already swelling the ranks of an underclass, where long-term unemployment and extremely low wages are endemic. More skilled and middle-class occupations are threatened: many who thought they had a career for life are being made redundant, while highly educated students are finding it more and more difficult to find suitable long-term employment. Pessimists predict the emergence of a highly uneven society, divided between the haves and have nots. It will also be a more rootless society, less confident of its ability to survive the future. Clearly such a scenario could provide the social roots for a new form of fascism.

The French futurologist Alain Minc has even envisaged the emergence of a "New Middle Ages," with areas of urban devastation untouched by the rule of law; where gangs rule and drugs provide diversion from the awful reality of poverty and disease. The argument has many insights, but it ignores a crucial political dimension: the fact that there was no democracy in the Middle Ages. Faced with the growth of a significant number of people living outside the community, especially as many could come from ethnic minorities, the main threat from extremism may not lie among the poorest themselves. Rather, a new wave of extremism could be based on those in employment who despise the "unproductive" and "immoral" breed who live outside the community. Certainly fascism historically was not especially strong among the unemployed or deprived: it appealed most to those who feared these developments, either on the personal or more social level.

Today, there are problems posed by national identity too. In Britain, allegiance to institutions like the Crown and Parliament is far weaker than it was fifty years ago. In France, there have been major fears about the threat to national identity posed by immigration from North African Muslim states, whose populations are growing rapidly. More particularly, but no less powerfully, there has been strong French anxiety over the implications of Algeria becoming Islamic Fundamentalist, which could lead to a flood of refugees—both legal and illegal. In Germany too there are fears about immigration, and a growing concern with the nature of what it is to be German. The rise of the regionalist Northern League in Italy has raised similar issues, which have been compounded by the rapidly declining power of antifascism as the basis of a broad national consensus.

More generally across Europe, the problem is growing of political allegiance based on largely self-centered economic factors rather than on social groupings, such as class or religion or nation. There is a sense in which this has become a "modern" political necessity, a reflection of the decline of traditional forms of political bond. It has proved a particularly powerful factor in the appeal of governing parties at a time of boom. Even in harder times governments have been able to use fear of the opposition's economic incompetence to their advantage: witness Britain at the time of the 1992 general election, or Germany in 1994. Yet basing political loyalty on material interest will pose major problems in the event of an economic downturn, when voters could become highly volatile and look to new radical parties. Certainly in the past, fascism emerged in countries in which elites had raised economic aspirations as a way of tying the masses to the nation—but which then found themselves faced with a serious economic crisis that required the taking of tough decisions.

Today political elites are under pressure once again. Their growing loss of self-confidence is partly the result of relative failure in the economic sphere, which has led to people's living standard expectations running ahead of possibilities. But there is a more general loss of faith among elites, which stems from the decline of the classic ideologies. There are few socialists who believe any longer in extensive state ownership or high taxation: as long ago as 1959 the German SPD gave up its radical program, and more recently the British Labor Party, the French socialists, and the Italian communists (now renamed the Party of Democratic Socialism) have effectively disowned much of their past. There are few conservatives—outside the right wing of the British Conservative Party—who have not realized that free-market economics can cause serious social division, without necessarily bringing new prosperity. Capitalism can be both a social glue and a solvent.

A more balanced view of the relationship between the private market and the state is necessary. Opinion polls are beginning to show that citizens are looking for a new synthesis, but the fashion-

able ideas—such as "communitarianism," popularized by the leading American sociologist Amitai Etzioni—seem to have little to say
about how to secure high living standards, the goal of most citizens.
Communitarianism teaches that rights must be matched by duties,
that the family and local community are vital sources of caring and
identity. There is much that is sensible here, though the historian of
ideas might add that little or nothing of this is new, especially the
quest for a less materialist "Third Way." Given communitarianism's
strong emphasis on liberty, it would be wrong to term it fascist, but
its emergence as an intellectual fashion underlines the return to at
least part of the political agenda that helped to spawn the first wave
of fascist ideology and movements.

For some time, "Europeanism" has seemed set to become a
substitute "ideology" among a large part of the political Establishment. It combines the promise of future economic prosperity with
a moral set of aspirations, such as the desire to transcend nationalism, to prevent further European wars, or for the rich areas to help
the poor. But recently European federalism has revealed itself to be
increasingly unpopular with many voters. Some political leaders
have responded by jumping on the populist bandwagon and adopting a more nationalist rhetoric. Many British Conservatives are
skeptical of a federal Europe, a position that seems to be shared by
Berlusconi in Italy. In France, Jacques Chirac played the nationalist
card at the time of his attack on the 1992 GATT accords, though in
general the French elite's commitment to "Europe" remains strong.
Europeanism also remains central to Christian Democrat German
politics, but here part of the point is growing confidence that Europe can be shaped in Germany's image.

There is much talk of yet further European integration being
inevitable, and the fact that this will require the creation of a new
European identity. Historically identity has tended to be created
around three poles: allegiance to a set of civic institutions, ethnicity,
or the demonization of "the Other." The first of these seems to offer little hope for Europe. It was possible in an established state and
over a period of considerable time to transfer allegiance—and the
willingness to die in war—from the feudal lord to the English
monarch and then to Parliament as the symbol of newfound liber-
ties. But it seems hard to imagine anyone feeling the same way

about the European Parliament, let alone the Bundesbank, or whatever the new central banking institution will be called.

If a more widespread European identity is to be created, a strengthening of cultural, even genetic, identity seems to be necessary. It is easy to see signs of this development in a variety of exhibitions and other forms that sponsor a sense of a shared European heritage stretching as far back as ancient Greece. And genetic theory, which has been out of fashion since 1945, is showing signs of making a comeback: in 1995 the *European* newspaper contained a two-page article on recent scientific research showing that Europeans really are different genetically from Africans—while the academic publishing sensation in America during 1994 was Charles Murray and Richard Herrnstein's book *The Bell Curve*, which purported to show that blacks had lower IQs than whites, though the Chinese were the most intelligent of all.

With Soviet communism dead and buried, fear of Islam, or other new forces such as the rapidly emerging China, offers ample opportunities for defining an "enemy." The growing fear of Islam has already been mentioned, but this could become far more intense during the next generation. The Gulf War in 1991, with its space-invader images of accurately zapping clinically defined targets, seemed to confirm that the West retains a vast technological lead. The war, however, also underlined the reluctance of many European countries to fight except for survival, and the speedy conclusion of the war owed much to Saddam Hussein's decision not to commit many of his best planes and troops. What would have happened to European opinion if the war had gone on for several weeks and the casualties had been high? What if, in a future war, Europe's enemies deployed nuclear weapons, which many will acquire in the near future? Little attention has been paid to the question of future war, though even the thought of it could revive end-of-the-nineteenth-century fears about Europe's ability to fight against a socially united and virile challenger—a dread that played its part in inspiring the first wave of fascist ideology and fascist leaders.

In general, postwar fascist chiefs have been an unimpressive bunch. Most of the early leaders, like Almirante or Mosley, were hangovers from the past who were tainted by their previous allegiances. But during the 1980s Le Pen helped to show, with his clean-cut, smart image and his ability to use cleverly constructed political rhetoric, that it was possible to attract a relatively widespread following among new generations of voters. In particular, Le Pen used a mixture of crude exploitation of fears about immigration and social trends with a more sophisticated vocabulary, which sought to place the Front National clearly within the mainstream French political tradition: his reward was fifteen percent of the vote in the 1995 presidential elections. The potential for neofascist progress in the 1990s is underlined even more clearly by the Italian case. Here Gianfranco Fini has managed to make himself the most popular politician on the Italian scene in 1994–6. Although the entry of his Italian Social Movement–National Alliance into government during 1994 stemmed directly from the sensational scandals that dramatically weakened the old governing parties, for some time beforehand there had been clear signs that Italian neofascism was being accepted as a legitimate, or semilegitimate, force. To reinforce this trend, during 1995 Fini appeared to bury much of fascism's past in the clear belief that this would help his "postfascist" party replace Berlusconi's troubled grouping as the main force on the right.

iii

SHORTLY BEFORE his suicide in 1945, the French fascist intellectual Pierre Drieu La Rochelle wrote: "I'm not only a Frenchman. I'm a European. But we played the game and I lost. I crave death." It is an enigmatic though interesting epitaph, for Drieu seems to have believed that fascism would have to die in order to be born again.

For much of the period since 1945, neofascism has been the province of nostalgics with no desire to renounce the past. This was especially true in the immediate postwar period, when parties like the MSI, SRP, or Union Movement were largely made up of people who had been active in the interwar years. Many had grown up as teenagers or young people under a fascist system and had been indoctrinated during a crucial phase of their lives. As such, these recidivist neofascists are a cohort that has not been replaced, and most of them have now died off.

Their place has been taken by growing bands of alienated

youths, who make up the bulk of parties like the German Alternative. In most cases their ideological commitment to fascism seems weak—though the leaders of these parties are usually overt fascist ideologues. They attract members because fascism remains a latter-day substitute for the Devil: it is a symbol of their rebellion—be it against parents, society, or whatever. Recidivist neofascist groups also provide a format for engaging in violence against ethnic communities, antifascists, gays, opposing soccer fans, or whoever is unlucky enough to be in their way. Social trends, like youth unemployment and the casualization of the labor market, seem likely to maintain a steady flow into these groups. Growing extremism and militancy on the part of ethnic populations too could spawn further recruits for violent neofascism. But it is hard to believe that here lies the basis of a future mass movement. For most people, this type of neofascism remains beyond the pale, though its potential for violence is considerable.

A second type of neofascist individual and group has seen more clearly the need for a break with the past: the radical neofascist, who holds that Hitler and Mussolini in some way betrayed fascism. A notable individual exponent of this view was Maurice Bardèche in France, who held that real fascism was socially radical and was best encapsulated in the first program of Italian fascism, or in its closing phase during the Salò Republic. Outside Italy, most radical neofascists have tended to look for roots more in Germany. The result has often been "Strasserism," the claim that Gregor Strasser and his brother Otto offered an alternative socialist form of Nazism, which was betrayed by Hitler in his quest to secure army and business support. Among the main groups it has influenced have been the NPD and British National Front during the 1980s. The radical form underlines that fascism was not a monolithic creed, but it is often based on debatable or one-sided readings of history: the Salò Republic, for instance, was characterized more by chaos and extensive violence than by social reform.

The most promising form of neofascist radicalism in terms of burying the past is the attempt to rehabilitate the German conservative revolutionaries, like Ernst Jünger (who celebrated his hundredth birthday in 1995), and key intellectuals who supported fascism, like Carl Schmitt and Martin Heidegger. Schmitt and Heidegger have the disadvantage that they supported the Nazi regime, but apologists claim—falsely in Heidegger's case—that this was mere opportunism. The French New Right, in particular its key theorist Alain de Benoist, has turned to the conservative revolutionaries and Schmitt for much of its inspiration, particularly to their ideas on the importance of re-creating national identity and providing a new meaning for work. Discussion of such thinkers means nothing to most neofascist activists, especially the young recidivists: in fact, it almost certainly loses rather than attracts support—especially among the electorate at large, who have no interest in esoteric discussions about the fascist tradition.

The importance of the radical neofascists, therefore, lies more in their ability to influence a third type of neofascist, the hybrid, or political debate more generally. The hybrid is the individual or party whose views have some clear links with the fascist past, but who in other ways seems to have broken with central tenets of fascism. Le Pen offers a good example of this category. His emphasis on national identity and the need for French rebirth has strong echoes of the fascist past, but his defense of more free-market views and of the democratic system—albeit with a strengthened presidency—seems totally alien to the fascist tradition. Here, however, it becomes necessary to read Le Pen more carefully. This is not simply a question of searching for gaffes, such as his claim that the Holocaust was a "detail of history": it involves looking at exactly what he said about the economy and the political system. Like all fascists, Le Pen is primarily interested in changing culture. Thus his defense of "democracy" is based on the belief that France must become a homogeneous society, not characterized by dangerous division.

Gianfranco Fini offers an even more important example of this hybrid neofascism. A man nurtured in the MSI since his teens, Fini has recently persuaded his party to rename itself the National Alliance and to disown fascist totalitarianism and racism. Once again this is a "conversion" that needs examining closely. The point is not simply the fact that a wave of Italian scandals has offered the neofascists a chance to establish themselves as a major party if they can only adopt a more respectable face. It is necessary to look at exactly what is being argued. Most Italian fascists in the interwar period never sought a totalitarian economy, if by this is meant a high level of state ownership or even control. Rather, they sought to produce a growing economy that would act in the national interest and integrate the workers into the nation and state. Fini's rejection of a highly statist policy is based on a similar philosophy: it has simply been updated to take into account that the Italian state now owns much inefficient industry. His rejection of racism should not be confused with accepting Italy as a multicultural society: it is more a form of New Right "differentialism," which accepts the right to other people's identities and cultures—in their own countries.

At the 1956 MSI Congress, a group of delegates chanted, "Fewer double-breasted suits—more brass knuckles." In countries where neofascist parties have managed to divorce themselves to some extent from the latter tradition, they have been able to attract some favorable media coverage and cooperation from at least part of the mainstream elite. In Italy Fini's fresh and relatively wholesome image was attracting media attention well before Berlusconi opened his television networks to the MSI leader. And even before the great wave of scandals in 1992, there were signs that the MSI was becoming treated as a party almost like the rest. During the last twenty-five years, the shrewder neofascists have learned that it is necessary to present a new face. This alone does not guarantee a political breakthrough: in Britain and Germany, the mainstream right has remained relatively strong—and in Britain the neofascists have been a remarkably motley crowd. But there are danger signs on the horizon for all of Europe. Mainstream parties are finding it increasingly difficult to maintain electoral loyalty. A future economic crisis poses particular dangers, given the general tendency today to fight elections on primarily materialist themes.

Fascism is on the march again. Its style may at times be very different, but the ideological core remains the same—the attempt to create a *holistic-national radical Third Way*. Should it ever gain power, it may prove that it has learned from the mistakes of the past. But an ideology that places so little emphasis on constitutions and rights, and so much on elite-inspired manipulation, must always be mistrusted. Beware of men—and women—wearing smart Italian suits: the color is now gray, the material is cut to fit the times, but the aim is still power, and the fantasy is the creation of a radical new culture.

Regardless of whether Fini makes it to the top, his success has been the result of a clear example of *syncretic legitimation*. Fini cleverly adapted the AN-MSI's appeal to help it break out of its largely ghettoized southern roots: he began to attract voters who were concerned by both economic and more affective national issues. More specifically, the AN-MSI made its major breakthrough when it began to achieve significant recognition from the Establishment and politically respectable sources, especially ones that opened more favorable media coverage.

In many ways, Fini's success has come from a specifically Italian crisis—further underlining the need for a clear national perspective when analyzing fascism. But the growing signs of major economic crisis, the loss of faith in mainstream elites, and the attraction of charismatic leadership (Fini's personal rating runs well ahead of that of his party) are features that can be found in all Western democracies. Fascism is on the move once more, even if its most sophisticated forms have had to learn to dress to suit the times. Can democracy triumph once again? Was the demise of classic fascism really so inevitable? Has German identity been forged in a more durable democratic mold, capable of withstanding serious economic depression? Is the Front National set for further gains? Could Britain be on the verge of a wave of radical nationalism? Never has the study of fascism—through all its history—been so timely.

Notes

The Birth of Fascist Ideology

1. See S. Payne, *Fascism: Definition and Comparison* (Madison 1980), for an excellent statement of this interpretation. See also his *A History of Fascism, 1914–1945* (Madison, 1995).

2. For a different presentation of the argument that fascism was a serious ideology, see R. Eatwell and A. Wright (eds.), *Contemporary Political Ideologies* (London, 1993), and R. Eatwell, "Towards a New Model of Generic Fascism," *Journal of Theoretical Politics* 2, 1992.

3. On the origins of left-right terminology, and for a more general analysis of types of right-wing thought, see R. Eatwell and N. O'Sullivan (eds.), *The Nature of the Right* (London, 1989).

4. Those who stress this aspect of fascism sometimes trace its origins to reactionary thinkers such as Joseph de Maistre. See, for example, I. Berlin, "Joseph de Maistre and the Origins of Fascism," in H. Hardy (ed.), *The Crooked Timber of Humanity* (London, 1991)

5. For instance, E. Nolte, *The Three Faces of Fascism* (New York, 1969), and especially J. L. Talmon, *The Origins of Totalitarian Democracy* (London, 1952).

6. For a widely influential academic attack on Plato and Hegel as the founding fathers of totalitarianism, see K. Popper, *The Open Society and its Enemies*, esp. vol. 2 (London, 1962), pp. 60–78.

7. See especially G. Mosse, *The Crisis of German Ideology* (New York, 1964), and F. Stern, *The Politics of Cultural Despair* (Berkeley, 1961).

8. See R. Soucy, *Fascism in France: the Case of Maurice Barrès* (Berkeley, 1972), and Z. Sternhell, *Maurice Barrès* (Paris, 1972). N.B. Soucy sees fascism as a form of conservatism.

9. On Chamberlain, see G. G. Field, *Evangelist of Race* (London, 1981). On the general rise of nineteenth century racist thought, see G. Mosse, *Toward the Final Solution* (New York, 1978).

10. The key writer to argue that a crucial factor in the rise of fascism was an attack on "positivism" is Z. Sternhell. The best introduction to his work in English is his essay "Fascist Ideology" in W. Laqueur (ed.), *Fascism: A Reader's Guide* (Harmondsworth, 1979). See also Z. Sternhell, M. Sznajder, and M. Asheri, *The Birth of Fascist Ideology* (Princeton, 1994).

11. See especially M. Burleigh, *Death and Deliverance: "Euthanasia" in Germany 1900–45* (London, 1994),

and P. Weindling, *Health, Race and German Politics between National Unification and Nazism, 1870–1945* (Cambridge, 1993).

12. For example, D. Beetham, "From Socialism to Fascism: the Relationship between Theory and Practice in the Work of Robert Michels," *Political Studies* 1 and 2, 1977. N.B., contrary to its popular left-wing image, early sociology both contributed to and exhibited fascist strands. See S. P. Turner and D. Käsler, *Sociology Responds to Fascism* (London, 1992).

13. For an introduction to Nietzsche, see J. P. Stern, *Nietzsche* (London, 1978). S. E. Aschheim, *The Nietzsche Legacy in Germany, 1980–1990* (Berkeley, 1993) offers an important survey and shows the connection between Nazism and Nietzsche. On Sorel-the-socialist, see J. Jennings, *Georges Sorel* (London, 1987). Cf. Sternhell et al., *Birth of Fascist Ideology*, who portray Sorel as an especially important figure in producing the synthesis of nationalism and socialism, which they see as lying at the heart of fascism.

14. On this important fascist philosopher, see V. Farias, *Heidegger and Nazism* (Philadelphia, 1989), and T. Rockmore, *On Heidegger's Nazism and Philosophy* (London, 1992).

15. Or the major Belgian theorist, Henri De Man. See Z. Sternhell's controversial *Neither Right nor Left* (Berkeley, 1986). On the left impact on fascism, see also the notable works of A. J. Gregor, especially *The Fascist Persuasion in Radical Politics* (Princeton, 1974).

16. The argument that fascist ideology focused on rebirth appears in its most sophisticated form in R. Griffin,

The Nature of Fascism (London, 1991). See also his edited selection of texts, *Fascism* (Oxford, 1995).

17. Cf. Sternhell's view that Nazism was not fascist on account of its form of racism. See also R. De Felice, *Interpretations of Fascism* (Cambridge, Mass., 1977), which sees Italian fascism as fundamentally different from Nazism on account of the latter's atavistic tendencies.

18. See Eatwell, "Towards a New Model" for an expansion of this argument, with examples taken more from the post-1918 period.

The National Roots of Fascist Movements

1. For more on the importance of national traditions, see R. Eatwell (ed.), *European Political Culture* (London, 1996).

2. For an excellent account of the emergence of British identity, especially during the eighteenth century, see L. Colley, *Forging the Nation* (London, 1992). See also R. Samuel (ed.), *Patriotism: the Making and Unmaking of British National Identities*, 3 vols. (London, 1989).

3. See W. H. Greenleaf, *The British Political Tradition*, 2 vols. (London, 1988).

4. See C. Holmes, *Anti-Semitism in British Society* (London, 1979), and G. Lebzelter, *Political Anti-Semitism in Britain* (London, 1978). See also D. Feldman, *Englishmen and Jews* (London, 1994).

5. G. Dangerfield, *The Strange Death of Liberal England* (London, 1938).

6. The concept of the importance of "space" for fascism to develop has

been developed especially by J. Linz, "Some Notes Toward a Comparative Study of Fascism in Sociological Historical Perspective," in W. Laqueur (ed.), *Fascism: A Reader's Guide* (Harmondsworth, 1979).

7. On the threats to the Conservatives, see F. Coetzee, *For Party or Country: Nationalism and the Dilemmas of Popular Conservatism in Edwardian England* (London, 1990), and E. H. H. Green, *The Crisis of Conservatism: the Politics, Economics and Ideology of the British Conservative Party, 1880–1914* (London, 1994).

8. For an account of popular propaganda, see K. Haste, *Keep the Home Fires Burning* (London, 1977).

9. See especially F. Braudel, *The Identity of France*, 2 vols. (London, 1989–90).

10. See N. O'Sullivan, *Fascism* (1983) and J. L. Talmon, *The Origins of Totalitarian Democracy* (London, 1952).

11. A claim made especially by Marxists: see the articles by Jost Dülffer, Gerard Botz, and Robert Wistrich in *The Journal of Contemporary History*, 4, 1976.

12. On the forging of modern national culture in this context, see E. Weber, *Peasants into Frenchmen* (London, 1979), and T. Zeldin, *A History of French Passions*, 2 vols. (Oxford, 1993).

13. On French anti-Semitism and the Dreyfus affair, see S. Wilson *Ideology and Experience: Antisemitism in France at the time of the Dreyfus Affair* (London, 1982).

14. See E. Weber's classic work, *Action Française* (Stanford, 1962).

15. The most notable commentator who has placed Maurras in the fascist tradition is E. Nolte in his enigmatic *Three Faces of Fascism* (New York, 1969). On Maurras as a reactionary, see H. S. McClelland, "The Reactionary Right," in R. Eatwell and N. O'Sullivan (eds.), *The Nature of the Right* (London, 1989). On links with the Sorelians, see P. Mazgaj, *The Action Française and Revolutionary Syndicalism* (Chapel Hill, 1979).

16. For the claim that France was the seedbed of fascism, see especially the works of Z. Sternhell, for example, the opening of *Neither Left nor Right* (Berkeley, 1986). For the conventional view, see R. Rémond, *The Right Wing in France: From 1815 to de Gaulle* (Philadelphia, 1969).

17. See B. Jenkins, *Nationalism in France: Class and Nation Since 1789* (London, 1990) and R. Tombs (ed.), *Nationhood and Nationalism in France: From Boulangism to the Great War, 1889–1918* (London, 1991).

18. This has bred a school of those who see Hitler as the last in a long line of "great" German leaders. See, for example, R. D. O'Butler, *The Roots of National Socialism* (London, 1941), W. M. McGovern, *From Luther to Hitler* (London, 1941), and W. Shirer, *The Rise and Fall of the Third Reich* (London, 1960).

19. G. Mosse, *The Crisis of German Ideology* (New York, 1964); F. Stern, *The Politics of Cultural Despair* (Berkeley, 1961).

20. For more on the impact of economic development and politics, including the argument that there was a special German form of development (*Sonderweg*), see B. Moore, Jr., *The Social Origins of Dictatorship and Democracy* (New York, 1966), and G. Eley,

From Unification to Nazism (London, 1991).

21. P. Pulzer, *Jews and the German State, 1848–1933* (Oxford, 1992).

22. Mosse (1964), p. 133. The Nazis erected a museum in his honor.

23. J. Retallack, *Notables of the Right* (London, 1988).

24. R. Chickering, *We Men Who Feel Most German* (London, 1984), p. 1. See also E. Eley, *Reshaping the German Right* (New Haven, 1980).

25. On this new populist, albeit manipulative, nationalism, see G. Mosse, *The Nationalization of the Masses* (New York, 1977).

26. See H.-U. Wehler, *The German Empire 1871–1914* (Leamington Spa, 1984) for an expansion of this argument (though he overstresses the cohesion of elites).

27. On the military, see G. Feldman, *Army, Industry and Labour in Germany, 1914–18* (New York, 1992), and M. Kitchen, *The Silent Dictatorship: the Politics of the German High Command 1916–8* (London, 1978). On the military's role in the state more generally, see G. Craig's classic *The Politics of the Prussian Army 1640–1945* (London, 1955). See also the controversial F. Fischer, *Germany's Aims in the First World War* (London, 1966), which holds that a broad section of the German elite held virtually the same aspirations as the Pan German League.

28. Wehler (1984), p. 216ff. See also J. Hatheway, "The Pre-1920 Origins of the National Socialist German Workers' Party," *Journal of Contemporary History* 2, 1994.

29. For the problems this caused political organization even a century later, see E. Banfield, "Amoral Familism," in M. Dogan and R. Rose, *European Politics* (London, 1971). See also G. Almond and S. Verba, *The Civic Culture* (Boston, 1963).

30. See J. N. Molony, *The Emergence of Political Catholicism in Italy* (London, 1977), and R. A. Webster, *The Cross and the Fasces: Christian Democracy and Fascism in Italy* (Stanford, 1961).

31. On Mussolini the revolutionary, see A. J. Gregor, *The Young Mussolini and the Intellectual Origins of Fascism* (Berkeley, 1979), and the very different interpretation of Mack Smith, *Mussolini* (London, 1981).

32. J. Gooch, *Army, State and Society in Italy, 1870–1915* (London, 1989), esp. pp. 73–95. See also J. Whittam, *The Politics of the Italian Army* (London, 1977).

33. A. De Grand, *The Italian Nationalist Association and the Rise of Fascism in Italy* (Lincoln, 1978). For further examples of radical nationalist thought, see A. Lyttelton (ed.), *Italian Fascism from Pareto to Gentile* (London, 1973).

34. E. Gentile, "Fascism as a Political Religion," *Journal of Contemporary History* 2–3, 1990.

35. On the new nationalism, see also W. Adamson, *Avant-Garde Florence* (Boston, 1993).

36. On the relationship of Italian socialism to fascism, see Gregor (1979), D. Roberts, *The Syndicalist Tradition in Italian Fascism* (Manchester, 1978), and Z. Sternhell, M. Sznajder, and M. Asheri, *The Birth of Fascist Ideology* (Princeton, 1994).

37. R. J. B. Bosworth, *Italy, the Least of the Great Powers: Italian Foreign Policy Before the First World War*

(Cambridge, 1979), Gooch (1989), and Whittam (1977).

38. On the importance of economic legitimation in Germany, see H. James, *A German Identity, 1770–1990* (London, 1990); for a more varied view, see J. Breuilly (ed.), *The State of Germany* (London, 1992).

39. I will be setting out these arguments in a more schematic way in a forthcoming publication.

Italy: The Rise of Fascism

1. For a good survey of the rise and early years of fascism, see A. Lyttelton, *The Seizure of Power* (London, 1987), and R. Vivarelli, *Storia delle origini del fascismo* (Bologna, 1991).

2. Compare the opportunistic Duce of D. Mack Smith, *Mussolini* (London, 1981) and most biographies with E. Gentile, *Le Origini dell'ideologia fascista, 1918–25* (Rome, 1975); A. J. Gregor, *The Young Mussolini and the Intellectual Origins of Fascism* (Berkeley, 1979); and Z. Sternhell, M. Sznajder and M. Asheri, *The Birth of Fascist Ideology* (Princeton, 1994). The relatively sympathetic multivolume biography of Mussolini by the leading Italian historian, R. De Felice, has not been translated into English. See R. De Felice, *Fascism: An Informal Introduction to Its Theory and Practice* (New Brunswick, 1976). For favorable accounts of his views, see E. Gentile, "Fascism in Italian Historiography," *Journal of Contemporary History* 2, 1986, and B. W. Parker, "Renzo De Felice and the History of Italian Fascism," *American Historical Review* 2, 1990.

3. See W. Adamson, *Avant-Garde Florence* (Boston, 1993), esp. pp. 140 and 258, and E. Gentile, *Le Voce*

(Bologna, 1976). See also W. L. Adamson, "The Language of Opposition in Early Twentieth-Century Italy: Rhetorical Continuities between Prewar Florentine Avant-gardism and Mussolini's Fascism," *Journal of Modern History* 1, 1992.

4. See J. Joll, *Three Intellectuals in Politics* (New York, 1960). See also G. L. Mosse, "The Political Culture of Italian Futurism: a General Perspective," *Journal of Contemporary History* 2–3, 1990, and A. Hewitt, *Fascist Modernism: The Aestheticization of Politics* (Stanford, 1992).

5. See C. Klopp, *Gabriele D'Annunzio* (New York, 1988), for a biography; P. Valesio, *Gabriele D'Annunzio* (New Haven, 1992) focuses more on the artistic side, which is increasingly regaining recognition.

6. On Italian diplomacy leading up to the conference, see H. J. Burgwyn, *The Legend of the Mutilated Peace: Italy, the Great War and the Peace Conference* (Westport, 1993).

7. See M. Ledeen, *The First Duce* (Baltimore, 1977), and R. De Felice, *D'Annunzio politico* (Milan, 1987).

8. A. Rhodes, *D'Annunzio* (London, 1965), p. 217.

9. M. Sznajder, "The 'Carto del Carnaro' and Modernization," *Tel Aviv Jahrbuch für deutsche Geschichte*, 1989.

10. For example, Ledeen, *The First Duce*, p. 201.

11. A. L. Cardoza, "The Long Goodbye: The Landed Aristocracy in North-Western Italy, 1880–1930," *European History Quarterly* 3, 1990.

12. M. Gribaudi, *Mondo operaio e mito operaio: Spazi e percorsi sociali a Torino nel primo novecento* (Turin, 1987).

13. A. Bull and P. Corner, *From*

Peasant to Entrepreneur (London, 1993), esp. pp. 70–1.

14. See D. J. Forsyth, *The Crisis of Liberal Italy: Monetary and Financial Policy, 1914–22* (Cambridge, 1993).

15. See J. N. Molony, *The Emergence of Political Catholicism in Italy* (London, 1977), and R. A. Webster, *The Cross and the Fasces* (Stanford, 1960).

16. See H. Fornari, *Mussolini's Gadfly: Roberto Farinacci* (Nashville, 1971), P. Nello, *Dino Grandi* (Bologna, 1987), G. Rochat, *Italo Balbo* (Turin, 1986), and C. G. Segrè, *Italo Balbo: A Fascist Life* (Berkeley, 1987). See also A. Cardoza, *Agrarian Elites and Italian Fascism: the Province of Bologna, 1901–1926* (Princeton, 1982), and the local studies in notes 18, 19, and 21 below.

17. For example, D. Mack Smith, *Mussolini*, p. 41.

18. P. Corner, *Fascism in Ferrara* (Oxford, 1975), p. 64.

19. See especially P. Snowden, *The Fascist Revolution in Tuscany, 1919–1922* (Cambridge, 1989), pp. 163–4.

20. Major commentators who have stressed the need to study fascism in terms of its concrete practice, rather than in terms of its alleged ideological origins or mercurial rhetoric, include: G. Allardyce, "What Fascism Is Not: Thoughts on the Deflation of a Concept," *American Historical Review* 2, 1979, and R. Vivarelli, "Interpretations of the Origins of Fascism," *Journal of Modern History* 1, 1991.

21. A. Kelikian, *Town and Country Under Fascism: The Transformation of Brescia, 1915–1926* (Oxford, 1986).

22. See E. Gentile, *Storia del partito fascista, 1919–1922* (Rome, 1989), and Lyttelton, *The Seizure of Power*.

23. P. Cannistraro (ed.), *Historical Dictionary of Fascist Italy* (Westport, 1982), p. xxi.

24. For a general account of business views see R. Sarti, *Fascism and the Industrial Leadership in Italy, 1919–1940* (Berkeley, 1971).

25. For an account of the king's relations with fascism, see D. Mack Smith, *Italy and its Monarchy* (London, 1989).

Italy: The Development of the Fascist Regime

1. For a good general account of the early years of Mussolini's governments, see A. Lyttelton, *Fascism: the Seizure of Power* (London, 1987).

2. On Mussolini, see R. De Felice, *Mussolini, il fascista* (Turin, 1966) and subsequent volumes in this massive biography, and D. Mack Smith, *Mussolini* (London, 1981).

3. On this development see D. Beetham, "From Socialism to Fascism: The Relation Between Theory and Practice in the Work of Robert Michels," *Political Studies* 1 and 2, 1977.

4. See G. Gentile, "The Philosophical Basis of Fascism," *Foreign Affairs*, 1927–8. See also his joint article on fascism with Mussolini in the *Enciclopedia Italiana* (Rome, 1932), which is reproduced in A. Lyttelton (ed.), *Italian Fascisms: From Pareto to Gentile* (London, 1973).

5. On their prefascist views, see A. De Grand, *The Italian Nationalist Association and the Rise of Fascism in Italy* (Lincoln, 1978).

6. On PPI dissidents, see J. Pollard, "Conservative Catholics and Italian Fascism: the Clerico-Fascists," in M. Blinkhorn (ed.), *Conservatives and*

Fascists (London, 1991). See also R. A. Webster, *The Cross and Fasces* (Stanford, 1960).

7. On Fascism in the south, see C. Duggan, *Fascism and the Mafia* (New Haven, 1989) and J. Steinberg, "Fascism in the Italian South," in D. Forgacs (ed.), *Rethinking Italian Fascism* (London, 1986).

8. On fascist support in elections, see M. Revelli, "Italy," in D. Mühlberger (ed.), *The Social Basis of European Fascist Movements* (London, 1987). N.B. far less detailed work has been done on voting for Italian fascism than for German National Socialism, mainly because relatively few free elections were contested by the former and because of the tendency to fight elections in alliance with others. For a social science work that tries to unravel the Italian case, see W. Brustein, "The Red Menace and the Rise of Italian Fascism," *American Sociological Review* 4, 1991.

9. A. Kelikian, *Town and Country under Fascism* (Oxford, 1986), esp. p. 83.

10. An argument made particularly by Renzo De Felice. See, for instance, *Fascism: An Informal Introduction to its Theory and Practice* (New Brunswick, 1976), esp. p. 12, and "Fascism and the Middle Classes" in S. Larsen et al. (eds.), *Who Were the Fascists?* (Bergen, 1980).

11. G. Salvemini, *The Fascist Dictatorship in Italy* (London, 1964), p. 250.

12. See D. Mack Smith, *Italy and its Monarchy* (London, 1989), esp. p. 254ff.

13. For more sophisticated examples of Mussolini's views, see Lyttelton (1973), and B. Mussolini, *Fascism: Doctrine and Institutions* (Rome, 1935).

14. See H. Fornari, *Mussolini's Gadfly: Roberto Farinacci* (Nashville, 1971).

15. R. Visser, "Fascist Doctrine and the Cult of the Romanità," *Journal of Contemporary History* 1, 1992. More generally on the many-faceted aspect of propaganda and the Mussolini cult, see L. Passerini, *Mussolini immaginario* (Rome, 1991).

16. De Felice argues that this was very different from Germany, where the idea of rebirth was stronger as many believed that Aryan man already existed, but had been suffocated by modernity. See De Felice, *Fascism*, esp. p. 56.

17. See Z. Brzezinski and C. Friedrich, *Totalitarian Autocracy and Dictatorship* (New York, 1961), and L. Schapiro, *Totalitarianism* (London, 1972).

18. E. Gentile, "Fascism as a Political Religion," *Journal of Contemporary History* 2–3, 1990, esp. p. 230. On the importance of myths, see also E. Gentile, *Il culto del littorio* (Rome, 1993).

19. J. Pollard, *The Vatican and Italian Fascism, 1929–1932* (London, 1985).

20. See especially R. Sarti, *Fascism and the Industrial Leadership in Italy, 1918–40* (Berkeley, 1971).

21. On De Ambris, see M. Sznajder, "Social Revolution and National Integration: Alceste De Ambris and Italian Fascism," *Canadian Review of Studies in Nationalism* 1–2, 1993.

22. See D. Roberts, *The Syndicalist Tradition and Italian Fascism* (Manchester, 1979).

23. For example, S. Woolf, "Italy," in Woolf (ed.), *Fascism in Europe* (London, 1981), p. 56.

24. See Roberts, *The Syndical Tradition*.

25. M. Ledeen, *Universal Fascism* (New York, 1972).

26. G. Salvemini, *Under the Axe of Fascism* (London, 1936), p. 10.

27. On the developmental aspect of the regime, see A. J. Gregor, *Italian Fascism and Developmental Dictatorship* (Berkeley, 1979). Cf. the more disorganized picture in G. Toniolo, *L'economia dell' italia fascista* (Rome, 1980).

28. Sarti, *Fascism and the Industrial Leadership*, p. 122, even argues that the Italian "economic miracle" which followed World War II was probably as much the result of the IRI as of developments such as the "European Common Market, foreign investments and the rise in domestic consumption."

29. De Felice especially has stressed the existence of a consensus, though he sees the key years as 1929–34: see *Mussolini, il duce* (Turin, 1974). This has been bitterly criticized within Italy, especially by those who seek to portray fascism as little more than a brutal repressive regime.

30. See V. de Grazia, *The Culture of Consent* (Cambridge, 1981).

31. See L. Caldwell, "Reproducers of the Nation: Women and Family in Fascist Policy," in Forgacs, *Rethinking Italian Fascism;* P. Corner, "Women in Fascist Italy: Changing Family roles in the Transition from an Agricultural to an Industrial Society," *European History Quarterly* 1, 1993; and V. de Grazia, *How Fascism Ruled Women* (Berkeley, 1993).

32. See T. Koon, *Believe, Obey, Fight: Political Socialization of Youth in Fascist Italy, 1922–43* (Chapel Hill, 1986), E. R. Tannenbaum, *Fascism in Italy: Society and Culture, 1922–1945* (London, 1973), and G. L. Williams, *Fascist Thought and Totalitarianism in Italy's Secondary Schools* (New York, 1994).

33. D. Thompson, *State Control in Fascist Italy* (Manchester, 1991).

34. See Duggan, *Fascism and the Mafia.*

35. L. Passerini, *Fascism in Popular Memory* (Cambridge, 1987), p. 94.

36. See I. Herzer, *The Italian Refuge* (Washington, 1992); M. Michaelis, *Mussolini and the Jews* (Oxford, 1978); J. Sternberg, *All or Nothing? The Axis and the Holocaust* (London, 1991); A. Stille, *Benevolence and Betrayal: Five Italian Families Under Fascism* (London, 1992); and S. Zuccotti, *The Italians and the Holocaust: Persecution, Rescue and Survival* (New York, 1987).

37. See C. Delzell (ed.), *The Papacy and Totalitarianism Between the Two World Wars* (New York, 1974).

Italy: War and Strife

1. See A. Cassells (ed.), *Italian Foreign Policy, 1918–1945* (Wilmington, 1991) and C. J. Lowe and F. Marzari, *Italian Foreign Policy, 1870–1940* (London, 1975). See also J. Whittam, *Fascist Italy* (Manchester, 1995).

2. See D. Mack Smith, *Mussolini's African Empire* (London, 1976), and E. M. Robertson, *Mussolini as Empire-Builder: Europe and Africa 1932–6* (London, 1977).

3. C. G. Segrè, *Italo Balbo: A Fascist Life* (Berkeley, 1987).

4. On the new nationalism see A. De Grand, *The Italian Nationalist Association and the Rise of Fascism in Italy* (Lincoln, 1979). See also C. G. Segrè, *The Fourth Shore* (Chicago, 1976).

5. See A. Sbacchi, *Ethiopia Under Mussolini* (London, 1985).

6. On changing attitudes toward Mussolini during the closing stages of the fascist regime, see R. De Felice *Mussolini, il duce,* vol. 2 (Turin, 1981).

7. See J. F. Coverdale, *Italian Intervention in the Spanish Civil War* (Princeton, 1975).

8. See P. Preston, *Franco* (London, 1993). See also the misleadingly titled S. Ben-Ami, *Fascism from Above: The Dictatorship of Primo de Rivera in Spain 1923–30* (Oxford, 1983). On the fascist Falange, see S. Payne's classic *Falange* (Stanford, 1962).

9. On fascist attitudes toward the United States before the late 1930s, see E. Gentile, "Impending Modernity: Fascism and the Ambivalent Image of the United States," *Journal of Contemporary History* 1, 1993.

10. On German responsibility for launching World War II, see D. C. Watt, *How War Came: the Immediate Origins of the Second World War* (London, 1989).

11. G. Ciano (ed. M. Muggeridge), *Ciano's Diaries 1939–1943* (London, 1947).

12. See M. Knox, *Mussolini Unleashed, 1929–41* (Cambridge, 1982).

13. D. Mack Smith, *The Italian Monarchy* (London, 1989), esp. p. 278ff.

14. J. I. Sadkovich, "The Italo-Greek War in Context: Italian Priorities and Axis Diplomacy," *Journal of Contemporary History* 3, 1993.

15. T. Koon, *Believe, Obey, Fight* (Chapel Hill, 1986), p. 249.

16. M. Knox, "Conquest, Foreign and Domestic in Fascist Italy and Nazi Germany," *Journal of Modern History* 1, 1984, sees this recurring desire to achieve radical change in both the domestic and foreign policy environments as a key similarity between the two major forms of fascism.

17. See A. De Grand, "Cracks in the Facade: The Failure of Fascist Totalitarianism in Italy, 1935–9," *European History Quarterly* 4, 1991. De Grand sees Mussolini as in many ways a weak dictator, who had parceled out power to others.

18. On the Resistance, see C. Delzell, *Mussolini's Enemies: The Italian anti-Fascist Resistance* (New York, 1974); C. Delzell, "The Italian anti-Fascist Resistance in Retrospect," *Journal of Modern History* 1, 1975; C. Pavone, *Una Guerra civile: saggio storico sulla moralità nella Resistenza* (Turin, 1991); and M. Wilhelm, *The Other Italy: Resistance in World War Two* (New York, 1988).

19. Mack Smith, *Mussolini,* p. 294.

20. For Mussolini's account of these events, see B. Mussolini (ed. R. Klibansky), *Benito Mussolini: Memoirs, 1942–3* (London, 1949).

21. O. Skorzeny, *Skorzeny's Special Missions* (London, 1959).

22. On this closing phase, see S. Bertoldi, *Salò: vita e morte della Repubblica Sociale Italiano* (Milan, 1976); G. Bocca, *La Repubblica di Mussolini* (Rome, 1977); F. W. Deakin, *The Brutal Friendship* (London, 1966); Part 2 appeared as *The Last Days of Mussolini* [London, 1966]); D. Ellwood, *Italy, 1943–5* (London, 1985); and R. Lamb, *War in Italy, 1943–5: A Brutal Story* (London, 1993).

23. See H. Fornari, *Mussolini's Gadfly: Roberto Farinacci* (Nashville, 1971).

24. G. Salotti, *Nicola Bombacci: da Mosca a Salò* (Rome, 1986).

25. H. Carpenter, *A Serious Charac-*

ter: The Life of Ezra Pound (New York, 1989).

Germany: The Rise of Nazism

1. For instance, R. G. L. Waite, *The Psychopathic God* (New York, 1987). However, the exact linkages between upbringing and later behavior are never fully made clear. For more balanced biographies, see A. Bullock, *Hitler: A Study in Tyranny* (Harmondsworth, 1963); W. Carr, *Hitler: A Study in Personality* (London, 1978); and I. Kershaw, *Hitler* (London, 1991).

2. J. P. Stern, *Hitler: The Führer and the People* (London, 1974), p. 184.

3. See A. Hitler, *Mein Kampf* (London, 1969), esp. p. 89ff.

4. The occult origins of Nazism have frequently been stressed. See, for example, C. Goodrick-Clarke, *The Occult Roots of Nazism* (Wellingborough, 1985). However, this argument is grossly overstated, though some Nazis, most notably the later leader of the SS, Heinrich Himmler, were interested in the occult.

5. See J. Noakes and G. Pridham (eds.), *Documents on Nazism, 1919–1945* (London, 1974), for a very useful set of key Nazi texts, including this program. For a detailed study of Hitler's early political career, see A. Tyrell, *Vom "Trommler" zum "Führer"* (Munich, 1975).

6. For good introductory surveys to the Weimar Republic, see R. Bessel, *Germany after the First World War* (London, 1993); M. Broszat, *Hitler and the Collapse of Weimar Germany* (Leamington Spa, 1987); E. J. Feuchtwanger, *From Weimar to Hitler* (London, 1993); E. Kolb, *The Weimar Republic* (London, 1988); A. J. Nich-

olls, *Weimar and the Rise of Hitler* (London, 1991); and D. J. K. Peukert, *The Weimar Republic* (London, 1992).

7. See K. Theweleit, *Male Fantasies*, 2 vols. (Cambridge, 1987–8); and J. M. Diehl, *Paramilitary Politics in Weimar Germany* (New York, 1977).

8. See G. Pridham, *Hitler's Rise to Power* (London, 1973), esp. p. 12.

9. Many have stressed Nazism's fear of communism, but the latter's more ideological influence has largely been neglected. See E. Nolte's highly controversial *Der Europäischen Bürgerkrieg* (Berlin, 1987).

10. For a history of the party, see D. Orlow, *The History of the Nazi Party*, 2 vols., (Newton Abbot, 1971).

11. On Strasser, see P. Stachura, *Gregor Strasser and the Rise of Nazism* (London, 1983).

12. For instance, Theweleit, *Male Fantasies*.

13. On Goebbels, see R. G. Reuth, *Goebbels* (London, 1994); see also J. Goebbels (ed. H. Heiber), *The Goebbels Diaries, 1925–6* (London, 1962).

14. For instance, Stachura, *Gregor Strasser*, p. 10.

15. For examples of their, and other, Nazi thought at this time, see B. M. Lane and S. Rupp (eds.), *Nazi Ideology Before 1993* (Manchester, 1978).

16. On these "conservative revolutionaries," see J. Herf, *Reactionary Modernism* (Oxford, 1984). On Moeller, see F. Stern, *The Politics of Cultural Despair* (Berkeley, 1961). On Jünger, see R. Woods, *Ernst Jünger and the Nature of Political Commitment* (Stuttgart, 1982). N.B. these commentators see such ideas as essentially conservative rather than syncretic. For a sympathetic account, see A. Mohler, *Die*

konservative Revolution in Deutschland, 1918–33 (Darmstadt, 1972).

17. On the links between Nazi membership and prior participation in other groups, see P. Merkl, *Political Violence Under the Swastika* (Berkeley, 1975), esp. p. 679.

18. See R. Lemmon, *Goebbels and 'Der Angriff'* (Nashville, 1994).

19. See, for instance, O. Strasser, *Hitler and I* (London, 1940). These helped establish the idea of a left-wing "Strasserite" alternative to Hitlerism, which later influenced some neofascists.

20. See H. James, *A German Identity 1770–1990* (London, 1989). On the economic crisis, see also G. Feldman, *The Great Divide: Politics, Economics, Society and the Great Inflation, 1914–24* (New York, 1993), H. James, *The German Slump: Politics and Economics 1924–36* (Oxford, 1987), and I. Kershaw (ed.), *Weimar: Why Did German Democracy Fail?* (London, 1990).

21. See R. J. Evans and D. Geary (eds.), *The German Unemployed* (London, 1987). For an alternative view, see C. Fischer, *The German Communists and the Rise of Nazism* (London, 1991), who shows that the Nazis exerted some appeal to communist supporters.

22. On Hugenberg, see J. A. Leopold, *Alfred Hugenberg* (New York, 1977).

23. S. Kracauer, *From Caligari to Hitler* (New York, 1963). The work has been criticized for being based on a narrow sample of films, but it reveals important cultural concerns.

24. J. Noakes, *The Nazi Party in Lower Saxony, 1921–1933* (Oxford, 1971), p. 198, and C. Koonz, *Mothers in the Fatherland* (New York, 1976), pp. 63–4.

25. See A. Bramwell, *Blood and Soil* (Kenilworth, 1985), and J. E. Farquharson, *The Plough and the Swastika: National Socialism and Farm Policy, 1928–33* (London, 1979).

26. For instance W. D. Allen, *The Nazi Seizure of Power* (London, 1966) shows that anti-Semitism played little part in campaigning in Thalburg. On the relative lack of anti-Semitism even among Nazi activists, see also Merkl, *Political Violence.*

27. For a major recent commentator who supports this line, see I. Kershaw, *The Hitler Myth: Image and Reality in the Third Reich* (Oxford, 1989). See also J. Fest, *The Face of the Third Reich* (Harmondsworth, 1973), esp. p. 130.

28. For the rural-middle class thesis see S. M. Lipset, *Political Man* (London, 1960), and M. Kater, *The Nazi Voter* (London, 1984). Supporters of the all-class position include: T. Childers (ed.), *The Formation of the Nazi Constituency, 1919–1933* (London, 1986); J. Falter, "The First German Volkspartei: The Social Foundations of the NSDAP," in K. Rohe (ed.), *Elections, Parties and Political Traditions* (New York, 1990); and D. Mühlberger, *Hitler's Followers* (London, 1991). See also J. Falter, *Hitlers' Wähler* (Munich, 1991).

29. See R. J. Evans, "German Women and the Triumph of Hitler," *Journal of Modern History* 1, 1976. See also Koonz, *Mothers in the Fatherland.*

30. Allen, *The Nazi Seizure of Power,* pp. 172 and 316n. On the SA's use of violence, see R. Bessel, *Political Violence and the Rise of Nazism: The Stormtroopers in Eastern Germany, 1925–34* (New Haven, 1984); C. Fischer,

Stormtroopers (New Haven, 1983); and E. G. Reiche, *The Development of the SA in Nurnberg, 1922–34* (New York, 1986).

31. E. Rosenhaft, *Beating the Fascists? German Communists and Political Violence, 1929–1933* (London, 1984,) argues that left unity was also hampered by indigenous resentment over social democrat moderation.

32. Some Marxists even at the time produced more sophisticated analyses. See D. Beetham (ed.), *Marxists in the Face of Fascism* (Manchester, 1983).

33. See R. Overy, *Göring* (London, 1983). See also D. Irving, *Göring* (London, 1989).

34. See H. A. Turner's important *German Big Business and the Rise of Hitler* (Oxford, 1985). Cf. D. Abraham, *The Collapse of the Weimar Republic* (Princeton, 1981), which goes out of its way to blame business for the collapse of the Weimar Republic. See also R. Neebe, *Grossindustrie, Staat und NSDAP* (Göttingen, 1981).

35. See Kershaw, *Weimar*. Esp. cf. the pessimistic views of Harold James, Dick Geary, and Richard Bessel with the more policy-failure oriented views of Carl-Ludwig Holtferich.

36. See M. Geyer, "Etudes in Political History: *Reichswehr*, NSDAP and the Seizure of Power," in P. Stachura (ed.), *The Nazi Machtergreifung* (London, 1983).

Germany: The Consolidation of the Nazi Dictatorship

1. For more on this important area of Nazi activity, see D. Welch (ed.), *Nazi Propaganda: The Power and the Limitations* (London, 1983); D. Welch, *The Third Reich: Politics and Propaganda* (London, 1993); Z. A. B. Zeman, *Nazi Propaganda* (Oxford, 1965).

2. See A. Speer, *Inside the Third Reich* (London, 1970).

3. G. Mosse, *The Nationalization of the Masses* (New York, 1977), esp. p. 190. On the syncretic aspects of many forms of Nazi art, see B. Taylor and W. van der Will (eds.), *The Nazification of Art* (Winchester, 1990).

4. For the classic totalitarian model applied to German, see K. D. Bracher, *The Nazi Dictatorship* (Harmondsworth, 1969); for a good example of the depiction of the Nazi state as a "polyocracy," see M. Broszat, *The Hitler State* (London, 1981). For more balanced surveys, see K. Fischer, *Nazi Germany: A New History* (London, 1995); J. Hiden and J. Farquharson, *Explaining Hitler's Germany* (London, 1989); and I. Kershaw, *The Nazi Dictatorship* (London, 1993). See also G. Schreiber, *Hitler: Interpretationen* (Darmstadt, 1984).

5. For a history of the party, see D. Orlow, *The History of the Nazi Party: 1933–45* (Newton Abbot, 1973). For brief accounts of the Nazi leaders, see R. Smelser and R. Zitelmann (eds.), *The Nazi Elite* (Basingstoke, 1993).

6. On Himmler, see P. Padfield, *Himmler: Reichsführer SS* (London, 1991). See also R. Gellately, *The Gestapo and German Society: Enforcing Racial Policy 1933–45* (Oxford, 1990).

7. See J. Caplan, *Government without Administration: State and Civil Service in Weimar and Nazi Germany* (Oxford, 1988).

8. J. Noakes, "German Conservatives and the Third Reich: An Ambiguous Relationship" in M. Blinkhorn (ed.), *Fascists and Conservatives* (London, 1991), p. 85.

9. On Schmitt, see J. W. Bendersky, *Carl Schmitt: Theorist of the Reich* (Princeton, 1983). Schmitt is increasingly being reassessed as one of the major political thinkers of the century. See, for instance, G. Sartori, "The Essence of the Political in Carl Schmitt," *Journal of Theoretical Politics* 1, 1989.

10. On Heidegger, see V. Farias, *Heidegger and Nazism* (Philadelphia, 1989); H. Ott, *Martin Heidegger: A Political Life* (London, 1993); and T. Rockmore, *On Heidegger's Nazism and Philosophy* (London, 1992).

11. On religion and the Nazis, see V. Barnett, *For the Soul of the People: Protestant Protest against Hitler* (London, 1992), and J. S. Conway, "National Socialism and the Christian Churches during the Weimar Republic," in P. Stachura (ed.), *The Nazi Machtergreifung* (London, 1983).

12. English language edition (Torrance, 1982).

13. See M. Burleigh and W. Wipperman, *The Racial State: Germany, 1933–45* (Cambridge, 1991); M. Burleigh, *Death and Deliverance: "Euthanasia" in Germany, 1900–1945* (London, 1994); H. Friedlander, *The Origins of Nazi Genocide: From Euthanasia to the Final Solution* (New York, 1995); J. Noakes, "Nazism and Eugenics: The Background to the Nazi Sterilisation Law of 14 July 1933," in R. J. Bullen et al. (eds), *Ideas into Politics* (London, 1984); and P. Weindling, *Health, Race and German Politics Between National Unification and Nazism, 1870–1945* (Cambridge, 1993).

14. See R. Smelser, *Robert Ley: Hitler's Labour Front Leader* (Oxford, 1988).

15. For a good example of this latter-day Marxist position, see N. Poulantzas, *Fascism and Dictatorship* (London, 1979). See also T. Mason, "The Primacy of Politics—Politics and Economics in National Socialist Germany," in H. A. Turner (ed.), *Nazism and the Third Reich* (London, 1972).

16. For example, H. James, *The German Slump: Politics and Economics 1924–36* (Oxford, 1987).

17. See W. E. Mosse, *Jews in the German Economy 1820–1935* (London, 1987).

18. See especially A. Barkai, *Nazi Economics* (Oxford, 1990). See also R. Overy, *The Nazi Economic Recovery, 1932–8* (London, 1982). Cf. C. Maier, "The Economics of Fascism and Nazism," in his *In Search of Stability* (Cambridge, 1987), who argues that it is an error to look for fascist economic views as such.

19. See Overy, *The Nazi Economic Recovery*; D. Irving, *Göring* (London, 1989); and R. Overy, *War and Economy in the Third Reich* (London, 1994).

20. See P. Hayes, *Industry and Ideology* (Cambridge, 1987).

21. See S. Reich, *The Fruits of Fascism* (Ithaca, 1990). Cf. M. Olson, *The Rise and Decline of Nations* (New York, 1982), which stresses the destructive impact of fascism.

22. On the army, see G. Craig, *The Politics of the Prussian Army, 1640–1945* (London, 1955); K. J. Muller, *Army, Politics and Society in Germany, 1933–45* (London, 1987); and R. J. O'Neill, *The German Army and the Nazi Party* (London, 1968).

23. P. Hoffmann, *The History of German Resistance, 1933–45* (London, 1977).

24. I. Kershaw, *The "Hitler Myth"*:

Image and Reality in the Third Reich (Oxford, 1989), p. 1.

25. On everyday life and attitudes, see D. F. Crew (ed.), *Nazism and German Society, 1933–45* (London, 1994); B. Engelmann, *In Hitler's Germany: Everyday Life in the Third Reich* (London, 1988); R. Grunberger, *A Social History of the Third Reich* (Harmondsworth, 1974); I. Kershaw, *Popular Opinion and Political Dissent in the Third Reich: Bavaria, 1933–45* (London, 1983); Kerhaw, *The "Hitler Myth,"* and D. J. K. Peukert, *Inside Nazi Germany* (London, 1987).

26. See A. Rabinbach, "The Aesthetics of Production," *Journal of Contemporary History* 4, 1976.

27. For instance, S. Salter, "Class Harmony of Class Conflict? The Industrial Working Class and the National Socialist Regime 1933–45," In J. Noakes (ed.), *Government, Party and People in Nazi Germany* (Exeter, 1980). Compare the mea culpa of the founding father of the British Nazi social history school in T. Mason, *Nazi Social Policy* (New York, 1993), where he argues that socio-class approaches ultimately reveal little about the extensive support the Nazis attracted. See also J. Caplan (ed.), *Nazism, Fascism and the Working Class* (New York, 1995).

28. See A. Bramwell, *Blood and Soil* (Kenilworth, 1985); G. Corni, *Hitler and the Peasants: Agrarian Policy in the Third Reich, 1930–39* (New York, 1990); and J. Farquharson, *The Plough and the Swastika* (London, 1979). See also W. Runderle and B. Norling, *The Nazi Impact on a German Village* (New York, 1993).

29. For the claim that Nazism had a proto-ecological side see Bramwell, *Blood and Soil* and A. Bramwell, *Ecology in the Twentieth Century* (New Haven, 1989).

30. On Nazism and women, see R. Bridenthal et al. (eds), *When Biology Became Destiny: Women in Weimar and Nazi Germany* (New York, 1984); C. Koonz, *Mothers in the Fatherland* (New York, 1976); T. Mason, "Women in Germany 1925–1940," 1 and 2, *History Workshop*, 1976; A. Owings, *Frauen: German Women Recall the Third Reich* (London, 1995); J. Stephenson, *The Nazi Organization of Women* (London, 1981), and *Women in Nazi Society* (London, 1975).

31. See H. Ulshöfer, *Liebesbriefe on Adolf Hitler* (Frankfurt, 1994), for other examples.

32. See W. Schumann, *Being Present: Growing up in Hitler's Germany* (New York, 1993), esp. p. 12.

33. See O. Bartov, *Hitler's Army: Soldiers, Nazis and the Third Reich* (Oxford, 1991); and Kershaw, *The "Hitler Myth,"* pp. 264–5.

34. F. K. M. Hillenbrand, *Underground Humour in Nazi Germany* (London, 1995).

35. See A. Merson, *Communist Resistance in Nazi Germany* (London, 1985).

36. See R. Chernow, *The Warburgs* (London, 1993). An interesting insight into Jewish life can also be gleaned from H. Freeden, *The Jewish Press in the Third Reich* (London, 1993).

37. For example, L. Dawidowicz, *The War Against the Jews 1933–45* (New York, 1977), esp. pp. 210–1.

38. See R. L. Merritt, *Public Opinion in Occupied Germany* (Urbana, 1970), esp. pp. 239–40.

39. For an excellent example, see Kershaw, *The Nazi Dictatorship*.

Germany: War and Death

1. On geopolitics, see G. Parker, *Western Geo-Political Thought in the Twentieth Century* (London, 1985). See also the special issue, "Historical Studies of Geopolitics," *Political Geography Quarterly* 2, 1987. N.B. there were crucial differences between Haushofer and Hitler: in particular, the former did not believe in racial biology.

2. See M. Burleigh, *Germany Turns Eastwards: A Study of "Ostforchismus" in the Third Reich* (London, 1988). On the background to Hitler's views, see W. Smith, *The Ideological Origins of Nazi Imperialism* (Oxford, 1986). See also R. Breitman, "Hitler and Genghis Khan," *Journal of Contemporary History* 2–3, 1990.

3. For a general account of German foreign policy at this time, see K. Hildebrand, *The Foreign Policy of the Third Reich* (London, 1973); D. Irving, *The War Path* (London, 1978); W. J. Mommsen and L. Kettenacker (eds.), *The Fascist Challenge and the Policy of Appeasement* (London, 1983); N. Rich, *Hitler's War Aims: Ideology, the Nazi State and the Course of Expansion*, 2 vols. (London, 1973); and G. Weinberg, *The Foreign Policy of Hitler's Germany: Starting World War II* (Chicago, 1980).

4. On relations between the military and Hitler, see W. Deist, *The Wehrmacht and German Rearmament* (New York, 1981); K. J. Müller, *The Army, Politics and Society in Germany, 1933–45* (London, 1987); and A. Seaton, *The German Army, 1933–45* (London, 1981).

5. See, for example, M. Michaelis, "World Power Status or World Dominion?" *Historical Journal* 2, 1972, and M. Hauner, "Did Hitler Want a World Dominion?" *Journal of Contemporary History* 1, 1978.

6. See for instance, T. Taylor (ed.), *Hitler's Secret Book* (New York, 1961), esp. p. 106.

7. For a classic statement of this position, see A. J. P. Taylor, *The Origins of the Second World War* (London, 1963). Taylor and followers argue that events like Hitler's November 1937 disquisition on expansion in the east (the Hossbach Memorandum) should really be interpreted as Hitler employing rambling monologues about future policy as a way of avoiding decisions on current policy.

8. M. Bloch, *Ribbentrop* (London, 1992). See also W. Michalka, *Ribbentrop und die deutsche Weltpolitik 1933–40* (Munich, 1980).

9. The importance of public opinion is usually stressed by social historians who believe that the Nazis had not overcome class opposition. See especially, T. Mason, *Nazi Social Policy* (New York, 1993).

10. On public opinion during the war, see J. Baird, *The Mythical World of Nazi War Propaganda* (New York, 1974); R. E. Herzstein, *The War that Hitler Won* (New York, 1978); and I. Kershaw, *The Hitler Myth* (Oxford, 1989). On the domestic impact of war generally, see M. Kitchen, *Nazi Germany at War* (London, 1995).

11. For a general work on Hess, see W. Schwarzwäller, *Rudolf Hess: The Deputy* (London, 1988); for a more speculative account of the flight, see J. Costello, *Ten Days to Destiny* (London, 1991). Hess was imprisoned for his pains and took his life—while still in captivity—in 1987.

12. V. Zuvorov, "Who Was Planning to Attack Whom?" *Journal of the Royal United Services Institute for Defence Studies*, June 1985. See also W. Maser, *Der Wortbruch: Hitler, Stalin und der Zweite Weltkrieg* (Munich, 1994).

13. For different interpretations of the Blitzkrieg economy, see A. Milward, *The German Economy at War* (London, 1965), and especially R. Overy, *War and Economy in the Third Reich* (London, 1994).

14. See R. H. S. Stolfi, *Hitler's Panzer's East* (Norman, 1993).

15. On the military's complicity in atrocities, see O. Bartov, *Hitler's Army: Soldiers, Nazis and the Third Reich* (Oxford, 1991). This work is mainly concerned with line fighters. For a more balanced view of the military, see T. Schulze, *The German Army and Nazi Policies in Occupied Russia* (London, 1989).

16. See R. Breitman, *The Architect of Genocide: Himmler and the Final Solution* (London, 1991). On the SS, see R. S. Koehl, *The Black Corps* (New York, 1983).

17. C. R. Browning, *The Path to Genocide* (Cambridge, 1992), p. 169ff.

18. For instance, see P. Burrin, *Hitler and the Jews* (London, 1993), and A. Mayer, *Why Did the Heavens Not Darken?* (New York, 1987). On the argument that Nazi genocide was in part a response to a fear of communism, and only one among many examples of genocide and mass killing, N.B. the 1980s German *"Historikerestreit."* On this, see R. J. Evans, *In Hitler's Shadow: West German Historians and the Attempt to Escape from the Nazi Past* (London, 1989), and C. S. Maier, *The Unmasterable Past: History,* *Holocaust and German National Identity* (Cambridge, 1988).

19. M. Gilbert, *The Holocaust* (London, 1986). For a good historiographical survey, see M. Marrus, *The Holocaust in History* (London, 1987), and M. Marrus, "Reflections on the Historiography of the Holocaust," *Journal of Modern History* 1, 1994.

20. For a good example, see D. Irving, *Hitler's War* (London, 1977). N.B. Irving was subsequently converted to the Holocaust Denial position. See his introduction in F. Leuchter, *The Leuchter Report* (London, 1989).

21. On Eichmann as the efficient technocrat, see H. Arendt, *Eichmann in Jersualem* (Harmondsworth, 1962).

22. On the impact of ideology, see M. Kater, *Doctors Under Hitler* (Chapel Hill, 1989); R. J. Lifton, *The Nazi Doctors* (New York, 1986), esp. pp. 423–71; and P. Weindling, *Health, Race and Politics between National Unification and Nazism, 1870–1945* (Cambridge, 1992).

23. Books stressing Hitler's role include G. Fleming, *Hitler and the Final Solution* (Oxford, 1986), and D. Cesarani (ed.), *The Final Solution* (London, 1994).

24. P. Levi, *If This Is a Man* (1987), p. 17.

25. D. Bankier, *The Germans and the Final Solution* (Oxford, 1992).

26. See W. Laqueur, *Auschwitz and the Allies* (London, 1982), who uses this distinction to help explain why the Allies did not make more of the Holocaust in wartime propaganda, or why they did not bomb the rail lines. See also M. Gilbert, *Auschwitz and the Allies* (Harmondsworth, 1985).

27. A. Speer, *Inside the Third Reich*

(London, 1970), esp. p. 498ff; Cf. G. Sereny, *Albert Speer: His Battle with Truth* (London, 1995).

28. On the morality of the attacks, see S. A. Garrett, *Ethics and Air Power in World War II* (New York, 1992). Britain lost approximately 40,000 civilians during the Battle of Britain air attacks. For a defense of the attacks, see R. Overy's excellent *Why the Allies Won* (London, 1995). For a controversial attack on the Allied bombings as war crimes, see D. Irving, *Dresden* (London, 1963).

29. On Goebbels and the Nazi "court" during the war, see J. Goebbels (ed. L. Lochner), *The Goebbels Diaries, 1942–3* (London, 1948), and J. Goebbels (ed. H. Trevor-Roper), *The Goebbels Diaries, 1945* (London, 1978)

30. Speer, *Inside the Third Reich*; Milward, *The German Economy at War*; and Overy, *War and Economy in the Third Reich*.

31. J. Erickson and D. Dilks (eds.), *Barbarossa: The Axis and the Allies* (London, 1994).

32. See R. Herzstein, *When Nazi Dreams Come True* (New York, 1982).

33. On the Waffen SS, see B. Wegner, *The Waffen-SS: Organisation, Ideals, Function* (Oxford, 1988). On Degrelle, see M. Conway, *Collaboration in Belgium: Léon Degrelle and the Rexist Movement* (Oxford, 1993).

34. See G. L. Weinberg, "German Plans for Victory, 1944–5," *Central European History* 2, 1993.

35. On resistance, see M. Balfour, *Withstanding Hitler in Germany, 1933–45* (London, 1988); P. Hoffmann, *The History of the German Resistance, 1933–45* (London, 1977); D. C. Large (ed.), *Contending with Hitler* (Cambridge, 1992);

and R. W. Weldon, *Ethics and Resistance in Nazi Germany* (London, 1993).

36. See H. Trevor-Roper, *The Final Days of Hitler* (London, 1948).

37. Major examples of those who have argued that the Nazis—largely inadvertently—led a social revolution include R. Dahrendorf, *Society and Democracy in Germany* (London, 1967), and D. Schoenbaum, *Hitler's Social Revolution* (London, 1966). For a radical view of Hitler-the-social-revolutionary, see R. Zitelmann, *Hitler: Selbstverständnis eines Revolutionärs* (Hamburg, 1987).

France: From Failure to the Firing Squad

1. Cf. E. Nolte, *Three Faces of Fascism* (New York, 1969), who sees the AF as fascist, with the more reactionary view of the AF in E. Weber, *Action Française* (Stanford, 1962).

2. See J. Blatt, "Relatives and Rivals: The Responses of the *Action Française* to Italian Fascism, 1919–26," *European Studies Review* 3, 1981.

3. On mainstream conservative politics in France, see M. Anderson, *Conservative Politics in France* (London, 1974). More specifically on the crucial 1930s, see R. Austin, "The Conservatives and the Far Right in France: The Search for Power, 1933–44" in M. Blinkhorn (ed.), *Fascists and Conservatives* (London, 1991); W. D. Irvine, "French Conservatives and the 'New Right' During the 1930s," *French Historical Studies* 4, 1974; and W. D. Irvine, *French Conservatism in Crisis* (Baton Rouge, 1979).

4. Cf. R. Soucy, *Fascism in France: The First Wave, 1924–33* (New Haven,

1986), and R. Soucy, "Centrist Fascism: The Jeunesses Patriotes," *Journal of Contemporary History* 2, 1981.

5. Most notably R. Rémond on his classic study of the French right, *The Right in France* (Philadelphia, 1969). Rémond argues that fascism came to France as a minor foreign import in the 1930s. For a more balanced view of the fascist tradition, see P. Milza, *Fascisme français: passé et présent* (Paris, 1987), and J. F. Sweets, "Hold that Pendulum: Redefining Fascism, Collaborationism and Resistance in France," *French Historical Studies* 4, 1988.

6. Soucy, *Fascism in France*, p. 199.

7. A. Douglas, "Violence and Fascism: The Case of the Faisceau," *Journal of Contemporary History* 4, 1984. See also Y. Guchet, *Georges Valois* (Paris, 1975).

8. On Valois's left leanings, see Z. Sternhell, *Neither Left Nor Right* (Berkeley, 1986). Sternhell sees Valois's linking of nationalism with socialism as the critical fascist synthesis.

9. See S. Berstein, *Le six février* (Paris, 1975); see also M. Beloff, "The Sixth of February," in J. Joll (ed.), *The Decline of the Third Republic* (London, 1955).

10. Cf. Soucy, *Fascism in France*. See also W. D. Irvine, "Fascism in France and the Strange Case of the Croix de Feu," *Journal of Modern History* 2, 1991, and R. Soucy, "French Fascism and the Croix de Feu: A Dissenting Interpretation," *Journal of Contemporary History* 1, 1991.

11. See C. Bernadec, *Dagore, les carnets secrets de la Cagoule* (Paris, 1977), and P. Bourdrel, *La Cagoule* (Paris, 1970).

12. For the views that this was a fascist organization, see Irvine, "Fascism in France," Soucy, "French Fascism," and R. Soucy, *Fascism in France: The Second Wave* (New Haven, 1995). Cf. Rémond, *The Right in France,* and Sternhell, *Neither Right nor Left,* who reject that the PSF was fascist.

13. The literature on the support for radical nationalism in interwar France is weaker than the work on ideology. For an introduction, see R. Soucy, "France," in D. Mühlberger (ed.), *The Social Basis of European Fascist Movements* (London, 1987).

14. See G. Allardyce, "The Political Transition of Jacques Doriot," *Journal of Contemporary History* 1, 1966; J.-P. Brunet, *Jacques Doriot: du communisme au fascisme* (Paris, 1986); P. Burrin, *La dérive fasciste: Doriot, Déat, Bergery, 1933–45* (Paris, 1986); and Soucy, *Fascism in France.*

15. P. Jankowski, *Communism and Collaboration: Simon Sabiani and Politics in Marseille, 1919–44* (New Haven, 1989).

16. The former position is argued especially by Sternhell, *Neither Right nor Left,* and in other works; see also B.-H. Lévy, *L'Idéologie française* (Paris, 1980). The classic statement of the latter is Rémond, *The Right in France.* Sternhell's views have been highly criticized in France. See A. Costa-Pinto, "Fascist Ideology Revisited: Zeev Sternhell and His Critics," *European History Quarterly* 4, 1986, and R. Wohl, "French Fascism, Both Left and Right: Reflections on the Sternhell Controversy," *Journal of Modern History* 1, 1991.

17. On Brasillach, see A. Brassie, *Robert Brasillach* (Paris, 1987); D. Carroll, *French Literary Fascists* (1995); and R. Tucker, *The Fascist Ego: A Political*

Biography of Robert Brasillach (Berkeley, 1975). On Maulnier and other radical nationalist thinkers see J.-L. Loubet del Blaye, *Les Non-conformistes des années 30* (Paris, 1969), and P. Sérant, *Les Dissidents de l'action française* (Paris, 1978).

18. See. P. Andreu and F. J. Grover, *Drieu La Rochelle* (Paris, 1979); Carroll, *French Literary Fascists*; and R. Soucy, *Fascist Intellectual. Drieu La Rochelle* (Berkeley, 1979).

19. On the revival of anti-Semitism, see P. J. Kingston, *Anti-Semitism in France During the 1930s* (Hull, 1983), and R. Schor, *L'antisémitisme en France pendant les années trente: prélude à Vichy* (Paris, 1992).

20. See P. Alméras, *Céline: entre haines et passions* (Paris, 1994); Carroll, *French Literary Fascists*; and N. Hewitt, *The Golden Age of Louis-Ferdinand Céline* (Leamington Spa, 1987).

21. See M. S. Alexander, *The Republic in Danger: General Maurice Gamelin and the Politics of French Defence, 1933–1940* (Cambridge, 1992). On the military, see also J. S. Ambler, *The Politics of the French Army, 1945–62* (Ohio, 1966), and A. Horne, *The French Army and Politics* (London, 1984).

22. On Pétain, see M. Ferro, *Pétain* (Paris, 1987); R. Griffiths, *Marshall Pétain* (London, 1970); and J.-M. Varaut, *Le Procès de Pétain* (Paris, 1995). See also P. Webster, *Pétain's Crime: The Full Story of French Collaboration in the Holocaust* (London, 1990).

23. J.-P. Azéma, *From Munich to the Liberation, 1938–44* (Cambridge, 1984), p. 39. For more on the human impact of occupation see H. Amouroux, *La Grande Histoire des Français sous l'Occupation*, 6 vols. (Paris, 1976).

24. On Laval, see J.-P. Cointet, *Pierre Laval* (Paris, 1993); F. Kupferman, *Laval, 1883–1945* (Paris, 1987); and G. Warner, *Pierre Laval and the Eclipse of France* (London, 1969).

25. For general works on the Vichy regime, see Azéma, *From Munich to the Liberation*; R. Paxton, *Vichy France* (New York, 1972); and F. F. Sweets, *Choices in Vichy France* (New York, 1986).

26. See W. D. Halls, *The Youth of Vichy France* (Oxford, 1981), and J. Hellman, *The Knight-Monks of Vichy France: Uriage, 1940–1945* (Montreal and Kingston, 1993).

27. On this side of economic policy, see A. Jones, "Illusions of Sovereignty: Business and the Organization of Committees of Vichy France," *Social History* 1, 1986; R. Kuisel, *Capitalism and State in Modern France* (Cambridge, 1981), esp. pp. 128–56; and A. Shennan, *Rethinking France: Plans for Renewal 1940–46* (Oxford, 1989).

28. On the wartime fascist parties, see Burrin, *La dérive fasciste*; B. M. Gordon, *Collaborationism in France during the Second World War* (Ithaca, 1980); G. Hirschfeld and P. Marsh (eds.), *Collaboration in France: Politics and Culture during the Nazi Occupation, 1944* (Oxford, 1989); and P. Ory, *Les Collaborateurs, 1940–45* (Paris, 1976).

29. C. de la Mazière, *The Captive Dreamer* (New York, 1972).

30. See P. Laborie, *L'Opinion française sous Vichy* (Paris, 1990), who underlines the problems of measuring opinion at this time. See also W. D. Halls, *Society and Christianity in Vichy France* (Oxford, 1995).

31. On this aspect, and general German attempts to exploit the French economy after 1940, see A. Milward, *The New Order and the French Economy* (London, 1970).

32. On Mitterrand's conversion from right-wing Vichy activist to member of the Resistance in 1943, see J. Péan, *Une jeunesse française* (Paris, 1994).

33. J. P. Fox, "How Far Did Vichy France Sabotage the Imperatives of Wansee?" in D. Cesarani (ed.), *The Final Solution* (London, 1994); see also A. Cohen, *Persécutions et sauvetage: Juifs et français sous l'occupation et sous Vichy* (Paris, 1993). Cf. R. Paxton and M. Marrus, *Vichy France and the Jews* (New York, 1981).

34. On the resistance, see R. Kedward, *Occupied France: Collaboration and Resistance, 1940–44* (Oxford, 1985), R. Kedward and R. Austin (eds.), *Vichy France and the Resistance: Ideology and Culture* (London, 1985); and R. Kedward, *In Search of the Maquis* (Oxford, 1993).

Britain: From Farce to Failure

1. On the Fascisti, see R. Thurlow, *Fascism in Britain: A History, 1918–1985* (Oxford, 1987). This is the best survey of interwar fascism and related movements.

2. See M. Cowling, *The Impact of Labour* (Cambridge, 1971). See also J. Hope, "British Fascism and the State, 1917–1927," *Labour History Review* 3, 1992, who argues that there was some willingness to tolerate the BFs where it was thought they were useful.

3. On Leese, see J. Morrell, "Arnold Leese and the Imperial Fascist League: The Impact of Racial Fascism," in K. Lunn and R. Thurlow (eds.), *British Fascism* (London, 1980), and Thurlow, *British Fascism*.

4. On Beamish and the Britons, see G. C. Lebzelter, "Henry Beamish and the Britons," in Lunn and Thurlow, *British Fascism*; and Thurlow, *Fascism in Britain*.

5. For instance, A. J. P. Taylor, *English History, 1914–45* (Oxford, 1965). See also R. Skidelsky, *Oswald Mosley* (London, 1975). N.B. Skidelsky later stated that he had perhaps played down Mosley's weak points. See his "Reflections on Mosley and British Fascism," in Lunn and Thurlow, *British Fascism*. On Mosley, see also R. Benewick, *The Fascist Movement in Britain* (London, 1972); D. S. Lewis, *Illusions of Grandeur* (Manchester, 1987); and Thurlow, *Fascism in Britain*. Sir O. Mosley, *My Life* (London, 1968) offers a strong, if at times disingenuous, defense of his career and views.

6. N. Mosley, *The Rules of the Game* (London, 1982); see also his *Beyond the Pale* (London, 1983).

7. See A. Marwick, "Middle Opinion in the Thirties: Planning, Progress and Political Agreement," *English Historical Review* 2, 1964.

8. On Conservatives' responses, see R. J. B. Bosworth, "The British Press, Conservatives and Mussolini, 1920–34," *Journal of Contemporary History* 2, 1970.

9. On BUF ideology, see especially S. Cullen, "The Development of the Ideas and Policy of the British Union of Fascists, 1932–40," *Journal of Contemporary History* 1, 1987; N. Nugent, "The Ideology of the British Union of Fascists," in N. Nugent and R. King (eds.), *The British Right*

(Aldershot, 1977); and Skidelsky, *Oswald Mosley*. See also Mosley, *My Life*.

10. On right-wing Conservative dissident ideology see G. Webber, *The Ideology of the British Right, 1918–1939* (London, 1986).

11. P. Ziegler, *King Edward VIII* (London, 1991), esp. pp. 208–9.

12. For surveys stressing the social basis of BUF membership, see J. Brewer, "Looking Back at Fascism: A Phenomenological Analysis of BUF Membership," *Sociological Review* 4, 1984; G. C. Webber, "Patterns of Membership and Support for the British Union of Fascists," *Journal of Contemporary History* 4, 1984; and G. C. Webber, "The British Isles," in D. Mühlberger (ed.), *The Social Basis of European Fascist Movements* (London, 1987).

13. For regional studies of the BUF, see J. Brewer, *Mosley's Men: The BUF in the West Midlands* (Aldershot, 1984); T. P. Lineham, *The British Union of Fascists in East London and South West Essex* (London, 1994); and S. Rawnsley, "The Membership of the British Union of Fascists," in Lunn and Thurlow, *British Fascism*.

14. See: M. Durham, "Women and the British Union of Fascists," in T. Kushner and K. Lunn (eds.), *The Politics of Marginality* (London, 1990), and M. Durham, "Gender and the British Union of Fascists," *Journal of Contemporary History* 3, 1992.

15. D. Mayall, "Rescued from the Shadows of Exile: Nellie Driver, Autobiography and the British Union of Fascists," in Kushner and Lunn, *The Politics of Marginality*.

16. On the BUF and anti-Semitism, see especially C. Holmes, *Anti-Semitism in British Society, 1976–1939*

(London, 1979); G. Lebzelter, *Political Anti-Semitism in England, 1918–39* (London, 1978); W. F. Mandle, *Anti-Semitism and the British Union of Fascists* (London, 1968); and Skidelsky, *Oswald Mosley*.

17. J. Gorman, "Another East End: A Remembrance," in G. Alderman and C. Holmes (eds.), *Outsiders and Outcasts: Essays in Honour of William J. Fishman* (London, 1993).

18. A point made in S. Cullen, "Political Violence: The Case of the BUF," *Journal of Contemporary History* 2, 1993—though the author plays down BUF provocation.

19. See R. Thurlow, *The Secret State* (Oxford, 1994). Thurlow argues that surveillance was a major factor in the failure of the BUF, but the forces of law and order from an early stage identified that the party was unlikely to gather significant support, and its failure has to be traced to more fundamental problems. See also R. Thurlow, "The Failure of British Fascism, 1932–40," in A. Thorpe (ed.), *The Failure of Political Extremism in Inter-War Britain* (Exeter, 1987).

20. See J. Guinness, *The House of Mitford* (London, 1984), and D. Mosley, *A Life of Contrasts* (London, 1977).

21. For instance, J. Charmley, *Churchill: The End of Glory* (London, 1993), who describes Mosley as "indubitably the most able" of the postwar politicians (p. 265). Presumably the reference is to his seductive powers.

22. See D. Farson, *Henry: An Appreciation of Henry Williamson* (London, 1982). See also M. D. Higginbottom, *Intellectuals and British Fascism: A Study of Henry Williamson* (London, 1992).

23. On fellow traveling with fascism,

especially the Nazis, see M. Cowling, *The Impact of Hitler* (Cambridge, 1975), and R. Griffiths, *Fellow Travellers of the Right* (Oxford, 1983). See also A. Schwarz, "Image and Reality: British Visitors to National Socialist Germany," *Journal of Contemporary History* 3, 1993.

24. For the argument that there was extensive public support for appeasement, see especially F. R. Gannon, *The British Press and Nazi Germany* (Oxford, 1971), and B. Granzow, *A Mirror of Nazism* (London, 1964).

25. On public opinion after the Munich conference, see R. Eatwell, "Munich, Public Opinion and Popular Front," *Journal of Contemporary* 3, 1973; on attitudes to Nazi persecution, see T. Kushner, "Beyond the Pale? British Reactions to Nazi Anti-Semitism, 1933–39," in Kushner and Lunn, *The Politics of Marginality.* For a revisionist view of 1940, see J. Charmley, *Churchill: The End of Glory* (London, 1993).

26. On the legal side of internment, see A. W. B. Simpson, *In the Highest Degree Odious: Detention Without Trial in Wartime Britain* (Oxford, 1992).

27. J. A. Cole, *Lord Haw-Haw* (London, 1964), and F. Selwyn, *Hitler's Englishman: The Crime of Lord Haw Haw* (London, 1987).

Neofascism in Italy

1. On the Resistance and the reemergence of politics, see D. Ellwood, *Italy 1943–5* (Leicester, 1985), and S. J. Woolf (ed.), *The Rebirth of Italy, 1943–50* (London, 1972).

2. L. Passerini, *Fascism in Popular Memory* (Cambridge, 1987), p. 100.

3. There is nothing substantial in English on the UQ. See S. Setta, *L'Uomo Qualunque, 1944–48* (Rome, 1975).

4. P. Allum, *Politics and Society in Post-War Naples* (Cambridge, 1973).

5. There is no detailed study of the early MSI in English. For general surveys, see R. Chiriani, "The Movimento Sociale Italiano: A Historical Profile," L. Cheles, R. Ferguson, and M. Vaughn (eds.), *Neo-Fascism in Europe* (London, 1991); F. Sidoti, "The Extreme Right in Italy: Ideological Orphans and Countermoblization," in P. Hainsworth (ed.), *The Extreme Right in Europe and the USA* (London, 1992); and L. Weinberg, *After Mussolini: Italian Neo-Fascism and the Nature of Fascism* (New York, 1979).

6. There is nothing substantial on Almirante in English. See the general works on the MSI listed above and below, and G. Almirante and F. Palamenghi-Crispi, *Il Movimento Sociale Italiano* (Rome, 1958), and G. Almirante, *Autobiografia di un "fucilatore"* (Milan, 1973).

7. G. del Boca, *Fascism Today* (London, 1967), p. 165. N.B. this is a journalistic work.

8. T. Sheehan, "Myth and Violence: The Fascism of Julius Evola and Alain de Benoist," *Social Research,* Spring 1981, esp. p. 47.

9. *Rivolta contro il mondo moderno* (Rome, 1934). Little of Evola's writings are available in English (though much has been translated into French). A rare exception is *The Doctrine of the Awakening* (London, 1951).

10. On Evola's thought, see F. Ferraresi, "Julius Evola: Tradition, Reaction, and the Radical Right," *European Journal of Sociology* 1, 1987; F. Ferraresi, "The Radical Right in Postwar Italy,"

Politics and Society 1, 1988; and R. Griffin, "Revolts against the Modern World," *Literature and History* 1, 1985.

11. R. Collin, *The De Lorenzo Gambit: The Italian Coup Manqué of 1964* (London, 1977). On American involvement in Italian politics, see P. Agee and L. Olf (eds.) *Dirty Work: The CIA in Western Europe* (London, 1978). As well as stressing the large sums of money spent, it claims the CIA would ultimately have backed the neofascists if they could have kept out the communists (see esp. p. 172).

12. On terrorism, see L. Weinberg and W. Eubank, *The Rise and Fall of Italian Terrorism* (Boulder, 1987), and L. Weinberg, "Patterns of Neo-Fascist Terrorism," *Terrorism* 2, 1979. See also N. Harris, *The Dark Side of Europe* (Edinburgh, 1993).

13. For a good specialist work, see R. Chiriani and P. Corsini, *Da Salò a Piazza della Loggia: Blocco d'ordine, neofascismo, radicalismo di destra a Brescia (1945–1974)* (Brescia, 1983).

14. Some idea of the networks involved can be gleaned from R. Cornwell, *God's Banker* (London, 1984).

15. L. Cheles, " 'Nostalgia dell'avvenire': The New Propaganda of the MSI between Tradition and Innovation," in Cheles, *Neo-Fascism in Europe.*

16. L. Cheles, "Dolce Stil Nero? Images of Women in the Graphic Propaganda of the Italian Neo-fascist Party," in Z. G. Baranski and S. W. Vinall (eds.), *Women and Italy* (London, 1991).

17. On MSI changes and voting during the 1970s–'80s, see M. Cacialgi, "The Movimento Sociale Italiano—Destra Nazionale and Neo-Fascism in Italy," *Western Euro-*

pean Poliitcs 2, 1988; P. A. Furlong, "The Extreme Right in Italy: Old Orders and Dangerous Novelties," *Parliamentary Affairs* 2, 1992; and P. Ignazi, "The Changing Profile of the Movimento Sociale Italiano," in P. Merkl and L. Weinberg (eds.), *Encounters with the Contemporary Radical Right* (Boulder, 1993). See also P. Ignazi, *Il polo escluso: profilo del Movimento Sociale Italiano* (Bologna, 1989).

18. R. De Felice, *Fascism: An Informal Introduction to Its Theory and Practice* (New Brunswick, 1976). See also the references to De Felice in chapter 3, n. 2.

19. For an interesting article relating this to Italian myths of fascism, see R. Bosworth, "Benardo Bertolucci, 1900 and the Myth of Fascism," *European History Quarterly* 1, 1989.

20. On changing interpretations see R. J. B. Bosworth, *Explaining Auschwitz and Hiroshima* (London, 1993), and N. Zapponi, "Fascism in Italian Historiography, 1986–1993: A Fading National Identity," *Journal of Contemporary History* 4, 1994.

21. See especially G. Tassani, "The Italian Social Movement: From Almirante to Fini," in R. Y. Nanetti and R. Catanzaro (eds.), *Italian Politics: A Review,* vol. 4 (London, 1990).

22. There is virtually nothing on Rauti in English.

23. On the Italian New Right and radical neofascism at this time, see F. Ferraresi et al., *La Destra Radicale* (Rome, 1984), and E. Raisi, *Storia de idee della nuova destra italiania* (Rome, 1990).

24. J. Andall, "New Migrants, Old Conflicts: The Recent Immigration into Italy," *The Italianist* 3, 1990, and L. Cheles, "The Italian Far Right:

Nationalist Attitudes and Views on Ethnicity and Immigration," in A. Hargreaves and J. Learman (eds.), *Racism, Ethnicity and Politics in Contemporary Europe* (London, 1995).

25. For a comparison between the two, see H.-G. Betz, *Radical Right-Wing Populism in Western Europe* (Basingstoke, 1994), and P. Ignazi, "New and Old Right-Wing Parties: The French Front National and the Italian Movimento Sociale," *European Journal of Political Research* 1, 1992.

26. On the Lega Nord, see I. Diamanti, *La Lega* (Rome, 1993); M. Gilbert, "The Lega Nord and Italian Politics," *Political Quarterly* 1, 1993; C. Ruzza and O. Schmidtke, "Roots of the Success of the Lega Lombarda," *Western European Politics* 2, 1993.

27. For instance, see U. Bossi, *Vento dal Nord* (Milan, 1992), esp. p. 141.

28. The fascist label has particularly been used by journalists, especially those on the left. See for instance the antifascist journal *Searchlight* during the 1980s and 1990s.

29. On these elections, see M. Bull and J. L. Newell, "Italy Changes Course? The 1994 Elections and the Victory of the Right," *Parliamentary Affairs* 1, 1995, and M. Sznajder, "Heirs of Fascism? Italy's Right Wing Coalition," *International Affairs* 1, 1995.

30. On changes in the MSI's visual propaganda, see L. Cheles, " 'Nostalgia dell'Avvenire': The Propaganda of the Italian Far Right between Tradition and Innovation," in L. Cheles, R. Ferguson, and M. Vaughn (eds.), *The Far Right in Western and Eastern Europe* (London, 1995).

31. See P. Francia, *Fini: la mia destra* (Rome, 1994), and F. Storace, *La*

Svolta (Rome, 1994); the latter indicates the good media coverage received by Fini after reassuming the leadership.

32. See. P. Ignazi, *Postfascisti? Dal Movimento Sociale Italiano ad Alleanza Nazionale* (Bologna, 1994).

Neofascism in Germany

1. On these trials, see E. Davidson, *The Trial of the Germans* (New York, 1966) and T. Taylor, *The Anatomy of the Nuremberg Trials* (New York, 1992); cf. B. F. Smith, *Reaching Judgment at Nuremberg* (New York, 1977), which is more critical of the whole process.

2. See. R. L. Merritt, *Public Opinion in Occupied Germany* (Urbana, 1970).

3. The most detailed work on these groups in the immediate postwar period is K. Tauber, *Beyond Swastika and Eagle,* 2 vols. (Middletown, 1967). A good survey of neo-Nazism in the postwar period can be found in R. Stöss, *Politics Against Democracy: Right-wing Extremism in West Germany)* (Oxford, 1991). For a shorter survey, see D. Childs, "The Far Right in Germany," in L. Cheles, R. Ferguson, and M. Vaughn (eds.), *The Far Right in Western and Eastern Europe* (London, 1995).

4. See R. L. Merritt, "Digesting the Past: Views of National Socialism in Semi-Sovereign Germany," *Societas* 2, 1977, and A. J. Merritt and R. L. Merritt (eds.), *Public Opinion in Semisovereign Germany* (Urbana, 1980).

5. For instance, E. Zimmermann, and T. Saalfeld, "The Three Waves of West German Right-Wing Ex-

tremism," in P. Merkl and L. Weinberg (eds.), *Encounters with the Contemporary Radical Right* (Boulder, 1993), esp. p. 65.

6. See D. C. Large, "Reckoning without the Past: The HIAG of the Waffen-SS and the Politics of Rehabilitation in the Bonn Republic, 1950–1961," *Journal of Modern History* 1, 1987; see also J. M. Diehl, *The Thanks of the Fatherland: German Veterans After the Second World War* (Chapel Hill, 1993).

7. *Rechtsradikalismus in der Bundesrepublik* (Bonn, 1964).

8. On the NPD, see J. D. Nagle, *The National Democratic Party: Right Radialism in the Federal Republic of Germany* (Berkeley, 1970).

9. T. A. Tilton, *Nazism, Neo Nazism and the Peasantry* (Bloomington, 1975).

10. For example, L. Niethammer, *Angepasster Faschismus: politische Praxis der NPD* (Munich, 1969).

11. E. Kolinsky, "Terrorism in West Germany," in J. Lodge (ed.), *The Threat of Terrorism* (London, 1988).

12. For a surprisingly sympathetic account of Kühnen, written by an antifascist journalist, see M. Schmidt, *The New Reich* (London, 1993).

13. On 1970s and 1980s fringe neo-Nazism, see C. Husbands, "Neo-Nazism in West Germany," in L. Cheles, R. Ferguson, and M. Vaughan (eds.), *Neo-Fascism in Europe* (London, 1991).

14. For English-language examples, see L. Degrelle, *Eastern Front* (Torrance, 1987), and *Hitler: Born at Versailles* (Torrance, 1992).

15. On the Holocaust Denial, see R. Eatwell, "The Holocaust Denial: A Study in Propaganda Technique,"

in Cheles, *Neo-Fascism in Europe;* P. Vidal-Nacquet, *The Assassins of Memory* (New York, 1992). See also R. Eatwell, "How to Revise History and Influence People," in Cheles, *The Far Right.*

16. T. Christophersen, *The Auschwitz Lie* (Torrance, 1979). The English-language edition was published in America, another notable source of Holocaust Denial activity. See especially D. Lipstadt, *The Holocaust Denial* (New York, 1993).

17. For instance, W. Stäglich's, *The Auschwitz Lie* (Torrance, 1980) was published in both English and in German.

18. D. Irving, *Hitler's War* (London, 1977).

19. A. Butz, *The Hoax of the Century* (Brighton, 1975). On Irving, see his "Introduction" to *The Leuchter Report* (London, 1989).

20. For an important attempt to rehabilitate the former, see A. Mohler, *Die konservative Revolution in Deutschland, 1918–1933* (Darmstadt, 1972).

21. M. Feit, *Die "Neue Rechte" in der Bundesrepublik* (Munich, 1987).

22. For instance, see E. Noelle-Neumann, *Die verlezte Nation* (Bonn, 1985).

23. For a good example of criticism, see R. J. Evans, *In Hitler's Shadow: West German Historians and the Attempt to Escape from the Nazi Past* (London, 1989), and C. Maier, *The Unmasterable Past* (Cambridge, 1988).

24. F. Schönhuber, *Ich war dabei* (Munich, 1981).

25. On the Republikaner, see H.-G. Betz, *Postmodern Politics in Germany* (London, 1991); E. Kolinsky, "A Future for Right Extremism in Germany?" in P. Hainsworth (ed.),

The *Extreme Right in Europe and North America* (London, 1992); T. Saalfeld, "The Politics of National Populism: Ideology and Politics of the German Republikaner Party," *German Politics* 2, 1993; H.-J. Veen, N. Lepszy, P. Mnich, *The Republikaner Party in Germany* (Washington, 1993). For a good work in German, see H. G. Jaschke, *Die Republikaner* (Bonn, 1994).

26. On the violence, see W. Bergman, "Xenophobia and Antisemitism after the Unification of Germany," *Patterns of Prejudice* 2, 1994, and M. Fulbrook, "The Threat of the Radical Right in Germany," *Patterns of Prejudice* 3/4, 1994.

27. On neo-Nazi violence at this time, see C. T. Husbands, "Militant Neo-Nazism in the Federal Republic of Germany in the 1990s," in Cheles, *The Far Right*. On the DA, see also the memoirs of a member: I. Hasselbach (with T. Reiss), *Führer-Ex: Memoirs of a Former Neo-Nazi* (London, 1996).

28. On anti-Semitism, see Bergmann, "Xenophobia and Anti-Semitism." See also W. Bergmann and R. Erb, *Antisemitismus in der Bundesrepublik Deutschland: Ergebnisse des empirischen Forschung von 1946–1989* (Munich, 1991).

29. For instance, U. Backes and P. Moreau, *Die Extreme Rechte in Deutschland: Geschichte, gengenwärtige Gefahren, Ursachen, Gegenmassnahmen* (Munich, 1993).

30. For instance, Searchlight, *Reunited Germany: The New Danger* (London, 1995).

31. See G. Almond and S. Verba, *The Civic Culture* (Boston, 1963). Cf. D. P. Conradt, "Germany," in G. Almond and S. Verba (eds.), *The Civic Culture Revisited* (New York, 1980).

Neofascism in France

1. H. R. Lottman, *The People's Anger: Justice and Revenge in Post-Liberation France* (London, 1988), and P. Novick, *The Resistance Versus Vichy: the Purge of Collaborators in Liberated France* (New York, 1968).

2. R. Aron, *Histoire de l'épuration*, vol. 1 (Paris, 1967), pp. 566–7, R. Faurisson, "A Dry Chronicle of the Purge," *Journal of Historical Review* 1, 1992. N.B. Faurisson is a leading light in the "Holocaust Denial" movement.

3. L. Wylie, *Village in the Vaucluse* (Cambridge, Mass., 1974), p. 210.

4. On the lingering impact of Vichy, see H. Rousso, *Vichy Syndrome* (New York, 1988).

5. On Gaullism, see J. Charlot, *Gaullisme d'opposition, 1946–58* (Paris, 1983). and J. Lacouture, *De Gaulle. Le Politique, 1944–59* (Paris, 1985). See also R. Vinen, *Bourgeois Politics in France, 1945–1951* (Cambridge, 1995).

6. For a good general account of post-1945 neofascist and related movements, see P. Milza, *Fascisme français: passé et présent* (Paris, 1987).

7. For the best single statement of his views, see *Qu'est ce que le fascisme?* (Paris, 1960).

8. See R. Eatwell, "Poujadism and Neo-Poujadism: From Revolt to Reconciliation," in P. Cerny (ed.), *Social Movements and Protest in Modern France* (London, 1982); S. Hoffman, *Le Mouvement Poujade* (Paris, 1956); and P. Poujade, *A. l'heure de la colère* (Paris, 1977).

9. For instance, R. Aron, *France: Steadfast and Unchanging* (London, 1969), esp. p. 36; Milza, *Fascisme français*.

10. On Poujadist voting, see M. Duverger et al., *Les élections du 2 Janvier 1956* (Paris, 1957), and Hoffman, *Le Mouvement Poujade.*

11. On the Algerian plotting and the return of de Gaulle, see J. S. Ambler, *The French Army in Politics 1945–62* (Ohio, 1966); B. Droz and E. Lever, *Histoire de la guerre d'Algérie* (Paris, 1982); A. Horne, *A Savage War of Peace* (London, 1977); and R. Rémond, *Le Retour de De Gaulle* (Paris, 1984).

12. On the OAS see F. Duprat, *Les Mouvements de l'extrême droite en France depuis 1944* (Paris, 1972), and R. Kauffer, *OAS Histoire d'une organisation secrète* (Paris, 1986).

13. For instance, Duprat, *Les mouvements de l'extrême droite,* esp. p. 63ff.

14. On Tixier, see Duprat, *Les Mouvements de l'extrême droite,* and Milza, *Fascisme français.*

15. On the new sixties groups, see Duprat, *Les Mouvements de l'extreme droite,* and Milza, *Fascisme français.*

16. On the ND, see A. Douglas, " 'La Nouvelle Droite': GRECE and the Revival of Radical Rightist Thought in Contemporary France," *Tocqueville Review* 2, 1984; D. Johnson, "The Nouvelle Droite," in L. Cheles, R. Ferguson, and M. Vaughan (eds.), *The Far Right in Western and Eastern Europe* (London, 1995), and T. Sunic, *Against Democracy and Equality: The European New Right* (New York, 1990). See also J. Brunn, *La Nouvelle Droite* (Paris, 1979), and especially, P.-A. Taguieff, *Sur la Nouvelle Droite* (Paris, 1994).

17. De Benoist's key work in the 1970s was *Vu du Droite* (Paris, 1977); see also his *Les idées à l'endroit* (Paris, 1979).

18. P. Harris and A. de Sédouy, *Qui n'est pas de droite?* (Paris, 1978), p. 385.

19. On the influence of Evola on de Benoist, see T. Sheehan, "Myth and Violence: The Fascism of Julius Evola and Alain de Benoist," *Social Research* 2, 1981.

20. For examples of those who see the ND as fascist, see R. Badinter (ed.), *Vous avez dites fascismes?* (Paris, 1985), and R. Griffin, *The Nature of Fascism* (London, 1991).

21. On the emergence of the ON, see Duprat, *Les Mouvements de l'extrême droite,* and Milza, *Fascisme français.*

22. For introductions to Le Pen and the FN, see P. Fysh and J. Wolfreys, "Le Pen, the National Front and the Extreme Right in France," *Parliamentary Affairs* 3, 1992; P. Hainsworth, "The Extreme Right in Post-War France: The Emergence and Success of the Front National," in P. Hainsworth (ed.), *The Extreme Right in Europe and the USA* (London, 1992); and M. Vaughan, "The Extreme Right in France: 'Lepenisme' or the Politics of Fear," in Cheles, *The Far Right.* See also J. Marcus, *The Front National in French Politics* (London, 1995).

23. On the impact of immigration since the 1970s, see A. Hargreaves, *Immigration in Post-war France* (London, 1987); O. Milza, *Les Français devant l'immigration* (Paris, 1988); and P. E. Ogden, "Immigration to France since 1945; Myth and Reality," *Ethnic and Racial Studies* 3, 1991.

24. On FN voting, see C. T. Husbands, "The Support for the Front National: Analyses and Findings," *Ethnic and Racial Studies* 3, 1991;

N. Mayer and P. Perrineau, "Why Do They Vote for Le Pen?" *European Journal of Political Research* 1, 1992; and S. Mitra, "The National Front in France—A Single Issue Movement?" *Western European Politics* 2, 1988.

25. C. Bourseiller, *Extrême Droite* (Paris, 1991), p. 161ff.

26. See especially, A. Tristan, *Au Front* (Paris, 1987).

27. On Faurisson and the Holocaust Denial, see P. Vidal-Nacquet, *The Assassins of Memory* (New York, 1992). See also P. Vidal-Naquet and L. Yagil, *Holocaust Denial in France* (Jerusalem, 1994).

28. See P. Birnbaum, *Antisemitism in France: A Political History from Léon Blum to the Present* (London, 1992).

29. For Le Pen's views see *Les Français d'abord* (Paris, 1984) and *La France est de retour* (Paris, 1985).

30. On the way in which Le Pen's views have become central to debate, see P.-A. Taguieff, *Face au racisme* (Paris, 1990), and Taguieff, *Sur la Nouvelle Droite*.

31. Among those seeing the FN as "Bonapartist" are R. Rémond, *Les droites en France* (Paris, 1982), and M. Winock, *Histoire de l'extrême droite en France* (Paris, 1993). Among those seeing it as "Poujadist" are W. Safran, "The Front National in France," in P. Merkl and L. Weinberg (eds.), *Encounters with the Contemporary Radical Right* (Boulder, 1993), and P. Bréchon and S. Mitra, "The National Front in France: The Emergence of an Extreme Right Protest Movement," *Comparative Politics* 4, 1992. Among those seeing it as fascist are Badinter, *Vous avez dites fascismes* (1985).

32. On Mégret's views, see *L'Im-*

pératif du renouveau (Paris, 1986), and *La Flamme* (Paris, 1990).

Neofascism in Britain

1. For a survey of postwar British fascism written in a more analystical way, see R. Eatwell, "Why Has the Extreme Right Failed in Britain," in P. Hainsworth (ed.), *The Extreme Right in Britain and the USA* (London, 1992). For an alternative overview history, see R. Thurlow, *Fascism in Britain* (Oxford, 1987).

2. On Mosley's postwar career, see especially R. Skidelsky, *Oswald Mosley* (London, 1975), and Thurlow, *Fascism in Britain*. See also Sir O. Mosley, *My Life* (London, 1968).

3. On the Union Movement, see J. Hope, "Mosley and the Union Movement," in M. Cronin (ed.), *The Failure of Fascism in Britain* (London, 1996).

4. J. H. Robb, *Working-Class Anti-Semite* (London, 1954), esp. p. 171.

5. See J. Hamm, *Action Replay: An Autobiography* (London, 1983).

6. Mosley's most interesting postwar books (he also wrote a considerable amount of journalism) are *The Alternative* (Ramsbury, 1947), *Europe: Faith and Plan* (London, 1958), and *Mosley—Right or Wrong?* (London, 1961). On Mosley's philosophy, see also R. Eatwell, "Continuity and Metamorphosis," in S. Larsen (ed.), *Modern Europe After Fascism* (Princeton, 1996), and Skidelsky, *Oswald Mosley*.

7. For instance, R. Skidelsky, "Sir Oswald Mosley: From Empire to Europe," *Twentieth Century Studies*, March 1969.

8. On the main parties' response to

immigration since 1945, see: Z. Layton-Henry, *The Politics of Immigration* (London, 1992), and A. Messina, *Race and Party Competition in Britain* (Oxford, 1989). See also F. Reeves, *British Racial Discourse* (Cambridge, 1983).

9. N. Mosley, *Beyond the Pale* (London, 1983). On the election campaign, see D. Butler and R. Rose, *The British General Election of 1959* (London, 1961).

10. For an account of the latter campaign, see J. Brewer, *Mosley's Men: The British Union of Fascists in the West Midlands* (Aldershot, 1984).

11. For instance, W. F. Mandle, *Anti-Semitism and the British Union of Fascists* (London, 1966), and C. Holmes, *Anti-Semitism in British Society, 1876–1939* (London, 1979). For a critique of their views, see D. L. Baker, "The Appeal of Fascism: Pathological Fantasy or Intellectual Coherence?" *Patterns of Prejudice* 3, 1986. See also D. L. Baker, "A. K. Chesterton, the Strasser Brothers and the National Front." *Patterns of Prejudice* 3, 1985.

12. For general accounts of the early NF, see S. Taylor, *The National Front in English Politics* (London, 1982), and M. Walker, *The National Front* (London, 1978).

13. See, for instance, Walker, *The National Front*, esp. p. 9.

14. On the Holocaust denial, see R. Eatwell, "The Holocaust Denial: A Study in Propaganda Technique," in L. Cheles, R. Ferguson and M. Vaughan (eds.), *Neo-Fascism in Europe* (London, 1991).

15. For the claim that the core of the NF's membership (though not necessarily voters) was attracted by its more fascist side, see M. Billig, *Fascists* (London, 1978).

16. On this club, which was founded in 1961 shortly after Prime Minister Harold Macmillan gave notice of Britain's intention to give up much of its remaining empire, see P. Seyd, "Factionalism in the Conservative Party: The Monday Club," *Government and Opposition* 4, 1972.

17. On Powell, see D. E. Schoen, *Enoch Powell and the Powellites* (London, 1977). Powell was a laissez-faire nationalist rather than a fascist, but he was also a great scholar of the Greeks and seems to have been influenced by the belief that politics depended on feeding the people myths. See J. Wood (ed.), *Freedom and Reality* (London, 1969), esp. p. 245. See also Tom Nairn, "Enoch Powell: The New Right," *New Left Review*, May June, 1970.

18. For instance, M. Steed, "The Results Analysed," in D. Butler and D. Kavanagh, *The British General Election of February 1974* (London, 1974) and M. Steed, "The National Front Vote," *Parliamentary Affairs* 3, 1978.

19. See C. Hartman and C. Husband, *Racism and the Mass Media* (London, 1974).

20. On NF support, see C. T. Husbands, *Racial Exclusionism and the City* (London, 1983). See also Taylor, *The National Front in English Politics*, and P. Whiteley, "The National Front Vote in the 1977 GLC Elections: An Aggregate Data Analysis," *British Journal of Political Science* 3, 1979.

21. M. Durham, "Women and the National Front," in Cheles, *Neo-Fascism in Europe*.

22. On this, see M. Barker, *The New Racism* (London, 1981).

23. D. Studlar, "Race in British Politics," *Patterns of Prejudice* 1, 1985.

24. See R. Eatwell, "The Esoteric Ideology of the National Front in the 1980s," in Cronin, *The Failure of British Fascism,* and G. Gable, "The Far Right in Contemporary Britain," in Cheles, *Neo-Fascism in Europe.*

25. See R. Hill and A. Bell, *The Other Face of Terror* (London, 1988), which is based on a television exposé of the more violent side of the NF.

26. See C. Husbands, "Racial Attacks: The Persistence of Racial Vigilantism in British Cities," in T. Kushner and K. Lunn (eds.), *Traditions of Intolerance* (Manchester, 1989). See also P. Panayi (ed.), *Racial Violence in Britain, 1840–1950* (London, 1993).

27. The BNP has attracted remarkably little serious academic attention. For a survey of contemporary developments see N. Copsey, "Contemporary Fascism in the Local Arena: The British National Party and 'Rights for Whites,' " in Cronin, *The Failure of British Fascism*; R. Eatwell, "Britain," in H.-G. Betz, and S. Immerfall (eds.), *New Party Politics of the Right* (Westview, 1997); and T. Kushner, "The Fascist as 'Other'? Racism and Neo-Nazism in Contemporary Britain," *Patterns of Prejudice* 1, 1994.

28. For instance, R. Miles and A. Phizacklea, *White Man's Country* (London, 1984), and N. Murray, "The Press and Ideology in Thatcher's Britain," *Race and Class* 3, 1986

Index